Math
Principles

For Food Service Occupations

FIFTH EDITION

Math
Principles

For Food Service Occupations

FIFTH EDITION

Anthony J. Strianese
Pamela P. Strianese

THOMSON

DELMAR LEARNING™

Australia · Brazil · Canada · Mexico · Singapore · Spain · United Kingdom · United States

THOMSON

DELMAR LEARNING

Math Principles for Food Service Occupations, 5E
by Anthony J. Strianese and Pamela P. Strianese

Vice President, Career Education Strategic Business Unit:
Dawn Gerrain

Acquisitions Editor:
Matthew Hart

Managing Editor:
Robert Serenka, Jr.

Product Manager:
Patricia M. Osborn

Editorial Assistant:
Patrick B. Horn

Director of Production:
Wendy A. Troeger

Senior Content Project Manager:
Matthew J. Williams

Director of Marketing:
Wendy E. Mapstone

Marketing Channel Manager:
Kristin McNary

Marketing Coordinator:
Scott Chrysler

Cover Design:
Joe Villanova

Cover Images:
Mitch Hrdlicka/Getty Images
Food Collection/Getty Images
Insy Shah/Getty Images
Photodisc/Getty Images
Stockdisc/Getty Images

For permission to use material from this text or product, contact us by
Tel   (800) 730-2214
Fax   (800) 730-2215
www.thomsonrights.com

Library of Congress Cataloging-in-Publication Data

Strianese, Anthony J.
  Math principles for food service occupations / Anthony J. Strianese,
Pamela P. Strianese.—5th ed.
      p. cm.
  Includes bibliographical references and index.
  1. Food service—Mathematics. I. Strianese, Pamela P.
II. Title.
  TX911.3.M33S75 2006
  647.9501′51—dc22

                                                    2006018688

NOTICE TO THE READER

Contents

Foreword . . . . *vii*

Preface . . . . *x*

Acknowledgments . . . . *xii*

Pretest: Math Skills . . . . *xv*

PART I

THE CALCULATOR 1

Chapter 1   Using the Calculator 2

PART II

REVIEW OF BASIC MATH FUNDAMENTALS 23

Chapter 2   Numbers, Symbols of Operations, and the Mill 24

Chapter 3   Addition, Subtraction, Multiplication, and Division 33

Chapter 4   Fractions, Decimals, Ratios, and Percents 55

PART III

MATH ESSENTIALS IN FOOD PREPARATION 79

Chapter 5   Weights and Measures 80

Chapter 6   Using the Metric System of Measure 98

Chapter 7   Portion Control 111

Chapter 8   Converting Recipes, Yields, and Baking Formulas 139

Chapter 9   Food, Recipe, and Labor Costing 159

PART IV

MATH ESSENTIALS IN FOOD SERVICE RECORD KEEPING 177

Chapter 10   Determining Cost Percentages and Pricing the Menu 179

Chapter 11   Inventory Procedures 201

Chapter 12   Purchasing and Receiving 224

Chapter 13   Daily Production Reports 234

PART V   ESSENTIALS OF MANAGERIAL MATH 249

Chapter 14   Front of the House and Managerial
             Mathematical Operations 250

Chapter 15   Personal Taxes, Payroll, and
             Financial Statements 280

Posttest: Math Skills.................................. 311

Appendix A 321

Glossary 323

Index.. 331

Foreword

Early in my life I became involved in the restaurant business, not really by choice, but at a time when my family (which was in the commercial fishing industry) was suffering quite a bit. This was back in the 1950s, when the industry collapsed. At that time, I was looking forward to experiencing some time on a fishing boat, but I did not see my future in it. My mother and father always spoke to me about an education, as my brother pursued a teaching career and became a famous water polo coach. My sisters, too, were geared toward the education field, and therefore I thought it would be good for me to pursue this avenue. By going to school, I began to learn the principles of mathematics and the importance it bears on any career.

I guess I knew from an early age that I wanted to be in business for myself, and, in order to do this, I would have to know my numbers. Any kind of business is based on math, which everyone needs to understand. I took accounting in high school and college, which helped me when I began keeping the books for five restaurants while continuing my college education. It gave me a better understanding of the use of numbers and how they work together for a bottom line, or a profit. You learn at an early point when you are involved in the operation of restaurants, as I was then and still am now, how important the numbers are.

I went into business in 1968 with my partner and developed the Sardine Factory Restaurant on Cannery Row, and we knew that the numbers were not great. With only $950 in cash to start with, we found a dilapidated old building on the wrong side of the tracks in an area that had depreciated due to the commercial industry collapse. The canneries turned into old buildings and structures that were just sitting there, empty. We created a gem within that realm, and the Sardine Factory is a restaurant that was designed to represent the Cannery Row era. We have pictures in what we call the "Cannery Row Bar/Lounge" that depict the commercial fishing industry, reflective of my family background, and some of the produce industry, reflective of my partner's family. We knew we had to make the restaurant a success, and it has been since day one.

We took the initiative with some unique ideas, such as using local produce and seafood, which was not being done, and we created an abalone soup that is still our signature soup today. The restaurant evolved from a small, 70-seat establishment to a five-room, 225-seat restaurant, which includes the elegant "Captain's Room," the beautiful glass-dome "Conservatory Room," and our unique "Downstairs Wine Cellar Room." The wine cellar has won the Wine Spectator Award consecutively over many years. And the restaurant, in general, has won many top awards for cuisine, service, and ambiance. We have sommeliers who serve the wine from our wine cellar, which holds close to 40,000 bottles of wine and 1,300 different types. Our seafood is brought in fresh to the restaurant, and we also serve some great steaks; we are known for both.

Many celebrities come to the restaurant, and we even had *Lifestyles of the Rich and Famous* tape a segment in the "Downstairs Wine Cellar Room." Famous actors and singers have dined here, including Bing Crosby, Phil Harris, and Paul Newman; and, of course, Clint Eastwood filmed the famous *Play Misty for Me* in our restaurant, and is still a good friend of ours to this day. Television personalities (such as Ray Romano), famous golfers (such as Tiger Woods), and many others like to come play golf and dine at great restaurants with great cuisine. In addition, we have hosted many politicians, such as governors, senators, assemblyman, and so forth from all over the United States, not to mention Leon Panetta—the former White House chief of staff—with whom I grew up.

I am proud to say that the restaurant has become world famous. We have been honored with the DiRōNA Award (Distinguished Restaurants of North America) and have received numerous other awards, such as the Mobile and the AAA, which have brought a tremendous amount of recognition to the restaurant. We are one of the few restaurants to receive these awards on the Monterey Peninsula, and we have set the pace for the local hospitality industry and have even brought national recognition to the area. Most recently, we were named one of the top 25 overall restaurants and one of the top 10 seafood restaurants in the country. With all the awards and recognitions, the restaurant continues to be a success because the numbers work. With food and labor costs, we are dealing in dollars and cents everyday, and that is what this book is about: giving you an opportunity to understand the importance of math and how it relates to your business success throughout the years, from when you first start out until you retire. The restaurant and hospitality business relies on numbers to work, and that relates to any restaurants operating independently, in hotels, and so forth. As chefs/owners, anything related to our business is based on numbers that will give us the facts and statistics for budgets that we hope will provide us continued success. By reading this book, and following its understanding of the role of math and how it can prepare you for employment in business, or if you eventually own your own business, this is a must-read for you to be a success and reach the goals you have set forth in your career to achieve.

> Bert Cutino, CEC, AAC
> Cofounder/COO, The Sardine Factory Restaurant
> 701 Wave Street, on the famous Cannery Row
> Monterey, CA 93942

Bert Cutino is a leader in the hospitality industry. He and his partner Ted Balestreri have been recognized as two of the "50 Power Players" in food service in the United States by *Nation's Restaurant News*. In 1968, they cofounded The Sardine Factory Restaurant in a nearly abandoned area known as Cannery Row. The restaurant was located in a building that once fed sardine workers. Cannery Row, with its approximately 30 restaurants, over 100 specialty shops, hotels, and visitor attractions, now draws 51% of the tourists that visit Monterey's Peninsula. The Sardine Factory was one of the innovators in serving California wines and implementing the premier wine program in the United States. From its 70-seat beginning, The Sardine Factory Restaurant has grown to five rooms and has more than tripled its seating capacity. The restaurant is one of the most successful, widely recognized, and highest grossing dining establishments in the United States. The Sardine Factory has been the recipient of virtually every major restaurant and wine award in the industry, including the prestigious DiRōNA, since 1993; with their 40,000 bottles of wine and close to 1,300 labels, the restaurant has earned *Wine Spectator's* Grand Award since 1982; the *Nation's Restaurant News* Hall of Fame Award (1981); *Restaurant & Institutions* Ivy Award (1980); and The Sardine Factory was also honored as one of 50 restaurants in the United States to serve at former president Ronald Reagan's inaugurations in 1981 and 1985. Chef Cutino has held national offices in the hospitality industry. He has served as head of the American Academy of Chefs (AAC) and has won both the American Culinary Federation's (ACF) Chef of the Year Award and Chef Professionalism Award. When asked about the success of the restaurant, he states that "success has been achieved through an unwavering commitment to quality. Every person on the staff, from waitpersons to kitchen staff, must be able to present him- or herself as a professional and strive for excellence!"

Preface

Many students, when told they are required to take a math course, react with fear due to the poor math experiences they have had in the past. Once students realize how important and relevant math is in the food service, they become motivated to learn, understand, and use math correctly to accomplish their goals of becoming a chef, baker, manager, or any of the many occupations in the food service industry. The authors of this fifth edition have had great success in teaching their students math skills and applications.

In researching this book, we have received interesting and passionate responses about the role that math plays in food service careers from chefs and managers throughout the United States and Canada. In conversations with these individuals, one fact became clearer and clearer: the more successful an individual was in his or her career, the more passionate he or she was in wanting to get the message to students about the importance of learning and using math to become a success in business. One common theme was articulated repeatedly by chefs and managers interviewed by the authors: with a knowledge and the proper usage of math, a business will succeed and the individual will succeed. Like cooking or baking, math is a sequential process. They pointed out that an individual must first master the basic skills before he or she can create a gourmet meal or spectacular dessert.

The fifth edition has been completely revised by the authors of the book. We have read and reread the fourth edition and have calculated every example and problem in the book. All examples have been checked for accuracy. New problems have been added to challenge the students. Step-by-step instructions for problems and concepts have been included. Throughout the book, the authors have added a series of TIPS (To Ensure Perfect Solutions) to assist the student in solving problems and understanding concepts of math. Each chapter has a Chef Sez feature, which is a quote from a manager or chef about the importance of math in his or her own particular operation.

The fifth edition has been completely revised to parallel the required knowledge and competencies mandated by the American Culinary Federation. We have consolidated the material in the book to 15 chapters and have eliminated information that our reviewers told us were not needed in a math book. In addition, the chapters have been set up in a format that follows a logical flow, starting with the basics of math and ending with financial statements. We added for the reader step-by-step calculator instructions through a series of table illustrations. The summary reviews are labeled consecutively in the book as Summary Review 1–1, 1–2, and so forth (the first number is the chapter, and the second number is the summary review). This will make it easier for the instructors and students to locate the summary reviews. We have added more critical thinking problems to make the math more relevant for the student. In addition, Chapters 8 to 15 have been completely revised. We have added behavioral objectives for the skills and strategies that are covered in each chapter. Throughout the book, the summary reviews have been developed to provide a written assessment for student mastery of the objectives. Of special interest and importance to the instructors who are using this new edition, the Instructor's Manual has been revised and all answers have been checked and double-checked for accuracy. Finally, this book is a "keeper." We have added an appendix with all formulas used in the book. This will be a valuable reference tool as you climb the career ladder.

As in the fourth edition, *Math Principles for Food Service Occupations* opens with a **Pretest** and concludes with a **Posttest** for the purpose of evaluating the student's math skills prior to, and upon completion of, the course. The new pretest and posttest consist of 100 math questions that assess the student's understanding of the concepts in the 15 chapters and are needed to have a successful career in the food service industry.

The content of the text has been divided into five coordinated parts to demonstrate subject association and simplify learning.

Part I, **The Calculator,** is placed at the beginning of the book. The authors believe that the calculator is an essential tool for math computation, just as a knife is a tool for the culinary professional. Since calculator skills and the use of calculators are being taught in elementary education, this chapter is placed in the front of the book. If the instructor does not feel that the chapter on calculators should be introduced until after the fundamentals are mastered, he or she can insert it into the class where appropriate.

Part II, **Review of Basic Math Fundamentals,** consists of three chapters intended to refresh and sharpen the student's math skills. The emphasis is placed on methods used to solve mathematical problems related to food service situations. This information should be thoroughly reviewed, with exercise problems worked and referred back to whenever necessary. The authors know that learning math is a sequential process. The student must have mastered the fundamentals and have an understanding of basic math concepts and computational skills before moving into more complicated problem solving.

Part III, **Math Essentials in Food Preparation,** consists of five chapters that focus on the math necessary to function in the preparation of both food and baked products. This part includes weights and measures, a revised section on using the metric system in the kitchen, portion control, converting and yielding recipes, as well as production and baking formulas. Chapter 9 has been completely revised to cover costing in recipes, food, and labor.

Part IV, **Math Essentials in Food Service Recordkeeping,** consists of four chapters concentrating on the math necessary for keeping important records accurate and current. This part covers determining cost percentages and how to price a menu. It also includes inventory procedures, purchasing and receiving, and daily production reports.

Part V, **Essentials of Managerial Math,** has been completely revised from the fourth edition. Chapter 14 concentrates on the math knowledge that is needed in front of house operations. Chapter 15 deals with payroll, taxes, and financial statements. A revised section has been added to this chapter on how to figure out the break-even point for a business. The information in Chapter 15 includes the types of math procedures that are typically the responsibility of management.

The material contained in this text will provide the student with sufficient math knowledge to demonstrate confidence and utilize skills that will lead to rapid job advancement in his or her career. Math, along with culinary skills and proper friendly service, is an essential part of the equation that makes a food service operation a success. Many talented chefs have succeeded in business, while others have failed. The authors want to emphasize that there is more to operating a successful food service operation than putting quality food before the guest.

Acknowledgments

When we decided to revise the fifth edition of *Math Principles for Food Service Occupations,* we knew that we would need help acquiring examples, information, and illustrations. We were fortunate that our travels have taken us to many locations where we could interview chefs and managers. Because of our many interests and participation at conventions and conferences, we have made important and meaningful contacts with influential leaders in the American Culinary Federation, New York State Hospitality and Tourism Association, New York State Restaurant Association, the Albany County Convention and Visitors Bureau, and graduates of the Hotel, Culinary Arts and Tourism program at Schenectady County Community College. Our experience in writing the three editions of *Dining Room and Banquet Management, The Food Service Industry Video Series,* and the fourth edition of *Math Principles for Food Service Occupations,* as well as numerous articles for local business publications, has allowed us many research opportunities. Both of us have masters' degrees: Pam in education and Toby in educational psychology. Toby has also been certified by the American Culinary Federation as a Certified Culinary Educator.

When undertaking this fifth edition, we asked ourselves how we could improve this textbook from the fourth edition. We wanted to make this book stand out from other math books in the hospitality and culinary field. The material in this fifth edition meets all the required knowledge and competencies in the knowledge area for business and math skills required by the American Culinary Federation. We knew we could bring a positive perspective about math to the student because of our combined 59 years of teaching experience at the elementary and college level. Also, we knew that we could call upon our hospitality experience throughout our various careers as cook, chef, bookkeeper, waitperson, food and beverage manager, butler, bartender, and banquet manager to reflect the importance of math in the food service industry to the student. But we wanted something more—we wanted to make the math meaningful. So, in each chapter, we added a section called "Chef Sez" in which the leaders in this industry explain to the reader why math is important. In alphabetical order, we list the following contributors and their titles:

Gail Allen, President, SYSCO Foods, Albany, New York;

Greg Benamati, Sous Chef, Whispering Canyon Café & Artist Point, Disney's Wilderness Lodge, Lake Buena Vista, Florida;

James V. Bigley, Vice President, HMB Consultants, Voorheesville, NY;

Bert P. Cutino, Certified Executive Chef, American Academy of Chefs, Chief Operating Officer, Cofounder, and Chef, The Sardine Factory Restaurant, Monterey, California;

Robert S. Faller, Director of Sales and Marketing, The Otesaga Resort Hotel, Cooperstown, New York;

George R. Goldoff, Vice President of Food and Beverage, Beau Rivage Resort and Casino, Biloxi, Mississippi;

Peter Huebner, President and Owner of Canada Cutlery Inc., Pickering, Ontario, Canada;

Matthew J. Kaperka, General Manager, The Mark of the Quad Cities, Sports & Entertainment, ARAMARK Corporation, Moline, Illinois;

William Leaver, Supervisor, Correctional Food Procurement & Distribution, State of New York, Department of Nutritional Services, Albany, New York;

Noble Masi, Certified Master Baker, Retired Senior Chef Instructor, The Culinary Institute of America;

Irene Maston, Certified Executive Chef, American Academy of Chefs, Chef/Owner, The Andrie Rose Inn, Ludlow, Vermont;

Bob Newell, Certified Executive Chef, Executive Chef, Sodexho, Fairview Southdale Hospital, Edina, Minnesota;

Rodney Renshaw, Executive Chef, The Savoy, Washington, DC;

Thomas Rosenberger, Certified Executive Chef, Director, Food and Beverage Management Programs, Department of Resorts and Gambling, Community College of Southern Nevada, North Las Vegas, Nevada;

Andre Soltner, Founder and Former Owner of Lutece, Master Chef Senior Lecturer, The French Culinary Institute, New York, New York;

Fritz Sonenschmidt, Certified Master Chef, Past Chairman of the American Academy of Chefs, Ambassador for the Culinary Institute of America, Hyde Park, New York;

Richard Wagner, Executive Pastry Chef, Oahu Country Club, Honolulu, Hawaii, and Chef/Instructor/Lecturer at the Kapiolani Community College at the Diamond Head Campus in Honolulu;

We were fortunate to have several editors at Thomson Delmar Learning who assisted us with this project. Jeff Burnham and Judy Roberts, who recruited us to write the book; Matthew Hart, our Acquisitions Editor and the driving force to expand the culinary and hospitality list at Delmar Learning; Patricia Osborn, our Product Manager; Matt Williams, our Content Project Manager who facilitated the production of this text; and Patrick Horn, Editorial Assistant.

Faculty and staff members at Schenectady County Community College assisted us with their knowledge and feedback on specific topics in this edition. We thank Professor Paul Krebs C.C.E. and Associate Professor Susan Hatalsky C.C.E., C.E.C. for their assistance with the concepts and math that deal with baking; Professor Gary Brenenstuhul for testing out concepts with his Math for Food Service classes and sharing his expertise, especially with his gallon, quart, and pints chart; Kevin Brown and Assistant Professor Kim Williams, who patiently checked out our Math for Managers section; Lynne King, our director of library services who researched and confirmed sources and citations for this edition; and Terry Treis, the duplicating machine operator who assisted and advised us with the duplication process of our copies.

Special thanks must be given to these individuals and organizations. To Cristina Lussi, the director of sales, and the staff at the Crowne Plaza Resort and Golf Club in Lake Placid, New York, for their gracious hospitality. We were able to write, edit, and finish the drafts of this edition in the picture-perfect area of Lake Placid, in their new Adirondack Great Room. To the American Culinary Federation (ACF), for developing their math standards for culinary professionals; and to Cancice Childers, the ACF accreditation manager, and Debbie Edge, the ACF accreditation assistant, who have offered Toby the opportunity to be part of the visiting teams to verify that both high schools and colleges are meeting the standards for accreditation. We owe a debt of gratitude to Nina Rodriguez, executive assistant to Bert Cutino, for communicating so quickly and efficiently with us in obtaining the foreword for this edition.

Finally, we would like to thank our employers for the support and encouragement they have given us to undertake this project: The North Colonie Central School District in Loudonville, New York, and Schenectady County Community College in Schenectady, New York. A special thanks goes to our sons, Mike and Larry, and to our family.

If you would like to contact us with questions, comments, or suggestions or any other pertinent information, you may contact either Delmar Thomson Learning or us directly by e-mail at strianaj@gw.sunysccc.edu.

Pamela P. Strianese   Anthony (Toby) J. Strianese

REVIEWERS

The authors and Delmar Learning would like to thank the following reviewers:

Victor Bagan, Instructor
Hibbing Community College
Grand Rapids, MI

Dan Golio, Instructor
Art Institute of New York City
New York, NY

Tom Dillard, Instructor
Seattle Central Community College
Seattle, WA

Linda Jaster, Instructor
Texas State Technical College
Waco, TX

Ann Dooley, Assistant Professor
Baltimore International College
Baltimore, MD

Tom J. Jones, Instructor
Sullivan University
Lexington, KY

Margie Gallo
Sullivan University
Louisville, KY

Joyce Martin, Instructor
East Central College
Union, MO

Robert Garlough, Professor
Grand Rapids Community College
Grand Rapids, MI

David Rosenthal, Department Chair
Contra Costa Community College
San Pablo, CA

William F. Gibson, Assistant Professor
Kauai Community College
Lihue, HI

Previous Edition

Doug Armstrong, Instructor
New Hampshire Community Technical College
Laconia, NH

Ron Jones, Department Chair
McIntosh College
Dover, NH

Joseph Crompton, Instructor
Heywood Career and Technology Center
Columbia, SC

Mary Petersen, Executive Director
Foodservice Educators Network International
Annapolis, MD

William Gibson, Instructor
Kauai Community College
Lihue, HI

Barbara Van Fossen, Associate Professor
Jefferson Community College
Steubenville, OH

Pretest

The pretest evaluates a student's math skills before the student begins the food service math course. This pretest helps both the student and the instructor to focus on the areas of greatest concern.

The instructor will determine the percentage of questions that must be answered correctly to show competency in mathematics in the food service industry.

Addition
1. $35.9 + 626.42 + 2,430.07 + 14.03 =$ _____

Subtraction
2. $\$7,569.75 - \$5,248.46 =$ _____

Multiplication
3. $46.8 \times 8 \times 13.3 \times 15.2 =$ _____

Division
4. $8,245.25 \div 182 =$ _____

Compute the following chain calculation.
5. $\$42,687.50 - \$31,628.75 + \$.05 =$ _____

Using a sales tax percentage of 8.25%, what is the amount of sales tax?
6. $8,169.43 _____

Using 40% as the desired food cost percentage, find the menu price based upon the raw food cost of the following questions. Round answers to the nearest cent.
7. $2.22 _____

8. $0.75 _____

Multiply the following problem.
9. $996.30 \times 6.5\%$ _____

Division problem.
10. $2890.00 \div 16.2\%$ _____

Figure out the total cost of the following problems.
11. $5892.15 + 16.8\%$ gratuity _____

12. $5192.14 - 11.6\%$ discount _____

13. Complete the following invoice, showing the extension amount price of all items.

Case	Size	Product	Unit	Price	Amount
7	#10	Sliced apples	Case	20.87	_____
5	#10	Sliced pineapples	Case	17.27	_____
9	#10	Tomato puree	Case	13.85	_____
8	#10	Green beans cut	Case	11.58	_____
4	#10	Tomatoes, whole peeled	Case	16.98	_____
3	10 lbs.	Fettuccine, long	Lbs.	6.56	_____
5	10 lbs.	Vermicelli, cut	Lbs.	4.20	_____
3	13 oz.	Pickling spices	Oz.	4.18	_____
4	6 oz.	Rubbed sage	Oz.	5.42	_____
3	11 oz.	Thyme, ground	Oz.	5.89	_____
4	46 oz.	Cranberry juice cocktail	Case	22.66	_____
5	50 lbs.	Granulated sugar	Bag	16.70	_____
		Total			_____

14. What is the total cost of the invoice?   _____

15. Twelve items were purchased at $13.60 each and six items at $9.95 each. If the sales tax on the total purchase was 8.25%, what was the total cost?   _____

16. A dessert cart was purchased for $1,880. A discount of 8.5% was given. What is the total cost if a sales tax of 7.5% is added to the purchase?   _____

Rewrite the following number by adding commas in the correct place(s).
17. 235620425   _____

Write out the words for the following dollar amount. For example, $195.23 would be written as "One hundred ninety five and 23/100 dollars."
18. $21,495.25   _____

Change the following amount to the nearest cent using the mill.
19. $55,678.526   _____

Find the sum in the following addition problem. Simplify the answer to lowest terms.
20. 20 4/5 + 16 3/15 + 20 3/10 =   _____

Find the difference in the following subtraction problem. Simplify the answer to lowest terms.
21. 28 4/5 − 16 3/15 =   _____

Find the product in the following multiplication problem.
22. 28 4/5 × 16 6/15 =   _____

Find the quotient in the following division problem.
23. 28 4/5 ÷ 2 6/15 =   _____

Change the following fractions to decimals.
24. 7/10 =   _____

25. 5/100 =   _____

Write the following decimals and mixed decimal fractions in words.

26. 0.7 = _____

27. 9.5 = _____

Write each of the following numbers as decimals.

28. Six tenths _____

29. Sixty-three ten thousandths _____

Compute the following problems.

30. $0.046 + 0.002 + 643 + 6.2675 =$ _____

31. $139.371 - 121.218 =$ _____

32. $7.323 \times 5.324 =$ _____

33. $54.25 \div 3.8 =$ _____

34. How much water should be used to cook 2 pints of barley using a ratio of 4 to 1 water to barley? _____

35. The Bears Restaurant sells 25 times as many orders of chateaubriand as chicken breasts. How many orders of chateaubriand were sold if 12 orders of chicken breasts were sold?

_____

Express the following common fraction as a percent.

36. 7/12 = _____

Express the following percent as a common fraction. Reduce the answer to the lowest common denominator.

37. 66% = _____

38. A 528-pound side of beef is ordered. The chuck cut weighs 76 pounds and the round cut weighs 58 pounds. What percent of the side is the chuck? _____

39. What percent is the round cut? _____

40. The food cost percentage for the month is 37%. If $25,485 was taken in on sales that month, how much of that amount went for the cost of food? _____

41. How many tablespoons are there in 12 teaspoons?

_____

42. One hundred and ten quarts equals how many gallons?

_____

43. A recipe calls for 4 pounds of apple juice. How much liquid would you use? _____

44. What is the range of ounces in a #10 can?

_____

45. Determine the cost of hamburger if the dial pointer on the portion scale points to the third mark beyond the 5 and the cost of 1 pound of ground beef is $3.99. _____

Find the amount of ounces in the following problems.

46. 17.23 pounds _____

47. 12.25 gallons _____

48. The Merlot Restaurant receives 10 ribs of beef weighing 22.75 pounds each. How many ounces of beef does this represent?

_____

Convert the following Fahrenheit temperature to Celsius. Round off the answer to two places to the right of the decimal point.

49. 140   _____

Convert the following Celsius temperature to Fahrenheit. Round off the answer to two places to the right of the decimal point.

50. 27   _____

Convert the following recipe from the American customary system to the metric system.

51. 1 lb. 6 oz. shortening   _____ g

52. 8 pounds of powdered sugar   _____kg

Convert the following recipe from the metric system to the American customary system. Answer should be carried out three places to the right of the decimal point.

53. 1 liter of mayonnaise   _____qt.

54. 5 milliliters of lemon juice   _____tsp.

55. A 2.5-pound box of frozen corn costs $2.55. How much does a 4-ounce serving cost?   _____

56. How many servings can be obtained from 15 gallons of soup if a ½-cup ladle is used?

_____

57. A 4-ounce serving of wax beans is served to each of 155 people. How many cans of wax beans are needed if each can weighs 14 ounces?

58. A 9-pound A.P. beef tenderloin is trimmed; 8 ounces are lost. How many E.P 6-ounce filets mignons can be cut from the tenderloin?

_____

59. For a wedding of 370 guests, an E.P. 8-ounce sirloin steak will be served. If each fabricated sirloin weighs 16 pounds, how many sirloins must be ordered?

_____

60. How many pounds of drawn fish should be ordered when preparing for a party of 188 guests?

_____

61. What is the yield percentage of a 22-pound turkey? The turkey lost 8 pounds and 5 ounces after fabrication and shrinkage.

_____

Find the working factor for the next two problems.

62. The standardized recipe is for 40 portions. The party is for 350 guests.

_____

63. The standardized recipe is for 50 portions. The party is for 30 guests.

_____

64. The following recipe yields nine 8-inch pies. Convert each ingredient to yield thirty-six 8-inch pies.

Amount of conversion   _____

4 lbs. flour   _____

3 lbs. 6 oz. granulated sugar   _____

1/2 oz. salt   _____

3 oz. lemon gratings   _____

1 lb. water   _____

8 oz. corn starch   _____

12 oz. egg yolks   _____

1 lb. 6 oz. lemon juice   _____

4 oz. butter, melted   _____

65. Determine the approximate yield of the following formula if each cookie is to contain 2½ ounces of dough.

1 lb. 6 oz. shortening   _____

1 lb. 6 oz. powdered sugar   _____

2 lb. 8 oz. pastry flour   _____

2 oz. liquid milk   _____

6 oz. raisins, chopped   _____

2 oz. pecans, chopped   _____

3 oz. pineapple, chopped   _____

2 oz. peaches, chopped   _____

8 oz. whole eggs   _____

1/4 oz. baking soda   _____

1/4 oz. vanilla   _____

1/2 oz. salt   _____

Find the approximate yield.   _____

66. Determine the amount of dry instant potato powder needed to prepare 6.5 gallons of mashed potatoes if the ratio calls for 1 lb. 13 oz. of powder for each gallon of milk.   _____

67. Find the baker's percentage of each ingredient used in the following formula. Round to the tenth place.

9 lbs. bread flour   _____

1 lb. pastry flour   _____

1 lb. shortening   _____

18 oz. sugar   _____

13 oz. eggs   _____

5 oz. salt   _____

8 oz. dry milk   _____

10 oz. compressed yeast   _____

5 lbs. cold water   _____

68. One loaf of bread was purchased for $2.89. There are 20 slices of bread in the package, but the 2 end pieces cannot be used. What is the cost of 2 slices of bread for an order of toast?

_____

69. A 9-pound (E.P.) leg of lamb costing $4.85 per pound is roasted. When the roast is removed from the oven, only 2/3 of the original amount is left. How much does an 8-ounce serving cost?

_____

70. Find the cost of the following recipe for soft dinner rolls. Recipe yields 16 dozen rolls.

Ingredients	Amount	Price	Cost
Sugar	1 lb.	$0.36 per pound	_____
Shortening	1 lb. 4 oz.	$0.48 per pound	_____
Dry milk	8 oz.	$1.93 per pound	_____
Salt	2 oz.	$0.42 per pound	_____
Eggs	3	$0.95 per doz.	_____
Yeast	6 oz.	$3.50 per pound	_____
Water	4 lbs.	$1.25 per gallon	_____
Bread flour	7 lbs.	$0.20 per pound	_____

71. Total cost of the recipe   _____

72. Cost of one dozen   _____

73. Cost of one roll   _____

74. The Chardonnay Café employees six culinary staff who each earn $11.50 per hour. During the week, they each work five 8-hour shifts. What is the cost of labor for the culinary staff?

_____

75. A fajita platter has a menu price of $13.95. The raw cost of food is $2.24. What is the food cost percentage?

_____

76. Determine the menu price if the raw food cost is $4.75 and the markup rate is 5/8.   _____

77. Determine the menu price if the raw food cost is $2.75 and a 38% food cost is desired.   _____

78. What was our food cost percentage for the month if we had sales of $111,213.25 and our purchases totaled $53,292?

_____

Find the monthly food cost percentage and the cost of food sold using the following information. Carry the food cost percentage two places to the right of the decimal.

Sales for the Month	$54,000.00
Beginning Inventory	$6,780.50
Purchases for the Month	$15,890.00
Food in Production	$2,005.10
Final Inventory	$4,852.27

79. The cost of food sold is _____

80. Monthly food cost percentage _____

81. Prepare a storeroom requisition form. Find the extension price and the total.

   Ten #10 cans peaches @ $3.71 per can _____

   Seven #10 cans tomatoes @ $2.83 per can _____

   12 heads lettuce @ $0.99 per head _____

   3 dozen apples @ $4.50 per dozen _____

   6 pounds of corn starch @ $0.56 per pound _____

   4 pounds of margarine @ $4.76 per pound _____

82. Total cost of this requisition _____

83. Complete the following counter production reports.

Item	Number of Portions For Sale	Number of Portions Not Sold	Number of Portions Sold	Unit Price	Value Sold
Hot Dogs	85	5		3.25	
Hamburgers	95	7		4.75	
Chicken Patty	65	18		4.75	
Barbecue	55	2		5.50	
Cube Steak	40	5		5.75	
Soda	120	21		1.75	
Shakes	60	8		3.25	
Milk	110	7		1.25	
Pie	48	12		3.50	
Ice Cream	60	15		3.75	
			Total Value Sold		

84. Calculate and total the following guest check. Three guests had lunch at the Lake Resort. They had two orders of coconut shrimp @ $8.25 each for appetizers; two glasses of Sauvignon Blanc @ $7.50 each; and three glasses of private Chardonnay @ $7.00 each. For their main courses, they had a turkey bacon wrap @ $8.25, a club sandwich @ $9.95, and a chicken wrap @ $9.50.

   _____

85. What is the sales tax amount if the sales tax is 6.5%?

   _____

86. What is the guest check total? _____

87. What will the tip be on the guest check if the tip is 15%?

   _____

88. Marisa works three shifts a week. If she sells nine additional $35.00 bottles of wine a night and the gratuity is 18%, what is her additional income?

Each shift   _____

Weekly total   _____

89. Complete the following cashier's daily report.

Today's date	
POS Register Readings or Total of Guest Check Sales	
Food Sales	$2,856.63
Beverage Sales	1,474.68
Miscellaneous Sales	191.21
Total Sales	
Add the Amount of Sales Tax	316.58
Gross Receipts	
Add—Start of Shift Money (Bank)	150.00
Total of Gross Receipts and Money Started With (Bank)	
Cash Collected from Guest Checks During the Shift	625.75
Less Total Cash Paid Out	
Total Cash in Drawer	
Credit Card Receipts	
American Express	1,550.56
Discover	315.45
MasterCard	900.37
Visa	975.25
House Accounts	528.82
Total Charge & House Receipts	
Add Cash in Drawer	
Total Cash and Charges (Should Equal the Amount of Gross Receipts)	
Over or (Short)	
Record of Cash Paid Out	
City Ice Company	31.50
Tips	16.85
Arkay Florist	18.75
Other	0.00
Total Cash Paid Out	
Signed by:	

90. Mr. Toby's restaurant charges $75 for an all-inclusive meal. The sales tax is 8.25% and the gratuity is 15%. What is the

Sales tax owed? _____

Amount of money for the restaurant _____

Gratuity amount? _____

91. A cook is paid a salary of $495 per week, plus a 2% commission on all food sales for the week in excess of $20,000. During the second week of March, the food sales amounted to $30,000. If the Social Security tax is 7.30%, how much Social Security tax was deducted from his earnings for that week? _____

92. How much tax would be paid if your net income is $45,880, and your tax is $380 plus 6% of the excess over $8,000?

_____

93. The food and beverage manager is paid a salary of $9,000 a month and receives two paychecks each month. On a recent paycheck, the deductions from his total earnings were as follows: $135.87 FICA tax; $450.00 federal withholding tax; $97.50 state income tax; and $36.50 city income tax.

What was his gross wage for this pay period? _____

What was his net pay? _____

Prepare a profit and loss statement. Find the cost of food sold, gross margin, total operating expenses, net profit, and the percent of sales. Round percentages to the tenth.

The Manor Restaurant had total sales for the month of November of $25,500. Their inventory at the beginning of the month was $6,280. During the month, they made purchases that totaled $8,200. The food in production cost was $225. The final inventory at the end of the month was $4,690.

Their expenses: salaries $3,220; Social Security taxes $115; rent $460; laundry $95; repairs and maintenance $421; advertising $75; taxes and insurance $195; supplies $120; depreciation $540; utilities $380; and miscellaneous expenses $210.

94. Cost of food sold _____ % _____

95. Gross margin _____ % _____

96. Total operating expenses _____ % _____

97. Net profit _____ % _____

98. Prepare a balance sheet. Find the total assets, total liabilities, and net worth.

Assets of May 15 : Home $138,000, home furnishings $26,085, automobile $22,750; speedboat $6,540, cash in savings accounts $38,670, cash in checking account $5,034, and stocks $4,824. Liabilities: home mortgage $85,500, auto loan $7,200, boat loan $3,900, note payable to loan company $4,500, and charge accounts $2,682.

Total assets _____

Total liabilities _____

Net worth _____

99. Determine the contribution rate, contribution rate percentage, and break-even point.

The Blue Bird Cafeteria did $120,000 in sales. Their variable costs were 40% of the total sales and the fixed costs were $24,000.

Contribution rate   _____

Contribution rate percentage   _____

Break-even point   _____

100. For a food service budget, the yearly income is $650,000. Find the dollar amount that was budgeted for each item listed.

    a. Food and Supplies   26%   _____

    b. Labor   24%   _____

    c. Workman's Compensation   4%   _____

    d. Fringe Benefits   8%   _____

    e. Utilities   11%   _____

    f. Printing Service   2%   _____

    g. New Equipment   10%   _____

    h. Equipment Service   5%   _____

    i. Telephone   3%   _____

    j. Profit   7%   _____

THE CALCULATOR

CHAPTER 1 • Using the Calculator

Chapter one introduces the calculator as an important tool in food service occupations. This chapter will provide instruction on the use of the calculator, utilizing the operations of addition, subtraction, multiplication, and division. Problem solving will be illustrated by using chain calculations, the constant function, the percent key, the memory function, and the plus/minus key to convert a positive number to a negative number, and vice versa.

CHAPTER 1

Using the Calculator

OBJECTIVES

At the completion of this chapter, the student should be able to use the calculator to:

1. Find sums, differences, products, and quotients.
2. Solve problems by using chain calculations.
3. Multiply or divide repeatedly using the constant function.
4. Find sums and differences by using a percent.
5. Find products and quotients by using a percent.
6. Solve problems using the memory function.
7. Use the plus/minus key to convert a positive number to a negative number, and vice versa.

KEY WORDS AND ABBREVIATIONS

calculator	CM or MC
C	MRC
CE	chain calculations
AC	constant function
M+	memory function
RM or MR	plus/minus key

The calculator is one of the most important tools used in food service occupations. It is portable, which means that an employee/owner can use it on the loading dock to check invoices, as well as in the kitchen to convert recipes. Calculators are easy to use and accurate.

There are so many different types of calculators on the market today that it becomes a major decision when a purchase must be made. To help reach a decision, it is best to read literature on the various kinds before finalizing your choice. In this age of electronics, there are many choices: solar-powered calculators, scientific calculators, full-featured solar-powered scientific calculators, solar mini-desktop calculators, and inexpensive handheld calculators, just to name a few. If a solar-powered calculator is purchased, it should have a battery backup. The authors also advise students to purchase a simple calculator, one that is not capable of performing scientific or financial calculations. An example of a simple calculator is shown in Figure 1–1.

Another important tool used in food service occupations is the computer. Computers have built-in calculators in software programs such as Excel and Lotus.

PURCHASING A CALCULATOR

If the calculator you use is for normal functions, it would be an advantage to purchase a solar calculator with fair-sized solar panels that can be used in just about any light. The solar calculator is recommended by the

Figure 1–1 *Hand held calculator (courtesy of Thorsten Rust/Shutterstock)*

T I P S . . . .   To Insure Perfect Solutions

Calculators work differently. Read *all* directions that come with your calculator.

authors in order to obtain the most accurate answers. A good-sized keyboard is another plus, as it is easier to calculate using the finger rather than the end of a pencil, which must be used on very small keyboards. The features required for most food service math functions can be found in most of the inexpensive handheld calculators. This is the kind of calculator used in this chapter to explain the necessary functions employed most often in the food service industry. Our intent is to help the student become more familiar with the main calculator functions and more comfortable using them. Every calculator does not have the same features, and even the keyboards vary from one model to another. For this reason, you should always read and study your calculator instruction booklet.

USING A CALCULATOR

The face of the small handheld calculator usually contains the keys listed in Figure 1–2. However, the operation key may have a different placement, depending on the calculator. Also listed are the functions these keys perform.

The instructions provided in this chapter will apply to most calculators. However, remember that some differences will exist between models. The following calculator functions are those that you will use during your food service career. The functions that would be of little use, such as the square root key, will not be discussed. The student should calculate

ON/OFF	Press to activate the power and turn the calculator on or disconnect power by turning it off. The off key usually clears the calculator, including the memory register. Not all solar calculators have an on/off switch.
C	When the power is on, this key is pressed to clear the calculator of all functions except the memory function.
CE	Press to clear an incorrect keyboard entry that has not been entered into the function. It does not clear the memory function.
CA or AC	If it is included on the keyboard, this key clears the calculator of all functions, including the memory function.
0–9	Numeral entry keys.
.	Decimal point key. Used to enter a decimal point into a number.
=	Equal or result key.
+	Plus or addition key.
−	Minus or subtraction key.
×	Times or multiplication key.
÷	Division key.
%	Percentage key—moves the decimal point two places to the left in the result.
√	Computes the square root of the number in the display. Not used in food service calculations. Used in scientific calculations.
+/−	Change sign key. Does not appear on all calculators. Used to convert a positive number to a negative number, and vice versa.
M+	Memory plus key. Adds display number to the memory.
M−	Memory minus key. Subtracts a number from the memory.
RM MR	Recall Memory or Memory Recall key Displays content in memory. Does not clear memory.
CM MC	Clear Memory or Memory Clear key Displays memory figures and clears the memory.
MRC	Memory Recall and Clear key. Recalls the memory and also clears the memory. When key is depressed once, memory is recalled. Depressed twice, memory is cleared.

Figure 1–2 *Calculator keys*

all examples presented to acquire practice and a complete understanding of the functions explained.

The first step in the use of any calculator is to make sure it is cleared and ready to receive calculations. This is done by depressing the **ON** key, meaning the power is "on" and the calculator is "clear." At this point, it is also wise to do a few simple problems to make sure the batteries and the calculator are functioning properly. The simple test problems may be addition and percent.

T I P S . . .   **To Insure Perfect Solutions**

Always press the clear key **before** you start to enter any new calculation.

The following problem is an example of a simple test addition problem.

At a banquet, a cook has to prepare two separate entrees: one for 37 prime ribs, the other for 65 boneless chicken breasts. How many clean plates must the cook have to serve the meals? If the cook used a calculator, the cook would solve the problem as illustrated in Table 1–1.

The following is an example of a simple percentage multiplication problem.

Mr. Ortiz booked a banquet for 600 guests. Because of the great speaker booked, he calls and states that he anticipates an increase of guests by 30%. How many meals would the chef have to prepare for Mr. Ortiz's banquet?

Think of this as 30% more meals than the original 600. Therefore, the answer will be greater than 600 meals. See Table 1–2 for the solution.

This means that the chef would have to increase the amount of meals by 180. Since the original number of meals was 600, the additional 180 meals would have to be added to the original number, as shown in Table 1–3.

The Four Basic Methods of Operation

The four basic methods of operation—addition, subtraction, multiplication, and division—are carried out on the calculator in the order that you would do the problem manually, or say the problem verbally. For

Use the following steps to solve the addition problem	Display Window
Press the keys three (3) seven (7)	37
Press the plus (+) key	+
Press the keys six (6) five (5)	65
Press the equal (=) key	=
The answer one hundred and two (102) shows in the display window	102

Table 1–1

Use the following steps to solve the percentage problem	Display Window
Press the keys six (6) zero (0) zero (0)	600
Press the multiplication (×) key	×
Press the keys three (3) zero (0)	30
Press the percentage (%) key	%
The answer one eighty (180) shows in the display window	180

Table 1–2

Use the following steps to solve the addition problem	Display Window
Press the keys six (6) zero (0) zero (0) (*the original amount of meals*)	600
Press the plus (+) key	+
Press the keys one (1) eight (8) zero (0) (*the 30% extra meals*)	180
Press the equal (=) key	=
The answer seven eighty (780) shows in the display window	780

Table 1–3

example, to add 8 and 6, you would enter 8 + 6 =. The answer, 14, would then appear in the display window. To subtract 6 from 14, you would enter 14 − 6 =. The answer, 8, would again appear in the display window.

Try the following practice exercises to see if you have mastered how to use a calculator for the four basic operations. Correct answers are given.

Addition practice exercises

a. 37 + 46 + 54 =   (*Answer:* 137)

b. 48 + 52 + 78 =   (*Answer:* 178)

c. 3,463 + 225 + 2,218 + 4,560 =   (*Answer:* 10466)

d. 32.5 + 519.43 + 2,226.06 + 18.03 =   (*Answer:* 2796.02)

e. 26,423 + 22.08 + 2,946 + 3,220 + 445.046 =

(*Answer:* 33056.126)

Subtraction practice exercises

a. 33,682 − 18,620 =   (*Answer:* 15062)

b. 3,895.28 − 1,620.29 =   (*Answer:* 2274.99)

c. 48,920.56 − 32,826.69 =   (*Answer:* 16093.87)

d. $8,668.78 − $4,878.28 =   (*Answer:* $3790.50)

e. 956 − 482.739 =   (*Answer:* 473.261)

Multiplication practice exercises

a. 86 × 256 =   (*Answer:* 22016)

b. 1,620 × 62 × 18 =   (*Answer:* 1807920)

c. 4,482 × 22 × 6.8 =   (*Answer:* 670507.2)

d. $46.5 \times 7 \times 12.2 \times 18.4 =$ (*Answer:* 73068.24)

e. $\$438.75 \times 34.5 =$ (*Answer:* $15136.875)

Division practice exercises

a. $2{,}175 \div 15 =$ (*Answer:* 145)

b. $7{,}137 \div 156 =$ (*Answer:* 45.75)

c. $6{,}256.25 \div 175 =$ (*Answer:* 35.75)

d. $82.9 \div 4.5 =$ (*Answer:* 18.422)

e. $6.5 \div .25 =$ (*Answer:* 26)

SUMMARY REVIEW 1–1

Addition

1. $48 + 59 + 215 =$ _____

2. $78 + 135 + 393 =$ _____

3. $269 + 458 + 680 =$ _____

4. $3{,}263 + 298 + 2{,}229 + 4{,}685 =$ _____

5. $35.6 + 626.42 + 2{,}430.07 + 14.03 =$ _____

Subtraction

6. $23{,}583 - 16{,}220 =$ _____

7. $4{,}596.26 - 2{,}723.25 =$ _____

8. $56{,}750.35 - 31{,}999.67 =$ _____

9. $\$7{,}567.75 - \$5{,}248.46 =$ _____

10. $987 - 452.634 =$ _____

Multiplication

11. $89 \times 372 =$ _____

12. $1{,}586 \times 82 \times 16 =$ _____

13. $4{,}556 \times 23 \times 8.9 =$ _____

14. $46.8 \times 8 \times 13.3 \times 12.2 =$ _____

15. $\$656.76 \times 33.5 =$ _____

Division

16. $1{,}675 \div 15 =$ _____

17. $6{,}280 \div 163 =$ _____

18. $8{,}245.25 \div 182 =$ _____

19. $92.7 \div 0.25 =$ _____

20. $7.5 \div 26 =$ _____

Chain Calculations

Since the calculator is portable, a chef or cook may use it in many areas of the food service operation, such as to calculate invoices or inventory. Invoices or inventory often require the food service employee to solve problems using chain calculations. Chain calculations involve a series of numbers and a variety of math operations. Many chain calculations involve all four basic operations. However, because specific math rules and steps apply when doing all four basic mathematical operations, we will limit the discussion of chain calculations to simple addition and subtraction problems. Chain calculations using addition and subtraction are carried out on the calculator in the same order as a person would say the problem verbally. For example:

$$29 + 120 - 38 + 25 - 12 = 124$$

29 plus 120 minus 38 plus 25 minus 12 equals 124.

TIPS . . . To Insure Perfect Solutions

When performing chain calculations, write down the intermediate results. Calculators do not provide an entry history. By writing down intermediate results, it is easier to find mistakes.

This is an example of how a chain calculation would be used in a restaurant setting. The prep cook has to figure out how many 10-ounce steaks are left on Thursday morning. She has to take into account how many she cut and how many the restaurant sold from Monday through Wednesday. On Monday she cut 150 steaks. The restaurant sold 86 steaks. Tuesday she cut 45 more steaks, and the restaurant sold 62 steaks. Wednesday she cut 25 steaks, and the restaurant sold 70 steaks. How many steaks are left for Thursday?

In order to solve the problem, it should be stated verbally as 150 minus 86 plus 45 minus 62 plus 25 minus 70 equals how many steaks are left. Table 1–4 illustrates how this problem will be solved.

Use the following steps to solve the chain calculation	Display Window
Press the keys one (1) five (5) zero (0) (*Monday's cut steaks*)	150
Press the minus (−) key	−
Press the keys eight (8) six (6) (*Monday's sold steaks*)	86
Press the plus (+) key	+
The display window shows six (6) four (4)	64
Press the keys four (4) five (5) (*Tuesday's cut steaks*)	45
Press the minus (−) key	−
The display window shows one (1) zero (0) nine (9)	109
Press the keys six (6) two (2) (*Tuesday's sold steaks*)	62
Press the plus (+) key	+
The display window shows four (4) seven (7)	47
Press the keys two (2) five (5) (*Wednesday's cut steaks*)	25
Press the minus (−) key	−
The display window shows seven (7) two (2)	72
Press the keys seven (7) zero (0) (*Wednesday's sold steaks*)	70
Press the equal (=) key	=
The display window shows two (2)	2
Answer: Two steaks are left on Thursday morning	

Table 1–4

Practice the following chain calculation exercises. Note, calculators do not have dollar ($) signs. Dollar signs have been added in problem d and also in several of the summary review problems.

a. 97 + 120 − 38 + 12 −25 = (answer 166)

b. 1,440 − 1,200 + 45 −2 + 6 = (answer 289)

c. 395 − 42 + 225 − 448 = (answer 130)

d. $53,785.25 − $32,726.85 + $2,253.75 = (answer $23,312.15)

e. 596 − 58 + 24,568 − 1,420.6 = (answer 23,685.4)

SUMMARY REVIEW 1–2

1. 67 + 230 − 89 − 6 + 3 =   _____

2. 1,260 − 1,051 + 290 − 2 + 3 =   _____

3. 365 − 52 + 290 − 545 =   _____

4. $42,685.50 − $31,628.75 + $0.05 =   _____

5. 592 − 65 − 28,562 + 1,325.8 =   _____

Constant Function

The **constant function** may be used to multiply or divide repeatedly by the same number. *The constant is entered first when multiplying and becomes the multiplier.* The multiplier remains in the calculator as a new multiplicand is entered. The = key is depressed to get the result. For example, find the product for each of the following:

T I P S . . .   **To Insure Perfect Solutions**

Make certain that **YOUR** calculator has a constant function. Not all calculators do!

The sales tax on meals is 6.5%. Using 6.5% as the constant, the restaurant manager must figure out the amount of sales tax for these three banquets.

a. $252.00

b. $79.00

c. $2,456.92

Remember that 6.5% must be changed to the decimal 0.065 (the decimal moves two places to the left when the % sign is removed) and entered first, followed by the × sign and then the multiplicand. Pressing the = key will give each product. The constant and × sign are entered only once.

Table 1–5 illustrates how these three problems are solved using the constant. The answers are rounded off to the nearest cent.

Use the following steps to solve the constant function problems	Display Window
Press the keys decimal (.) zero (0) six (6) five (5) (*sales tax %*)	.065
Press the multiplication (×) key	×
Press the keys two (2) five (2) two (2) (*banquet a*)	252
Press the equal (=) key	=
The answer sixteen dollars and thirty-eight cents (16.38) shows in the display window, which is the sales tax for banquet a	16.38
Press the keys seven (7) nine (9) (*banquet b*)	79
Press the equal (=) key	=
The answer five dollars thirteen and a half cents (5.135) shows in the display window, which is the sales tax for banquet b	5.135
The answer is rounded off to the nearest cent, 5.14	5.14
Press the keys two (2) four (4) five (5) six (6) decimal (.) nine (9) two (2) (*banquet c*)	2456.92
Press the equal (=) key	=
The answer one hundred fifty-nine dollars and sixty-nine and ninety-eight tenths cents (159.6998) shows in the display window, which is the sales tax for banquet c	159.6998
The answer is rounded off to the nearest cent, 159.70	159.70

Table 1–5

As you can see, the constant and × sign are entered only one time. New multiplicands are entered without reentering the constant or × sign.

SUMMARY REVIEW 1-3

What is the amount of sales tax on the following amounts, if the 6.5% sales tax rate is used as the constant? Round answers to the nearest cent.

1. $289.00 _____

2. $78.50 _____

3. $2,450.95 _____

4. $5,236.55 _____

5. $8,169.43 _____

DIVIDING BY A CONSTANT

In division, the constant is entered after the first dividend is entered. It becomes the divisor and remains in the calculator as each new dividend is entered. For example, find the quotient in the following:

A restaurant manager may use division to set the price of menu items once the raw food cost is known. The formula to set the menu price is raw food cost divided by the desired food cost percentage. Using 40% as the desired food cost, the restaurant manager sets the menu price for the three items using the above formula. Therefore, 40% is the constant.

a. 2.95

b. 3.27

c. 12.22

Use the following steps (with constant) to determine menu prices	Display Window
Press the keys two (2) decimal (.) nine (9) five (5) (*raw cost a*)	2.95
Press the division (÷) key	÷
Press the keys decimal (.) four (4) zero (0) (*desired food cost %*)	.40
Press the equal (=) key	=
The answer seven dollars and thirty-seven and five-tenths (7.375) shows in the display window for menu item a	7.375
The menu price is rounded off to the nearest cent, 7.38	7.38
Press the keys three (3) decimal (.) two (2) seven (7) (*raw cost b*)	3.27
Press the equal (=) key	=
The answer eight dollars and seventeen and a half (8.175) shows in the display window for menu item b	8.175
The menu price is rounded off to the nearest cent, 8.18	8.18
Press the keys one (1) two (2) decimal (.) two (2) two (2) (*raw cost c*)	12.22
Press the equal (=) key	=
The menu price thirty dollars and fifty-five cents (30.55) shows in the display window for menu item c	30.55

Table 1–6

Remember that 40% must first be changed to the decimal 0.40 (the decimal moves two places to the left when the % sign is removed) and entered after the first dividend. The procedure for entering would be the dividend followed by the ÷ sign, which is entered only once, as is the constant, which is entered last. Pressing the = key will give each quotient.

The restaurant manager uses the steps in Table 1–6 to determine the three menu prices.

SUMMARY REVIEW 1-4

Using 35% as the desired food cost percentage, find the menu price based upon the raw food cost of the following questions. Round answers to the nearest cent.

1. $2.22   _____

2. $0.75   _____

3. $8.97   _____

4. $5.68   _____

5. $3.48   _____

DISCUSSION QUESTION 1-A

If you were the restaurant manager, would you keep the prices at exactly a 35% food cost, or would you change the menu prices? How would you do it, and why?

Chef Sez...

"The use of calculators in food service is just as important to the success of an operation as the quality of its food. Without calculators or more important, the proper use of them, no establishment will be successful."

William Leaver
Supervisor, Correctional Food
Procurement & Distribution
State of New York
Department of Nutritional Services

The Office of Nutritional Services establishes all menus, portion sizes, equipment requirements, and purchases of all food items for the 70 correctional facilities (with a population of over 70,000) in New York State. This amounts to almost $40 million a year. Mr. Leaver supervises the par stocks and all purchasing for the correctional facilities. He is a member of the executive team at a cook-chill plant that produces 130,000 portions of food per day. They currently ship their products to 41 correctional facilities and the Training Academy.

Multiplying, Dividing, Adding, and Subtracting by a Percent

Many times in the food service business, a monetary discount is given for buying goods in bulk. This discount is expressed in the form of a percentage. For example, if a business buys five slicing machines, they may receive a 10% discount. In order to know the amount of the discount, the chef/owner must be able to multiply by a percent. Chefs, banquet managers, cooks, or any food service employees need to understand how to multiply using percentages because, many times, their bonus or gratuity depends on a percentage of the gross or net sales. As stated previously in the chapter, a chef/owner may divide by a desired food cost percentage to set a menu price once the raw cost is determined.

Multiplication and division by a percent are functions that are performed just as you would express the problem orally. For example, you would say 580 dollars times 5.5 percent, so on the calculator you enter $580 \times 5.5\%$, and the correct answer appears in the display window as 31.9 (this is $31.90). Or you can change 5.5% to the decimal 0.055 and proceed to find the solution by entering $580 \times 0.055 = 31.90$. The calculator will automatically place the decimal point, but the dollar sign must be added.

Multiplying by a percent Table 1–7 will demonstrate how to multiply by a percentage.

Problem: $896.25 \times 7.5\%$ or $0.075 =$

Use these steps to determine how to multiply by a percent	Display Window
Press the keys eight (8) nine (9) six (6) decimal (.) two (2) five (5)	896.25
Press the multiplication (×) key	×
Enter the percent amount. Press the keys decimal (.) zero (0) seven (7) five (5)	.075
Press the equal (=) key	=
The answer sixty-seven dollars and twenty-one and eight-tenths cents (67.218) shows in the display window	67.218
Round off the amount to sixty-seven dollars and twenty-two cents (67.22)	67.22

Table 1–7

Use these steps to determine how to divide with a percent	Display Window
Press the keys eight (8) nine (9) six (6) decimal (.) two (2) five (5)	896.25
Press the division (÷) key	÷
Enter the percent amount. Press the keys decimal (.) seven (7) five (5)	.75
Press the equal (=) key	=
The answer one thousand one hundred and ninety-five dollars (1,195.00) *shows in the display window*	(1,195.00)

Table 1–8

Exercises:

Try the following practice exercises to see if you have mastered multiplying by a percentage. Answers are rounded to the nearest cent.

   a. $652.40 × 6.7% or 0.067 =   *(Answer: $43.71)*

   b. $2,900 × 35% or 0.35 =   *(Answer: $1,015.00)*

   c. $7,200.00 × 15.6% or 0.156 =   *(Answer: $1,123.20)*

   d. $958.20 × 7.9% or 0.079 =   *(Answer: $75.70)*

Dividing by a percent When dividing by a percent, as stated before, the problem is entered just as you would express it orally. For example, you say 580 dollars divided by 5.5 percent, and the correct answer appears in the display window as 10545.454, or you can change the 5.5% to the decimal 0.055 and proceed to find the solution by entering 580 ÷ 0.055 =. Again, the calculator will automatically place the decimal point, but the dollar sign must be added.

A word of caution to the readers: it is common to have the results of the problem seem strange or wrong because the resulting answer is larger than the original dividend. For example, a baker makes five pies for a restaurant. The restaurant manager will sell individual pieces of the pie as dessert. If the pies are cut into 10 slices, each slice represents 10% of one pie. What is the total amount of slices will we get from five pies? The problem, 5 ÷ 10%, will result in the answer of 50 pieces of pie. The number 50 is larger than the dividend of 5.

The following problem reads: $896.25 ÷ 75% or 0.75 =

The steps to solve the problem are shown in Table 1–8.

Exercises:

Try the following practice exercises to see if you have mastered dividing by a percentage. Answers are rounded to the nearest cent.

   a. $652.40 ÷ 6.7% or 0.067 =   *(Answer: $9,737.31)*

   b. $2,900.00 ÷ 35% or 0.35 =   *(Answer: $8,285.71)*

   c. $7,200.00 ÷ 15.6% or 0.156 =   *(Answer: $46,153.85)*

   d. $958.20 ÷ 7.9% or 0.079 =   *(Answer: $12,129.11)*

SUMMARY REVIEW 1-5

Multiplication

  1. $996.30 × 8.5%   _____

  2. $565.45 × 7.5%   _____

3. $2,800.00 × 16.4%   _____

4. $7,452.85 × 6.8%   _____

5. $788.99 × 7.75%.   _____

Division

6. $425.60 ÷ 76%   _____

7. $352.75 ÷ 7.4%   _____

8. $2,890.00 ÷ 15.2%   _____

9. $7,252.80 ÷ 6.4%   _____

10. $956.26 ÷ 8.9%   _____

Adding by a percent When adding by a percentage two steps are needed. First, you have to multiply to find the amount of money that you will add to the original price. Second, the amount of money that has been found has to be added to the original price. Table 1–9 illustrates the following problem.

Problem: The Showboat Restaurant purchased $593.51 worth of kitchen equipment. The sales tax was 5.5%. What was the total cost of the equipment?

Subtracting by a percent Discounts are a normal part of doing business in the food service industry. Whenever a discount is given to a business, two steps must be calculated to solve the problem. First, the food service professional must multiply by a percentage to determine the amount of the discount. Second, that amount has to be subtracted from the original price. Table 1–10 shows how to subtract after finding the amount of a discount.

Problem: Kelly Hart purchased a new slicing machine for $2,560. She was given a 15% discount. What was the total cost?

Use the following steps to determine how to add by a percent	Display Window
Enter the price of the kitchen equipment. Press the keys five (5) nine (9) three (3) decimal (.) five (5) one (1)	593.51
Press the multiplication (×) key	×
Enter the sales tax percent. Press the keys decimal (.) zero (0) five (5) five (5)	.055
Press the equal (=) key	=
The answer thirty-two dollars and sixty-four cents and three-tenths (32.643) shows in the display window	32.643
The sales tax is rounded off to 32.64	32.64
Enter the price of the kitchen equipment. Press the keys five (5) nine (9) three (3) decimal (.) five (5) one (1)	593.51
Press the plus (+) key	+
Enter the amount of sales tax. Press the keys three (3) two (2) decimal (.) six (6) four (4)	32.64
Press the equal (=) key	=
The total cost of the equipment, six hundred twenty-six dollars and fifteen cents (626.15), shows in the display window	626.15

Table 1–9

Use these steps to determine how to subtract by a percent	Display Window
Enter the price of the slicing machine. Press the keys two (2) five (5) six (6) zero (0)	2560
Press the multiplication (×) key	×
Enter the discount percent. Press the keys decimal (.) one (1) five (5)	.15
Press the equal (=) key	=
The answer three hundred eighty-four dollars (384) shows in the display window	384
Enter the price of the slicing machine. Press the keys two (2) five (5) six (6) zero (0)	2560
Press the minus (−) key	−
Enter the amount of the discount. Press the keys three (3) eight (8) four (4)	384
Press the equal (=) key	=
The total cost of the equipment, two thousand one-hundred seventy-six dollars (2,176.00), shows in the display window	2176

Table 1–10

SUMMARY REVIEW 1–6

Figure out the total costs of the following problems.

1. $284.62 + 3.5% tax   _____

2. $4,892.15 + 16.8% gratuity   _____

3. $636.22 − 6.5% discount   _____

4. $4,192.14 − 11.6% discount   _____

5. $982.40 − 7.5% discount   _____

The Memory Function

The **memory function** is used to retain figures in the calculator. Even when the power is turned off, some calculators will retain figures. This function makes totaling an invoice or figuring other totals simpler when multiplying by a percent. Since the keys of some calculators may vary slightly, it is wise to check a calculator's instruction booklet before using its memory function. For example:

Before starting, press the C and CM keys to clear the calculator and its memory. The following is a step-by-step outline of how to use the memory function to complete an invoice (see Figure 1–3). Each step corresponds to a line of the invoice, as shown in Figure 1–4.

Using the calculator, check the accuracy of the completed invoice of Webb Food Company, Inc. (Figure 1–5). Multiply the number of cases times the price to check the accuracy of the amount given on each line. When mistakes appear, make the necessary corrections. Also check the total invoice price by adding all figures in the amount column. You may do this exercise with or without the memory function. However, using the memory function for practice will increase your confidence in the

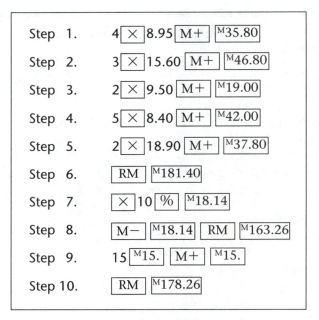

Step 1.	4 $\times$ 8.95 M+ ^{M}35.80
Step 2.	3 $\times$ 15.60 M+ ^{M}46.80
Step 3.	2 $\times$ 9.50 M+ ^{M}19.00
Step 4.	5 $\times$ 8.40 M+ ^{M}42.00
Step 5.	2 $\times$ 18.90 M+ ^{M}37.80
Step 6.	RM ^{M}181.40
Step 7.	$\times$ 10 % ^{M}18.14
Step 8.	M− ^{M}18.14 RM ^{M}163.26
Step 9.	15 ^{M}15. M+ ^{M}15.
Step 10.	RM ^{M}178.26

Figure 1–3 *Step-by-step outline for use of the memory function*

Distributor:	Haines Foods, Inc.	Phone: 771-8800
		Date: April 20, 20___
Address:	70 Greenbrier Avenue	
	Ft. Mitchell, KY 41017	

Distributors of Fine Food Products — Wholesale Only

No. of Pieces	Salesperson	Order No.	Invoice #
5	Joe Jones	2860	J 2479

Packed by: Sold To: Mr. John Doe
   R.H.   Street: 120 Elm Avenue
               City/State: Covington, KY

Case	Pack	Size	Canned Foods	Price	Amount
4	6	#10 can	Sliced Apples	8.95	35.80
3	6	#10 can	Pitted Cherries	15.60	46.80
2	12	#5 can	Apple Juice	9.50	19.00
5	24	1 lb.	Cornstarch	8.40	42.00
2	24	#2$\frac{1}{2}$ can	Asparagus	18.90	37.80
			Total Amount		181.40
			Less: Special Discount 10%		18.14
			Total Net Price		163.26
			Plus: Delivery Charge		15.00
			Total Invoice Price		178.26

Figure 1–4 *Invoice form*

future. To start checking the invoice using the memory function, the first line would be calculated as follows:

Problem: 6 cases of sliced apples at $20.87 for each case =
4 cases of sliced pineapple at $17.27 for each case =
Table 1–11 demonstrates the first two steps using the memory function.

Use these steps with the memory function	Display Window
Press the key six (6)	6
Press the multiplication (×) key	×
Press the keys two (2) zero (0) decimal (.) eight (8) seven (7)	20.87
Press the memory + (M+) key	M+
The answer one hundred twenty-five and twenty-two cents shows in the display window with an M	125.22M
Press the key four (4)	4
Press the multiplication (×) key	×
Press the keys one (1) seven (7) decimal (.) two (2) seven (7)	17.27
Press the memory + (M+) key	M+
The answer sixty-nine dollars and eight cents shows in the display window with an M	69.08M
Press the Memory Retain key (MR)	MR
The answer one hundred ninety-four dollars and thirty cents (194.30) shows in the display window with an M	194.3M
Continue on with the problem in Figure 1–5	

Table 1–11

Complete each line by following the procedure given in the above example. To find the total invoice price, press the RM key (recall memory).

Webb Food Company, Inc.
1225 South Street
Mechanicville, New York 12118
518.637.2592

webbfc@nycap.rr.com

Invoice Number 12223

Tancredi's Restaurant
Depot Square
Mechanicville, NY 12118

Case	Size	Product	Unit	Price	Amount
6	#10	Sliced apples	Case	20.87	125.22
4	#10	Sliced pineapple	Case	17.27	69.08
8	#10	Tomato puree	Case	13.85	110.80
7	#10	Green beans, cut	Case	11.58	81.06
3	#10	Tomatoes, whole peeled	Case	16.98	50.94
2	10 lbs.	Fettuccine, long	Lbs.	6.56	13.12
4	10 lbs.	Vermicelli, cut	Lbs.	4.20	20.80
2	13 oz.	Pickling spices	Oz.	4.18	8.36
3	6 oz.	Rubbed sage	Oz.	5.42	16.26
2	11 oz.	Thyme, ground	Oz.	5.89	64.79
5	46 oz.	Cranberry juice cocktail	Case	22.66	113.30
3	50 lbs.	Granulated sugar	Bag	16.70	50.10
		Total			723.83

Figure 1–5 *Completed invoice form*

DISCUSSION QUESTION 1–B

Are any of the figures incorrect? What could have happened to cause the mistake(s)? What is the correct total? As the chef/owner, what steps would you take to correct the bill?

SUMMARY REVIEW 1-7

1. Complete the following invoice, using your calculator and its memory function.

Distributor:	Miller Foods, Inc.		Phone: 772-9654
			Date: April 22, 20—
Address:	2033 Elm Avenue		
	Norwood, Ohio 45212		
	Distributors of Fine Food Products—Wholesale Only		

No. of Pieces	Salesperson		Order No.	Invoice #
4	James Jones		2861	J 2480
Packed by:	Sold To:	Mr. Tim O'Connell		
R.H.	Street:	916 Montague Street		
	City/State:	Cincinnati, Ohio 45202		

Case	Pack	Size	Canned Foods	Price	Amount
5	6	#10 can	Sliced Pears	$10.95	_____ a.
3	6	#10 can	Sliced Peaches	12.85	_____ b.
6	12	#5 can	Tomato Juice	9.50	_____ c.
4	24	1 lb.	Cornstarch	8.40	_____ d.
3	24	#2$\frac{1}{2}$ can	Asparagus	18.90	_____ e.
			Total Amount		_____ f.
			Less: Special Discount 12%		_____ g.
			Total Net Price		_____ h.
			Plus: Delivery Charge		$12.00
			Total Invoice Price		_____ i.

Multiplying by a Percent Using the Memory Function

Remember that percentage is a key function when developing a food service career. It is, as previously stated, the language of the food service industry. When discussing labor costs, food costs, and so forth, the figures are given by percent. With this in mind, you can see the importance of understanding and developing confidence in using this function and dealing with percentages. For example:

The purchasing agent at Morrisey's Restaurant purchased five food items at $18.50 each and three food items at $12.60 each. If the sales tax on the total purchase was 6.5%, what was the total cost of the purchase? Table 1–12 demonstrates the steps in this calculation.

Use these steps with the memory function	Display Window
Press the key five (5) (*five food items purchased*)	5
Press the multiplication (×) key	×
Press the keys one (1) eight (8) decimal (.) five (5) zero (0)	18.50
Press the memory plus (M+) key	M+
The answer ninety-two dollars and fifty cents shows in the display window with an M	92.5M
Press the key three (3) (*three food items purchased*)	3
Press the multiplication (×) key	×
Press the keys one (1) two (2) decimal (.) six (6) zero (0)	12.60
Press the memory plus (M+) key	M+
The answer thirty-seven dollars and eighty cents shows in the display window with an M	37.8M
Press the memory recall key (MR)	MR
The answer one-hundred thirty dollars and thirty cents shows in the display window with an M	130.3M
Press the multiplication (×) key	×
Press the keys decimal (.) zero (0) six (6) five (5)	.065
Press the equal key (=)	=
The answer eight dollars and forty-six and ninety-five hundredths of a cent shows in the display window with an M	8.4695M
The sales tax must be added, so press the memory plus (M+) key	M+
Press the memory recall key (MR)	MR
The answer one hundred thirty-eight dollars and seventy-six and ninety-five hundredths of a cent shows in the display window with an M	138.7695M
The answer is rounded off to one hundred thirty-eight dollars and seventy-seven cents (138.77), which is the cost of the food items plus the sales tax	138.77

Table 1–12

SUMMARY REVIEW 1–8 (Round answers to nearest cent)

1. Chenusa Jones purchased 12 items at $12.60 each. Sales tax was 6.5%. What was the total cost?

2. Bob Shirley purchased eight items at $6.25 each, and six items at $8.95% each. If the sales tax on the total purchase was 7.5%, what was the total cost?

3. Bill Thompson made purchases costing $10.40, $54.80, $7.35, $8.98, and $0.56. If the sales tax was 7.75% of the total amount, what was the total cost?

4. Hillary Meyers purchased 15 items at $16.20 each, and 4 items at $20.50 each. If the sales tax on the total purchase was 5.25%, what was the total cost?

5. Sheryar Khan purchased items costing $89.95, $16.75, and $9.25. If the sales tax was 6.75% of the total amount, what was the total cost?

Use these steps with the plus/minus key	Display Window
Press the keys two (2) eight (8) zero (0) zero (0) (*cost of equipment*)	2800
Press the multiplication (×) key	×
Press the keys decimal (.) zero (0) eight (8) (*discount*)	.08
Press the minus key (−)	−
The answer two hundred twenty-four dollars shows in the display window	224
Press the keys two (2) eight (8) zero (0) zero (0) (*cost of equipment*)	2800
Press the equal (=) key	=
The answer two thousand five-hundred seventy-six dollars shows in the display window with a minus sign after it, showing the answer is a negative number	2576−
Press the plus/minus (+/−) key	+/−
The answer two thousand five-hundred seventy-six dollars shows in the display window without the minus sign, showing it is now a positive number	2576
Press the multiplication key (×)	×
Press the keys decimal (.) zero (0) six (6) five (5) (*sales tax*)	.065
Press the equal (=) key	=
The answer one hundred sixty-seven dollars and forty-four cents shows in the display window (sales tax cost)	167.44
Press the plus key (+)	+
Press the equal (=) key	=
The answer two thousand seven-hundred forty-three dollars and forty-four cents (2743.44) shows in the display window. This is the total cost of the used equipment with the sales tax.	2743.44

Table 1–13

Using the Plus/Minus Key

This change sign key is used to convert a positive number to a negative number, and vice versa. The key is only used on certain occasions and would not be considered a popular key, like the 3 or 1 key. For example:

The Blue Bird Restaurant purchased some used equipment for $2,800. It was given a special discount of 8% plus a sales tax of 6.5%. What was the total cost? Table 1–13 illustrates how to use the plus/minus key.

In the above calculation, the 2576 appears with a minus sign, which is a negative number. To add the 6.5% sales tax, that negative sign must be converted to a positive sign so the sales tax amount can be added to the cost. This is accomplished by pressing the plus/minus key after the amount 2576− appears in the display window.

SUMMARY REVIEW 1-9 (Round answers to nearest cent)

1. The Chateau Restaurant purchased a dessert cart for $1,680. Because the cart was slightly damaged, they were given an 8.5% discount. A sales tax of 6.5% was added to the purchase price. What was the total cost?

2. The Sky Lark Restaurant purchased new china for $4,868.54. Because they chose a discontinued pattern, they were given a 9% discount. A sales tax of 7.5% was added to the purchase price. What was the total cost?

3. A party was catered for 60 people. The bill came to $480. A senior citizen discount of 5.5% was given. A sales tax of 7% was added to the bill. What was the total bill?

4. A party for 90 people was served. The bill was $810. A discount of 4.5% was given because it was a school group. A sales tax of 7.5% was added to the bill. What was the total bill?

5. Four bakers' balance scales were purchased for $880. A 4% discount was given because the scales were purchased in quantity. A sales tax of 8% was added to the bill. What was the total bill?

PART II

REVIEW OF BASIC MATH FUNDAMENTALS

CHAPTER 2 • Numbers, Symbols of Operations, and the Mill

CHAPTER 3 • Addition, Subtraction, Multiplication, and Division

CHAPTER 4 • Fractions, Decimals, Ratios, and Percents

Part II contains a review of the basic math fundamentals used in most food service operations. Basic mathematical concepts are covered using whole numbers, fractions, decimals, and percents. Commonsense guidelines in the use of the mill and rounding up when it comes to business situations are discussed. Competency in each area of this review section is essential for ensuring accuracy in working the math exercises presented in this work text and for accurate record keeping when performing math functions in the food service industry.

Numbers, Symbols of Operations, and the Mill

OBJECTIVES

At the completion of this chapter, the student should be able to:

1. Read and write numbers.
2. Identify the symbols for the four basic operations of addition, subtraction, multiplication, and division.
3. Identify the mill and use it in solving problems.
4. Understand the reasoning for rounding up in a food service operation.

KEY WORDS

whole numbers	symbols of operations
unit	cent
numerals	mill
digits	rounding up
period	

The information presented in this chapter is intended to refresh your knowledge of basic mathematical terms and principles that you learned in your early school years but may not have put into practice often enough to retain. These terms and principles are important to all math functions. They will be used throughout the book, and they need to be fully understood for you to increase your math skills and function effectively in the workplace.

The food service industry, in the 21st century, will continue to require employees to possess math skills. The industry is extremely competitive, and controlling costs (e.g., food, beverage, labor, etc.) is vital to the survival of any business venture.

Math skills start with the understanding of terms such as **whole numbers, units, numerals,** and **digits.**

You may feel you fully understand all these terms, but it is still important that you study this chapter, if only to adjust your attitude to a more enthusiastic approach toward refreshing your math skills.

NUMBERS

Whole numbers are numbers such as 0, 1, 2, 3, 4, 5, 6, 7, 8, and 9 that are used to represent whole units rather than fractional units. A **unit** is a standard quantity or amount. Units, of course, are not limited to

Chef Sez...

"What is your labor cost, your food cost, your beverage cost, your increase in covers over last month, your variable expenses, your overhead, your breakeven, your cost of capital, your revenue per square foot, your inventory turnover or your profitability? All of these are questions, which you will need to know to operate an effective and profitable business. All of these questions can be answered by having the ability to understand and analyze numbers through mathematics. But many food service operators have difficulty interpreting these relationships, thus, they are only able to make decisions based on limited knowledge of the situation. A food service manager does not need to be an accountant to operate a profitable enterprise, but a food service manager does need to have a working knowledge of basic mathematics to make daily decisions on the health of their business."

George R. Goldoff
Vice President of Food and Beverage
Beau Rivage Resort and Casino
Biloxi, Mississippi

Mr. Goldoff oversees the success of the 14 restaurants and outlets that serve food, along with the four bars and five service bars at this prestigious hotel, resort, and gaming complex. Revenue from food and beverage sales is $75,000,000 (yes, that's right, 75 million dollars). Beau Rivage employs 275 cooks and 1,100 food and beverage employees. Among the restaurants that Mr. Goldoff is responsible for is the Port House. This restaurant has won the Best Award of Excellence from *Wine Spectator* magazine, is a four-diamond award winner from AAA, and has earned the prestigious Distinguished Restaurants of North America (DiRōNA) award. The Beau Rivage Resort and Casino has been named by *Travel and Leisure* magazine one of the top 500 hotels in the world.

manufactured products. A unit may be a single quantity of like products, such as a case of apple juice. Units are often established by producers or manufacturers. The unit they establish is usually a quantity that is convenient for both the consumer and producer. Some convenient and sensible units for individuals could include a quart or gallon of milk, a pound of butter, a pint or quart of strawberries, or a dozen oranges. In the food service industry, convenient and sensible units might include a 10-pound can of fruit or vegetables, a 100-pound bag of flour, or a 5-pound box of bacon. Convenient and sensible units also help a manufacturer or business keep track of inventories.

Numerals are used to represent or express numbers. For example, 8, 21, 450, II, and X are numerals, because they express numbers. The individual numbers on a clock are numerals as well.

Digits are any of the numerals that combine to form numbers.

There are 10 digits, as shown in Figure 2–1, with names that you should be quite familiar with.

0	1	2	3	4	5	6	7	8	9
zero	one	two	three	four	five	six	seven	eight	nine

Figure 2–1 *Digits.*

Figure 2–2 *Place value columns within each period.*

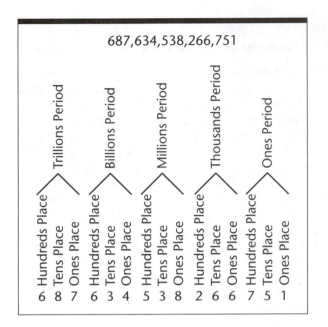

Digits can be combined in various ways to produce different numbers. For example, 457 and 745 are both combinations of the digits 7, 5, and 4. The value of each digit depends on where it is placed in the combination of numbers. For example, the 4 in the number 457 is valued at 400. However, the 4 in the number 745 is valued at 40. Each place has a different name and therefore a different value, as shown in Figure 2–2.

In large groups of numbers made up of four or more digits, the digits are placed into groups of three. Each of these groups is called a **period,** as shown in Figure 2–2. Periods are separated with commas. (In the metric system, to be discussed later in this text, periods are separated by spaces rather than commas.) The value of each digit is determined by its position in the place value columns. In Figure 2–2, the digit 5 is used twice. When it appears in the tens place of the ones period, the 5 represents 50. When it is used in the hundreds place of the millions period, it represents 500 million. As you can see, *place* is very important when numbers are grouped.

In the food service industry, the billions and trillions periods are very seldom or ever required. These periods are used by big business and our government when discussing budgets and the national debt. Major restaurant chains and some popular restaurant establishments will present and use figures in the millions place, but that is usually the extent of profit or loss figures.

Commas are used to separate periods. They are used for financial records, such as profit and loss statements and balance sheets. Commas are also used when writing checks, both professionally and personally.

Readers should be aware that in many non-English-speaking countries, spaces or periods are used to separate numeric periods in place of commas. For example, an invoice from France for toothpicks may be shown as 1 500 or even 1.500 instead of 1,500.

T I P S . . .   To Insure Perfect Solutions

When placing commas, start at the right, then count three places and insert a comma.

A chef/owner—or, for that matter, any person—must know how to write a bank check to pay bills. For most people, daily, monthly, or weekly checks are generally written in the hundreds of dollars. But there will be times when a person must write a check in the ten thousands and maybe even in the hundred thousands. Summary Reviews 2–1 and 2–2 will allow the student to practice check-writing techniques using both numbers and words.

SUMMARY REVIEW 2–1

Rewrite the following numbers by adding commas in the correct place(s).

1. 4956 _____

2. 10495 _____

3. 245620425 _____

4. 26495 _____

5. 218873296 _____

6. 48973 _____

7. 210000000 _____

8. 41213728 _____

9. 97822732642 _____

10. 8725351280 _____

As stated before in this chapter, most food service professionals will have to write checks with smaller numbers, such as $195.23. This would be written as one hundred ninety five and 23/100 dollars. When writing words or numbers on a check, always start at the far left. If not, unscrupulous merchants may add an extra number or word. Figure 2–3 illustrates the correct way to write a check, while Figure 2–4 illustrates the improper way to write a check.

ROBERT SMITH	No. ___19___	$\frac{56\text{-}95}{42}$
	HAMILTON, OHIO ___feb. 2___ 20 ___	
PAY TO THE ORDER OF ___SYSCO Foods___		$ 195.23
One hundred ninety five and 23/100 ___ DOLLARS		
	___Robert Smith___	

Figure 2–3 *Correctly written check.*

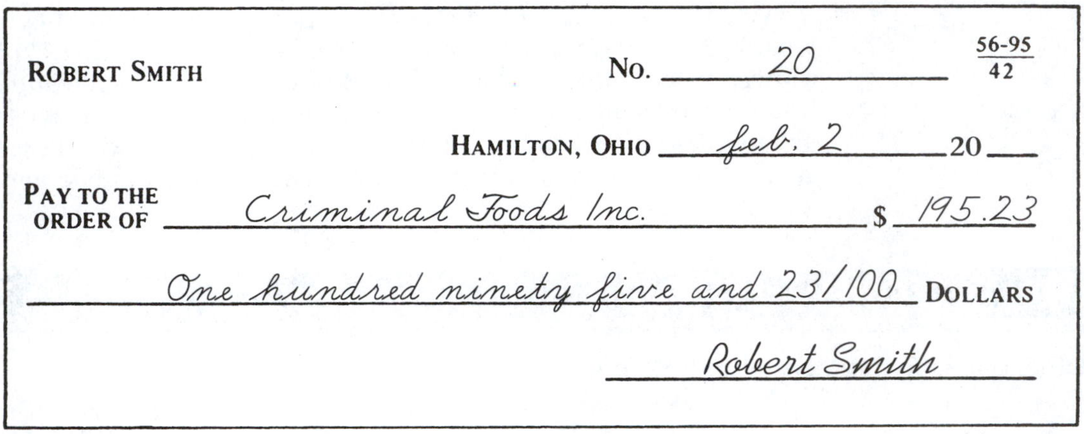

ROBERT SMITH

No. _____ 20 _____ $\frac{56\text{-}95}{42}$

HAMILTON, OHIO _____ feb. 2 _____ 20 ___

PAY TO THE
ORDER OF _____ Criminal Foods Inc. _____ $ 195.23

_____ One hundred ninety five and 23/100 _____ DOLLARS

_____ Robert Smith _____

Figure 2–4 *Incorrectly written check (there is room to add thousands of dollars).*

Figure 2–5 *Place values*

8,925,451,260

Billions	Hundred Millions	Ten Millions	Millions	Hundred Thousands	Ten Thousands	Thousands	Hundreds	Tens	Ones
8	9	2	5	4	5	1	2	6	0

Large numbers are also expressed with the names shown in Figure 2–5. The digit 0 in the ones column is needed to hold a place and to give the other digits their proper value. The digit 6 in the tens place would be 6, not 60, without the zero. The complete number shown in Figure 2–3 is read "eight billion nine-hundred twenty-five million four-hundred fifty-one thousand two-hundred sixty." Zeroes are not read. The number 149,000,000 is read "one hundred forty-nine million." The word "and" is not used in reading whole numbers.

SUMMARY REVIEW 2–2

Write out the words for the following dollar amounts. For example, $195.23 would be written as one hundred ninety five and 23/100 dollars.

1. $1,956.12 _____

2. $20,495.25 _____

3. $35.32 _____

4. $492.49 _____

5. $52,678.52 _____

6. $63,682.63 _____

7. $781.75   _____

8. $8.88   _____

9. $92.91   _____

10. $105.16 _____

SYMBOLS OF OPERATIONS

There are four basic arithmetic operations: addition, subtraction, multiplication, and division. Math symbols are used to indicate which of these four operations is required in any given transaction or arithmetic problem. The importance of math symbols can be demonstrated by selecting two

Figure 2–6 *Mathematical symbols.*

Symbol	Name	Meaning	Examples
+	plus sign	add to, or increase by	8 + 99 = 107 2 + 19 = 21 361 + 12 = 373
−	minus sign	subtract from, take away from, decrease by, or less	17 − 9 = 8 23 − 5 = 18 49 − 9 = 40
× or *	multiplication or times sign	multiply by, or the product of	2 × 12 = 24 9 × 3 = 27 5 * 25 = 125
÷ or /	division sign	divided by	4/2 = 2 27 ÷ 9 = 3 100 ÷ 20 = 5
___	fraction bar	separates numerator and denominator	$\frac{6}{3} = 2$ $\frac{10}{5} = 2$ $\frac{20}{5} = 4$
.	decimal point	indicates the beginning of a decimal fraction	0.321 1.877 117.65
%	percent sign	parts per 100, by the hundredths	15% 12% 6%
=	equal sign	the same value as, or is equal to	1 = 1
$	dollar sign	the symbol placed before a number to indicate that it stands for dollars	$12.00
@	at or per	used to indicate price or weight of each unit when there is a quantity of a unit	5 doz. doughnuts @ $1.15/doz. 25 bags of potatoes @ 10 lb./bag 100 ice cream cones @ $0.25 per cone

numerals and setting up problems using each of the four basic math symbols. The problems appear to be similar until the symbol is added.

(a)	10	(b)	10	(c)	10	(d) $10 \div 2 = 5$
	+2		−2		×2	or $\frac{10}{2} = 5$
	12		8		20	or $10/2 = 5$

As you can see, the math symbol used will yield different results and dictates the direction the problem will take.

Example (a), of course, is addition, (b) is subtraction, (c) is multiplication, and (d) is division. Figure 2–6 provides the names, meanings, and some examples of the symbols commonly used in the food service industry.

SUMMARY REVIEW 2–3

In the problems or statements following, the symbol of operation has been omitted. In each instance, determine the symbol that should be placed in the blank.

1. Meaning by the hundredths. _____

2. Used to indicate price of each unit. _____

3. Used to separate the numerator from the denominator when dealing with fractions. _____

4. Indicates the beginning of a decimal fraction. _____

5. A symbol placed before a monetary figure. _____

6. 24 _____ 15 = 360

7. 284 _____ 4 = 71

8. He purchased a dozen _____ $1.99 per dozen.

9. 28 × 2 _____ 56

10. A waitress is usually tipped 15 _____ of the total bill.

11. 1540 _____ 5 = 308

12. 1850 _____ 360 = 1490

13. 2075 _____ 190 = 2265

14. The food cost for the month was 38 _____.

15. The restaurant purchased six cases of sliced apples _____ $12.50 per case.

THE MILL

When dealing with monetary numbers, **cent** is used to represent the value of one hundredth part of a dollar. The third place to the right of the decimal is called a **mill** and represents the thousandth part of a dollar, or one-tenth of one cent.

When the final result of a monetary number includes a mill, it is usually rounded to a whole number of cents. To round a number to the nearest cent, the third digit (the mill) is dropped if it is less than 5. If that digit is **5 or more,** another cent is added to the digit before it. For example:

$4.626 rounded to the nearest cent is $4.63 because 6 mills are more than 5.

$4.623 rounded to the nearest cent is $4.62 because 3 mills are less than 5.

$4.625 rounded to the nearest cent is $4.63 because the digit 5 means another cent is added to the digit before it.

The mill is an important figure in the food service industry because the production cost of an item and the cost of menu food items are figured to the mill to obtain the exact cost of the item. The exact cost is very important when figuring a menu or selling price. For example, when producing rolls, it is necessary to know that each roll may cost $0.043 to produce, making the cost of one dozen rolls $0.516, or $0.52. In the case of a menu item, the manager must determine the cost of a serving before he or she can determine a selling or menu price.

T I P S . . .   To Insure Perfect Solutions

Find the answer to the problem. The *LAST* step is rounding to the mill.

SUMMARY REVIEW 2–4

Answer the following questions about the mill.

1. How many mills are contained in one cent? _____

2. How many mills are contained in 10 cents? _____

3. How many mills are contained in $1.00? _____

4. What is the rule to follow if the mill is 4 or less? _____ .

   Five or more? _____

Change the following amounts to the nearest cent using the mill.

5. $0.045 _____

6. $0.591 _____

7. $0.058 _____

8. $0.052 _____

9. $0.073 _____

10. $0.074 _____

11. $0.012 _____

12. $0.134 _____

13. $638.514 _____

14. $8,425.793 _____

15. $542.247 _____

The value of rounding up

In the food service industry, it is essential to make intelligent financial decisions in order to have a profitable business or maintain a budget in a nonprofit organization. Industry leaders often say, "Don't step over pennies to pick up nickels." Instead of stepping over pennies, pick them up and use them to make a profit or balance a budget! Those pennies that are picked up will assist in having a financially successful operation. For instance, an owner of a quick service operation selling french fries determines that each portion of fries costs 0.134 cents to produce. The owner—now that the raw food cost is determined—can set the menu price. Even though it is mathematically incorrect to round up when the hundredth place (the mill) is 4 or less, it makes sense business-wise to round up. Rounding off correctly, mathematically, would result in each portion of fries costing 13 cents. Business-wise, the quick service owner decides to round up the portion of fries to 14 cents, and sets the desired food cost percentage as 20%. As stated in Chapter 1, the formula to determine the menu price is: raw food cost divided by the desired food cost percentage. Mathematically correct, the 13-cent portion of fries divided by 20% would create a menu price of 65 cents for each portion of fries. But if the owner rounds up to the next penny (14 cents), the menu price is now determined to be 70 cents. Selling a million orders of french fries would result in an income gain of $50,000!

CHAPTER

3

Addition, Subtraction, Multiplication, and Division

OBJECTIVES

At the completion of this chapter, the student should be able to:

1. Find sums.
2. Find differences.
3. Check subtraction by adding.
4. Find products using the multiplication table.
5. Use a step-by-step procedure to find products.
6. Check the accuracy of the multiplication product.
7. Find quotients.
8. Find the remainder.
9. Check the accuracy of the division quotient.

KEY WORDS

addition	multiplier
sum	product
subtraction	subproducts
minuend	division
subtrahend	dividend
difference	divisor
trading (borrowing)	quotient
multiplication	remainder
multiplicand	

In this chapter, the four most basic, and essential, math functions—addition, subtraction, multiplication, and division—will be covered. In these pages, you will not only revisit the foundation of all computation, but you will also see how these computations are integral to food service operations.

T I P S . . .   To Insure Perfect Solutions

We read words from left to right. We solve math problems working from right to left.

Chef Sez...

Math was never one of my favorite subjects in high school. I kept thinking, "Why do I need to know math?" Today, as executive chef at Fairview Southdale Hospital, I use math every minute of the day!

My budget for food is $96,000 a month based on 31 days, and $93,000 for a 30-day month. This food budget is used for all patient meals, café service, catering, and foods used for floor stock. Daily, we average 225 patient meals, 150 "meals on wheels," and 1,800 guests in our café. My per-meal cost for a patient is $1.33, with another $1.25 in snacks and nourishments per day.

The challenge my staff and I face is this: as we increase revenue in our café, the amount of money I spend on my monthly food purchases should not increase. I must find ways to control my costs without spending any more money on food. This is accomplished through forecasting and knowing our patient census. We take this information to our production system and calculate our food production process. This allows me to control the amount of food to order and prepare, resulting in minimal leftovers and waste. My goal is to operate the café at about 40% food cost, with catering at 35% externally and internally at cost.

Every day, I am using all four functions of math—adding, subtracting, multiplying, and dividing—to keep my costs in line!

Bob Newell, Certified Executive Chef (CEC)
Executive Chef
Sodexho
Fairview Southdale Hospital
Edina, Minnesota

Fairview Southdale Hospital, located in a suburb of Minneapolis, Minnesota, is a 390-bed facility. The hospital has a staff of over 1,000 physicians, 2,200 health providers, and more than 500 volunteers. Mr. Newell has had a varied career as a chef for a variety of hospitals, as well as for private industry like the Dow Corning Corporation, Alma College, and hotels. He has also operated his own catering business.

ADDITION

Addition can be considered one of the most popular math functions because it means an increase is taking place. In any business venture, it is the desire of the operator that the increase shows up in the form of a nice profit.

Addition is the act of putting things together, or combining things or units that are alike, to obtain a total quantity. This total quantity is called the **sum.** If you have $6.00 and are given $10.00, you have a total of $16.00. This simple addition problem can be written two different ways. For example:

$$\$6.00 + \$10.00 = \$16.00$$

Written with the numbers placed in a row or line, this is called the *horizontal position*. The horizontal position is seldom used in a problem involving large numbers because the way the numbers are positioned makes it difficult to calculate the answer.

This same problem can also be written in what is called the *vertical* or *column position*.

$$\begin{array}{r} \$\ 6.00 \\ +\ 10.00 \\ \hline \$16.00 \end{array}$$

Figure 3–1 *How many servings of Cappuccino? Simple addition is used in food service everyday (2 + 2 = 4).*

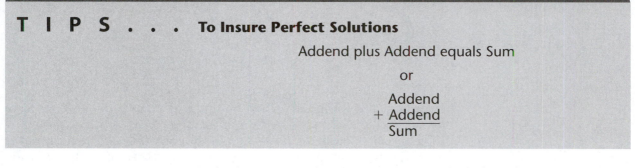

T I P S . . . **To Insure Perfect Solutions**

Addend plus Addend equals Sum

or

Addend
+ Addend
Sum

In both instances the plus sign, a symbol of operation, is used to indicate that the numbers are to be added. Figure 3–1 shows an example of how addition is used in food service.

As another example, when serving a sirloin steak dinner, if there are 25 steaks ready to be served, 18 cooking on the broiler, and 125 stored in the refrigerator, the food service establishment has a total of 168 steaks on hand. Since all of the units to be added are alike, it is unnecessary to write out what the units are. Therefore, the addition can be written in either of the following ways:

$$25 + 18 + 125 = 168 \quad \text{(or)} \quad \begin{array}{r} 25 \\ 18 \\ +125 \\ \hline 168 \end{array}$$

It is not necessary to use the plus sign when three or more numbers are added together in the vertical position because it cannot be confused with any other arithmetic operation. Remember that each digit must be placed in the correct column to give it the proper value.

Computing addition problems manually may be considered a task of the past because everyone uses calculators today. Nevertheless, it is still wise to understand the rules and proper steps for solving addition problems this way because situations may arise when a calculator is unavailable, or, worse yet, the battery may go dead while you are performing an important calculation. It is never wise to depend entirely on calculators or adding machines. Absorb the information and examples presented in this chapter so that you can add rapidly and accurately, should automation ever fail you.

Guidelines

There are several basic guidelines that can be followed in arithmetic problems to save time and improve accuracy.

Be Neat. If you are interested in a food service career, neatness is essential in both your physical appearance and personal hygiene. Neatness is also important in math. It does not require additional time to write neatly and carefully, placing each number in the proper column directly under the number above it, as shown below.

```
      2 1 5 8
          3 6
        5 2 6
        2 0 9
          8 5
  + 1 9 2 2
    4 9 3 6
```

T I P S . . .   To Insure Perfect Solutions

Always write down trades (carryovers).

Neatness is also important when trading (carrying) numbers over from one column to the next. The sum of the ones column in the preceding problem is 36 and not 6. The 3 (actually 30) is traded (carried over) to the tens column. When the trade (carryover) 3 is written, it is placed neatly at the top of the tens column so that it is not overlooked when counting that column. The sum of the tens column is 23 (actually 230). The 2 is traded (carried over) to the hundreds column. Again, place the 2 neatly over the top of the hundreds column. Follow this procedure for each column in the problem as shown below:

```
    ① ② ③
    2 1 5 8
        3 6
      5 2 6
      2 0 9
        8 5
+ 1 9 2 2
  4 9 3 6
```

Check Your Work. All work must be checked, even when using a calculator, to be sure your addition is correct. Mistakes can be made even when calculating automatically. Even if you find, through checking, that your work is always correct, the practice should still be continued. The penalty for mathematical errors in the classroom is only a lower grade; the penalty for errors in a food service operation can result in a monetary loss for both you and your employer.

The common method of checking addition is to add the individual columns in reverse order. For example, if you originally added the columns from top to bottom, which is the usual practice, you can check your work by adding a second time, from bottom to top. Just reverse your procedure.

Increase Your Accuracy and Speed. Addition is often simplified if numbers are combined and then added. For example, in the problem 7 + 3 +

$8 + 2 + 5 + 3 = 28$, the addition is greatly simplified by combining 7 and 3 into 10, and 8 and 2 into 10, which adds up to twenty. Adding the remaining numbers (5 and 3) gives 8, which makes a total of 28.

Eliminate unnecessary steps when adding. One method of increasing your speed and accuracy is that instead of thinking 7 plus 3 equals 10, automatically see the 7 and 3 combination as 10. When adding the problem in the previous paragraph, do not think that 10 plus 10 equals 20, plus 5 equals 25, plus 3 equals 28. Think 10, 20, 28.

If these guidelines are followed, they will help you to ensure the accuracy and speed required for any type of addition problem, especially those related to food service. Some of these guidelines, such as neatness and checking your work, apply to all arithmetic operations.

SUMMARY REVIEW 3-1

Find the sum of each of the following addition problems. Use the methods and guidelines suggested in this chapter. To improve your math skills, calculate these problems manually and then check your work.

1.
```
    6
  + 7
```

2.
```
    4
    7
    6
  + 3
```

3. $3 + 5 + 8 + 17 =$ _____

4. $24 + 19 + 12 + 28 =$ _____

5.
```
    259
  + 148
```

6.
```
    338
    225
  + 648
```

7.
```
  $56.17
   49.54
   26.38
 + 18.67
```

8.
```
    312
    422
    345
    239
  + 751
```

9.
```
  $366.26
   441.31
   374.43
   223.23
  +154.73
```

10.
```
      8
     28
    335
   2765
    222
    589
     17
    259
  + 126
```

11.
```
  $ 43.16
    42.19
    41.20
    38.72
    31.42
    29.73
    25.42
    27.63
    18.64
  + 12.25
```

12.
```
  $555.25
   216.11
   140.18
   310.20
   713.14
   726.12
   289.82
   326.22
   129.10
 + 222.12
```

13. If a person's guest check includes an omelette @ $6.99, French toast @ $5.99, and coffee @ $1.25, how much is the total check?

_____

14. When preparing a fruit salad bowl, the following items were used: oranges $1.98, apples $0.79, grapes $0.92, bananas $1.69, strawberries $2.68, peaches $1.47, and pineapple $0.98. What was the total cost of the fruit salad bowl?

_____

15. The restaurant had 203 orders of chicken in the freezer, 126 in the walk-in refrigerator, and 109 in the reach-in refrigerator. How many orders of chicken did they have on hand?

_____

SUBTRACTION

Subtraction means to take away. It is the removal of one number of things from another number of things (see Figure 3–2). The word "subtract" is very seldom used except in its mathematical sense. The popular word used in the business world is "deduct," which also means to take away. For example, instead of saying "he *subtracted* a discount of $2.00 from my bill," the statement would be "he *deducted* a discount of $2.00 from my bill."

Figure 3–2 *Subtraction is taking place when a serving portion is removed from others (10 − 2 = 8).*

If you have $12.00 and spend $8.25, the subtraction problem is written as follows:

$$
\begin{array}{r}
\$12.00 \\
-\ 8.25 \\
\hline
\$\ 3.75
\end{array}
$$

The minus sign ($-$) must always be used so that the problem is not confused with another mathematical operation.

Each of the factors in subtraction has a name. The original number before subtraction, or before anything is removed, is called the **minuend.** In the example above, the minuend is $12.00. The number removed from the minuend is called the **subtrahend.** Finally, the amount left over or remaining after the problem is completed is called the **difference.**

$$
\begin{array}{r}
1585 \quad \text{Minuend} \\
-\ 742 \quad \text{Subtrahend} \\
\hline
843 \quad \text{Difference}
\end{array}
$$

Trading (Borrowing)

Subtraction frequently requires **trading (borrowing).** When trading, add ten to the ones column of the minuend. At the same time, diminish the number in the tens column by one. Although the minuend is usually a larger number than the subtrahend, a particular digit in the minuend may be less than the digit beneath it in the subtrahend, so trading (borrowing) is required. Example: $1{,}723 - 688 = 1{,}038$. When this problem is set up in the vertical position, it looks like this:

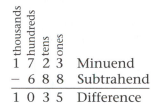

$$
\begin{array}{r}
1\ 7\ 2\ 3 \quad \text{Minuend} \\
-\ 6\ 8\ 8 \quad \text{Subtrahend} \\
\hline
1\ 0\ 3\ 5 \quad \text{Difference}
\end{array}
$$

T I P S . . .   To Insure Perfect Solutions

Minuend minus Subtrahend equals Difference

or

$$
\begin{array}{r}
\text{Minuend} \\
-\ \text{Subtrahend} \\
\hline
\text{Difference}
\end{array}
$$

T I P S . . .   To Insure Perfect Solutions

Always write down trades (carryovers).

The minuend (1,723) is clearly a larger number than the subtrahend (688). However, the digit 8 in the ones column of the subtrahend is larger than the digit 3 in the ones column of the minuend. Since 8 cannot be subtracted from 3, it becomes necessary to trade (borrow) from the tens column.

To indicate that a ten has been traded (borrowed), cross out the 2 in the tens column and write 1 above it. If this step is neglected, you may sometimes forget that you traded (borrowed).

$$\begin{array}{r} {\scriptstyle 1\ 13} \\ 1\ \cancel{7}\ \cancel{2}\ \cancel{3} \\ -\ \ \ 6\ 8\ 8 \\ \hline \end{array}$$

Add the traded (borrowed) ten to the 3 in the ones column, which increases the 3 to 13. Then subtract $13 - 8 = 5$. The 5 is written beneath the bar in the ones column.

$$\begin{array}{r} {\scriptstyle 1\ 13} \\ 1\ \cancel{7}\ \cancel{2}\ \cancel{3} \\ -\ \ \ 6\ 8\ 8 \\ \hline 5 \end{array}$$

In the tens column, 8 cannot be subtracted from 1 (actually 80 from 10), so it is necessary to trade (borrow) a hundred from the hundreds column. This is done by crossing out the numeral 7 in the hundreds column and writing 6 above it.

$$\begin{array}{r} {\scriptstyle 6\ 11\ 13} \\ 1\ \cancel{7}\ \cancel{2}\ \cancel{3} \\ -\ \ \ 6\ 8\ 8 \\ \hline 5 \end{array}$$

Return to the tens column, and subtract 8 from 11 (actually 80 from 110) to get 3 (actually 30). Write the 3 in the tens column beneath the bar.

$$\begin{array}{r} {\scriptstyle 6\ 11\ 13} \\ 1\ \cancel{7}\ \cancel{2}\ \cancel{3} \\ -\ \ \ 6\ 8\ 8 \\ \hline 3\ 5 \end{array}$$

Moving to the hundreds column, 6 can be subtracted from 6 (which is actually 600 from 600). Even though nothing will remain, a zero is used to hold a place. Trading (borrowing), therefore, is unnecessary in this column.

$$\begin{array}{r} {\scriptstyle 6\ 11\ 13} \\ 1\ \cancel{7}\ \cancel{2}\ \cancel{3} \\ -\ \ \ 6\ 8\ 8 \\ \hline 0\ 3\ 5 \end{array}$$

The problem is completed by bringing down the 1 that remains in the thousands column. The completed problem appears below:

$$\begin{array}{r} {\scriptstyle 6\ 11\ 13} \\ 1\ \cancel{7}\ \cancel{2}\ \cancel{3} \\ -\ \ \ 6\ 8\ 8 \\ \hline 1\ 0\ 3\ 5 \end{array}$$

Checking Subtraction

Checking any math problem is always a wise step to take, even when using a calculator, because errors are so easily made. The common way of checking a subtraction answer is to add together the subtrahend and the difference. The sum of these two numbers should equal the minuend.

Subtraction: Check:

```
  3 6 4 2   Minuend                    2 1 3 2   Subtrahend
- 2 1 3 2   Subtrahend              + 1 5 1 0   Difference
  1 5 1 0   Difference                3 6 4 2   Minuend
```

SUMMARY REVIEW 3-2

Find the difference in the following subtraction problems. Calculate these problems manually and then check your work.

1. 955 − 314 = _____   2. 688 − 520 = _____

3. 4925 − 1649 = _____

4.   743   5.   828   6.   5197
       − 526   − 593   − 2058

7. $24.43   8. $76.32   9. $132.77
      − 18.20   − 56.54   − 59.99

10. $7,333.64   11. $221,004.03
    − 6,132.45   − 79,625.07

12. The bill for the wedding party came to $1,585.21. They were given a discount of $121.00 because the guaranteed number of people attended. What was the total bill?

_____

13. The restaurant thought they had 76 live lobsters on hand. Taking a quick inventory, it was discovered that 29 were dead. How many live lobsters did the restaurant have left?

_____

14. A restaurant had 240 chickens in the freezer. They used 31 for a special party. How many did they have left?

_____

15. A restaurant purchased 268 pounds of sirloin. Forty-eight pounds were lost in boning and trimming. How many pounds were left?

_____

MULTIPLICATION

Multiplication is another math operation where an increase takes place. Methods that bring forth an increase, such as addition, seem to be most popular, especially if the increase is spelled "profit" or carries a dollar sign. Multiplication can be thought of as a shortcut for a certain type of addition problem. In **multiplication,** a whole number is added to itself a specified amount of times. For example, $4 \times 2 = 8$ is another way of expressing $4 + 4 = 8$. The number 4 is added to itself two times.

Since a relationship exists between addition and multiplication, it does not matter which operation is used in simple problems such as the one above. However, when the problem consists of problems involving large numbers (such as $4531 \times 6580 = ?$), addition is an impractical way of solving it. This is when multiplication becomes useful as a shortcut for addition. Working out the preceding problem is quite lengthy using multiplication, as shown in the following example. Now just imagine what would be involved if done by addition:

$$
\begin{array}{r}
6580 \\
\times\ 4531 \\
\hline
6580 \\
19740 \\
32900 \\
26320 \\
\hline
29813980
\end{array}
$$

T I P S . . . . To Insure Perfect Solutions

Multiplier times Multiplicand equals Product

or

$$
\begin{array}{l}
\text{Multiplier} \\
\times\ \text{Multiplicand} \\
\hline
\text{Product}
\end{array}
$$

Each number involved in the multiplication process has a name. The number that is added to itself (4 in the example, $4 \times 2 = 8$) is called the **multiplicand** (which means "going to be multiplied"). The number representing the amount of times the multiplicand is to be added to itself is called the **multiplier** (number 2 in the example). The result of multiplying the multiplicand by the multiplier is called the **product.** The product in our example is 8.

The following example gives the names and functions of the various numbers involved in the multiplication operation.

$$
\begin{array}{r}
362 \\
\times\ 32 \\
\hline
724 \\
10860 \\
\hline
11584
\end{array}
\quad
\begin{array}{l}
\text{Multiplicand} \\
\text{Multiplier} \\
\text{Subproduct} \\
\text{Subproduct} \\
\text{Product}
\end{array}
$$

Function	Name
Number to be added to itself	Multiplicand
Number of times to be added to itself	Multiplier
Product of the ones column	Subproduct
Product of the tens column	Subproduct
Final result (answer)	Product

In this example, subproducts are shown. **Subproducts** (sub meaning under, below, or before; product being the result of multiplying) occur whenever the multiplier consists of two or more digits. In this case, the multiplier is 32. The first subproduct is the result of the product $362 \times 2 = 724$. The second subproduct (10,860) is the result of multiplying 362×30. The zero at the end of this subproduct is not necessary, because $4 + 0 = 4$. It does not affect the outcome of the problem, and is only shown here to illustrate that the product of multiplying 362×30 is 10,860 and not 1,086. It also helps keep all of the digits in their proper columns (ones in the ones column, tens in the tens column, and so forth), as mentioned earlier in relation to subtraction.

Once all of the subproducts are determined, they are added together to obtain the final total or product (in this example, 11,584). The multiplication sign (also called the times sign) is always used in a multiplication problem to distinguish it from any other type of arithmetic operation.

The Multiplication Table

It has now been demonstrated to you through examples that multiplication is a shortcut for certain types of addition problems. A shortcut method is only valuable if it can be used efficiently and accurately. The key to using multiplication efficiently is the multiplication table (see Figure 3–3, giving products up to 12×12). Accuracy depends on your efforts and how well you have developed your multiplication skills.

Practice the multiplication table until it is memorized. To test how well you have memorized this table, write each problem on one side of an index card and the product on the other side. You should be able to look at a problem and know its answer within five seconds, without looking at the other side.

T I P S . . . .   **To Insure Perfect Solutions**

Remember the old saying: practice makes perfect.

1 × 1 = 1	5 × 1 = 5	9 × 1 = 9
1 × 2 = 2	5 × 2 = 10	9 × 2 = 18
1 × 3 = 3	5 × 3 = 15	9 × 3 = 27
1 × 4 = 4	5 × 4 = 20	9 × 4 = 36
1 × 5 = 5	5 × 5 = 25	9 × 5 = 45
1 × 6 = 6	5 × 6 = 30	9 × 6 = 54
1 × 7 = 7	5 × 7 = 35	9 × 7 = 63
1 × 8 = 8	5 × 8 = 40	9 × 8 = 72
1 × 9 = 9	5 × 9 = 45	9 × 9 = 81
1 × 10 = 10	5 × 10 = 50	9 × 10 = 90
1 × 11 = 11	5 × 11 = 55	9 × 11 = 99
1 × 12 = 12	5 × 12 = 60	9 × 12 = 108
2 × 1 = 2	6 × 1 = 6	10 × 1 = 10
2 × 2 = 4	6 × 2 = 12	10 × 2 = 20
2 × 3 = 6	6 × 3 = 18	10 × 3 = 30
2 × 4 = 8	6 × 4 = 24	10 × 4 = 40
2 × 5 = 10	6 × 5 = 30	10 × 5 = 50
2 × 6 = 12	6 × 6 = 36	10 × 6 = 60
2 × 7 = 14	6 × 7 = 42	10 × 7 = 70
2 × 8 = 16	6 × 8 = 48	10 × 8 = 80
2 × 9 = 18	6 × 9 = 54	10 × 9 = 90
2 × 10 = 20	6 × 10 = 60	10 × 10 = 100
2 × 11 = 22	6 × 11 = 66	10 × 11 = 110
2 × 12 = 24	6 × 12 = 72	10 × 12 = 120
3 × 1 = 3	7 × 1 = 7	11 × 1 = 11
3 × 2 = 6	7 × 2 = 14	11 × 2 = 22
3 × 3 = 9	7 × 3 = 21	11 × 3 = 33
3 × 4 = 12	7 × 4 = 28	11 × 4 = 44
3 × 5 = 15	7 × 5 = 35	11 × 5 = 55
3 × 6 = 18	7 × 6 = 42	11 × 6 = 66
3 × 7 = 21	7 × 7 = 49	11 × 7 = 77
3 × 8 = 24	7 × 8 = 56	11 × 8 = 88
3 × 9 = 27	7 × 9 = 63	11 × 9 = 99
3 × 10 = 30	7 × 10 = 70	11 × 10 = 110
3 × 11 = 33	7 × 11 = 77	11 × 11 = 121
3 × 12 = 36	7 × 12 = 84	11 × 12 = 132
4 × 1 = 4	8 × 1 = 8	12 × 1 = 12
4 × 2 = 8	8 × 2 = 16	12 × 2 = 24
4 × 3 = 12	8 × 3 = 24	12 × 3 = 36
4 × 4 = 16	8 × 4 = 32	12 × 4 = 48
4 × 5 = 20	8 × 5 = 40	12 × 5 = 60
4 × 6 = 24	8 × 6 = 48	12 × 6 = 72
4 × 7 = 28	8 × 7 = 56	12 × 7 = 84
4 × 8 = 32	8 × 8 = 64	12 × 8 = 96
4 × 9 = 36	8 × 9 = 72	12 × 9 = 108
4 × 10 = 40	8 × 10 = 80	12 × 10 = 120
4 × 11 = 44	8 × 11 = 88	12 × 11 = 132
4 × 12 = 48	8 × 12 = 96	12 × 12 = 144

Figure 3–3 *Multiplication table of numbers from 1 through 12*

1	2	3	4	5	6	7	8	9	10	11	12	13	14	15	16	17	18	19	20	21	22	23	24	25
2	4	6	8	10	12	14	16	18	20	22	24	26	28	30	32	34	36	38	40	42	44	46	48	50
3	6	9	12	15	18	21	24	27	30	33	36	39	42	45	48	51	54	57	60	63	66	69	72	75
4	8	12	16	20	24	28	32	36	40	44	48	52	56	60	64	68	72	76	80	84	88	92	96	100
5	10	15	20	25	30	35	40	45	50	55	60	65	70	75	80	85	90	95	100	105	110	115	120	125
6	12	18	24	30	36	42	48	54	60	66	72	78	84	90	96	102	108	114	120	126	132	138	144	150
7	14	21	28	35	42	49	56	63	70	77	84	91	98	105	112	119	126	133	140	147	154	161	168	175
8	16	24	32	40	48	56	64	72	80	88	96	104	112	120	128	136	144	152	160	168	176	184	192	200
9	18	27	36	45	54	63	72	81	90	99	108	117	126	135	144	153	162	171	180	189	198	207	216	225
10	20	30	40	50	60	70	80	90	100	110	120	130	140	150	160	170	180	190	200	210	220	230	240	250
11	22	33	44	55	66	77	88	99	110	121	132	143	154	165	176	187	198	209	220	231	242	253	264	275
12	24	36	48	60	72	84	96	108	120	132	144	156	168	180	192	204	216	228	240	252	264	276	288	300
13	26	39	52	65	78	91	104	117	130	143	156	169	182	195	208	221	234	247	260	273	286	299	312	325
14	28	42	56	70	84	98	112	126	140	154	168	182	196	210	224	238	252	266	280	294	308	322	336	350
15	30	45	60	75	90	105	120	135	150	165	180	195	210	225	240	255	270	285	300	315	330	345	360	375
16	32	48	64	80	96	112	128	144	160	176	192	208	224	240	256	272	288	304	320	336	352	368	384	400
17	34	51	68	85	102	119	136	153	170	187	204	221	238	255	272	289	306	323	340	357	374	391	408	425
18	36	54	72	90	108	126	144	162	180	198	216	234	252	270	288	306	324	342	360	378	396	414	432	450
19	38	57	76	95	114	133	152	171	190	209	228	247	266	285	304	323	342	361	380	399	418	437	456	475
20	40	60	80	100	120	140	160	180	200	220	240	260	280	300	320	340	360	380	400	420	440	460	480	500
21	42	63	84	105	126	147	168	189	210	231	252	273	294	315	336	357	378	399	420	441	462	483	504	525
22	44	66	88	110	132	154	176	198	220	242	264	286	308	330	352	374	396	418	440	462	484	506	528	550
23	46	69	92	115	138	161	184	207	230	253	276	299	322	345	368	391	414	437	460	483	506	529	552	575
24	48	72	96	120	144	168	192	216	240	264	288	312	336	360	384	408	432	456	480	504	528	552	576	600
25	50	75	100	125	150	175	200	225	250	275	300	325	350	375	400	425	450	475	500	525	550	575	600	625
1	2	3	4	5	6	7	8	9	10	11	12	13	14	15	16	17	18	19	20	21	22	23	24	25

Figure 3–4 *Multiplication table of numbers from 1 through 25*

Another method of presenting the multiplication table is shown in Figure 3–4. This unique table gives the products of numbers up to 25 × 25 = 625. It is relatively simple to use. For example, to find the product of 8 × 9, locate the number 8 in the vertical (up and down) column to the far left. Then move your finger to the right until the 9 is located in the horizontal (left to right) column at the top of the table. The number 72 is in the place where the 8 column and the 9 column intersect. Therefore, 72 is the product of 8 × 9. Look one place below the 72 and find the number 81. This is the product of 9 × 9. Drop down another place to find that 10 × 9 = 90.

Simplifying Multiplication by a Step-By-Step Procedure. This multiplication example is intended to illustrate the step-by-step procedures involved in finding the product. As mentioned earlier, multiplication is a

T I P S . . .   To Insure Perfect Solutions

Placing a card or sheet of paper across the table horizontally is helpful in locating the products of the various numbers.

variation of, and has a very close association with, addition. In this example, it will be shown that the product of the problem is the result of adding together the subproducts of each step of the problem.

Example: 924
                                       × 65

Ones column:
   Step 1.   5 × 4 =   20
   Step 2.   5 × 20 =   100
   Step 3.   5 × 900 =   4,500
   Subproduct of ones column   4,620

Tens column:
   Step 4.   60 × 4 =   240
   Step 5.   60 × 20 =   1,200
   Step 6.   60 × 900 =   54,000
   Subproduct of tens column   55,440

Add subproducts:
   Step 7.   4,620 + 55,440 =   60,060 (Product)

This example shows the steps in finding the product of 924 × 65. Generally when the problem is worked, the unneeded zeros are eliminated, but carryover numbers are used, as shown in the following example:

```
    9 2 4   Multiplicand
    × 6 5   Multiplier
    4 6 2 0   Subproduct of ones column
    5 5 4 4   Subproduct of tens column
    6 0 0 6 0   Product
```

2 is the carryover number for the ones column.
1 is the carryover number for the tens column.

Notice that the subproduct of the ones column in both methods of working the problem is 4,620. The same is true for the subproduct of the tens column, 55,440. The zero is left off the subproduct in the second method because its only purpose is to hold a place. As long as the other figures are in their proper places, the zero is unnecessary.

Checking the Product

The accepted and common method of checking the accuracy of a multiplication product is to invert, or turn over, the multiplicand with the multiplier and work the problem from a reverse position.

Original Multiplication   Problem Checked
      3 4 8   Multiplicand   5 4   Multiplier
      × 5 4   Multiplier   × 3 4 8   Multiplicand
    1 3 9 2   Subproduct   4 3 2   Subproduct
    1 7 4 0   Subproduct   2 1 6   Subproduct
    1 8 7 9 2   Product   1 6 2   Subproduct
                                             1 8 7 9 2   Product

If the problem is worked accurately in both instances, the products will be the same. If two different products are obtained, invert the problem back to its original form and try again with a little better effort. Today, checking can be done on a calculator. However, it is a good practice to work problems through manually and then double-check the work on a calculator. Remember that doing problems manually sharpens your math skills, and that times will arise when you must function without automation.

Guidelines

A few guidelines are offered here to help provide speed and accuracy to multiplication work.

Be Neat. Neatness is very important, as pointed out earlier in this chapter. The customary method of multiplying eliminates end zeroes (zeroes that appear at the end of a number), and you must therefore be very careful in writing each number in its proper place.

Be Careful with Carryover Numbers. Remember that carryover numbers are added to the product of the two numbers being multiplied. The carryover numbers are not multiplied, as pointed out in the following example. (Note: It is unnecessary to write the carryover numbers as shown in the following example.)

$$
\begin{array}{r}
④\ ⑤\ \ \\
7\ 5\ 8 \\
\times\ 7 \\
\hline
5\ 3\ 0\ 6
\end{array}
$$

The first numbers to multiply are $7 \times 8 = 56$. Write the 6 in the ones column beneath the bar and carry the 5 over to the tens column. Next, $7 \times 5 = 35$. To this we add the carryover number 5. So, $35 + 5 = 40$. Write the 0 in the tens column beneath the bar and carry the 4 to the hundreds column. The next step in proper order is $7 \times 7 = 49$. To this, add the carryover number 4. This becomes $49 + 4 = 53$. Write the 3 in the hundreds column beneath the bar and the 5 in the thousands column beneath the bar. $7 \times 758 = 5,306$.

T I P S . . . .   To Insure Perfect Solutions

When the multiplier consists of two or more numerals, be careful to note the carryover numbers.

To Quickly Determine the Product When Multiplying by 10, 100, 1000, and so forth Add the Correct Number of Zeroes to the Multiplicand. For example: $10 \times 222 = 2,220$. Since there is one zero in 10, add one zero to 222 to obtain the product. When multiplying by 100, two zeroes would be added. $100 \times 222 = 22,200$. When multiplying by 1000, three zeroes are added.

Use Units in the Product When They Are Used in the Multiplicand. A unit was explained in a previous lesson as a single quantity of like things. Most multiplication problems in the world of work involve some sort of designated units. If a chicken processing plant has 45 chickens each in 15 separated pens, how many chickens does it have on hand? ($45 \times 15 = 675$) The product is not simply 675, but 675 chickens. This type of unit does not have to be written next to the multiplicand when working the problem, but remember what type of units are being multiplied so the result will be a certain number of those designated units.

SUMMARY REVIEW 3-3

Find the answer to the following multiplication problems. If units are indicated, write the unit in the answer. Do these problems manually and then check your work. Round to the nearest cent.

1.   156
        × 3

2.   5682
        × 76

3.   3562
        × 29

4.   372
        × 121

5.   9763
        × 1847

6. $355.46
        × 32

7. $5,351.44
        × 53

8. $8,421.55
        × 1.69

9. A side of beef weighs 323 pounds and costs $2.73 per pound. How much does the side cost?

10. If a foresaddle of veal weighs 46 pounds and costs $7.60 per pound, what is the total cost?

11. Jim's catering truck gets 13 miles to every gallon of gas. How many miles can it travel on 128 gallons of gas?

12. When preparing meat loaf, it is required that four pounds of ground beef go into each loaf. How many pounds of ground beef must be ordered when preparing 65 loaves?

13. Ribs of beef weigh 24 pounds and cost $2.97 per pound. What is the total cost of the ribs?

14. A wedding reception is catered for 575 people. The caterer charges $25.75 per person. What is the total bill?

_____

15. A cook earns $125.00 a day. How much is earned in a year if the cook works 328 days?

_____

DIVISION

Division is the act of separating a whole quantity into parts. It is a sharing of that whole part, a process of dividing one number by another. Division is basically the method of finding out how many times one number is contained in another number. It is, in a sense, a reverse of multiplication, as shown below:

Multiplication $5 \times 8 = 40$
Division $40 \div 8 = 5$
                  $40 \div 5 = 8$

Look at division from another viewpoint. Assume that your employer promises to pay you $8.00 per hour. After putting in eight difficult hours, you receive a check for only $56.00 (before deductions, of course). Just looking at the total, you know something is wrong. A simple division problem will show you that $56 \div 8 = 7. You were only being paid $7.00 an hour, or you were paid only for seven hours. Using division can thus help you find out that a mistake was made.

Division is frequently used in the food service business because foods are constantly being divided. A strip sirloin is divided into steaks, vegetables into portions, cakes into servings, and so forth (see Figure 3–5, which shows another example). An example illustrating the division of food can be seen by observing how a solution is found to the following problem:

A No. 10 can of applesauce contains about 105 ounces. How many guests can be served if each guest receives a 3-ounce portion?

$$105 \div 3 = 35$$

Thirty-five guests can be served from the 105-ounce can of applesauce. Using division has helped the cook to know how many cans must be opened when serving a certain number of people.

In division, the number to be divided is called the **dividend.** In the problem $80 \div 4 = 20$, the number 80 is the dividend. The name for the number by which the dividend is divided (number 4, in this example) is the **divisor.** The result of dividing the dividend by the divisor is called the **quotient.** The quotient in this example is the number 20.

T I P S . . . .   To Insure Perfect Solutions

Dividend divided by Divisor equals Quotient

$$\overset{\text{Quotient}}{\text{Divisor}\overline{)\text{Dividend}}}$$

Figure 3–5 *Division is the method of operation used when dividing roll dough into units.*

T I P S . . . .   **To Insure Perfect Solutions**

When dividing using the calculator, enter the dividend *first.*

In situations where the divisor is not contained in the dividend an equal or exact number of times, the figure left over or remaining is called the **remainder.** For example: 83 ÷ 4 = 20 with 3 left over, because 4 is too large to be contained in 3. In this problem, 3 is the remainder.

There are several division signs that can be used when working division problems. Usually the sign selected depends on how long or difficult the problem may be. Up to this point in our examples of the division operation, division has been indicated by a bar with a dot above and below (÷). This symbol is mainly used when the problem is simple or when first stating a division problem that is to be solved. Simple problems are also written using the fraction bar. For example, 84 ÷ 7 = 12 can also be written $\frac{84}{7}$ = 12.

For what is known as a long division problem, the accepted sign to use has the appearance of a closed parenthesis sign with a straight line coming out of the top:

Step-By-Step Division

When reviewing basic mathematical operations, division is usually discussed last because it involves both multiplication and subtraction in its operation (including carryover numbers and trading). For example: $8,295 \div 15 = ?$

Since this problem would be considered a lengthy one, the long division form is used.

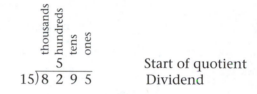

A long division problem is started from the left, rather than from the right, as in addition, subtraction, and multiplication. The first step is to estimate how many times 15 is contained in 82 (actually 8,200). It is known that $5 \times 15 = 75$, so your first estimate would be 5. The 5 is written above the division bar in the hundreds place.

Start of quotient
Dividend

To make sure that 5 is the correct figure, it is multiplied by 15. The product is 75. The 7 is written in the thousands column, under the 8, and the 5 in the hundreds column, under the 2. Then 75 is subtracted from 82. If the difference is less than 15, the estimate of 5 in the hundreds place of the quotient is correct. $82 - 75 = 7$. Since 7 is less than 15, the estimate is correct.

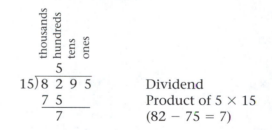

Dividend
Product of 5×15
$(82 - 75 = 7)$

The next step is to bring the 9 in the tens place of the dividend down to the right of the 7, giving 79. We estimate that 79 contains 15 only 5 times. $79 - 75 = 4$, which is smaller than 15. (Note that sometimes the estimate is too low or too high. When this happens, the estimate must be increased or decreased accordingly.)

So far our problem has advanced to this point:

$$
\begin{array}{r}
5\ 5 \\
15\overline{)8\ 2\ 9\ 5} \\
7\ 5 \\
\hline
7\ 9 \\
7\ 5 \\
\hline
4
\end{array}
$$

Dividend

Product of 5×15
$(79 - 75 = 4)$

The next step is to bring down the remaining figure 5 from the ones column and place it to the right of the 4 (left over from subtracting

75 from 79). Again, estimate how many times 45 contains 15. It is easy to see that 3 should be the estimated figure, making the problem come out even. The completed problem is shown as follows:

$$
\begin{array}{r}
5\ 5\ 3 \\
15\overline{)8\ 2\ 9\ 5} \\
7\ 5 \\
\hline
7\ 9 \\
7\ 5 \\
\hline
4\ 5 \\
4\ 5 \\
\hline
\end{array}
$$

Quotient
Dividend

Product of 3×15

The Remainder

As explained earlier, the figure in a division problem that may be left over when the dividend does not contain the divisor exactly is called the remainder. For example:

$$
\begin{array}{r}
6\ 5 \\
33\overline{)2\ 1\ 6\ 3} \\
1\ 9\ 8 \\
\hline
1\ 8\ 3 \\
1\ 6\ 5 \\
\hline
1\ 8 \\
\end{array}
$$

Quotient
Dividend
Product of $6 \times 33 = 198$

Product of $5 \times 33 = 165$
Remainder

At this point, there are no more numerals to bring down from the dividend. There are no 33s contained in the number 18. Therefore, the leftover 18 is called the remainder. Therefore, the solution would be 65 R18. The remainder can also be written in fractional or decimal form, as shown below:

$$2{,}163 \div 33 = 65\tfrac{18}{33} \text{ (a fraction) or } 65.545 \text{ (a decimal)}$$

Checking Division

The common method of checking division is to multiply the quotient by the divisor. The product of multiplying the divisor and quotient together should be the same as the dividend.

Division:

Divisor

$$
\begin{array}{r}
1\ 3\ 2 \\
22\overline{)2\ 9\ 0\ 4} \\
2\ 2 \\
\hline
7\ 0 \\
6\ 6 \\
\hline
4\ 4 \\
4\ 4 \\
\hline
0 \\
\end{array}
$$

Quotient
Dividend

Remainder

To check the division:

$$
\begin{array}{r}
1\ 3\ 2 \\
\times\ \ 2\ 2 \\
\hline
2\ 6\ 4 \\
2\ 6\ 4 \\
\hline
2\ 9\ 0\ 4 \\
\end{array}
$$

Quotient
Divisor

Dividend

When the quotient includes a remainder, multiply the quotient by the divisor as shown in the previous example, then add the remainder to the product.

```
                    2 7 5        Quotient
        Divisor 31 )8 5 4 4      Dividend
                    6 2
                    2 3 4
                    2 1 7
                      1 7 4
                      1 5 5
                        1 9      Remainder
```

To check the division with a remainder present:

```
            2 7 5        Quotient
        ×     3 1        Divisor
            2 7 5
          8 2 5
          8 5 2 5        Product
        +     1 9        Remainder
          8 5 4 4        Dividend
```

SUMMARY REVIEW 3–4

Find the quotient for the following division problems. Carry answers three places to the right of the decimal point. Calculate these problems manually and then check all work.

1.   45 ÷ 15 = _____   2.   96 ÷ 3 = _____

3.   7)770   4.   8)1696   5.   46)2250

6.   58)896.74   7.   29)648.28   8.   344)988.42

9. A 480-pound side of beef is purchased for $950.40. What is the cost per pound?

_____

10. In one week, the Prime Time Catering Company's delivery truck traveled 336 miles. They used 24 gallons of gasoline. How many miles did they average per gallon?

   _____

11. The chef at the Starlight Restaurant earns $43,200 per year. If this chef works 48 weeks per year, how much does she earn in one week?

   _____

12. The preparation cook at the Blue Star Restaurant works five days a week and earns $356.00 per week. How much does he earn in one day?

   _____

13. A restaurant orders 392 pounds of pork loins. Each loin weighs 14 pounds. How many loins are contained in the shipment?

   _____

14. The Deluxe Catering Company's delivery truck averages 13 miles per gallon of gasoline. During 30 days of operation, the truck travels 2,028 miles. How much gasoline is used?

   _____

15. One hundred twenty-eight ounces of orange juice are contained in one gallon. How many 8-ounce glasses of juice can be served?

   _____

CHAPTER 4

Fractions, Decimals, Ratios, and Percents

OBJECTIVES

At the completion of this chapter, the student should be able to:

1. Simplify (or express) a fraction in lower terms without changing the value of the fraction.
2. Add, subtract, multiply, and divide fractions.
3. Change fractions to decimals.
4. Write decimals and mix decimal fractions in words.
5. Write numbers as decimals.
6. Find sums, differences, products, and quotients in decimal problems.
7. Solve problems by using given ratios.
8. Write common fractions as percents.
9. Write percents as common fractions, whole numbers, or mixed numbers.
10. Find the percents of meat cuts.

KEY WORDS

fractions	least common denominator
numerator	decimal
denominator	decimal fractions
proper fractions	decimal point
factor	mixed decimal fractions
improper fractions	ciphers
mixed number	ratio
simplification	proportion
like fractions	percent
unlike fractions	

Now that you have learned about the roles that addition, subtraction, multiplication, and division play in food service operations, it is time to learn about the equally important roles played by fractions, decimals, ratios, and percents.

FRACTIONS

Fractions are sometimes used in a restaurant operation. They may play an important part when converting standard recipes, dealing with the contents of a scoop or dipper, and dividing certain items into serving portions, but compared to most other math operations, the use of fractions is limited. This does not mean, however, that the knowledge of fractions is unimportant. Situations will occur in your workplace and everyday life where knowledge of this subject will be required, so review this section just as intensely as the others.

A **fraction** indicates one or more equal parts of a unit. For example, a cake is usually divided into eight equal pieces. (See Figure 4–1.) If this is done, the following statements are true about the parts or slices of the cake:

One part is $\frac{1}{8}$ of the cake.

Three parts are $\frac{3}{8}$ of the cake.

Seven parts are $\frac{7}{8}$ of the cake.

Eight parts are $\frac{8}{8}$ of the cake or the whole cake.

Another example of this same teaching tool is the division of a 9-inch pie into slices. A 9-inch pie is usually cut into seven equal servings. In this case, the fractional parts would be a little different but the same theory shown for the sliced cake would hold true:

One part is $\frac{1}{7}$ of the pie.

Three parts are $\frac{3}{7}$ of the pie.

Six parts are $\frac{6}{7}$ of the pie.

Seven parts are $\frac{7}{7}$ of the pie or the whole pie.

Figure 4–1 *An example of a fractional part is shown when cutting a cake. Usually $\frac{1}{8}$ is a serving portion.*

TIPS . . . **To Insure Perfect Solutions**

The parts of a fraction are the numerator (top number) and the denominator (bottom number). Think of the letter *d* in denominator as the *d* in down (in other words, the bottom number).

$$\frac{\text{Numerator}}{\text{Denominator}}$$

Since fractions indicate the division of a whole unit into equal parts, the numeral placed above the division or fraction bar indicates the number of fractional units taken and is called the **numerator.** The numeral below the bar represents the number of equal parts into which the unit is divided and is called the **denominator.** Thus, if a cantaloupe is cut into eight equal wedges, but only five of those wedges are used on a fruit plate, the wedges used are represented by the fraction $\frac{5}{8}$.

A common fraction is written with a whole number above the division bar and a whole number below the bar. For example:

$$\frac{5}{8} \quad \text{Numerator} \atop \text{Denominator}$$

A **proper fraction** is a fraction whose numerator is smaller than its denominator. For example:

$$\frac{5}{8} \quad \text{Numerator} \atop \text{Denominator}$$

This type of fraction is in its lowest possible terms when the numerator and denominator contain no common factor. A **factor** refers to two or more numerals that, when multiplied together, yield a given product. For example: 3 and 4 are factors of 12. The fraction $\frac{5}{8}$ is in its lowest possible terms because there is no common number by which both can be divided. (See "The Simplification of Fractions" later in this chapter.)

An **improper fraction** is a fraction whose numerator is larger than its denominator, and whose value is greater than a whole unit. If, for instance, $1\frac{3}{4}$ hams is expressed as an improper fraction, it is expressed as $\frac{7}{4}$ since the one whole ham would be $\frac{4}{4}$, and the extra $\frac{3}{4}$ makes it $\frac{7}{4}$. Such fractions can be expressed as a mixed number by dividing the numerator by the denominator, as shown below:

$$\frac{7}{4} = 1\frac{3}{4} \text{ mixed number}$$

A **mixed number** is a whole number mixed with a fractional part. For example:

$$1\frac{1}{3}, \, 3\frac{3}{4}, \text{ and } 8\frac{2}{3}$$

The Simplification of Fractions

Simplification is a method used to express a fraction in lower terms without changing the value of the fraction. This is achieved by dividing the numerator and denominator of a fraction by the greatest factor (number) common to both. For example:

$$\frac{12}{28} \quad \begin{array}{l}(\div\ 4\ \text{greatest factor}) = \\ (\div\ 4\ \text{greatest factor}) =\end{array} \quad \frac{3}{7}$$

$$\frac{16}{24} \quad \begin{array}{l}(\div\ 8\ \text{greatest factor}) = \\ (\div\ 8\ \text{greatest factor}) =\end{array} \quad \frac{2}{3}$$

The value of these fractions is unchanged, but they have been simplified or reduced to their lowest possible terms.

A mixed number is usually expressed as an improper fraction when it is to be multiplied by another mixed number, a whole number, or a fraction. The first step is to express the mixed number as an improper fraction. This is done by multiplying the whole number by the denominator of the fraction, and then adding the numerator to the result. The sum is written over the denominator of the fraction. For example:

$$1\tfrac{3}{4} \times 4\tfrac{1}{4} = \tfrac{7}{4} \times \tfrac{17}{4} = \tfrac{119}{16} = 7\tfrac{7}{16}$$

In this example, the whole number (1) is multiplied by the denominator of the fraction (4). To this result (4), the numerator (3) is added. The sum (7) is written over the denominator (4), creating the improper fraction $\tfrac{7}{4}$. The same procedure is followed in expressing the mixed number $4\tfrac{1}{4}$ as the improper fraction $\tfrac{17}{4}$. When the two mixed numbers are expressed as improper fractions, the product is found by multiplying the two numerators together and the two denominators together, resulting in the improper fraction $\tfrac{119}{16}$, and simplifying (reducing) it to the lowest terms, $7\tfrac{7}{16}$.

Adding and Subtracting Fractions

Fractions are used most often to increase and decrease recipe ingredients. Ingredients such as herbs and spices generally appear in a recipe in fractional quantities. The addition and subtraction of fractions are used most often when adjusting recipes. However, all operations dealing with fractions will be required at some point on the job or in everyday activity. One example of the use of fractions in food service is illustrated in Figure 4–2.

Before fractions can be added or subtracted, they must have the same denominator. **Like fractions** are fractions that have the same denominator. To add or subtract like fractions, add or subtract the numerators and write the result over the common denominator. Examples of adding and subtracting like fractions are shown below:

$$\frac{2}{9} + \frac{5}{9} = \frac{7}{9} \qquad \frac{5}{9} - \frac{3}{9} = \frac{2}{9}$$

Note how simple it is to add and subtract like fractions. The next step, dealing with unlike fractions, becomes a little more difficult.

Figure 4–2 *Fractions are used in recipes by adding $\frac{3}{4}$ cup + $2\frac{1}{2}$ cups.*

T I P S . . . .   **To Insure Perfect Solutions**

When adding like fractions, add the numerators only (the top numbers of the fractions). The denominators (the bottom numbers of the fractions) remain unchanged.

When subtracting like fractions, subtract the numerators only (the top numbers). The denominators (the bottom numbers) remain unchanged.

To determine the **least common denominator,** multiply the two denominators by each other. For example, $\frac{3}{4}$ plus $\frac{5}{7}$ equals what? We multiply 4 by 7, which equals 28. So, the least common denominator is 28. There are times when multiplying the two denominators does not result in the least common denominator. For example, $\frac{7}{12} - \frac{1}{2}$ has a denominator of 24; but that is not the least common denominator. First, determine whether the 12 could be the least common denominator. Divide the 2 into the 24, and you discover that it is! A little practice and detective work in this area will help determine the least common denominator.

Unlike fractions have different denominators. They are more difficult because only like things can be added or subtracted. Therefore, to add or subtract fractions that have unlike denominators, the fractions must first be expressed so the denominators are the same. To find this common denominator, multiply the two denominators together ($5 \times 4 = 20$). The product will, of course, be common to both. For example:

$$\frac{2}{5} + \frac{3}{4} = \frac{?}{20}$$

When a number is found that is a multiple of both denominators, the fractions are then expressed in terms of the common denominator, so $\frac{2}{5}$ is $\frac{8}{20}$ and $\frac{3}{4}$ is $\frac{15}{20}$. These fractions have now become like fractions that can be added or subtracted without too much difficulty, as shown below:

Add	Subtract
$\frac{2}{5} = \frac{8}{20}$	$\frac{3}{4} = \frac{15}{20}$
$+\frac{3}{4} = \frac{15}{20}$	$-\frac{2}{5} = \frac{8}{20}$
$\frac{23}{20} = 1\frac{3}{20}$ Sum	Difference $\frac{7}{20}$

In adding and subtracting unlike fractions, the common denominator may be any number that is a multiple of the original denominators. However, always use the least common denominator to simplify the work. The **least common denominator** is the smallest number that is a multiple of both denominators. For example: if $\frac{1}{3}$ and $\frac{2}{5}$ are to be added, the least common denominator is 15, since it is the smallest multiple of both 3 and 5.

$$\frac{1}{3} = \frac{5}{15}$$
$$+\frac{1}{5} = \frac{3}{15}$$
$$\frac{8}{15}$$

Multiplying Fractions

Multiplying fractions is considered the simplest operation with fractions. When multiplying two fractions, multiply the two numerators and place the results over the result obtained by multiplying the two denominators. For example:

$$\frac{2}{3} \times \frac{7}{8} = \frac{14}{24} = \frac{7}{12}$$

Note: $\frac{14}{24}$ expressed in lowest terms is $\frac{7}{12}$.

If multiplying a whole number by a fraction, multiply the whole number by the numerator of the fraction, place the result over the denominator of the fraction, and divide the new numerator by the denominator. For example:

$$\frac{17}{1} \times \frac{3}{4} = \frac{51}{4} = 12\frac{3}{4}$$

Sometimes it is possible to simplify the problem before multiplying. In the example below, 6 is a factor of 24 because 24 contains 6 exactly 4 times. This step is commonly called *canceling:*

$$\frac{\overset{4}{\cancel{24}}}{1} \times \frac{5}{\underset{1}{\cancel{6}}} = 20$$

If the numerator and denominator can be divided evenly by the same number, simplify to lowest terms. For example:

$\frac{32}{48}$ Numerator and denominator can be divided evenly by the common factor 16, resulting in: $\frac{2}{3}$

If multiplying by one or two mixed numbers, express the mixed number or numbers as improper fractions and proceed to multiply as with two fractions. For example:

$$\frac{8}{1} \times 3\frac{5}{8} = \frac{8}{1} \times \frac{29}{8} = 29$$

$$2\frac{1}{3} \times 4\frac{3}{5} = \frac{7}{3} \times \frac{23}{5} = \frac{161}{15} = 10\frac{11}{15}$$

A note of caution: when dividing by a fraction (which is less than 1), the answer is greater than the dividend. For example, a serving of a hamburger is $\frac{1}{3}$ pound. How many hamburgers can be obtained from five pounds of ground beef?

$$5 \div \frac{1}{3} = x$$

$$5 \times \frac{3}{1} = x$$

$$\frac{5}{1} \times \frac{3}{1} = x$$

$$15 = x$$

From five pounds of ground beef, 15 hamburgers (weighing $\frac{1}{3}$ pound each) can be obtained.

Dividing Fractions

Dividing fractions is perhaps the most difficult operation because it involves the process of inverting (turning over) the divisor. Always be careful to invert the correct fraction. Mistakes can be easily made when inverting takes place. After inverting the divisor, proceed to operate the same as you would when multiplying fractions.
Example A:

$$\frac{5}{8} \div \frac{1}{2} = \frac{5}{8} \times \frac{2}{1} = \frac{5}{4} \times \frac{1}{1} = \frac{5}{4} = 1\frac{1}{4}$$

Step 1:   The divisor $\frac{1}{2}$ is inverted to $\frac{2}{1}$.
Step 2:   Cancel a factor of 2 from the 8 and 2.
Step 3:   Multiply $\frac{5}{4} \times \frac{1}{1}$ to get $\frac{5}{4}$.
Step 4:   The result $\frac{5}{4}$ is an improper fraction and must be reduced to a mixed number, which would be $1\frac{1}{4}$.
Example B:

$$\frac{14}{1} \div \frac{1}{2} = \frac{14}{1} \times \frac{2}{1} = 28$$

Step 1:   The divisor $\frac{1}{2}$ is inverted to $\frac{2}{1}$.

Step 2:   Multiply $\frac{14}{1} \times \frac{2}{1} = 28$.

Example B results in a whole number so, of course, reducing is not necessary.

SUMMARY REVIEW 4-1

Find the sum in each of the following addition problems. Simplify all answers to lowest terms.

1. $\dfrac{3}{7}$ $+\dfrac{3}{7}$

2. $\dfrac{4}{9}$ $+\dfrac{2}{9}$

3. $\dfrac{6}{9}$ $+\dfrac{2}{9}$

4. $\dfrac{1}{2}$ $+\dfrac{1}{8}$

5. $\dfrac{7}{16}$ $+\dfrac{2}{4}$

6. $\dfrac{3}{4}$ $+\dfrac{1}{8}$

7. $1\dfrac{5}{16}$ $+3\dfrac{3}{4}$

8. $\dfrac{23}{32}$ $+\dfrac{15}{16}$

9. $2\dfrac{1}{2}$ $3\dfrac{3}{4}$ $+6\dfrac{1}{8}$

10. $\dfrac{4}{9}$ $\dfrac{5}{12}$ $+\dfrac{5}{18}$

11. $\dfrac{1}{2}$ $\dfrac{1}{3}$ $+\dfrac{1}{5}$

12. $6\dfrac{5}{6}$ $10\dfrac{5}{12}$ $+13\dfrac{2}{3}$

13. $20\dfrac{4}{5}$ $16\dfrac{3}{15}$ $+18\dfrac{3}{10}$

14. $12\dfrac{1}{6}$ $9\dfrac{1}{3}$ $+7\dfrac{1}{9}$

15. $12\dfrac{3}{8}$ $6\dfrac{1}{4}$ $+10\dfrac{1}{2}$

SUMMARY REVIEW 4-2

Find the difference in each of the following subtraction problems. Simplify all answers to lowest terms.

16. $\dfrac{3}{7}$ $-\dfrac{1}{7}$

17. $\dfrac{4}{9}$ $-\dfrac{2}{9}$

18. $\dfrac{7}{16}$ $-\dfrac{3}{16}$

19. $\dfrac{3}{4}$ $-\dfrac{1}{3}$

20. $3\dfrac{3}{4}$ $-1\dfrac{3}{16}$

21. $12\dfrac{1}{4}$ $-5\dfrac{5}{16}$

22. $14\dfrac{7}{24}$ $-6\dfrac{5}{16}$

23. $45\dfrac{5}{8}$ $-32\dfrac{7}{16}$

24. $18\dfrac{7}{16}$ $-13\dfrac{1}{4}$

25. $23\dfrac{5}{18}$ $-7\dfrac{5}{12}$

26. $42\dfrac{23}{32}$ $-23\dfrac{15}{16}$

27. $43\dfrac{5}{8}$ $-18\dfrac{1}{4}$

28. $21\frac{3}{16}$ 29. $15\frac{5}{9}$ 30. $25\frac{5}{12}$

$-\ 16\frac{1}{8}$ $-\ 8\frac{2}{3}$ $-\ 12\frac{3}{16}$

SUMMARY REVIEW 4–3

Find the product in each of the following multiplication problems.

31. $\frac{5}{8} \times \frac{1}{2} =$ _____   39. $\frac{2}{3} \times 12\frac{1}{3} =$ _____

32. $\frac{7}{8} \times \frac{2}{4} =$ _____   40. $24\frac{1}{3} \times 7\frac{2}{3} =$ _____

33. $5\frac{1}{2} \times 3\frac{1}{2} =$ _____   41. $22\frac{5}{16} \times 4 =$ _____

34. $1\frac{3}{4} \times 4\frac{5}{8} =$ _____   42. $8\frac{2}{9} \times 3\frac{1}{2} =$ _____

35. $36 \times 5\frac{3}{4} =$ _____   43. $10\frac{3}{4} \times 3\frac{1}{2} =$ _____

36. $45 \times 7\frac{1}{2} =$ _____   44. $22 \times 5\frac{1}{4} =$ _____

37. $4\frac{3}{4} \times 5\frac{1}{2} =$ _____   45. $3\frac{5}{8} \times \frac{1}{2} =$ _____

38. $18 \times 9\frac{5}{9} =$ _____

SUMMARY REVIEW 4–4

Find the quotient in each of the following division problems:

46. $\frac{15}{16} \div \frac{3}{4} =$ _____   54. $\frac{5}{16} \div 3 =$ _____

47. $\frac{15}{16} \div 2 =$ _____   55. $2\frac{1}{4} \div 1\frac{1}{2} =$ _____

48. $\frac{3}{4} \div \frac{3}{16} =$ _____   56. $7\frac{5}{8} \div 2\frac{1}{4} =$ _____

49. $\frac{7}{16} \div \frac{3}{16} =$ _____   57. $9\frac{3}{8} \div \frac{3}{4} =$ _____

50. $1\frac{1}{2} \div 6 =$ _____   58. $10\frac{2}{3} \div \frac{1}{2} =$ _____

51. $2\frac{5}{8} \div 7 =$ _____   59. $\frac{7}{8} \div \frac{1}{4} =$ _____

52. $\frac{1}{4} \div 10 =$ _____   60. $12\frac{3}{4} \div \frac{2}{3} =$ _____

53. $\frac{3}{4} \div 2 =$ _____

DECIMALS

A decimal is based on the number 10. The decimal system refers to counting by tens and powers of 10. The term **decimal** refers to decimal fractions. **Decimal fractions** are those fractions that are expressed with denominators of 10 or powers of 10. For example:

$$\frac{1}{10} \qquad \frac{9}{100} \qquad \frac{89}{1,000} \qquad \frac{321}{10,000}$$

T I P S . . .   **To Insure Perfect Solutions**

A little trick to help remember the decimal: keep in mind that a decade equals 10 years. Therefore, a decimal is based on the number 10.

Instead of writing a fraction, a point (.) called a **decimal point** is used to indicate a decimal fraction. For example:

$$\frac{1}{10} = 0.1 \qquad\qquad \frac{9}{100} = 0.09$$

$$\frac{89}{1,000} = 0.089 \qquad\qquad \frac{321}{10,000} = 0.0321$$

Individuals should know and memorize the relationship of decimals to common fractions that is used in the food service industry. If a food service employee is working at a delicatessen and a guest asks for $\frac{1}{2}$ pound of cheese, the employee must know that when the scale reads 0.5, that represents $\frac{1}{2}$ pound, based on the decimal system. Table 4–1 illustrates common fractions that are used in the food service industry and their decimal equivalents. It is helpful for a food service professional to memorize this information.

Table 4–1 *Relationship between fractions and decimals*

Fraction	Decimal Equivalent
$\frac{1}{8}$	.125
$\frac{1}{5}$	.2
$\frac{1}{4}$	.25
$\frac{1}{3}$	.33333...
$\frac{2}{5}$	.4
$\frac{1}{2}$	.5
$\frac{2}{3}$	.66666...
$\frac{3}{4}$	.75
$\frac{7}{8}$	.875

Numbers go in both directions from the decimal point. The place value of the numbers to the left starts with the units or ones column, and each column (moving left) is an increasing multiple of 10.

Thousands	Hundreds	Tens	Units or Ones
1,000	100	10	1

To the right of the decimal point, each column is one-tenth of the number in the column immediately to its left. For example, one-tenth of one is $\frac{1}{10}$. Thus, the decimals to the right of the decimal point are 0.1, 0.01, 0.001, 0.0001, and so on. These numbers stated as decimal fractions are $\frac{1}{10}$, $\frac{1}{100}$, $\frac{1}{1,000}$, and $\frac{1}{10,000}$.

Decimal fractions differ from common fractions because they have 10 or a power of 10 for a denominator, whereas common fractions can have any number for the denominator. To simplify writing a decimal fraction, the decimal point is used. For example, to express the decimal fraction $\frac{725}{1,000}$ as its equivalent using a decimal point:

1. Convert the decimal fraction to a decimal first by writing the numerator (725).

2. Count the number of zeroes in the denominator and place the decimal point according to the number of zeroes. There must always be as many decimal places as there are zeroes in the denominator (0.725).

Often, when writing a decimal fraction as a decimal, it is necessary to add zeroes to the left of the numerator before placing the decimal point to indicate the value of the denominator. For example: $\frac{725}{10,000}$ = 0.0725, which should be read as seven hundred twenty-five ten thousandths.

When a number is made up of a whole number and a decimal fraction, it is referred to as a **mixed decimal fraction.** To write a mixed decimal fraction, the whole number is written to the left of the decimal point and the fractional part to the right of the decimal point. For example: $7\frac{135}{1,000}$ = 7.135. The decimal point is read as "and," so to read this mixed decimal fraction, the whole number is read first, then the decimal point as "and." Next, read the fraction as a whole number and state the denominator. Following this procedure, 7.135 is read "seven and one-hundred thirty-five thousandths."

To add or subtract decimal fractions, keep all whole numbers in their proper column and all decimal fractions in their proper column. Remember that the decimal point separates whole numbers from fractional parts. It is therefore very important that decimal points are directly in line with one another. For example, in adding decimal fractions:

2.135	Addend
7.43	Addend
4.008	Addend
+ 1.125	Addend
14.698	Sum

Note that the decimal point in the sum goes under the decimal point of the other numbers.

When subtracting decimal fractions:

$$
\begin{array}{rl}
9.825 & \text{Minuend} \\
-\ 5.450 & \text{Subtrahend} \\
\hline
4.375 & \text{Difference}
\end{array}
$$

Note that the decimal point in the difference goes under the decimal point in the minuend and subtrahend.

To multiply decimal fractions, follow the same procedure as when multiplying whole numbers to find the product. To locate the decimal point in the product, count the number of decimal places in both the multiplicand and the multiplier. The number of decimal places counted in the product is equal to the sum of those in the multiplicand and multiplier. For example:

$$
\begin{array}{rl}
4.32 & \text{Multiplicand} \\
\times\ 0.06 & \text{Multiplier} \\
\hline
0.2592 & \text{Product}
\end{array}
$$

There are four decimal places in the multiplicand and multiplier. Therefore, four decimal places are counted from right to left in the product.

In many cases, the total number of decimal places in the multiplicand and multiplier exceeds the number of numerals that appear in the product. In such cases, **ciphers** (zeroes) are added to the left of the digits in the product to complete the decimal places needed:

$$
\begin{array}{rl}
0.445 & \text{Multiplicand} \\
\times\quad 0.16 & \text{Multiplier} \\
\hline
2670 & \\
445 & \\
\hline
0.07120 & \text{Product}
\end{array}
$$

Note that a cipher is added to the product to complete the five decimals places required.

To divide decimal fractions, proceed as if the numbers were whole numbers and place the decimal point as follows:

1. When dividing by whole numbers, place the decimal point in the answer directly above the decimal point in the dividend.

$$
\begin{array}{l}
\phantom{\text{Divisor } 6)}0.06 \quad \text{Quotient} \\
\text{Divisor } 6\overline{)0.36} \quad \text{Dividend} \\
\phantom{\text{Divisor } 6)}\underline{0.36}
\end{array}
$$
Use zeroes as needed in the quotient to hold a place.

$$
\begin{array}{l}
\phantom{\text{Divisor } 5)}0.8 \quad \text{Quotient} \\
\text{Divisor } 5\overline{)4.0} \quad \text{Dividend} \\
\phantom{\text{Divisor } 5)}\underline{4.0}
\end{array}
$$
Zeroes are not needed in the quotient to hold a place.

T I P S . . .   To Insure Perfect Solutions

Dividend divided by Divisor equals Quotient

$$
\dfrac{\text{Quotient}}{\text{Divisor})\overline{\text{Dividend}}}
$$

T I P S . . .   **To Insure Perfect Solutions**

When dividing using the calculator, enter the dividend *first*.

---

2. When dividing a whole number or mixed decimal by a mixed decimal or decimal fraction, change the divisor and dividend so the divisor becomes a whole number. This is accomplished by multiplying both the dividend and divisor by the same power of 10. The divisor and dividend can be multiplied by the same power of 10 without changing the value of the division.

$$
\begin{array}{r}
12. \\
\text{Divisor } 0.25\overline{)3.00.} \\
\underline{2\,5} \\
50 \\
\underline{50}
\end{array}
\quad
\begin{array}{l}
\text{Quotient} \\
\text{Dividend}
\end{array}
$$

In the preceding example, the divisor 0.25 is made into the whole number 25 by multiplying by 100, moving the decimal point two places to the right. Since the dividend must also be multiplied by 100, the decimal point in the dividend is also moved two places to the right, so 3 becomes 300. The decimal point in the quotient is always placed directly over the decimal point in the dividend. The answer is 12, a whole number. Note that when moving a decimal point, an arrow is used to show where the decimal point is to be moved.

SUMMARY REVIEW 4–5

Change the following fractions to decimals.

1. $\frac{9}{10}$ = _____   6. $\frac{49}{100}$ = _____

2. $\frac{3}{10}$ = _____   7. $\frac{79}{100}$ = _____

3. $\frac{47}{100}$ = _____   8. $\frac{83}{100}$ = _____

4. $\frac{7}{10}$ = _____   9. $\frac{67}{100}$ = _____

5. $\frac{81}{100}$ = _____   10. $\frac{3}{10}$ = _____

Write the following decimals and mixed decimal fractions in words.

11. 0.6 _____   16. 0.67187 _____

12. 0.29 _____   17. 6.3 _____

13. 0.85917 _____ 18. 7.42 _____

14. 0.002 _____   19. 9.135 _____

15. 0.0578 _____   20. 3.41 _____

Write each of the following numbers as decimals.

21. Five tenths _____

22. Fourteen hundredths _____

23. Sixteen hundredths _____

24. Sixty-eight ten thousandths _____

25. One hundred twenty-two thousandths _____

26. Sixty-four hundred thousandths _____

27. Three and five tenths _____

28. Sixteen hundred thousandths _____

29. One hundred thousandths _____

30. Eight and nine hundredths _____

Find the sum in each problem.

31. $0.45 + 0.062 + 8.169 + 0.046 =$ _____

32. $0.58 + 0.675 + 6.225 + 9.323 =$ _____

33. $0.015 + 0.702 + 10.318 + 12.792 =$ _____

34. $0.056 + 0.015 + 0.711 + 6.25 + 16.37 =$ _____

35. $0.046 + 0.002 + 643 + 6.1675 =$ _____

Find the difference in each problem.

36. $9.765 - 0.046 =$ _____

37. $10 - 0.123 =$ _____

38. $1 - 0.685 =$ _____

39. $0.0622 - 0.0421 =$ _____

40. $139.371 - 123.218 =$ _____

Find the product in each problem. Round the answers to the nearest ten-thousandth when necessary.

41. $412 \times 0.52 =$ _____

42. $0.822 \times 1.52 =$ _____

43. $0.0524 \times 0.132 =$ _____

44. $6.53 \times 0.38 =$ _____

45. $7.323 \times 5.452 =$ _____

Find the quotient in each problem. Give quotients three decimal places when necessary.

46. $0.49 \div 7 =$ _____   51. $4 \div 0.25 =$ _____

47. $16 \div 4.8 =$ _____   52. $2.65 \div 1.5 =$ _____

48. $945 \div 500 =$ _____   53. $6.5 \div 2.45 =$ _____

49. $0.0684 \div 24 =$ _____   54. $45.5 \div 3.5 =$ _____

50. $46.76 \div 400 =$ _____   55. $54.25 \div 4.8 =$ _____

RATIOS

The term *ratio* is used in food service to express a comparison between two numbers. A **ratio** between two quantities is the number of times one contains the other. An example of using a ratio as a comparison is shown in the following problem:

Last week, the Sirloin Steak Restaurant sold five times as many steaks as pork chops. How many steaks were sold last week?

To determine how many steaks were sold, the amount of pork chops sold must be known. The restaurant sold 425 orders of pork chops.

Multiplying the amount of pork chops that were sold by the number 5 will solve this problem.

Mathematically, the problem will be set up this way:

$425 \times 5 = 2{,}125$

Therefore, 2,125 steaks were sold last week at the Sirloin Steak Restaurant. Another way to state this fact is by saying that steaks outsold pork chops by 5 to 1.

T I P S . . . To Insure Perfect Solutions

All answers should be checked for reasonableness. Think about and estimate what the correct answer should be. In the previous problem, if the answer came out to be 425 or less, the answer would not be reasonable. If a ratio is set up the wrong way, the answer will not be reasonable.

SUMMARY REVIEW 4–6

Determine the answers to the following questions using ratios.

1. The Cabernet Café sold six times as much Cabernet Sauvignon as Zinfandel. How many bottles of Cabernet Sauvignon were sold if they sold 5 bottles of Zinfandel?

   _____

2. Lanci's sold eight times as much osso bucco as veal marsala. How many orders of osso bucco were sold if they sold 33 orders of veal marsala?

   _____

3. The Bears Restaurant sells 15 times as many orders of chateaubriand as chicken breasts. How many orders of chateaubriand were sold if 12 orders of chicken breasts were sold?

   _____

4. The Casola Dining Room sold half as many orders of appetizers as desserts. How many appetizers were sold if the restaurant sold 250 desserts?

   _____

5. Scotti's sold 25 times as many orders of sausage and cheese pizzas than plain cheese pizzas. How many sausage and cheese pizzas were sold if they sold 280 cheese pizzas?

PROPORTIONS

Mathematical or word problems that include ratios may be solved by using proportions. A **proportion** is defined as a relation in size, number, amount, or degree of one thing compared to another. For example, when preparing baked rice, the ratio is 2 to 1, that is, 2 parts liquid to 1 part rice. If cooking 1 quart of raw rice, the formula calls for 2 quarts water or stock. The order in which the numbers are placed when expressing a ratio is important. If you say that the ratio when cooking barley is 4 to 1, meaning 4 parts water to 1 part barley, it is not the same as saying 1 to 4, which would reverse the ratio and mean 1 part water to every 4 parts of barley (which would cause the barley to scorch and burn).

How to Use Proportions to Solve Problems

The problem reads: How much water is needed to cook 8 quarts of barley using a ratio of 4 to 1 liquid to barley?

Step 1 Set up a written equation Right now, you don't know how much water is needed to cook 8 quarts of barley. Since the amount of water is an unknown, that unknown quantity will be named x. X is the amount of water to be determined; it does not mean to multiply. Facts you must know to do a proportion The water is represented by an x, since that is the answer to be determined. "Is to" in a mathematical equation is represented by a full colon (:) The numbers on the outside of the equation are called *extremes* The numbers on the inside of the equation are called *means*
Step 2 Set up a mathematical equation $x : 8 = 4 : 1$
Step 3 Multiply the means together 8 times 4 = 32, and put the answer on the right of the = sign Multiply the extremes together x times 1 = 1x, and put the answer on the left of the = sign
Step 4 The mathematical equation looks like this: $1x = 32$
Step 5 Divide both sides of the equation by the number next to the x $x/1 = x$ (the 1 cancels out the 1) $32/1 = 32$ Therefore $x = 32$, or 32 quarts of water is needed to end up with 8 quarts of barley.

SUMMARY REVIEW 4–7

Solve the following problems using the proportions given.

1. How much water is needed to bake $\frac{3}{4}$ gallon of rice using a ratio of 2 to 1 liquid to rice?

_____

2. How much water is required to soak $\frac{1}{2}$ gallon of navy beans using a ratio of 3 to 1 water to beans?

_____

3. How much water should be used to cook 1 pint of barley using a ratio of 4 to 1 water to barley?

_____

4. How much water is needed to prepare orange juice using $1\frac{1}{2}$ pints of orange concentrate and a ratio of 3 to 1 water to concentrate?

_____

5. How much water is needed to prepare lemonade using $1\frac{3}{4}$ pints of frozen lemonade and a ratio of 4 to 1 water to lemonade?

_____

6. How much chicken stock is needed to bake $1\frac{1}{4}$ quarts of rice using a ratio of 2 to 1 stock to rice?

_____

7. How much water will it take to simmer $1\frac{3}{4}$ quarts of barley using a ratio of 4 to 1 water to barley?

_____

8. How much water will it take to soak $\frac{3}{4}$ gallon of red beans using a ratio of 3 to 1 water to beans?

_____

9. How much water is needed to prepare orange juice using $1\frac{3}{4}$ quarts of orange concentrate and a ratio of 4 to 1 water to concentrate?

_____

10. How much water is required when making fruit punch if $1\frac{1}{4}$ pints of frozen punch concentrate is used and the ratio is 5 to 1 water to concentrate?

PERCENTS

Percent plays a big part in food service language. It is used to express a rate when dealing with important business matters such as food costs, labor costs, profits, and even that undesirable figure called loss. When management meets with food service employees and wishes to emphasize points that need improving, the message conveyed is usually done by expressing a percentage. For example: last month our food cost was 45%. We must bring this figure under control.

Percent (%) means "of each hundred." Thus, 5% means 5 out of every 100. This same 5% can also be written 0.05 in decimal form. In fraction form, it is $\frac{5}{100}$. The percent sign (%) is, in reality, a unique way of writing 100.

Percents are a special tool used to express a rate of each hundred. If 50% of the customers in a restaurant select a seafood entree, a rate of a whole is being expressed. The whole is represented by 100% and all of the customers entering the restaurant would represent the whole, or 100%. Another example of percent in food service is shown in Figure 4-3.

To find what percent one number is of another number, divide the number that represents the part by the number that represents the whole. For example: a hindquarter of beef weighs 240 pounds. The round cut weighs 52 pounds. What percent of the hindquarter is the round cut?

The 240-pound hindquarter represents the whole. The 52-pound round cut represents only a fractional part of the hindquarter. As a fraction, it is written $\frac{52}{240}$. Simplified or reduced to lowest terms, it is $\frac{13}{60}$. To express a common fraction as a percent, the numerator is divided by the denominator. The division must be carried out two places (hundredth place) for the percent. Carrying the division three places behind the

Figure 4–3 *An example of percent in food service—20% of the truffles are dark.*

decimal gives the tenth of a percent, which makes the percent more accurate. The finished problem looks like this:

$$
\begin{array}{r}
0.2166 \text{ is equal to } 21.7\% \\
240\overline{)52.0000} \\
-48\ 0 \\
\hline
4\ 00 \\
-2\ 40 \\
\hline
1\ 600 \\
-1\ 440 \\
\hline
1600 \\
-1440 \\
\hline
160
\end{array}
$$

Percent means hundredths, so the decimal is moved two places to the right when the percent sign is used.

This same percent could be obtained by converting the fraction $\frac{13}{60}$ into a percent by dividing the denominator into the numerator, as shown in the following example:

$$
\begin{array}{r}
0.2166 \text{ is equal to } 21.7\% \\
60\overline{)13.0000} \\
-12\ 0 \\
\hline
1\ 00 \\
-\ \ 60 \\
\hline
400 \\
-\ 360 \\
\hline
400 \\
-\ 360 \\
\hline
40
\end{array}
$$

When a percent is expressed as a common fraction, the given percent is the numerator and 100 is the denominator. For example:

$$40\% = \frac{40}{100} \text{ or } \frac{2}{5};$$

$$20\% = \frac{20}{100} \text{ or } \frac{1}{5}.$$

When a percent is changed to a decimal fraction, the percent sign is removed and the decimal point is moved two places to the left. For example:

$$24.5\% = 0.245$$

$$75.7\% = 0.757$$

When a decimal fraction is expressed as a percent, move the decimal point two places to the right and place the percent sign to the right of the last figure. For example:

$$0.234 = 23.4\%$$

$$0.826 = 82.6\%$$

The preceding percents are read as twenty-three and four-tenths percent, and eighty-two and six-tenths percent.

Remember the following points when dealing with percents:

- When a number is compared with a number larger than itself, the result is always less than 100%. For example:

  72 is 80% of 90 since $\frac{72}{90} = \frac{4}{5} = 80\%$.

- When a number is compared with itself, the result is always 100%. For example:

72 is 100% of 72 since $\frac{72}{72} = 1 = 100\%$.

- When taking a percent of a whole number, the method of operation is to multiply. For example:

If a restaurant takes in $9,462 in one week, but only 23% of that amount is profit, what is the profit?

$$
\begin{array}{r}
\$ 9{,}462 \\
\times\ 0.23 \\
\hline
28386 \\
18924 \\
\hline
\$2{,}176.26 \quad \text{Profit}
\end{array}
$$

Finding Percents of Meat Cuts

Since the use of percents in expressing a rate is a common practice in the food service business, this exercise is included for two reasons. First, to show the student how the sides of beef, veal, pork, and, lamb are blocked out into wholesale or primal cuts, and, second, to provide another opportunity to practice and understand percents.

A side is half of the complete carcass. A saddle, used in reference to the lamb carcass, is the front or hind half of the complete carcass that is cut between the twelfth and thirteenth ribs of lamb. The side or saddle is blocked out into wholesale or primal cuts at the meat processing plant.

Shown below is a blocked out side of beef and how the percentage of each wholesale cut is found. For the side of beef in Figure 4–4, find the percentage of each wholesale cut.

To find a percentage, divide the whole into the part. In this case, the whole is represented by the total weight of the side of beef, 444 pounds. The part is represented by the weight of each individual wholesale cut. For example, the percentage of chuck is found as follows:

$$
\begin{array}{r}
0.252 \text{ is equal to } 25.2\% \quad \text{Percentage of chuck} \\
\text{Total weight of side of beef } 444\overline{)112.000} \qquad\qquad \text{Weight of chuck} \\
-\ 88\ 8 \\
\hline
23\ 20 \\
-\ 22\ 20 \\
\hline
1\ 000 \\
888 \\
\hline
112
\end{array}
$$

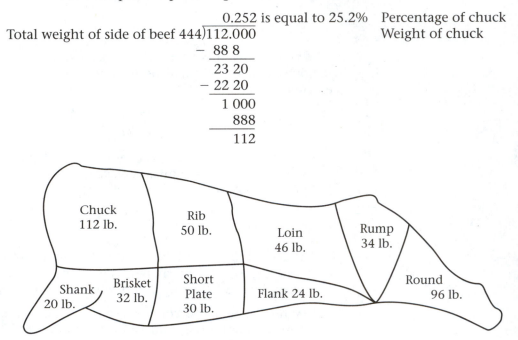

Figure 4–4 *A side of beef divided into cuts*

Chef Sez...

"When developing a new chef's knife, the percentage of each raw material going into that item must be precisely calculated. If the metal alloys chromium, molybdenum, and vanadium contained in the knife blade steel are not present in the correct amounts, the knife blade could be too soft, too hard, or too brittle. If the percentages were incorrect, we'd end up with a poor-quality knife that would be unacceptable for culinary professionals to use."

Peter Huebner
President and Owner of Canada Cutlery
Inc. Pickering, Ontario, Canada

Canada Cutlery Inc. is a supplier of professional quality cutlery and kitchen tools. They have been marketing professional chef's knives and tools since 1954. Their CCI Superior Culinary Master® professional knives and tools are manufactured in state-of-the-art facilities to not only meet, but to exceed, the demands of the professional chef. Only the highest quality, European, high-carbon, stainless surgical steel is used. (http://www.canadacutlery.com)

The percentages of the other eight beef cuts are found by following the same procedure. Carry three places to the right of the decimal. When the exercise is completed and the percentages are totaled, the result should be 99% plus a figure representing a tenth of a percent. In the following example, the figure expressing the sum is 99.7%. A 100% result will be unlikely, since the individual percents will almost never figure out evenly.

25.2%	Chuck
4.5%	Shank
7.2%	Brisket
6.7%	Short plate
11.2%	Rib
10.3%	Sirloin
5.4%	Flank
7.6%	Rump
21.6%	Round
99.7%	Total

SUMMARY REVIEW 4–8

Express the following common fractions as percents.

1. $\frac{3}{8}$ = _____

2. $\frac{5}{9}$ = _____

3. $\frac{3}{10}$ = _____

4. $\frac{5}{12}$ = _____

5. $\frac{3}{16}$ = _____

6. $\frac{5}{8}$ = _____

7. $\frac{5}{6}$ = _____

8. $\frac{4}{9}$ = _____

9. $\frac{2}{3}$ = _____

10. $\frac{3}{4}$ = _____

Express the following percents as common fractions, whole numbers, or mixed numbers. Reduce to the lowest common denominator.

11. 3% = _____

12. 40% = _____

13. 75% = _____

14. 60% = _____

15. 100% = _____

16. 38% = _____

17. 68% = _____

18. 200% = _____

19. 65% = _____

20. 140% = _____

Solve the following problems. Round answers to the nearest hundredth.

21.	5% of 85 = _____	26.	75% of $750.00 = _____
22.	30% of 678 = _____	27.	43% of $468.00 = _____
23.	42% of 500 = _____	28.	65% of $2,480.00 = _____
24.	14.5% of 92 = _____	29.	26% of $4,680.00 = _____
25.	39% of $38.20 = _____	30.	79% of $2,285.00 = _____

31. A 526-pound side of beef is ordered. The chuck cut weighs 76 pounds and the round cut weighs 58 pounds. What percent of the side is the chuck?_____ What percent is the round?

_____

32. A party for 325 people is booked. The cost of the party is $8,125. If they are given an 8% discount on their total bill, what is the cost of the party?

_____

33. A party for 120 people is booked. The cost of the party is $3,000. If they are given a 12% discount on their total bill, what is the cost of the party?

_____

34. If a restaurant takes in $25,680 in one week and 26% of that amount is profit, how much is profit?

_____

35. Mrs. Hill purchased three new coffee urns at $1,586 each. For buying in quantity, she is given a $3\frac{1}{2}$% discount on the total bill. What is the amount she paid?

_____

36. If a 48-pound beef round is roasted and 9 pounds are lost through shrinkage, what percent of the round is lost through shrinkage?

_____

37. The food cost percentage for the month is 38%. If $26,485 was taken in that month, how much of that amount went for the cost of food?

_____

38. If a restaurant's gross receipts for one week total $12,000, of which $8,000 is profit, what percent of the gross receipts is profit?

_____

39. If a restaurant's gross receipts for one day total $18,500, of which $5,600 are expenses, what percent of the gross receipts are expenses?

_____

40. If a 45-pound round of beef is roasted and 9 pounds are lost through shrinkage, what percent of the round is lost through shrinkage?

_____

41. If a restaurant's gross receipts for one week total $22,080 but only 24% of that amount is profit, how much are expenses?

_____

42. If a 52-pound round is roasted and 9 pounds are lost through shrinkage, what percent of the round roast is lost through shrinkage?

_____

43. If a restaurant's gross receipts for one week is $42,682 and 26% of that amount is for labor, 37% for food cost, and 15% for miscellaneous items, how much is the profit?

_____

Find the percentage of beef and pork wholesale cuts in the following problems.

44. Find the percentage of each cut of beef that makes up the side of beef shown in the figure.

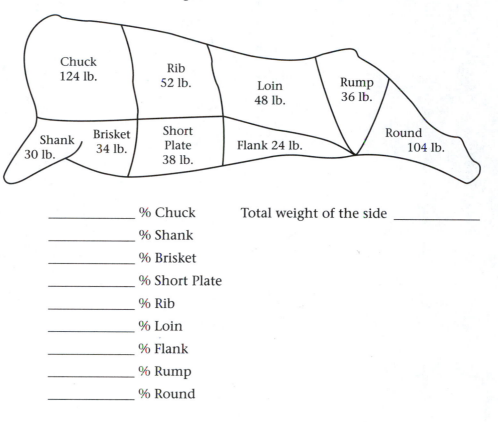

_____ % Chuck   Total weight of the side _____

_____ % Shank

_____ % Brisket

_____ % Short Plate

_____ % Rib

_____ % Loin

_____ % Flank

_____ % Rump

_____ % Round

45. Find the percentage of each cut of pork that makes up the side of pork shown in the figure.

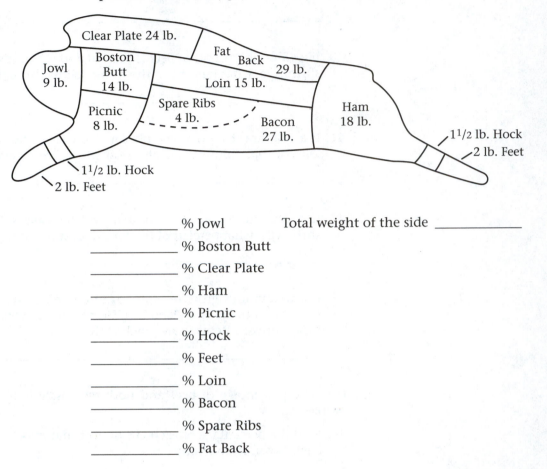

_____ % Jowl   Total weight of the side _____

_____ % Boston Butt

_____ % Clear Plate

_____ % Ham

_____ % Picnic

_____ % Hock

_____ % Feet

_____ % Loin

_____ % Bacon

_____ % Spare Ribs

_____ % Fat Back

PART III

MATH ESSENTIALS IN FOOD PREPARATION

CHAPTER 5 • Weights and Measures

CHAPTER 6 • Using the Metric System of Measurement

CHAPTER 7 • Portion Control

CHAPTER 8 • Converting Recipes, Yields, and Baking Formulas

N ow that the review is completed and you have refreshed your math skills, it is time to approach the math functions used in kitchen production by the preparation crew.

In the past, the preparation crew was hired to perform individual production tasks such as broiling, sauteing, and roasting. Other details concerned with math skills were the responsibility of management. In addition, management sets standards for controlling portions, converts recipes, and writes food production reports. Today, controls in all areas of production have become everyone's job. Math skills must be learned and developed by all personnel. This is the only way management can control the high cost of food and labor as well as keep menu prices competitive. Developing math skills is also a step in moving up the ladder to a management position or from employee to employer.

There are a number of daily situations in the preparation area of a commercial kitchen where math skills are required for the operation to run efficiently. These situations require the attention of each member of the crew.

Since more products are being packaged and more recipes are being written using the metric system, this part of the book explains the importance of understanding and using the metric system of measure.

Kitchen personnel responsible for food preparation usually consist of the chef, sous-chef, cooks, butcher, baker, and pantry or salad person. Every member of this crew should understand the math functions presented in this section of the text. Remember that the steps up the ladder of promotion and success are not difficult ones to climb if you are prepared when the opportunity arrives.

CHAPTER 5

Weights and Measures

OBJECTIVES

At the completion of this chapter, the student should be able to:

1. Identify the equivalent measures commonly used in food service operations.
2. Find equivalent measures.
3. Tell what as purchased (A.P.) and edible portion (E.P.) mean.
4. Identify abbreviations of weights and measures.
5. Use a baker's balance scale.
6. Demonstrate how to convert decimal weights into ounces.
7. Identify different types of portion scales (dial and digital) and know how to use them.

KEY WORDS

as purchased (A.P.)
edible portion (E.P.)
drained weight test
scoops
dippers

ladles
baker's balance scale
volume
portions
portion scale

The careful use of weights and measures is an essential part of a food service operation. It is a method used to obtain accuracy and consistent quality in all food products and to control cost. Uniform products mean repeat sales.

There are two essential kinds of measurement practiced in a food service operation. Both are extremely important for having and maintaining a successful operation. They are:

- Ingredient measurement
- Portion measurement

In this chapter, the equipment used in weighing and measuring is discussed. The use of these devices is explained and the two basic kinds of measurement are discussed. In following chapters, portion control will be emphasized and clarified.

THE USE OF WEIGHTS AND MEASURES

Recipes or formulas used in food establishments are stated in weights and measures. The more exact recipes or formulas are stated in weights, and a balance baker's scale is used. In this way, ingredient amounts can be found more accurately, and accuracy is of major importance—especially in baked products. An unbalanced baked product is sure failure. When measuring ingredients, one is very seldom exact; much depends on how firmly the ingredients are packed into the measuring device and what the

tsp. or small "t"	teaspoon
tbsp. or large "T"	tablespoon
C.	cup
pt.	pint
qt.	quart
gal.	gallon
oz.	ounce
lb.	pound
bch.	bunch
doz.	dozen
ea.	each
crt.	crate

Figure 5–1 *Common abbreviations of weights and measures*

individual considers a full measure. The common measures used are teaspoons, tablespoons, cups, pints, quarts, and gallons. These are usually abbreviated when stated in recipes. Figure 5–1 gives the common abbreviations used.

When weighing most ingredients in a bakery preparation, you can usually proceed without much concern. Just be sure you are using an accurate scale. When weighing ingredients that must be cleaned, peeled, or trimmed, however, you must be aware of the difference between **A.P. (as purchased) weight** and **E.P. (edible portion) weight.**

- **A.P.** is a term used to refer to the weight of a product as it was purchased.

- **E.P.** is a term used to refer to the weight of a product after it has been cleaned, trimmed, boned, and so forth. At this point, all the nonedible parts have been removed.

A recipe or formula should indicate which weight is being referred to by using A.P. or E.P. when listing ingredients. If this step is neglected, you must attempt to judge from the instructions in the method of preparation. When the instructions state that the item must first be trimmed, peeled, and boned, then you can be certain that A.P. weight is stated. If the instructions indicate the item has already been cleaned, trimmed, and peeled, you know E.P. weight is called for.

Liquid measures are sometimes measured by volume. This practice is usually faster than weighing and just as accurate. As pointed out, volume measures are not recommended for measuring dry ingredients unless the amount is too small to weigh. An example of this would be $\frac{1}{4}$ teaspoon of salt or $\frac{1}{2}$ teaspoon of cinnamon.

EQUIVALENTS OF WEIGHTS AND MEASURES

To compete in the culinary world, a chef or culinarian must be able to weigh and measure ingredients used for recipes. Being knowledgeable about how to use mathematics to convert ingredients for different recipes is essential for success in this industry. The culinarian must know how many ounces make up a pound; how many ounces are in a # 10 can; how many quarts make up a gallon and so on. Figure 5–2 is a useful tool that Professor Gary Brenenstuhl uses with his culinary arts

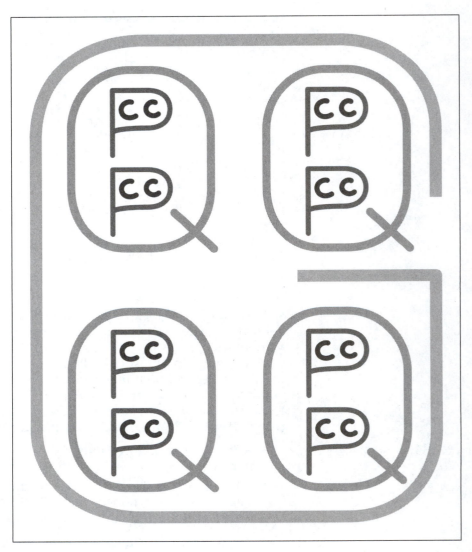

Figure 5–2 *Professor Brenenstuhl's useful measurement tool*

students at Schenectady County Community College. The large G signifies a gallon of liquid. Inside the G are four Qs, which signify that 4 quarts make up one gallon. Inside each Q are two Ps, which signify that 2 pints make up one quart. Each P has two Cs, which signify that 2 cups are equal to 1 pint.

Figure 5–3 illustrates the relationship of the common equivalent weights and measures used in this tool.

A culinarian can use this information to control food costs and use up products that may spoil and have to be thrown out. For example, at

Unit of measure	Amount of fluid ounces	Equivalent relationship
1 gallon	128	4 quarts
1 quart	32	2 pints
1 pint	16	2 cups
1 cup	8	

Figure 5–3 *Relationships between gallons, quarts, pints, and cups in measurements*

an elementary school, the cook has to prepare a recipe that calls for a gallon of milk. The cook, after taking inventory of milk, discovers that there is an excess of 8-oz. containers of milk that, if not used, would spoil in a day. Instead of opening up a new gallon container of milk, the cook uses 16 of the 8-oz. containers of milk. Mathematically, $16 \times 8 = 128$. There are 128 ounces in a gallon.

The relationship of the various measures and weights is given in Figure 5–4. This figure can be used to convert from measures to weights or weights to measures, and can help save production time. For example, if 2 pounds of liquid milk are required in a recipe, this can be quickly measured by volume as 1 fluid quart since 2 pounds of liquid equals 1 fluid quart, or if 1 pound of whole eggs is needed, this can be measured as fluid pint.

T I P S . . . .   To Insure Perfect Solutions

When weighing liquids, be aware that all liquids do not weigh the same. A cup of water does not weigh the same as a cup of oil. Therefore, the old saying "a pound is a pint the world around" is not necessarily true!

Figure 5–4 *Equivalents of weights and measures*

1 pinch	=	$\frac{1}{8}$ teaspoon (approx)
3 teaspoons	=	1 tablespoon
2 tablespoons	=	1 oz.
4 tablespoons	=	$\frac{1}{4}$ cup
8 tablespoons	=	$\frac{1}{2}$ cup
12 tablespoons	=	$\frac{3}{4}$ cup
16 tablespoons	=	1 cup
2 cups	=	1 pint
4 cups	=	1 quart
16 cups	=	1 gallon
2 pints	=	1 quart
4 quarts	=	1 gallon
5 fifths	=	1 gallon
2 quarts	=	1 magnum
8 quarts	=	1 peck
4 pecks	=	1 bushel
8 ounces	=	1 fluid cup
16 ounces	=	1 pound
1 pound	=	1 fluid pint
2 pounds	=	1 fluid quart
8 pounds	=	1 fluid gallon
12 dozen	=	1 gross
32 ounces	=	1 quart
64 ounces	=	$\frac{1}{2}$ gallon
128 ounces	=	1 gallon

Figure 5–5 *An assortment of measuring and weighing utensils used in food service operations*

DISCUSSION QUESTION 5-A

A recipe calls for $\frac{1}{2}$ gallon of milk. Using the information from Figure 5–4, calculate the possible solutions if the restaurant only has the following containers of milk: quarts; pints; cups.

SUMMARY REVIEW 5-1

Fill in the correct measure using information found in Figure 5–4.

1. 9 teaspoons   equal   _____ tablespoons

2. 8 tablespoons   equal   _____ cup

3. 2 pinches   equal   _____ teaspoon(s)

4. 16 tablespoons   equal   _____ cup(s)

5. 120 quarts   equal   _____ gallons

6. 1 magnum   equals   _____ quarts

7. 4 pounds   equal   _____ fluid quarts

8. 64 ounces   equal   _____ quarts

9. 20 gallons   equal   _____ quarts

10. 1 peck   equals   _____ quarts

11.   4 pints   equal   _____ quarts

12.   64 ounces   equal   _____ pounds

13.   8 cups   equal   _____ ounces

14.   1 bushel   equals   _____ pecks

15.   18 cups   equal   _____ pints

In food preparation and baking, a recipe or formula will call for so many pounds or ounces of liquid, and a scale may not be available or it would be more convenient to measure the liquid. Assume this is the situation for the following problems. For each, state the amount of volume measure you would use.

16.   The recipe calls for 1 pound 8 ounces of water. _____

17.   The recipe calls for 4 pounds of apple juice. _____

18.   The recipe calls for 5 pounds of apple juice. _____

19.   The recipe calls for 2 pounds and 12 oz. milk. _____

20.   The recipe calls for 6 pounds of skim milk. _____

DISCUSSION QUESTION 5-B

Why does a food service professional have to know how to convert measurements to equivalent weights and measures? Give two examples of how this knowledge would be used in a food service operation.

Size of Cans In the food service industry, many products are packed in cans. A culinarian has to know how much is in each can. Figure 5–6 shows can numbers and their equivalent measurements. Because a can of vegetables or fruit has a varying amount of liquid, measurements are not exact. The food service operator must perform a "can cutting" to determine the quality of the product, how much of the ingredients of the can is product, and how much is liquid. This is called a **drained weight test.** For example, the operator will open up a # 10 can of tomatoes, pour the liquid into one container, and pour the tomatoes into another. Both containers are weighed, which shows the operator the liquid weight and the tomato weight separately. This will explain why there is a variation in the amount of measurements in the can.

Size of can	Measurement	Equivalent ounces
Number 1 or Picnic	$1\frac{1}{4}$ Cups	$10\frac{1}{2}$ to 12
Number 300	$1\frac{3}{4}$ Cups	14 to 16
Number 303	2 Cups	16 to 17
Number 2	$2\frac{1}{2}$ Cups	20
Number $2\frac{1}{2}$	$3\frac{3}{4}$ Cups	27 to 29
Number 3	$5\frac{3}{4}$ Cups	51
Number 10	3 Quarts	6 lbs. 8 oz. to 7 lbs. 5 oz.

Figure 5–6 *Common can numbers and their equivalents. Source:* Albany Times Union, *March 26, 2004.*

MEASURING AND WEIGHING DEVICES

There are many measuring and weighing instruments used in food service operations. They include an assortment of cups, spoons, ladles, dippers or scoops; baker's balance scales, digital platform scales, and portion scales; kitchen or serving spoons; and pints, quarts, and gallons that are used as a substitute for weighing liquid measures. Some of these are illustrated in Figure 5–5 and described in the following paragraphs.

SUMMARY REVIEW 5-2

Fill in the correct measure using Figure 5–6 and making conversions where needed.

1. What is the range of ounces in a number 10 can? _____ to _____.
2. How many pints are in a number 10 can? _____ to _____.
3. How many tablespoons are in a number 303 can? _____.
4. How many quarts are in a number 3 can? _____
5. How many teaspoons are in a number 1 can? _____

Scoops or Dippers

Scoops or **dippers** are used to serve many foods as well as to control the portion size. The various sizes are designated by a number that appears on the lever that mechanically releases the item from the scoop. The number that appears on the lever indicates the number of level scoops it will take to fill a quart. Figure 5–7 gives the relationship of the scoop number to the approximate capacity in ounces and volume content for both customary and metric measure.

Customary or United States Measure			Metric Measure	
Scoop number	Volume	Approximate weight	Volume	Approximate weight
6	$\frac{2}{3}$ cup	5 oz.	160 mL	140 g
8	$\frac{1}{2}$ cup	4 oz.	120 mL	110 g
10	3 fl. oz.	3 to $3\frac{1}{2}$ oz.	90 mL	85 to 100 g
12	$\frac{1}{3}$ cup	$2\frac{1}{2}$ to 3 oz.	80 mL	70 to 85 g
16	$\frac{1}{4}$ cup	2 to $2\frac{1}{2}$ oz.	60 mL	60 to 70 g
20	$1\frac{1}{2}$ fl. oz.	$1\frac{3}{4}$ oz.	45 mL	50 g
24	$1\frac{1}{3}$ fl. oz.	$1\frac{1}{2}$ oz.	40 mL	40 g
30	1 fl. oz.	1 oz.	30 mL	30 g
40	0.8 fl. oz.	0.8 oz.	24 mL	23 g
60	$\frac{1}{2}$ fl. oz.	$\frac{1}{2}$ oz.	15 mL	15 g

Figure 5–7 *Scoop or dipper sizes and approximate weights and measures in both customary and metric units. Weights vary with different foods. This is only a guide and not exact. Source: Chart comes from Gisslen, Wayne, (2003). Professional cooking (5th ed.). New York: John Wiley & Sons.*

Figure 5–8 *This chef is using a ladle to measure the exact serving of sauce.*

Figure 5–9 *Ladle sizes*

Size	Weight
$\frac{1}{4}$ cup	2 oz.
$\frac{1}{2}$ cup	4 oz.
$\frac{3}{4}$ cup	6 oz.
1 cup	8 oz.

Ladles

Ladles are used to serve stews, soups, sauces, gravies, dressings, cream dishes, and other liquids or semiliquids, when portioning and uniform servings are desired or required. (See Figure 5–8.) They come in assorted sizes, holding from 2 to 8 ounces. The size, in ounces, is stamped on the handle. Figure 5–9 shows the ladle sizes most frequently used.

DISCUSSION QUESTION 5-C

Why does a food service professional have to know the sizes of scoops and ladles? How will this affect the cost of food and the appearance of the plates?

The Baker's Balance Scale

The **baker's balance scale** is the best type of scale to use because it ensures accuracy with the use of weight. The scale has a twin platform.

Figure 5–10 *Measuring scale*

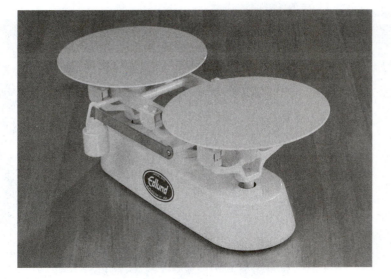

Figure 5–11 *Baker's scale beam graduated in $\frac{1}{4}$ ounces up to 16 ounces (1 pound)*

(See Figure 5–10.) On the platform to the left is placed a metal scoop, in which the food to be weighed is placed. On the platform to the right is placed a special weight equal to the weight of the scoop. (See Figure 5–10.) If another container is used on the left platform, balance the scale by placing counterweights on the right side or by adjusting the ounce weight on the horizontal beam. This horizontal beam runs across the front of the scale. The beam has a weight attached to it and is graduated in $\frac{1}{4}$ ounces. The weight is placed on the number of ounces one wishes to weigh. The ounce weight can be graduated to 16 ounces (1 pound). (See Figure 5–11.) This scale can be used to weigh ingredients up to 10 pounds.

If a larger amount of food is to be weighed, additional metal weights of 1, 2, and 4 pounds are provided. When using this scale, always balance it before setting the weights for a given amount. It must balance again after the ingredients are placed on the scale.

When weighing 8 ounces of egg yolks, for example, place a container large enough to hold the yolks on the left platform and balance the scale. Move the weight on the horizontal beam 8 additional ounces. Then add the yolks to the container until the scale balances again.

If 1 pound $6\frac{1}{2}$ ounces of flour are to be weighed, place the metal scoop on the left-hand platform and the special balance weight on the right-hand platform. This brings the two platforms to a complete balance. The 1-pound weight is placed on the platform to the right, and the weight on the scaling beam is set on $6\frac{1}{2}$ ounces. Flour is placed in the metal scoop until the two platforms balance a second time. For weighing small amounts, such as $1\frac{3}{4}$ ounces of baking powder, a piece of paper or a small paper plate should be placed on both platforms. To weigh the baking powder, slide the hanging weight (the weight on the horizontal beam attached to the scale) to $1\frac{3}{4}$ ounces. Pour the baking powder onto the paper on the left platform until it balances.

Figure 5–12 *An example of a baker's scale to determine quantities.*

Why the Baker's Balance Scale Is Important

Baking is fundamentally a science, so ingredients have to be accurate. A major challenge in baking is realizing that volume measures and measures of weights are different. For instance, if a recipe is written in **volume,** that is, the recipe states to add 2 cups of flour, then the baker would measure 2 cups of flour by volume. But if the recipe calls for weighing out 16 ounces of flour, that may or may not be the same amount as the 2 cups of volume measure. The baker has to have the skill to use the balance scale accurately in order for the finished product to be a success.

To prove our point, obtain two 8-ounce measuring cups. Fill one with cotton balls and the other with crushed stone. Both of them measure 8 ounces of ingredients by volume, but do they both weigh the same amount? Of course not! To check our conclusion, practice by weighing both items using a baker's balance scale.

In the workplace, you will be expected to be able to use the baker's scale correctly. Practice is necessary to become competent, so, whenever possible, set the scale at various settings and weigh whatever items are usually on hand. (See Figure 5–12.) Use items such as flour, salt, sugar, rice, and water.

T I P S . . . To Insure Perfect Solutions

The weight of one cup of cotton balls **does not** equal the weight of one cup of crushed stone.

This is further illustrated in Figure 5–14, which gives approximate weights and measures of common foods. For instance, compare the weight of a cup of cooked diced beef with a cup of fresh bread crumbs. A cup of beef weighs $5\frac{1}{2}$ ounces, while a cup of bread crumbs weighs 2 ounces.

SUMMARY REVIEW AND HANDS-ON ACTIVITY 5–3

Total the amounts of each ingredient in the five formulas given and write the total below each formula.

For Example:

Ingredients	Pounds	Ounces
Sugar	1	8
Flour	4	6
Salt	—	1
Shortening	1	12
TOTAL	**6 lb.**	**27 oz. = 7 lb. 11 oz.**

(Note: There are 16 ounces in a pound, so for each 16 ounces, carry 1 pound to the pound column. Twenty-seven ounces equals 1 pound and 11 ounces, so 6 pounds 27 ounces equals 7 pounds 11 ounces.)

Then, for hands-on practice, weigh each ingredient separately using sugar or rice to represent each ingredient. When this is done, add up the total amount of all ingredients weighed. The amount should equal the sum of all the weights of ingredients listed.

Formula 1:

Ingredients	Pounds	Ounces
Shortening	1	6
Bread Flour	3	12
Salt	—	1
Sugar	2	10
Baking Powder	—	3
TOTAL		

Formula 2:

Ingredients	Pounds	Ounces
Shortening	1	8
Pastry Flour	2	10
Baking Powder	—	4
Baking Soda	—	$\frac{1}{2}$
Sugar	1	12
Salt	—	$2\frac{1}{4}$
TOTAL		

Formula 3:

Ingredients	Pounds	Ounces
Sugar	2	6
Baking Powder	—	$\frac{3}{4}$
Salt	—	$\frac{1}{2}$
Flour	4	10
Cornstarch	—	5
TOTAL		

Formula 4:

Ingredients	Pounds	Ounces
Butter	1	12
Pastry Flour	4	6
Dry Milk	—	$3\frac{1}{2}$
Shortening	1	6
Sugar	2	10
Salt	—	$\frac{3}{4}$
TOTAL		

Formula 5:

Ingredients	Pounds	Ounces
Butter	—	12
Cake Flour	—	10
Sugar	2	14
Baking Powder	1	$1\frac{3}{4}$
Dry Milk	—	6
Water	1	11
TOTAL		

Chef Sez...

"In bread and roll production, the student must weigh out ingredients. This is an important step because of:

A. Balanced formula—varying the percent of ingredients will change the formula;

B. Consistent production of the required quantity—varying the ingredients may result in too large or too small a quantity;

C. Consistent production of quality;

D. Uniformity regardless of changes in mixing personnel;

E. Uniformity in fermentation times;

F. Control of costs."

Chef Noble Masi, Certified Master Baker,
Professor Emeritus
The Culinary Institute of America
Hyde Park, NY

Noble Masi was the 1999 American Culinary Chef of the Year. He was a professor of baking and pastry at The Culinary Institute of America. He was also the recipient of the 1996 ACF Chef Professionalism Award. He is an ACF-certified judge and a frequent speaker at seminars. He presented a seminar on signature breads at the American Culinary Federation National Convention.

Portion Scale

Portion scales are used for measuring food servings, or **portions.** Sometimes, ingredients are measured as well if a baker's balance scale is not available. A **portion scale** is operated by the use of a spring and can easily be unbalanced, so it is recommended that ingredients be weighed using the baker's balance scale if at all possible.

Portioning foods for service is a control method used in industry to ensure that the correct amount of an item or preparation is acquired and

Figure 5–13 *Portioning meat on a portion scale helps control serving size and cost.*

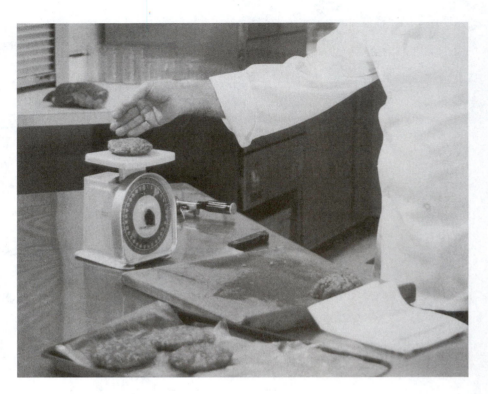

served. The scale would be used to portion a 3-ounce serving of baked ham, a $2\frac{1}{2}$-ounce serving of roast turkey, a 5-ounce hamburger steak, or a $4\frac{1}{2}$-ounce patty of pork sausage. If the exact cost of each item sold is to be determined, it is necessary to know the yield of each food. For example, if 15 pounds of beef round cost $27.75, the cost per serving cannot be determined until a serving portion and yield are established after the meat has been roasted.

The portion scale shown in Figure 5–13 is used to weigh quantities up to 32 ounces (2 pounds). Each number on the movable dial represents 1 ounce. Each mark between the numbers represents $\frac{1}{4}$ ounce. For instance, the first mark past the pointer is $\frac{1}{4}$ ounce. The longer line next to it is $\frac{1}{2}$ ounce. The short line next in order is $\frac{3}{4}$ ounce, and the long line that comes next is 1 full ounce.

The platform at the top of the portion scale is attached to a metal stem that fits into the scale. It is made of stainless steel and can be removed for washing, but care must be taken when replacing it to ensure that it fits properly and performs accurately. When the platform is properly placed, the pointer rests on 0, which also represents 32 ounces when weighing takes place. When weighing amounts that fit on the platform, first place waxed paper or some type of patty paper on the platform. Then, using the handle to move the scale dial, move the dial to the left until the pointer is again at zero. This action accounts for the weight of the paper. Place enough of the item being weighed on the paper until the pointer is exactly at the amount needed. For example, if portioning a 3-ounce crab cake, place enough of the mixture on the platform so that the pointer points directly at the 3, indicating that 3 ounces have been obtained. When weighing amounts that do not fit properly on the platform, use a light aluminum cake or pie pan to hold the item. Before weighing the item, however, be sure to balance the pan, using the same method as for balancing the paper.

Some approximate weights and measures of common foods are listed in Figure 5–14.

Food Product	Tbsp.	Cup	Pt.	Qt.
Allspice	$\frac{1}{4}$ oz.	4 oz.	8 oz.	1 lb.
Apples, Fresh, Diced	$\frac{1}{2}$ oz.	8 oz.	1 lb.	2 lb.
Bacon, Raw, Diced	$\frac{1}{2}$ oz.	8 oz.	1 lb.	2 lb.
Bacon, Cooked, Diced	$\frac{2}{3}$ oz.	$10\frac{1}{2}$ oz.	1 lb. 5 oz.	2 lb. 10 oz.
Baking Powder	$\frac{3}{8}$ oz.	6 oz.	12 oz.	1 lb. 8 oz.
Baking Soda	$\frac{3}{8}$ oz.	6 oz.	12 oz.	1 lb. 8 oz.
Bananas, Sliced	$\frac{1}{2}$ oz.	8 oz.	1 lb.	2 lb.
Barley	—	8 oz.	1 lb.	2 lb.
Beef, Cooked, Diced	$\frac{3}{8}$ oz.	$5\frac{1}{2}$ oz.	11 oz.	1 lb. 6 oz.
Beef, Raw, Ground	$\frac{1}{2}$ oz.	8 oz.	1 lb.	2 lb.
Bread Crumbs, Dry	$\frac{1}{4}$ oz.	4 oz.	8 oz.	1 lb.
Bread Crumbs, Fresh	$\frac{1}{8}$ oz.	2 oz.	4 oz.	8 oz.
Butter	$\frac{1}{2}$ oz.	8 oz.	1 lb.	2 lb.
Cabbage, Shredded	$\frac{1}{4}$ oz.	4 oz.	8 oz.	1 lb.
Carrots, Raw, Diced	$\frac{5}{16}$ oz.	5 oz.	10 oz.	1 lb. 4 oz.
Celery, Raw, Diced	$\frac{1}{4}$ oz.	4 oz.	8 oz.	1 lb.
Cheese, Diced	—	$5\frac{1}{2}$ oz.	11 oz.	1 lb. 6 oz.
Cheese, Grated	$\frac{1}{4}$ oz.	4 oz.	8 oz.	1 lb.
Cheese, Shredded	$\frac{1}{4}$ oz.	4 oz.	8 oz.	1 lb.
Chocolate, Grated	$\frac{1}{4}$ oz.	4 oz.	8 oz.	1 lb.
Chocolate, Melted	$\frac{1}{2}$ oz.	8 oz.	1 lb.	2 lb.
Cinnamon, Ground	$\frac{1}{4}$ oz.	$3\frac{1}{2}$ oz.	7 oz.	14 oz.
Cloves, Ground	$\frac{1}{4}$ oz.	4 oz.	8 oz.	1 lb.
Cloves, Whole	$\frac{3}{16}$ oz.	3 oz.	6 oz.	12 oz.
Cocoa	$\frac{3}{16}$ oz.	$3\frac{1}{2}$ oz.	7 oz.	14 oz.
Coconut, Macaroon, Packed	$\frac{3}{16}$ oz.	3 oz.	6 oz.	12 oz.
Coconut, Shredded, Packed	$\frac{3}{16}$ oz.	$3\frac{1}{2}$ oz.	7 oz.	14 oz.
Coffee, Ground	$\frac{3}{16}$ oz.	3 oz.	6 oz.	12 oz.
Cornmeal	$\frac{5}{16}$ oz.	$4\frac{3}{4}$ oz.	$9\frac{1}{2}$ oz.	1 lb. 3 oz.
Cornstarch	$\frac{1}{3}$ oz.	$5\frac{1}{3}$ oz.	$10\frac{1}{2}$ oz.	1 lb. 5 oz.
Corn Syrup	$\frac{3}{4}$ oz.	12 oz.	1 lb. 8 oz.	3 lb.
Cracker Crumbs	$\frac{1}{4}$ oz.	4 oz.	8 oz.	1 lb.
Cranberries, Raw	—	4 oz.	8 oz.	1 lb.

Figure 5–14 *Approximate weights and measures of common foods*

(continued)

Food Product	Tbsp.	Cup	Pt.	Qt.
Currants, Dried	$\frac{1}{3}$ oz.	$5\frac{1}{3}$ oz.	11 oz.	1 lb. 6 oz.
Curry Powder	$\frac{3}{16}$ oz.	$3\frac{1}{2}$ oz	—	—
Dates, Pitted	$\frac{5}{16}$ oz.	$5\frac{1}{2}$ oz.	11 oz.	1 lb. 6 oz.
Eggs, Whole	$\frac{1}{2}$ oz.	8 oz.	1 lb.	2 lb.
Egg Whites	$\frac{1}{2}$ oz.	8 oz.	1 lb.	2 lb.
Egg Yolks	$\frac{1}{2}$ oz.	8 oz.	1 lb.	2 lb.
Extracts	$\frac{1}{2}$ oz.	8 oz.	1 lb.	2 lb.
Flour, Bread	$\frac{5}{16}$ oz.	5 oz.	10 oz.	1 lb. 4 oz.
Flour, Cake	$\frac{1}{4}$ oz.	$4\frac{3}{4}$ oz.	$9\frac{1}{2}$ oz.	1 lb. 3 oz.
Flour, Pastry	$\frac{5}{16}$ oz.	5 oz.	10 oz.	1 lb. 4 oz.
Gelatin, Flavored	$\frac{3}{8}$ oz.	$6\frac{1}{2}$ oz.	13 oz.	1 lb. 10 oz.
Gelatin, Plain	$\frac{5}{16}$ oz.	5 oz.	10 oz.	1 lb. 4 oz.
Ginger	$\frac{3}{16}$ oz.	$3\frac{1}{4}$ oz.	$6\frac{1}{2}$ oz.	13 oz.
Glucose	$\frac{3}{4}$ oz.	12 oz.	1 lb. 8 oz.	3 lb.
Green Peppers, Diced	$\frac{1}{4}$ oz.	4 oz.	8 oz.	1 lb.
Ham, Cooked, Diced	$\frac{5}{16}$ oz.	$5\frac{1}{4}$ oz.	$10\frac{1}{2}$ oz.	1 lb. 5 oz.
Horseradish, Prepared	$\frac{1}{2}$ oz.	8 oz.	1 lb.	2 lb.
Jam	$\frac{5}{8}$ oz.	10 oz.	1 lb. 4 oz.	2 lb. 8 oz.
Lemon Juice	$\frac{1}{2}$ oz.	8 oz.	1 lb.	2 lb.
Lemon Rind	$\frac{1}{4}$ oz.	4 oz.	8 oz.	1 lb.
Mace	$\frac{1}{4}$ oz.	$3\frac{1}{4}$ oz.	$6\frac{1}{2}$ oz.	13 oz.
Mayonnaise	$\frac{1}{2}$ oz.	8 oz.	1 lb.	2 lb.
Milk, Liquid	$\frac{1}{2}$ oz.	8 oz.	1 lb.	2 lb.
Milk, Powdered	$\frac{5}{16}$ oz.	$5\frac{1}{4}$ oz.	$10\frac{1}{2}$ oz.	1 lb. 5 oz.
Molasses	$\frac{3}{4}$ oz.	12 oz.	1 lb.	3 lb.
Mustard, Ground	$\frac{1}{4}$ oz.	$3\frac{1}{4}$ oz.	$6\frac{1}{2}$ oz.	13 oz.
Mustard, Prepared	$\frac{1}{4}$ oz	4 oz.	8 oz.	1 lb.
Nutmeats	$\frac{1}{4}$ oz.	4 oz.	8 oz.	1 lb.
Nutmeg, Ground	$\frac{1}{4}$ oz.	$4\frac{1}{4}$ oz.	$8\frac{1}{2}$ oz.	1 lb. 1 oz.
Oats, Rolled	$\frac{3}{16}$ oz.	3 oz.	6 oz.	12 oz.
Oil, Salad	$\frac{1}{2}$ oz.	8 oz.	1 lb.	2 lb.
Onions	$\frac{1}{3}$ oz.	$5\frac{1}{2}$ oz.	11 oz.	1 lb. 6 oz.
Peaches, Canned	$\frac{1}{2}$ oz.	8 oz.	1 lb.	2 lb.

Figure 5–14 *Approximate weights and measures of common foods (continued)*

Food Product	Tbsp.	Cup	Pt.	Qt.
Peas, Dry, Split	$\frac{7}{16}$ oz.	7 oz.	14 oz.	1 lb. 12 oz.
Pickle Relish	$\frac{5}{16}$ oz.	$5\frac{1}{4}$ oz.	$10\frac{1}{2}$ oz.	1 lb. 5 oz.
Pickles, Chopped	$\frac{1}{4}$ oz.	$5\frac{1}{4}$ oz.	$10\frac{1}{2}$ oz.	1 lb. 5 oz.
Pimentos, Chopped	$\frac{1}{2}$ oz.	7 oz.	14 oz.	1 lb 12 oz.
Pineapple, Diced	$\frac{1}{2}$ oz.	8 oz.	1 lb.	2 lb.
Potatoes, Cooked, Diced	—	$6\frac{1}{2}$ oz.	13 oz.	1 lb. 10 oz.
Prunes, Dry	—	$5\frac{1}{2}$ oz.	11 oz.	1 lb. 6 oz.
Raisins, Seedless	$\frac{1}{3}$ oz.	$5\frac{1}{3}$ oz.	$10\frac{3}{4}$ oz.	1 lb. 5 oz.
Rice, Raw	$\frac{1}{2}$ oz.	8 oz.	1 lb.	2 lb.
Sage, Ground	$\frac{1}{8}$ oz.	$2\frac{1}{4}$ oz.	$4\frac{1}{2}$ oz.	9 oz.
Salmon, Flaked	$\frac{1}{2}$ oz.	8 oz.	1 lb.	2 lb.
Salt	$\frac{1}{2}$ oz.	8 oz.	1 lb.	2 lb.
Savory	$\frac{1}{8}$ oz.	2 oz.	4 oz.	8 oz.
Shortening	$\frac{1}{2}$ oz.	8 oz.	1 lb.	2 lb.
Soda	$\frac{7}{16}$ oz.	7 oz.	14 oz.	1 lb. 12 oz.
Sugar, Brown, Packed	$\frac{1}{2}$ oz.	8 oz.	1 lb.	2 lb.
Sugar, Granulated	$\frac{7}{16}$ oz.	$7\frac{1}{2}$ oz.	15 oz.	1 lb. 14 oz.
Sugar, Powdered	$\frac{5}{16}$ oz.	$4\frac{3}{4}$ oz.	$9\frac{1}{2}$ oz.	1 lb. 3 oz.
Tapioca, Pearl	$\frac{1}{4}$ oz.	4 oz.	8 oz.	1 lb.
Tea	$\frac{1}{6}$ oz.	$2\frac{1}{2}$ oz.	5 oz.	10 oz.
Tomatoes	$\frac{1}{2}$ oz.	8 oz.	1 lb.	2 lb.
Tuna Fish, Flaked	$\frac{1}{2}$ oz.	8 oz.	1 lb.	2 lb.
Vanilla, Imitation	$\frac{1}{2}$ oz.	8 oz.	1 lb.	2 lb.
Vinegar	$\frac{1}{2}$ oz.	8 oz.	1 lb.	2 lb.
Water	$\frac{1}{2}$ oz.	8 oz.	1 lb.	2 lb.

Figure 5–14 *Approximate weights and measures of common foods (continued)*

SUMMARY REVIEW 5–4

Directions: determine both the weight and the cost of the food product for the following problems.

1. Determine the cost of a hamburger if the dial pointer on the portion scale points to the second mark beyond the 5, and the cost of 1 pound of lean ground beef is $3.99.

2. Determine the cost of a portion of corn beef if the dial on the portion scale points to the third mark beyond the 2, and the cost of 1 pound of cooked corn beef is $5.25.

_____

3. Determine the cost of a portion of cooked ham if the dial pointer on the portion scale points to the first mark beyond the 3, and the cost of 1 pound of cooked ham is $3.45.

_____

4. Determine the cost of a portion of roast loin of pork if the dial pointer on the portion scale points to the second mark beyond the 4, and the cost of 1 pound of cooked pork loin is $3.99.

_____

5. Determine the cost of a filet mignon if the dial pointer on the portion scale points to the second mark beyond the 8, and the cost of 1 pound of beef tenderloin is $9.95.

_____

CONVERTING DECIMAL WEIGHTS INTO OUNCES

As the food service industry moves toward using weights of ingredients based on the decimal system, the professional must know how to convert the amount of a decimal into weights.

Manufacturers are selling scales based upon the decimal system, where the base number is 10. This causes people to become confused, because 0.5 is actually 8 ounces (0.5 times 16 is equal to 8)—0.5 is not 5 ounces.

Many recipes state ingredients in ounces. For example, a soup recipe requires 5 ounces of pepperoni or a salad dressing requires 6 ounces of blue cheese. In the past, the food service professional used the ounce scale. It was, and still is, easy to weigh the ingredients on the scale. However, purveyors are selling and pricing ingredients based on the decimal system. It is common to have food products listed on invoices in pounds and the decimal of the pound. The blue cheese on the invoice may be listed as 5.637 pounds. How will the chef determine how many ounces have been received? The blue cheese must be converted to ounces. There are 16 ounces in a pound. Therefore, 5 pounds times 16 is equal to 80 ounces. That is the easy part. But how many ounces of blue cheese does the 0.637 represent? In order to find the answer, 16 must be multiplied by 0.637 ounces, which equals 10.192 ounces.

T I P S . . . **To Insure Perfect Solutions**

The food service professional must realize that 0.5 on a digital scale is not 5 ounces, but instead equals 8 ounces or half of a pound (16 × 0.5 = 8 ounces).

How to calculate the math:

Decimal amount of ounces	
Multiplied by	.637
Number of ounces in a pound	× 16
Total ounces	10.192 ounces

SUMMARY REVIEW 5–5

Find the amount of ounces in the following problems based on a pound. Do not round off.

1. .45 lb. _____

2. .75 lb. _____

3. .25 lb. _____

4. .333 lb. _____

5. .618 lb. _____

6. .737 lb. _____

7. .921 lb. _____

8. .279 lb. _____

9. Chef Bhutta orders and receives 156.25 ounces of chicken. If each guest receives a 10-ounce portion of chicken, how many guests can be served?

   _____

10. The Merlot Restaurant receives 10 ribs of beef weighing 22.72 pounds each. How many ounces of beef does this represent?

   _____

CHAPTER 6

Using the Metric System of Measure

OBJECTIVES

At the completion of this chapter, the student should be able to:

1. Recite the basic measure of the metric system.
2. Compute length using meters.
3. Compute mass or weight using kilograms or grams.
4. Compute volume using liters.
5. Compute temperature using degrees Celsius.
6. Recognize the increase in the use of metrics in the U.S. food service industry.
7. Change measurements from the customary system to the metric system.
8. Find the cost of food and beverage products using the metric system.

KEY WORDS

metric system
milliliters
grams
kilograms
meters
liters or cubic meters
degrees Celsius
prefixes

decimeter
centimeter
millimeter
dekameter
hectometer
kilometer
cubic centimeter

HISTORY OF THE METRIC SYSTEM IN THE UNITED STATES

*What is the **metric system**?*

The **metric system** of measure is a decimal system based on the number 10. It is difficult to understand why this system of measure has never been adopted for exclusive use in the United States. This system is more accurate than the system that is used in the United States, which relies on quarts, pounds, ounces, and so forth. It is especially useful in baking, because baking is a science where exact measurements are needed to produce consistent quality baked products.

France introduced the **metric system** to the world during the French Revolution. France's lawmakers, during that period of history, asked their scientists to develop a system of measurement based on science rather than custom. They developed a system of measurement that was based upon a length called the meter.

The meter has been used in a limited capacity over the last 30 years, but never to its fullest extent. Perhaps it can be blamed on the fact that most people resist change. There have been attempts over the years to bring about the change. In 1971, the Department of Commerce recommended that the United States adopt the system in a report made to Congress. The report stated that the question was not whether the United States should go metric, but how the switch should take place. It proposed that the switch be made over a 10-year period, as done in Great Britain and Canada. A key element in the Great Britain and Canadian conversion was education. It became the only system taught in the primary schools. The general public was taught the metric system and language by means of magazines, posters, television, newspapers, radio, and so forth. A demonstration center was even set up so that the public could practice purchasing food using the metric system. In the United States, little action was taken on this report until December 23, 1975. At that time, President Ford signed into law the Metric Conversion Act, establishing a national policy in support of the metric system and supposedly ending the dilemma that had continued for so long.

With the signing of the new law it was understood that, through a national policy of coordinating the increasing use of metrics in the United States, the conversion to the metric system would be done on a voluntary basis. The government also created a metric board, appointed by the president with the advice and consent of the Senate. The board was made up of individuals from the various economic sectors that would be influenced most by the metric changeover. Included were people representing labor, science, consumers, manufacturing, construction, and so forth. The function of this board was to create and carry out a program that would allow the development of a sensible plan for a voluntary changeover. This all took place in the 1970s. Today, little is heard of this law or program, although slowly some progress is being made. In 1988, President Bush ordered every federal agency to go metric. However, again the president was not specific as to when the change should occur. No timetable was set—the president left it to each individual federal agency. Some of these agencies have set a date for the change, while others have not. The Federal Highway Administration, for example, moved forward and ordered states to use the metric system in designing all roads that were built after September 30, 1996. If states did not comply, a penalty was assessed.

INDUSTRIES THAT USE THE METRIC SYSTEM

Some industries, notably science, pharmaceutical, engineering, and automotive, have found it necessary to go metric in order to participate in world trade. The medical field has also joined in the use of metric language. Doctors learn early in their training to specify drug dosage in metric units.

Today, over *90 percent* of the world's population uses the metric system. It is also used by over *nine-tenths* of the world's *nations*.

In the United States, metric measurements are gradually being introduced and used in many industries, among them the food and beverage industry. For example, when a person buys a beverage (soda, coffee, etc.), the measurement often appears on the package in both metrics and the customary measurements that have always been used. For instance, the authors purchased a "to go" cup of coffee, and on the paper cup was printed "12 ounces," along with the metric measurement of "355 ml" (which stands for **milliliters**). When we received a package of potato chips with our sandwich, the package listed the weight as 1 oz. or 28 g (which stands for **grams**). Because the metric system is exact, it is better to use this system in baking since ingredients are usually weighed rather than measured. The textbook *Professional Baking, 4th edition* by Wayne Gisslen has all the recipes in customary (or, as he states, the "U.S.") measurements, along with metric measurements.

Therefore, as the United States changes to the metric system, the people who will be affected most are those whose jobs are concerned with weights and measures. This is certainly the case for food service workers. Instead of pints, quarts, and gallons, they will have to adjust to liters. Instead of pounds and ounces, they will use kilograms and grams; and instead of degrees Fahrenheit, temperature will be in degrees *Celsius* (previously known as *Centigrade*). The purpose of this chapter, therefore, is to make these terms and others dealing with the metric system more familiar to the food service student.

DISCUSSION QUESTION 6-A

Find five food or beverage products that you have at home that have their contents listed in metric measurements. Why are companies listing their contents in metrics?

In recent years, food service students in the United States have been exchanged with students from foreign countries in similar programs. When an exchange like this takes place, certainly recipes and formulas are exchanged, making knowledge of the metric system an asset. The student should be able to convert recipes and formulas both ways, that is, from customary to metric and vice versa.

The metric system is a decimal system based on the number 10. For example, when the meter is divided by 10, it produces 10 *decimeters;* a decimeter divided by 10 produces 10 *centimeters;* and a centimeter divided by 10 produces 10 *millimeters*. To put it another way, one meter equals 1000 millimeters, or 100 centimeters, or 10 decimeters. (Note: the comma is not used in metric notation; instead, a space is left. Example: 1000 millimeters.) This system of measure seems more practical when compared to our customary units of measure—the yard, which is divided into 3 feet (or 36 inches); and the foot, which is divided into 12 inches.

The metric system also provides standard rules for amounts of its units through prefixes. For example, *a milligram* is one-thousandth of a gram (weight), *a milliliter* is one-thousandth of a liter (volume), and a *millimeter* is one-thousandth of a meter (length). When the unit is increased and the prefix *kilo* is added, a *kilogram* is 1000 grams and a *kilometer* is 1000 meters. The customary system lacks this kind of uniformity.

Breaking Down the Metric System

T I P S . . . To Insure Perfect Solutions

Meters (m) measure lengths; **liters** (l) measure volume; **grams** (g) measure weight; and temperature is measured in **Celsius** (°C).

Chef Sez...

"The knowledge of mathematics is so important in baking because it insures the result is the same with each formula produced, regardless of its amount or volume. Scaling and measuring accurately are absolutely imperative.

The United States is the only major country that uses a complex system of measurements (pounds, ounces, etc). The rest of the world uses the metric system. Most people think the metric system is harder than it actually is. Metric kitchens do not work with impractical numbers, such as 454 g = 1 lb., 28.35 g = 1 oz., or 191 °C. No surprise, most people are scared of the metric system. American industry will probably adopt the metric system sometime in the future."

Richard Wagner

Chef Richard Wagner is the executive pastry chef at the Oahu Country Club in Honolulu, Hawaii. This exclusive, premier diamond country club is the oldest private club west of the Rockies; it was founded on June 8, 1906. Chef Wagner has had a vast amount of experience as a pastry chef on cruise ships and in first-class hotels and pastry shops, both domestic and international. Chef Wagner is also a chef/instructor/lecturer at the Kapiolani Community College at the Diamond Head Campus in Honolulu. Chef Wagner was awarded a master's degree in patisserie and confiserie from the Culinary Institute of Vienna in 1972.

UNITS OF MEASURE IN THE METRIC SYSTEM

The best way to learn the metric system is to forget all about the customary measurements and simply think metric. To think metric is to think in terms of 10 and to understand the following basics: the **meter** represents *length;* **grams,** or, in most cases, **kilograms,** represent *mass;* **liters** or **cubic meters** represent *volume;* and **degrees Celsius** deals with *temperature.* To compare these new units of measure with familiar ones, a meter is about 39 inches, which is slightly longer than the yard. The gram is such a small unit of mass, approximately 0.035 of an ounce, that to make a comparison it is necessary to take 1,000 grams or 1 kilogram, which is equal to 2.2 pounds. The liter is equal to about 1.0567 quarts, which means it is about 5 percent larger than a quart. There are other units of measure in the metric system, but the ones mentioned are those that will be of most concern to the people involved in food service.

LENGTHS

It was stated that to think metric is to think in terms of 10. To show how this is done, take the base unit of length (the *meter*), and multiply or divide it by 10. Each time the meter is multiplied or divided by 10, special names are attached on the front of the word to indicate the value. These names are called **prefixes.** Lengths smaller than a meter are divided by 10, and the result is called a **decimeter.** Dividing a decimeter by 10 gives a **centimeter.** When the centimeter is divided by 10, it is called a **millimeter.**

1 decimeter   = 0.1 meter
1 centimeter = 0.01 meter
1 millimeter = 0.001 meter

T I P S . . .   To Insure Perfect Solutions

The length of a *meter* is about *one giant step*.

So for the units smaller than a meter, the prefixes are *deci* (a tenth of a meter), *centi* (a hundredth of a meter), and *milli* (a thousandth of a meter).

For lengths larger than a meter, multiply by 10. For 10 meters, the prefix *deka* is used. For 100 meters, the prefix is *hecto*. The prefix for 1,000 is *kilo*. So, 10 meters are called a **dekameter,** 100 meters a **hectometer,** and 1000 meters a **kilometer.** *Kilo* is a very popular prefix because most distances on roadways are given in kilometers.

1 kilometer   = 1000 meters
1 hectometer = 100 meters
1 dekameter = 10 meters

VOLUME AND CAPACITY

When measuring volume and capacity, it is first necessary to understand what a cubic meter is before learning what a liter represents. A **cubic meter** is a cube with the sides each one meter long. In other words, a cubic meter equals the length of one meter, the width of one meter, and the height of one meter. If a metal container is $\frac{1}{10}$ of a meter (one decimeter) on each side, it is referred to as one *liter*. It would contain one liter of liquid and the liquid would weigh one kilogram. When measuring liquid by the American customary system, it is said that *"A pint is the pound the world around."* In the metric system, it can be changed to *"A liter is a kilogram the world around,"* meaning that every liter of liquid weighs one kilogram, or 2.2 pounds. For units smaller than a liter, a container that has sides one centimeter long is called a **cubic centimeter.** It would hold one milliliter of water, and one milliliter weighs one gram. From this, of course, it can be seen that, in the metric system, there is a very direct relationship among length, volume, and mass.

MASS OR WEIGHT

The base unit for mass is the gram, but (as stated before) the gram is such a small unit of weight that it did not prove practical for application, so the kilogram (1000 grams) is used as the base unit. It is the only base unit that contains a prefix. When the metric system is adopted, all weights will be given in grams or kilograms. Since the kilogram is a fairly large unit, it may be too large to be a convenient unit for packing most foodstuffs, so the half-kilo (500 grams) may become a more familiar unit. Prefixes such as deci, centi, milli, hecto, and deka may be used with the gram, but they are not practical in everyday life, so the gram and kilogram are the common terms used.

When using the metric system, it has proven difficult to remember the names of all the units and terms, so abbreviations are used. (See Figure 6–1.)

Figure 6–1 *Metric units and their symbols*

Quantity	Unit	Symbol
Length	meter	m
	decimeter	dm
	centimeter	cm
	millimeter	mm
	kilometer	km
	hectometer	hm
	dekameter	dam
Volume	cubic centimeter	cm^3
	cubic meter	m^3
Capacity	milliliter	ml
	liter	l
Mass	gram	g
	kilogram	kg
Temperature	degrees Celsius	°C

T I P S . . .   To Insure Perfect Solutions

One **gram** is about the **weight** of a **paper clip**. One **kilogram** is about the **weight** of a **large book** or **dictionary**.

Temperature

In the metric system, temperature is measured in degrees Celsius (°C). On the Celsius scale, the boiling point of water is 100° and the freezing point is 0°. On the Fahrenheit (F) scale, the boiling point is 212° and the freezing point is 32°. (See Figure 6–2.) Actually, the official metric temperature scale is the Kelvin scale, which has its zero point at absolute zero. Absolute zero is the coldest possible temperature in the universe. The Kelvin scale is used often by scientists and very seldom, if ever, in everyday life.

> **To convert Fahrenheit temperature to degrees Celsius:** Subtract 32 from the given Fahrenheit temperature and multiply the result by $\frac{5}{9}$.

Your restaurant calls for cooking hamburgers to 155 °F. What is the temperature in degrees Celsius?

Step 1: Subtract 32 from the given Fahrenheit temperature.	$155 - 32 = 123$
Step 2: Multiply the result by $\frac{5}{9}$	$123 \times \frac{5}{9} = \frac{615}{9}$
Step 3: Divide by 9	$\frac{615}{9} = 68.33$
Step 4: The answer is	68.33 °C

> **To convert Celsius degrees to Fahrenheit:** Multiply the Celsius temperature by $\frac{9}{5}$ and add 32 to the result.

Figure 6–2 *Some common temperatures expressed in Fahrenheit and Celsius*

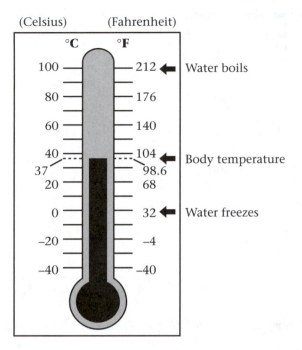

Your new job is in a country that gives the temperature in Celsius degrees. What is the Fahrenheit temperature when it is reported to be 25 °C?

Step 1: Multiply the Celsius temperature by $\frac{9}{5}$	$25 \times \frac{9}{5} = 45$
Step 2: Add 32 to the results	$45 + 32 = 77$
The answer: 25 °C is 77 °F	77 °F

SUMMARY REVIEW 6–1

Convert the following Fahrenheit temperatures to Celsius. Round off all answers to two places to the right of the decimal point.

1.   23   _____

2.   41   _____

3.   45   _____

4. 140   _____

5.   32   _____

6. 200   _____

7. 450   _____

8. 350   _____

9. 325   _____

10. −10   _____

Convert the following Celsius temperatures to Fahrenheit. Round off all answers to two places to the right of the decimal point.

11. 10   _____

12.   3   _____

13. 27   _____

14. 56   _____

15. 16   _____

16. 75   _____

17. 43   _____

18. 12   _____

19. 18   _____

20. 4   _____

Converting Recipes from Customary Measurements to the Metric System

A tremendous amount of recipes have been written since this country was founded. Almost all of these recipes are written in customary measurements. Some of these recipes are family favorites that the culinarian would like to duplicate in the food service occupation in which he or she works. To assist in helping the U.S. cooks learn about both the customary and metric systems, companies like Ohaus are developing and selling scales that weigh by the pound, decimal ounce, fractional ounce, gram, and kilogram.

Figure 6–3 is a chart that provides the multiplier to the culinarian in order to convert customary measurements to metric units.

Using the information from Figure 6–3, we will illustrate how to convert a fricassee of veal recipe, as shown in Figure 6–4.

The first ingredient (18 pounds of veal) is multiplied by the kilogram multiplier of 0.4535925, found in the Mass or Weight section in Figure 6–3.

	When you know	Multiply by	To find	Symbol
Length	Inches	2.54	Centimeters	cm
	Feet	0.3048	Centimeters	cm
	Yards	0.9144	Meters	m
	Miles	1.609347	Kilometers	km
Capacity	Teaspoons	5	Milliliters	ml
	Tablespoons	15	Milliliters	ml
	Fluid Ounces	29.574	Milliliters	ml
	Ounces	0.031	Liters	1
	Cups	0.241	Liters	1
	Pints	0.04732	Liters	1
	Quarts	0.951	Liters	1
	Gallons	37853	Liters	1
Mass or Weight	Ounces	28.35	Grams	g
	Pounds	0.4535925	Kilograms	kg

Figure 6–3 *Conversion from customary to metric units*

How to convert the recipe				
Ingredients	**Multiply by**		**Metric**	
18 pounds of veal shoulder cut into 1-inch cubes To solve the problem: multiply 18 times (×)	0.4535925	=	8.164665 kilograms	
3 gallons of water	3.7853	=	11.3559 liters	
2 pounds of shortening	0.4535925	=	0.907185 kilograms	
1 pound 8 ounces of flour (change this to ounces) 1 pound = 16 ounces + 8 = 24 ounces To solve the problem: multiply 24 times (×)	28.35	=	680.4 grams	
Salt and pepper to taste				

Figure 6–4 *Converting a recipe from customary measurements to metric measurements*

The result is 8.164665 kilograms. The last item, flour, is converted to ounces and multiplied by the grams multiplier. When Figure 6–3 is consulted, notice that we are multiplying like amounts; for instance, we multiply pounds by the multiplier for kilograms, we do not multiply pounds by the multiplier for grams. It is necessary to change items into correct categories—otherwise, the answer will be wrong. Follow this same procedure to convert a recipe from the metric system to the customary system, as shown in Figure 6–6.

Figure 6–5 is a table for converting metric measurements to customary measure.

Figure 6–6 illustrates how to convert an éclair dough recipe from metric to customary measurements. This also demonstrates why metric measurements are more exact. When converting the butter, the metric

	When you know	Multiply by	To find	Symbol
Length	Millimeters	0.04	Inches	in.
	Centimeters	0.39	Inches	in.
	Meters	3.28	Feet	ft.
	Meters	1.09	Yards	yd.
	Kilometers	0.62	Miles	mi.
Capacity	Milliliters	0.2	Teaspoons	tsp.
	Milliliters	0.07	Tablespoons	tbsp.
	Milliliters	0.03	Fluid ounces	fl. oz.
	Liters	30	Ounces	oz.
	Liters	4.23	Cups	C.
	Liters	2.11	Pints	pt.
	Liters	1.06	Quarts	qt.
	Liters	0.026412	Gallons	gal.
Mass or Weight	Grams	0.03527	Ounces	oz.
	Kilograms	2.2046	Pounds	lb.

Figure 6–5 *Conversion from metric measurements to customary measurements*

Ingredients in metric	Multiply by		Customary
500 ml water			
To solve the problem: multiply 500 times (×)	0.03	=	15 fl. oz.
5 ml salt	0.2	=	1 tsp.
22 ml sugar	0.07	=	1.54 or 1½ tbsp.
450 g butter or margarine	0.03527	=	15.87 oz. or 1 lb. (16 oz.)
450 g bread flour	0.03527	=	15.87 oz. or 1 lb. (16 oz.)
16 eggs			16 eggs

Figure 6–6 *Recipe conversion from metric to customary measurements*

Metric		Customary
1 gram	=	0.03527 ounce
1 kilogram	=	2.2 pounds
28.35 grams	=	1 ounce
4535925 grams	=	1 pound
5 milliliters	=	1 teaspoon
15 milliliters	=	1 tablespoon
241 milliliters	=	1 cup
0.4732 liters	=	1 pint
0.951 liters	=	1 quart
1 liter	=	1.06 quarts

Figure 6–7 *Weights and measures equivalents*

measurement is exact at 450 g, but to weigh out 15.87 oz. will be difficult, so the baker adds a pound of butter.

Figure 6–7 provides equivalents of weights and measures between the customary and metric measurements that may be used as a quick reference, and may prove helpful to the food service professional.

SUMMARY REVIEW 6–2

1. Convert recipes (a) through (e) from the American customary system to the metric system. Use the conversion table shown in Figure 6–3.

   (a) **White cream icing ingredients**

       1 lb. 4 oz. shortening   _____ g

       $\frac{1}{4}$ oz. salt   _____ g

       5 oz. dry milk   _____ g

       14 oz. water   _____ ml

       5 lb. powdered sugar   _____ kg

       vanilla to taste   _____ to taste

(b) **Yellow cake ingredients**

2 lb. 8 oz. cake flour	_____ kg
1 lb. 6 oz. shortening	_____ g
3 lb. 2 oz. granulated sugar	_____ kg
1 oz. salt	_____ g
$1\frac{3}{4}$ oz. baking powder	_____ g
4 oz. dry milk	_____ g
1 lb. 4 oz. water	_____ g
1 lb. 10 oz. whole eggs	_____ g
12 oz. water	_____ ml
vanilla to taste	_____ to taste

(c) **Italian meringue ingredients**

1 lb. egg whites	_____ g
1 lb. 8 oz. water	_____ ml
1 lb. 12 oz. sugar	_____ g
$1\frac{1}{2}$ oz. egg white stabilizer	_____ ml
$\frac{1}{8}$ oz. vanilla	_____ ml

(d) **Vanilla pie filling ingredients**

12 lb. liquid milk	_____ kg
4 lb. granulated sugar	_____ kg
1 lb. cornstarch	_____ g
$\frac{1}{4}$ oz. salt	_____ g
2 lb. whole eggs	_____ g
6 oz. butter	_____ g
vanilla to taste	_____ to taste

(e) **Fruit glaze ingredients**

2 lb. water	_____ g
2 lb. 8 oz. granulated sugar	_____ kg
8 oz. water	_____ ml
4 oz. modified starch	_____ g
4 oz. corn syrup	_____ ml
1 oz. lemon juice	_____ ml
food color as desired	

2. Convert recipes (a) through (e) from the metric system to the American customary system. Use the conversion table shown in Figure 6–5. Answer should be carried out three places to the right of the decimal point.

(a) **Chicken a la king ingredients**

4.5 kilograms boiled chicken or
   turkey, diced   _____ lb.

0.45 kilograms green peppers, diced   _____ lb.

227 grams pimentos, diced   _____ oz.

0.9 kilograms mushrooms, diced   _____ lb.

2.8 liters chicken stock   _____ qt.

0.74 kilograms flour   _____ lb.

0.9 kilograms shortening   _____ lb.

2.8 liters milk   _____ qt.

240 milliliters sherry wine   _____ fl. oz.

(b) **Tartar sauce ingredients**

110 grams dill pickles, chopped fine   _____ oz.

60 grams onions, chopped fine   _____ oz.

0.14 grams parsley, chopped fine   _____ oz.

1 liter mayonnaise   _____ qt.

5 milliliters lemon juice   _____ tsp.

(c) **Cocktail sauce ingredients**

0.95 liters catsup   _____ qt.

0.6 liters chili sauce   _____ oz.

0.24 liters prepared horseradish   _____ oz.

120 milliliters lemon juice   _____ oz.

30 milliliters Worcestershire sauce   _____ oz.

hot sauce to taste   _____ to taste

(d) **Spicy peach mold ingredients**

0.95 liters peaches, canned,
   sliced, drained   _____ qt.

0.45 liters peach syrup   _____ oz.

0.45 liters hot water   _____ oz.

0.95 liters cold water   _____ oz.

0.24 liters vinegar   _____ oz.

0.36 liters sugar   _____ C.

28 grams cinnamon stick   _____ oz.

15 milliliters whole cloves   _____ tsp.

392 grams orange gelatin   _____ oz.

(e) **Brussels sprouts and sour cream ingredients**

2.7 kilograms brussels sprouts	_____ lb.
30 milliliters salt	_____ tsp.
112 grams onions, minced	_____ oz.
140 grams butter	_____ oz.
0.90 kilograms sour cream	_____ oz.
water to cover, boiling	

CHAPTER 7

Portion Control

OBJECTIVES

At the completion of this chapter, the student should be able to:

1. Identify methods of controlling portion size.
2. Identify portion sizes.
3. Find cost per serving.
4. Identify portion sizes using scoops or dippers.
5. Identify and find amounts of food to prepare.
6. Define and identify the terms E.P. (edible portion) and A.P. (as purchased).
7. Find the approximate number of serving portions.
8. Find the amount of food to order.
9. Find the amount of cost per portion.

KEY WORDS

portion control
portion size
edible portion (E.P.)
as purchased (A.P.)

cost per serving
shrinkage
yield
yield percentage

There is a saying in food service that a good rich stock is the key to kitchen production. However, portion control is the key to profits.

Portion control is a term used in the food service industry to ensure that a specific or designated amount of an item is served to the guest. It is also the method used to acquire the correct number of servings from a standardized recipe, a roast, vegetable preparation, cake, or pie. In addition, portion control is helpful in controlling food production, pricing the menu, purchasing, and controlling food cost.

ACHIEVING PORTION CONTROL

The best way to control portions is to use standardized recipes that state the number of servings a preparation will produce. However, a standardized recipe gives only the stated number of portions if the servings are uniform in size. To ensure uniform servings or portions, the preparation crew and serving personnel must be instructed in the use of ladles, scoops, scales, spoons, and similar measuring devices when portioning food.

Another method of achieving a successful portion control program is intelligent buying. Buy foods in sizes that portion well. Work out buying specifications that suit the portion need. For example, cooked smoked

Figure 7–1 *The chef is converting a recipe to determine the amounts needed to produce the required number of servings.*

ham can be purchased in many types and sizes. Purchase the kind that will produce a ham steak the diameter desired and one that produces little or no waste. Most link sausage, such as wieners, pork links, and frankfurters, can be purchased at a certain number (6, 8, or 10) to each pound. Purchase the count per pound that best suits the portion requirement. Select veal, pork, lamb, and beef ribs and loins that provide the size chop or slice desired. Appearance is important. If the food does not look appetizing, the first bite may never be taken.

Many foods can be purchased ready-to-cook and are purchased for absolute portion control. This is another controlling device to consider. Fish fillets, steaks, chops, and cutlets are all cut to the exact ounce desired. (See Figure 7–1.) The cost per pound is much higher because the more labor involved in fabricating a product, the higher the cost. To many food service operators the final cost is, in reality, lower when considering the following factors:

- no leftovers
- less storage required
- no waste
- no cutting equipment to purchase
- less labor cost

T I P S . . . . To Insure Perfect Solutions

Always know the exact cost of the food that is placed on the plate in front of the guest.

Methods of Controlling Portion Size

There are five basic methods used in the food service industry to control portion size. They are listed in Figure 7–2 with a few examples of how each can be achieved.

Method	Examples
Weight	5 oz. pork cutlet 8 oz. roast beef 6 oz. roast pork
Count	8 fried scallops per order 2 Italian meatballs per order 3 corn fritters per order
Volume	2 oz. portion of Hollandaise sauce over vegetables No. 12 scoop of baked rice 3 oz. slotted spoonful of green beans
Equal Portions	Cake cut into 8 equal slices Pie cut into 7 equal wedges Pan of baked lasagna cut into 12 equal servings
Portioned Fill	8 oz. casserole of chicken pot pie 5 oz. glass of apple juice 4 oz. cup of chocolate mousse

Figure 7–2 *Methods of portion control*

Portioning Food

When portioning food for a particular establishment, remember that portions can be too large as well as too small. Therefore, before a portion policy is established, the manager (as well as the chef) should know the customers. This knowledge can be acquired by carefully observing the plates brought into the dishwashing area. Too much uneaten food left in a bowl or on a plate indicates that a portion is too large, or that the quality of the food does not satisfy the customer. In either case, the situation tells a story and must be corrected to improve customer satisfaction and control food cost. Too small a portion is usually indicated by plates and bowls that are scraped entirely clean. A satisfied guest usually leaves a very small amount of food on the plate or in the bowl.

When portioning food by weight, it is easy to find how much raw food is needed and how much should be prepared for a specific number of people. (See Figure 7–3.)

As an example, the Raven's Nest Restaurant expects to serve 325 hamburgers on Saturday evening. Each hamburger weighs 8 ounces before it is cooked. The following box illustrates how to determine how much raw hamburger to order.

Step 1: Number to be served = 325 hamburgers
Step 2: Multiply this number by the raw weight of each hamburger, 8 ounces
Step 3: $325 \times 8 = 2600$ ounces
Step 4: Divide the 2600 by 16 (ounces in one pound)
Step 5: The answer is 162.5 pounds, or 162 pounds and 8 ounces

Therefore, the formulas are as follows:
Number to be served × portion size = number of ounces needed
Number of ounces needed ÷ 16 (ounces in one pound) = number of pounds needed

Figure 7–3 *Precise portion control results in cost management.*

By finding the cost per ounce, a total cost is easy to calculate. Many chefs and managers become tired of hearing employees ask, *"How much should I prepare?"* By observing portion control charts posted in the preparation area and doing some simple figuring, employees can answer their own questions.

Once a portion policy is established, it should be posted in the kitchen. A typical portion chart is shown in Figure 7–4.

Chef Sez...

"Math is the most important subject to learn because, as a chef/owner, I use it all the time. I have to use math to price my prix fixe menu at a cost that will allow me to make a profit. It also has to be priced so my guests perceive a value, so they will return to the inn. I must keep a guest history of what items sell the best on my menu, so I can forecast how many of each appetizer, entrée, and dessert we will sell. Once I forecast my menu, I have to purchase the correct amount of food so I don't have too much (which would result in spoiled food) or too little (which would result in unhappy guests). The success of the Andrie Rose Inn is dependent on my culinary skills, along with a correct understanding and use of math."

Irene Maston
Certified Executive Chef
American Academy of Chefs
The Andrie Rose Inn
Ludlow, Vermont

Chef Maston and her husband, Michael, are the owners and innkeepers of The Andrie Rose Inn. They provide gracious accommodations in a circa-1829 country village inn with luxury suites. The Andrie Rose Inn has received the three-diamond rating from the American Automobile Association and an A+ Triple Crown Excellent rating from the American Bed and Breakfast Association's *Inspected, Rated & Approved Bed & Breakfasts and Country Inns*. The *New York Magazine* called it "a place not to be missed," and *USA TODAY* selected The Andrie Rose Inn as one of the "Top 10 Romantic Inns in the USA" in 1999. Chef Maston serves a four-course meal every Friday and Saturday, and changes her menu seasonally.

STEWS, BLANQUETTES, HASHES, ETC.

Beef Goulash	7 oz.
Beef Stew	7 oz.
Veal Blanquette	6 oz.
Lamb Blanquette	7 oz.
Lamb Stew	7 oz.
Veal Stew	7 oz.
Oxtail Stew	10 oz.
Roast Beef Hash	6 oz.
Corned Beef Hash	6 oz.
Chicken Hash	6 oz.
Beef Stroganoff	7 oz.
Beef a la Deutsch	7 oz.

STARCH AND POTATO PREPARATIONS

Baked	6 oz.
Au Gratin	4 oz.
Delmonico	4 oz.
French Fried	5 oz.
Mashed	5 oz.
Julienne	4 oz.
Lyonnaise	5 oz.
Croquette	5 oz.
Hash Brown	5 oz.
Escallop	4 oz.
Candied Sweet	5 oz.
Rice	4 oz.

VEGETABLES

Asparagus, Spears	4 or 5 spears
Asparagus, Cut	4 oz.
Beans, Limas	4 oz.
Beans, String	4 oz.
Beans, Wax	4 oz.
Beets	4 oz.
Brussels Sprouts	5 oz.
Cabbage	5 oz.
Cauliflower	5 oz.
Carrots	4 oz.
Corn on the Cob	1 cob
Corn, Whole Kernel	4 oz.
Corn, Cream Style	5 oz.
Mushrooms, Whole	4 oz.
Onions	5 oz.
Peas	4 oz.
Squash	4 oz.
Succotash	3 oz.
Tomatoes, Stewed	4 oz.
Eggplant	4 oz.

DESSERTS

Baked Alaska	1 slice—per Alaska
Compotes	5 oz.
Cake	1 slice—8 per cake
Ice Cream	4 oz.
Jubilee	5 oz. ice cream, 2 oz. cherries
Parfaits	5 oz. ice cream, 3 oz. sauce
Pie	1 slice—6 per pie
Pudding	5 oz.
Sherbets	4 oz.

SALADS

Cole Slaw	4 oz.
Garden Salad	5 oz.
Ham Salad	5 oz.
Julienne	5 oz.
Macaroni	4 oz.
Potato	5 oz.
Toss	5 oz.
Waldorf	5 oz.

Figure 7–4 *Standardized portion chart (continued)*

STEAKS	
Chateaubriand (for 2 guests)	16 oz.
Filet Mignon	8 oz.
Sirloin	10 oz.
NY Strip	12 oz.
T-bone	12 oz.
Club	10 oz.
Porterhouse	14 oz.
Salisbury	8 oz.
Ham	6 oz.
Veal Steak	6 oz.
Lamb Steak	7 oz.

CHOPS AND CUTLETS	
Pork Chops (2)	4 oz. each
Lamb Chops (2)	4 oz. each
Veal Chop	6 oz.
English Lamb Chop	6 oz.
Veal Cutlet	6 oz.
Pork Cutlet	6 oz.
Escallop of Veal	7 oz.
Noisette of Lamb (2)	$3\frac{1}{2}$ oz. each
Pork Tenderloin	8 oz.
Beef Tournedos (2)	4 oz. each

POULTRY	
Fried Chicken	$\frac{1}{2}$ fryer ($3\frac{1}{2}$ lb. chicken)
Broiled Chicken	$\frac{1}{2}$ broiler (2 lb. chicken)
Roast Chicken	$\frac{1}{2}$ chicken (3 lb. chicken)
Roast Turkey	$2\frac{1}{2}$ oz. white meat (3 oz. dark)
Turkey Steak	5 oz. white meat
Boneless Turkey Wings	2 wings
Chicken a la King	6 oz.
Chicken Pot Pie	8 oz. plus crust
Chicken a la Maryland	$\frac{1}{2}$ fryer, 1 oz. bacon, 2 oz. cream sauce, 2 oz. corn fritters, 2 croquettes, 6 oz.
Chicken Cutlets (2)	6 oz.
Roast Duck	8 oz.
Roast Squab	1 bird
Roast Bnls Chicken Breast	5 oz. breast
Baked Stuffed Chicken Leg	1 leg, 3 oz. stuffing

Figure 7–4 *Standardized portion chart (continued)*

SEAFOOD	
Lobster, Broiled Whole	16 oz.
Lobster Newburg	5 oz. meat
Fried Shrimp	6 jumbo—8 medium
Shrimp Newburg	7 medium
Sauteed Shrimp	6 jumbo—8 medium
Softshell Crabs	2 crabs
Clam Roast	8 cherrystone
Steamed Clams	8 cherrystone
Fried Clams	8 cherrystone
Fried Oysters	7 select
Oyster Stews	6 select
Fried Scallops	8 small—6 large
Sauteed Scallops	8 small—6 large
Halibut	7 oz.
Cod	7 oz.
Sea Bass	7 oz.
Pampano	7 oz.
Red Snapper	6 oz.
Frog Legs	8 oz.
Mahi Mahi	7 oz.
Lake Trout	7 oz.
Rainbow Trout	8 oz.
Brook Trout	8 oz.
Smelt	6 fish, about 7 oz.
Salmon	7 oz.
Shad Roe	4 oz.
English and Dover Sole	7 oz.

Figure 7–4 *Standardized portion chart (continued)*

ROASTED MEATS	
Roast Rib of Beef	8 oz.
Roast Tenderloin of Beef	6 oz.
Roast Sirloin of Beef	6 oz.
Roast Round of Beef	5 oz.
Roast Leg of Lamb	5 oz.
Roast Loin of Pork	6 oz.
Roast Leg of Veal	5 oz.
Roast Fresh Ham	6 oz.
Baked Ham	6 oz.

Figure 7–4 *Standardized portion chart (continued)*

Example:

Appetizer	4 oz.
Salad	4 oz.
Entree	8 oz.
Potato	4 oz.
Vegetable	4 oz.
Bread & Butter	3 oz.
Dessert	6 oz.
Beverage	7 oz.
	40 oz. = $2\frac{1}{2}$ pounds

Figure 7–5 *Ideal portion sizes for one meal*

A point to remember when figuring portion sizes is that the average human stomach can only hold approximately $2\frac{1}{2}$ pounds of solid and liquid food comfortably. Therefore, oversized portions do not make customers satisfied, and usually create more waste. The intelligent restaurant operator figures portion sizes so that the customer has room left for dessert. An example of how the portion sizes for one meal should add up is given in Figure 7–5.

Cost Per Serving

To find the cost per serving, the total weight of the item is converted into ounces and divided into the total cost to find the cost of one ounce. The cost of one ounce is multiplied by the number of ounces being served. See the following formula to simplify this explanation.

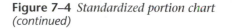

Total weight × 16 = total ounces.
Total cost ÷ by total ounces = cost of 1 ounce.
Cost of 1 ounce × number of ounces served = cost per serving.

Example: A 5-pound box of frozen lima beans costs $6.24. How much does a 4-ounce serving cost?

Weight 5 lbs. $\times$ 16 = 80 ounces.
$6.24 (total cost) $\div$ 80 (ounces) = 0.078 cost of 1 ounce.
0.078 (cost of 1 ounce) $\times$ 4 (ounces served) = 0.312 = $0.31 (cost of a 4-ounce serving).

The division is carried to three places to the right of the decimal point. Remember that the third digit is the mill, or $\frac{1}{10}$ of a cent.

Of course, if a cost per pound is given rather than a total, the number of pounds given must be multiplied by the cost per pound to find a total cost.

Example: Find the cost of a 3-ounce serving of succotash (mixture of two vegetables) if the following ingredients are used.

5-pound box lima beans @ $1.23 per pound.
$2\frac{1}{2}$-pound box corn @ $0.58 per pound.
To state this function as a math formula, it would be expressed as:
Total weight $\times$ unit price = total cost.
5 pounds $\times$ $1.23 = $6.15 total cost of lima beans.
$2\frac{1}{2}$ pounds $\times$ $0.58 = $1.45 total cost of corn.
$6.15 + $1.45   = $7.60 total cost of succotash.

To complete the problem, follow the same steps explained in the previous example.

$7\frac{1}{2}$ pounds $\times$ 16 = 120 ounces.
$7.60 total cost $\div$ 120 ounces = $0.063 cost of 1 ounce.
$.063 cost of 1 ounce $\times$ 3 ounces = $0.189 or $.019 cost of a 3-ounce serving.

SUMMARY REVIEW 7–1

Work each problem. Round answers to the nearest cent.

1. A $2\frac{1}{2}$-pound box of frozen corn costs $1.55. How much does a 4-ounce serving cost?

   _____

2. When preparing succotash, a $2\frac{1}{2}$-pound box of frozen corn costs $0.58 per pound, and a 5-pound box of frozen lima beans costs $1.18 per pound. How much does a 3-ounce serving cost?

   _____

3. A $2\frac{1}{2}$-pound box of frozen peas and onions costs $0.72 per pound. How much does a $3\frac{1}{2}$-ounce serving cost?

   _____

4. If frozen asparagus spears cost $11.95 for a 5-pound box, how much does a 3-ounce serving cost?

_____

5. If a $2\frac{1}{2}$-pound box of frozen cut broccoli costs $1.70, what is the cost of a $3\frac{1}{2}$-ounce serving?

_____

6. A 5-pound box of frozen asparagus spears costs $2.39 per pound. How much does a $2\frac{1}{2}$-ounce serving cost?

_____

7. A $2\frac{1}{2}$-pound bag of frozen oriental vegetable mix costs $0.78 per pound. How much does a 4-ounce serving cost?

_____

8. A 3-pound bag of frozen Scandinavian vegetable mix costs $1.29 per pound. How much does a $3\frac{1}{2}$-ounce serving cost?

_____

9. A 2-pound bag of frozen whole baby carrots costs $0.82 per pound. How much does a 3-ounce serving cost?

_____

10. Find the cost of a $5\frac{1}{2}$-ounce serving of a beef stir-fry if the following items were used:

3-pound bag frozen stir-fry vegetables @ $1.45 per pound.

5 pounds of sliced fresh beef @ $3.80 per pound.

_____

PORTIONING WITH SCOOPS OR LADLES

Scoops, as mentioned in Chapter 5, are used to serve and portion such foods as dressings, rice, meat patties, croquette mixtures, ice cream, and muffin batters. Two examples are shown in Figure 7–6. They have a metal bowl or cup of known capacity, an extended handle, and a thumb-operated lever to release the item being portioned or served. A movable strip of metal on the inside of the bowl releases its contents. This metal strip contains a number to indicate the size of the metal cup; the larger the number, the smaller the cup. The number indicates the number of scoops it will take to make a quart. Figure 7–7 relates each scoop number to its approximate capacity in ounces and also to the approximate content of each scoop size in cups or tablespoons.

Figure 7–6 *Two examples of food scoops (courtesy of Hamilton Beach)*

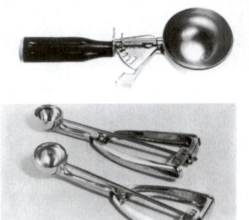

United States Measurements			Metric Measurements	
Scoop number	Volume	Approximate weight	Volume	Approximate weight
6	$\frac{2}{3}$ cup	5 oz.	160 ml	140 g
8	$\frac{1}{2}$ cup	4 oz.	120 ml	110 g
10	3 fl. oz.	3 to $3\frac{1}{2}$ oz.	90 ml	85 to 100 g
12	$\frac{1}{3}$ cup	$2\frac{1}{2}$ to 3 oz.	80 ml	70 to 85 g
16	$\frac{1}{4}$ cup	2 to $2\frac{1}{2}$ oz.	60 ml	60 to 70 g
20	$1\frac{1}{2}$ fl. oz.	$1\frac{3}{4}$ oz.	45 ml	50 g
24	$1\frac{1}{3}$ fl. oz.	$1\frac{1}{3}$ oz.	40 ml	40 g
30	1 fl. oz.	1 oz.	30 ml	30 g
40	0.8 fl. oz.	0.8 oz.	24 ml	23 g
60	$\frac{1}{2}$ fl. oz.	$\frac{1}{2}$ oz.	15 ml	15 g

Figure 7–7 *Scoop or dipper sizes and approximate weights and measures in both U.S. and metric units. Weights vary with different foods; this is only a guide and is not exact.*

Ladles are used to portion sauces, gravies, soups, and other liquids. They come in assorted sizes, holding from 2 to 8 ounces. When ladles are used, portions will be consistent. The size, in ounces, is stamped on the handle. Figure 7–8 shows the ladle sizes most frequently used.

Figure 7–8 *Ladle sizes*

Ladle Sizes	
Size	Weight
$\frac{1}{4}$ cup	2 oz.
$\frac{1}{2}$ cup	4 oz.
$\frac{3}{4}$ cup	6 oz.
1 cup	8 oz.

DETERMINING NUMBER OF SERVINGS USING SCOOPS OR LADLES

Chefs and cooks must portion food out uniformly for both customer satisfaction and cost control. To find the number of servings of a particular amount of food or liquid when portioning with a scoop or ladle, divide the amount contained in the scoop or ladle into the amount being served. This function, as a formula, appears as follows:

Amount portioned ÷ scoop or ladle content = number of servings

Example: How many servings can be obtained from 4 gallons of ice cream if a No. 8 scoop is used to portion out the ice cream?

Step 1: Consult the chart in Figure 7–7 and find the No. 8 scoop. The chart says that the volume will result in $\frac{1}{2}$ cup. Note: we use the volume, rather than the weight, because different foods weigh different amounts. As we said in Chapter 5, the weight of one cup of cotton balls **does not** equal the weight of one cup of crushed stone.

Step 2: Since the volume of a No. 8 scoop is expressed in cups, we must convert the 4 gallons of ice cream to cups; to divide, like amounts are necessary. In other words, we can't divide cups into gallons; cups have to be divided into cups.

1 gallon contains 16 cups
4 gallons times (×) 16 = 64 cups
64 cups are in 4 gallons

Step 3: Cups are divided by the volume size of the scoop.

64 divided by (÷) $\frac{1}{2}$ cup

$\frac{64}{1} \times \frac{2}{1} = 128$ servings

Example: How many servings of soup can be obtained from 5 gallons of soup, using a $\frac{3}{4}$-cup ladle?

Step 1: Consult the chart in Figure 7–8 and find the $\frac{3}{4}$-cup ladle. The chart says that the volume will result in 6 oz.

Step 2: Since the volume of a $\frac{3}{4}$-cup ladle is expressed in cups and also ounces, we must convert the 5 gallons of soup into cups or ounces; to divide, like amounts are necessary. In other words, we can't divide cups into gallons; cups have to be divided into cups.

1 gallon contains 16 cups
5 gallons times (×) 16 = 80 cups
80 cups are in the 5 gallons
        OR
1 gallon contains 128 ounces
5 gallons times (×) 128 = 640 ounces
640 ounces are in the 5 gallons

Step 3: Cups are divided by the volume size of the ladle.
80 divided by (÷) $\frac{3}{4}$ cup

$\frac{80}{1} \times \frac{4}{3} = \frac{320}{3} = 106.67$ servings

We can obtain 106 servings; the remainder is dropped, because it is not a complete portion.

OR

Ounces are divided by the ounce size of the ladle

640 divided by (÷) 6 ounces = 106.67

We can obtain 106 servings; the remainder is dropped, because it is not a complete portion.

In the above example, the authors used either cups or ounces because the ounces in a ladle are expressed in fluid ounces rather than weight. Therefore, the answer will come out the same.

SUMMARY REVIEW 7–2

In working the following problems, use information from Figures 7–7 and 7–8 to solve the problems. Use the maximum weight, if figuring out the problem with weight. For instance, if the problem calls for a No. 10 scoop, use $3\frac{1}{2}$ oz., not 3 oz. Only record complete servings; drop any remainders.

1. How many servings can be obtained from 15 gallons of soup if a $\frac{1}{2}$-cup ladle is used?

   _____

2. How many servings can be obtained from a quart of Cabernet Sauvignon reduction if a $\frac{1}{4}$-cup ladle is used?

   _____

3. Determine how many servings can be obtained from 12 pounds of bread pudding if a No. 10 scoop is used to portion?

   _____

4. How many servings can be obtained from 5 quarts of strawberry mousse if a No. 6 scoop is used to portion?

   _____

5. How many individual salads can be obtained from 7 pounds of tuna fish salad if a No. 10 scoop is used to portion?

   _____

6. How many clam fritters can be obtained from 5 pounds of batter if a No. 24 scoop is used to portion?

   _____

7. How many blueberry muffins can be obtained from $2\frac{1}{2}$ gallons of batter if a No. 12 scoop is used to portion?

   _____

8. How many servings can be obtained from $\frac{1}{2}$ gallon of cold pack cheese if a No. 16 scoop is used to portion?

_____

9. How many hush puppies can be obtained from $2\frac{1}{2}$ pounds of batter if a No. 30 scoop is used to portion?

_____

10. How many servings can be obtained from 12 pounds of mashed potatoes if a No. 8 scoop is used to portion?

_____

FIGURING AMOUNTS TO PREPARE

In any food service operation, it is constantly necessary to figure how many cans, boxes, or packages of certain food items are needed or must be opened in order to have enough food to serve a given number of people. This problem is solved by multiplying the number of people to be served by the portion size, giving the number of ounces needed. Next, the weight of the can, box, or package is converted into ounces, and the given amount is divided into the number of ounces needed. If a remainder results from the division, an additional container must be opened. By utilizing mathematics in this situation, guesswork can be eliminated and food preparation can be controlled. Steps to simplify this function are as follows:

> **Number of people to be served × portion size = ounces needed.**
> **Pounds in container × 16 + ounces = ounces in one container.**
> **Ounces needed ÷ ounces in one container = containers needed.**

Example: How many No. 10 cans of green beans are needed to serve a party of 260 people if each person is to receive a 3-ounce serving and each can contains 4 pounds 6 ounces?

Step 1:
260 × 3 ounces = 780 ounces
Number of people to be served × portion size
= ounces needed to serve 260 people.

Step 2:
4 pounds × 16 ounces per pound
= 64 ounces + 6 = 70 ounces
Pounds in container × 16 + ounces in container
= content of 1 container.

Step 3:
780 ÷ 70 ounces = 11.14 cans
Ounces needed to serve 260 people ÷ content of one container
= 12 No. 10 cans needed to serve 260 people.

The preceding example shows that 12 No. 10 cans are needed to serve each of the 260 people a 3-ounce serving. When dividing the content of the can into the number of ounces needed, a remainder resulted, so an additional can was required.

SUMMARY REVIEW 7–3

1. A 3-ounce serving of peas is to be served to each of 180 people. How many boxes of frozen peas should be cooked if each box weighs $2\frac{1}{2}$ pounds?

2. A 3-ounce serving of wax beans is served to each of 55 people. How many cans of wax beans are needed if each can weighs 14 ounces?

3. How many No. $2\frac{1}{2}$ cans of pork and beans are required to serve 84 people if each can weighs 1 pound 10 ounces and each serving is 5 ounces?

4. A 3-ounce serving of peas is to be served to each of 110 people. How many boxes of frozen peas are needed if each box weighs 5 pounds?

5. How many No. 10 cans of green beans are needed to serve a party of 270 people if each person is to receive a $3\frac{1}{2}$-ounce serving and each can weighs 4 pounds 4 ounces?

6. How many No. 5 cans of potato salad are required to serve 96 people if each can weighs 3 pounds 6 ounces and each serving is $5\frac{1}{2}$ ounces?

7. How many $2\frac{1}{2}$-pound bags of corn will be needed to serve 360 people if each person is to receive a $3\frac{1}{2}$-ounce serving?

8. How many boxes of frozen chopped spinach are needed to serve a party of 186 people if each person is to receive a 3-ounce serving and each box weighs 4 pounds?

9. How many 5-pound boxes of frozen lima beans are needed to serve a party of 350 people if each person is to receive a 4-ounce serving?

_____

10. A $3\frac{1}{2}$-ounce serving of frozen peas and pearl onions is to be served to 145 people. How many 5-pound boxes will be needed?

_____

11. How many No. 10 cans of cut green beans are needed to serve a party of 180 people if each person is to receive a 3-ounce serving and each can weighs 5 pounds 10 ounces?

_____

12. How many 2-pound bags of Scandinavian vegetable mix will be required to serve a party of 85 people if each person is to receive a 4-ounce serving?

_____

13. How many No. $2\frac{1}{2}$ cans of diced beets are needed to serve a party of 42 people if each person is to receive a $4\frac{1}{2}$-ounce serving and each can weighs 2 pounds 5 ounces?

_____

14. How many No. 5 cans of tomato juice will be needed to serve 132 people if each person is to receive a 4-ounce serving and each can contains 48 fluid ounces?

_____

15. How many No. $2\frac{1}{2}$ cans of diced carrots are needed to serve a party of 168 people if each person is to receive a 3-ounce serving and each can weighs 1 pound 12 ounces?

_____

FINDING THE APPROXIMATE NUMBER OF SERVING PORTIONS

Finding approximately how many servings can be acquired from a given amount of food (as shown in Figure 7–9), or how much of a certain meat, fish, vegetable, or liquid food product should be ordered, are additional portion control concerns. For example, how many 12-ounce strip steaks can be cut from a short loin? How many 2-ounce meatballs can be acquired from a certain amount of ground beef? How many pounds of fish steaks must be ordered for a party of 80 people? How many gallons of orange juice must be ordered to serve a party of 250 people?

Figure 7–9 *The top picture illustrates appropriate portion control. The bottom picture illustrates an unappealing presentation and inappropriate portion control.*

The arithmetic involved in these problems is quite simple, and it is an essential part of a food service operation. This arithmetic must be accurate to keep inventories at a minimum, to control waste, and to maintain an effective portion control program.

As Purchased (A.P.)

When a raw food product is purchased in its natural state, this is called **as purchased (A.P.).** Before serving the food to the guests, an employee has to clean the product and prepare it for consumption. In the cleaning and preparation of the product, there will be a portion of the product that is discarded or can't be used. This is true of many products, whether it is meat (tenderloin of beef), poultry (whole turkey), vegetables (case of romaine lettuce), or fruits (for fruit salad). The tenderloin cannot be taken from the case and put in the oven. It must be fabricated before it is ready to be cooked.

Edible Portion (E.P)

A product that is ready to be served to the guests is called an **edible portion (E.P.).** There are many products being offered to the food service industry ready to cook and serve without any waste.

Types of Edible Portion (E.P.) Products **Edible portion (E.P.)** products can be described in three ways. The easiest to understand are products that are purchased already fabricated and ready to be cooked. The second and third deal with products that belong to the **as purchased (A.P.)** definition. The second definition occurs when a chef purchases a product and has to trim it and fabricate it into equal portions. The third type of **edible portion (E.P.)** product occurs after food (generally meat) is roasted. It is removed from the oven and cut into equal portions.

The first example of an **Edible Portion (E.P.)** is when a chef has to order chicken breasts for a banquet of 300 guests. Each guest will receive one chicken breast weighing 8 ounces. The only preparation needed before the breast is cooked is for the chef to add his or her special ingredients or marinades. There is no waste in buying the product. The chef knows the exact cost, weight, and portion size of all 300 breasts when purchased.

The second example can be shown as follows: A chef purchases a short loin of beef. After fabricating the short loin, the loin is cut into steaks. The chef now has steaks that are in the state of **edible portion (E.P.).** They can be grilled and served to the guests.

When a chef roasts a prime rib of beef, a certain percentage of the weight of the product is lost through cooking (this is called **shrinkage**). After the roast is taken from the oven and rests the proper time, it is cut into desired portion weights and served to the guests in an **edible portion (E.P.).**

Therefore, the food service professional can purchase products **as purchased (A.P.)** and fabricate them to get them to their desired state of **edible portion (E.P.),** or buy products ready to cook or even, in some instances, ready to be served directly to the guests without any preparation.

It is critical that food service professionals know how to determine the **edible portion (E.P.)** of products, both for determining serving portions and figuring out the food cost of the product. Two key factors that must be considered in the **edible portion (E.P.)** are **shrinkage** and **yield.**

How to Determine the Number of Servings (Yield) To find out how many servings can be obtained from a given product (yield), the amount of the **edible portion (E.P.)** must first be established. Using our three examples from above, we will illustrate how to obtain the yield.

In the first example, the chef simply has to place an order for the 300 chicken breasts. The chef knows that the yield will result in 300 (8-oz.) chicken breasts.

For the second example, the restaurant purchases an 18-pound short loin of beef in the **as purchased (A.P.)** state. When the prep cook trims and bones the short loin the resulting waste of bone, fat, and skin cannot be used; in effect, they are lost to the restaurant. This loss amounts to 2 pounds and 10 ounces. When the cook weighs the trimmed short loin, it now weighs 15 pounds and 6 ounces (18 pounds − 2 pounds and 10 ounces). The amount of short loin left is the **edible portion (E.P.)** before cooking. Once the cook knows the **edible portion (E.P.),** the amount of servings can be determined. The formula is as follows:

Edible portion (E.P.) divided by (÷) serving portion = number of servings.

Using our short loin from above, we will illustrate how to determine the number of servings that the prep cook will obtain.

Step 1: Convert the **as purchased (A.P.)** 18-pound short loin into ounces (16 ounces in a pound).

18 times (×) 16 = 288 ounces **as purchased (A.P.)**

Step 2: Convert the resulting waste from the short loin, 2 pounds and 10 ounces, into ounces.

2 times (×) 16 = 32 + 10 = 42 ounces of waste

Step 3: Subtract the waste (42 ounces) from the **as purchased (A.P.)** ounces (288)

288 minus − 42 = 246 ounces. This is now the **edible portion (E.P.).**

Step 4: The portion size of the steak is determined based upon restaurant specifications (12 ounces). This is the **edible portion (E.P.)** for one steak.

Step 5: The **edible portion (E.P.)** of the short loin (246 ounces) is divided by the portion size of one steak (12 ounces).

246 divided by (÷) 12 = 20.5 steaks

Therefore, 20 (12-ounce) steaks is the **yield** that results from this **E.P.,** which equals 240 ounces. This leaves 6 ounces from the short loin that cannot be used, because it is not the correct portion size.

Shown as long division:

$$
\begin{array}{r}
20.5 \\
12\overline{)246.0} \\
\underline{24} \\
60 \\
\underline{60}
\end{array}
\qquad \textbf{E.P. Amount}
$$

Each steak is to weigh 12 ounces, so the weight of each steak is divided into 246 ounces **E.P.** amount. This shows that 20 steaks can be cut from the sirloin. It was necessary to convert the **E.P.** amount to ounces because you can only divide like amounts.

In the third example, the chef will roast a pork loin after it has been fabricated. The pork loin weighs 13 pounds. One pound and 2 ounces are lost through shrinkage. How many 8-ounce portions can be obtained after cooking?

Step 1: Convert the fabricated pork loin into ounces (16 ounces in a pound).

13 times (×) 16 = 208 ounces

Step 2: Convert the amount of shrinkage into ounces.

One pound = 16 ounces + 2 ounces = 18 ounces of shrinkage

Step 3: Subtract the shrinkage from the fabricated pork loin.

208 ounces minus (−) 18 ounces = 190 ounces

Step 4: The **edible portion (E.P.)** of the pork loin (190 ounces) is divided by the portion size (8 ounces).

190 divided by 8 (or 190 ÷ 8) = 23.75 portions

Therefore, 23 (8-oz). portions is the **yield** that results from this **E.P.,** which equals 184 ounces. This leaves 6 ounces from the pork loin that cannot be used, because it is not the correct portion size.

SUMMARY REVIEW 7–4

1. A 7-pound **A.P.** beef tenderloin is trimmed; 8 ounces are lost. How many 6-ounce filet mignons can be cut from the tenderloin?

   _____

2. How many 5-ounce pork chops can be cut from a pork loin weighing 15 pounds **A.P.** if the tenderloin, which is removed, weighed 9 ounces, and 3 pounds 5 ounces are lost through boning and trimming?

   _____

3. How many orders of meatballs can be obtained from 40 pounds **E.P.** of ground beef if each meatball is to weigh 2 ounces and two meatballs are served per order?

   _____

4. How many orders of Swedish meatballs can be obtained from 32 pounds **E.P.** of ground pork and veal if each meatball weighs $1\frac{1}{2}$ ounces and four meatballs are served with each order?

   _____

5. How many 5-ounce Swiss steaks can be cut from a beef round weighing 44 pounds **A.P.** if 4 pounds 3 ounces are lost in boning and trimming?

   _____

6. When preparing pork sausage, 16 pounds **A.P.** of pork picnic is purchased. One-fourth of the amount is lost through boning and trimming. How many 4-ounce patties can be obtained?

_____

7. How many 5-ounce glasses of orange juice can be obtained from 2 gallons of orange juice?

_____

8. Forty-six pounds **(A.P.)** of turkey breast are purchased. Four pounds 4 ounces are lost through boning and skinning. How many turkey steaks can be obtained if each steak is to weigh 5 ounces?

_____

9. A 13-pound **(A.P.)** pork loin is roasted. One pound 2 ounces are lost through waste. How many $2\frac{1}{2}$-ounce servings can be obtained from the cooked loin?

_____

10. A 14-pound **(A.P.)** ham is trimmed. Twelve ounces are lost. How many ham steaks can be cut from the ham if each steak is to weigh 6 ounces?

_____

11. A 19-pound **(A.P.)** rib eye is purchased. Two pounds 14 ounces are lost through trimming. How many rib steaks can be cut from the rib eye if each steak is to weigh 8 ounces?

_____

12. A 12-pound **(E.P.)** pork loin is purchased. How many $4\frac{1}{2}$-ounce pork cutlets can be cut from the loin?

_____

13. Eleven pounds of chicken croquette mixture is prepared. How many croquettes will the mixture produce if each croquette is to weigh $2\frac{1}{2}$ ounces?

_____

14. A 20-pound **(A.P.)** leg of veal is purchased. Six pounds 6 ounces are lost through trimming and boning. How many 5-ounce veal cutlets can be obtained from the leg of veal?

_____

15. How many $5\frac{1}{2}$-ounce hamburgers can be obtained from 45 pounds **(E.P.)** of ground chuck?

ORDERING FOOD

Controlling amounts to order is another important food service function. Ordering close to the proper amount needed will reduce inventories and help control food cost and waste. When ordering food for a specific number of people, the amount to order can be found by multiplying the amount of the serving portion by the number of people to be served. The result will be the number of ounces required. Next, convert the common purchasing quantity into ounces and divide this amount into the number of ounces needed. (Of course, in the case of meat, fish, etc., consideration must be given to the amount that may be lost through boning and trimming.) A suggested formula is as follows:

> **Amount of portion × number of people served**
> **= number of ounces required.**
> **Common purchase quantity × 16**
> **= number of ounces in pound**
> **Number of ounces required ÷ ounces in pound**
> **= number to order.**

Example: How many pounds of ground chuck **E.P.** should be ordered if 42 people are to be served and each person is to receive a 5-ounce portion?

Step 1:
5 ounces × 42 = 210 ounces.
Amount of portion × number to be served
= number of ounces required to serve 42 people.

Step 2:
210 ounces ÷ 16 ounces = $13\frac{1}{8}$ = 14 pounds.
Number of ounces required ÷ 16 ounces in one pound
= amount to order.

This example can also be shown as follows:

$$
\begin{array}{rl}
42 & \text{Number of people to be served} \\
\times\ 5 & \text{Serving portion 5 ounces} \\
\hline
210 & \text{Number of ounces to serve 42 people}
\end{array}
$$

$$
\begin{array}{r}
13\frac{1}{8} \qquad \text{14 pounds must be ordered} \\
16\overline{)210 \text{ oz.}} \\
\underline{16} \\
50 \\
\underline{48} \\
2
\end{array}
$$

A total of 210 ounces will be required to serve 42 people. The common purchase quantity for meat is pounds. Since there are 16 ounces in a pound, 16 is divided into the number of ounces required. The result is 13 and $\frac{1}{8}$ remaining, so the actual number of pounds to be ordered must be 14 pounds. The remainder indicates that 13 pounds will not produce enough portions to serve 42 people.

SUMMARY REVIEW 7–5

1. For a wedding of 270 guests, an **E.P.** 8-oz. sirloin steak will be served. If each fabricated sirloin weighs 16 pounds, how many sirloins must be ordered?

   _____

2. Salisbury steak is to be served to a party of 195 people. Each portion is to weigh 7 ounces. How many **E.P.** pounds of ground beef must be ordered?

   _____

3. How many **E.P.** pounds of pork sausage should be ordered for 68 people if each person is to receive two $2\frac{1}{2}$-ounce patties?

   _____

4. How many gallons of orange juice must be ordered for a party of 175 people if each person is to receive a 5-ounce glass?

   _____

5. How many pounds of bacon should be ordered when serving a breakfast party of 96 people if each person is to receive 3 slices of bacon and there are 16 slices of bacon to each pound?

   _____

6. When preparing a breakfast for 220 people, how many pounds of link sausage must be ordered if each person is to receive three sausages and there are eight sausages to each pound?

   _____

7. How many **E.P.** pounds of short ribs should be ordered when preparing for 80 people if each person is to receive a 12-ounce portion?

   _____

8. How many pounds of ground beef must be ordered to serve spaghetti and meatballs to 130 people if each person is to receive two $2\frac{1}{2}$-ounce meatballs.

   _____

9. Pot roast of beef is being served to 110 people. Each person is to receive a 5-ounce serving. It is estimated that 3 pounds will be lost in shrinkage. How many **A.P.** pounds of beef brisket should be ordered?

_____

10. When preparing a breakfast for 138 people, how many pounds of Canadian bacon must be ordered if each person is to receive a $2\frac{1}{2}$-ounce portion?

_____

11. How many pounds of ground beef must be ordered when preparing meat loaf for 76 people if each person is to receive a $5\frac{1}{2}$-ounce serving?

_____

12. How many gallons of apple juice must be ordered to serve a party of 115 people if each person is to receive a 4-ounce glass of juice?

_____

13. How many **E.P.** pounds of pork loin must be ordered when serving 4-ounce breaded pork chops to a party of 210 people?

_____

14. How many **E.P.** pounds of spare ribs should be ordered when preparing for 65 people if each person is to receive a 12-ounce portion?

_____

15. How many **A.P.** pounds of beef tenderloin should be ordered to serve a party of 105 people if each person is served a 6-ounce tenderloin steak, and 1 pound 7 ounces are allowed for trimming?

_____

PURCHASING FRESH FISH

The quantity of fresh fish to purchase depends on three things: the number of people being served, the portion size, and the market form desired. Figure 7–10 is a suggested guide associating the market form to the amount to purchase.

The formula shown below will simplify the ordering procedure:

Amount per person × number served = amount to order.

Market Form	Amount per person
Fish sticks, steaks & fillets **(E.P.)**	$\frac{1}{3}$ pound
Dressed fish **(E.P.)**	$\frac{1}{2}$ pound
Drawn fish **(A.P.)**	$\frac{3}{4}$ pound
Whole fish or fish in the round (just as it comes from the water) **(A.P.)**	1 pound

Figure 7–10 *Chart for purchasing fresh fish*

Example One: How many pounds of fish steaks must be ordered for serving a party of 84 people? (Use guide.)

$$\frac{1}{3} \times \frac{84}{1} = 28 \text{ pounds}$$

Example Two: How many pounds of dressed fish should be ordered when preparing for a group of 72 people? (Use guide.)

$$\frac{1}{2} \times \frac{72}{1} = 36 \text{ pounds}$$

Example Three: How many pounds of drawn fish should be ordered when preparing for a party of 56 people? (Use guide.)

$$\frac{3}{4} \times \frac{56}{1} = 42 \text{ pounds}$$

SUMMARY REVIEW 7–6

Determine the answers to the following 10 questions using the information from Figure 7–10.

1. How many pounds of drawn fish should be ordered when preparing for a party of 88 people?

_____

2. How many pounds of fish steaks should be ordered when preparing for a group of 78 people?

_____

3. How many pounds of fish fillets should be ordered when preparing for a party of 75 people?

_____

4. How many pounds of fish sticks should be purchased when preparing for a group of 96 people?

_____

5. How many pounds of drawn fish should be purchased when preparing for a party of 140 people?

_____

6. How many pounds of dressed fish should be purchased when preparing for a party of 94 people?

_____

7. How many pounds of fish steaks should be ordered when preparing for a group of 135 people?

_____

8. How many pounds of fish fillets should be ordered when preparing for a party of 114 people?

_____

9. How many pounds of fish sticks should be purchased when preparing for a group of 123 people?

_____

10. How many pounds of drawn fish should be ordered when preparing for a party of 168 people?

_____

YIELD PERCENTAGE OF AN A.P. PRODUCT

Once it has been determined how much of an **A.P.** product is waste and how much is **E.P.,** the person ordering food can convert this to a yield percentage. The purchaser can keep records of the yield percentage of items used and will know how much to purchase for future orders. As an example, we will use the information from our 18-pound short loin of beef in the **as purchased (A.P.)** state. We discovered that, when the prep cook trimmed and boned the short loin, the resulting loss in waste amounted to 2 pounds and 10 ounces. The remaining trimmed short loin weighs 15 pounds and 6 ounces (18 pounds − 2 pounds and 10 ounces). The yield percentage of the short loin is determined in this manner:

> **Edible portion (E.P.) divided by (÷) as purchased (A.P.) = yield percentage.**

Using our short loin from above, we will illustrate how to determine the yield percentage.

Step 1: Convert the **as purchased (A.P.)** 18-pound short loin into ounces (16 ounces in a pound).

18 times (×) 16 = 288 ounces **as purchased (A.P.)**

Step 2: Convert the resulting waste from the short loin, 2 pounds and 10 ounces, into ounces.

2 times (×) 16 = 32 + 10 = 42 ounces of waste

Step 3: Subtract the waste (42 ounces) from the **as purchased (A.P.)** ounces (288)

288 minus (−) 42 = 246 ounces. This is now the **edible portion (E.P.)**

Step 4: Divide the **E.P.** by the **A.P.** to equal the yield percentage.

246 ÷ 288 = 85.4% **yield percentage**

How to Use the Yield Percentage

Once the purchaser knows how to determine the yield percentage of products, each product should be tested for the yield percentage. When the yield percentage is determined, this number must be saved for future ordering. The individual purchasing the product will have to take the yield percentage into account when purchasing products.

To figure out the amount of food to order, we will continue with our short loin example from above. For instance, your chef tells you to order enough short loin to serve each of 100 guests an 8-oz. portion. The purchaser has determined, through previous experiences, that a short loin results in a yield percentage of 85.4%. This can be solved by figuring out the amount of **edible portion (E.P.)** that is needed, and then dividing it by the **yield percentage.**

Step 1: Determine the amount of **E.P.** of short loin needed for the 100 guests.

100 guests × 8 oz. portion = 800 ounces of **E.P.** needed

Step 2: Number of ounces needed by **E.P.** divided by (÷) yield percentage = number of ounces of short loin needed.

800 ounces ÷ 85.4% = 936.76814 ounces of short loin needed

Step 3: Convert the ounces into pounds by dividing the amount of ounces needed by 16.

936.76814 ÷ 16 = 58.548008 pounds

Step 4: The purchaser would order 59 pounds of short loin.

Based on the authors' research, most purchasers and chefs determine the yield percentage one time and then they order based on experience. For example, one chef told us that for every prime rib he roasts, he obtains 17 regular cuts and 20 English cuts from the size of the rib he specifies. When he has a party for 200 guests, he divides the 200 by 17 and determines that he must order 12 prime ribs. Another purchasing agent told us that he knows, when a romaine salad is on the menu, that the cooks obtain 100 portions from the purchased case of romaine that he buys. Therefore, if he projects to serve 300 romaine salads, he orders three cases of romaine lettuce.

SUMMARY REVIEW 7–7   Yield Percentage

Answers should be shown in this manner: 98.1%.

1. What is the yield percentage of a 24-pound turkey? The turkey lost 8 pounds and 5 ounces after fabrication and shrinkage.

   _____

2. What is the yield percentage of an 8-pound pork tenderloin? The tenderloin lost 1 pound and 5 ounces after fabrication and shrinkage.

   _____

3. What is the yield percentage of 50 pounds of potatoes? The potatoes lost 6 pounds and 3 ounces after fabrication.

   _____

4. What is the yield percentage of a 15-pound salmon? The salmon lost 3 pounds and 9 ounces after fabrication and shrinkage.

   _____

5. What is the yield percentage of a 7-pound chicken? The chicken lost 4 pounds and 2 ounces after fabrication and shrinkage.

   _____

Questions 6 through 10 have to be solved using the yield percentage for ordering food.

6. If the yield percentage for a prime rib roast is 50%, how many pounds will have to be ordered to serve 300 guests? Each guest will receive an 8-ounce portion.

   _____

7. If the yield percentage for a chicken breast is 29.6%, how many pounds will have to be ordered to serve 250 guests? Each guest will receive a 6-ounce portion.

   _____

8. If the yield percentage for salmon is 45%, how many pounds will have to be ordered to serve 150 guests? Each guest will receive a 7-ounce portion.

   _____

9. If the yield percentage for a cantaloupe melon is 58.1%, how many pounds will have to be ordered to serve 75 guests? Each guest will receive a 4-ounce portion.

_____

10. If the yield percentage for strawberries is 91.9%, how many pounds will have to be ordered to serve 300 guests? Each guest will receive a 3-ounce portion.

_____

DISCUSSION QUESTION 7–A

Your produce salesman offers to sell you bags of salad ingredients (cleaned and ready to eat). You have been buying the ingredients individually, and cleaning and preparing them with your current workforce. What considerations will you take into account when determining whether you should purchase ready-to-serve salad ingredients versus ones that your staff will have to clean and prepare? Provide three considerations.

CHAPTER

8

Converting Recipes, Yields, and Baking Formulas

OBJECTIVES

At the completion of this chapter, the student should be able to:

1. Find the working factor to convert recipes.
2. Convert standard recipes from larger to smaller amounts, or from smaller to larger amounts.
3. Find approximate recipe yields.
4. Use ratios and proportions to convert ingredients for recipes.
5. Find percents for bakers' formulas.

KEY WORDS

standardized recipe   ratios
working factor   proportions
yield   bakers' percentages

During your food service career, occasions will frequently occur when you will be required to convert recipes to amounts that will differ from the original recipe. These amounts may be more or less than the recipe yield. For example, the recipe you have may yield 50 portions, but the need is for 25 or 100 portions.

Some food service establishments produce food from what is referred to as a **standardized recipe.** This is a recipe that will produce the same quality and quantity each and every time. Standardized recipes are ideal for certain food service operations such as nursing homes, retirement villages, and some school cafeterias. However, food production will vary in most food service operations, so converting recipes is a very important technique to master. (See Figure 8–1.)

CONVERTING STANDARD RECIPES

It is a simple matter to double or cut a recipe in half. Many times this can be done mentally with little or no effort. However, when it becomes necessary to change a recipe from 12 to 20 portions or from 50 to 28, it appears to be more complicated. Actually, the procedure is the same for both and involves a fairly simple function of finding a **working factor** and multiplying each ingredient quantity by the working factor. The working factor is the number that will be used to multiply the amount of the original ingredients in a recipe to either increase or decrease a recipe.

Figure 8–1 *The chef is converting a recipe to determine the amounts needed to produce the required number of servings.*

The first step in converting a recipe is to find the **working factor.** This is done as follows:

Step 1: Divide the yield desired by original recipe yield.

$$\frac{\text{New yield}}{\text{Old yield}} = \text{Working factor}$$

Step 2: Multiply each ingredient in the original recipe by the working factor.

Working factor × old quantity = new quantity (desired quantity).

To simplify this procedure, change ingredient pounds to ounces before starting to multiply. This way, it is only necessary to multiply ounces. After multiplying, convert the product back to pounds and ounces. If you are using the metric system, this step is not necessary.

Example: A standardized recipe yields 40 portions. Only 30 portions are desired.

First, you must find the working factor by following the formula given in Step 1.

$$\frac{30 \text{ New yield}}{40 \text{ Old yield}} = \frac{3}{4} \text{ Working factor or } .75$$

Next, convert the quantity of each ingredient in the original recipe to ounces and multiply each ingredient by $\frac{3}{4}$ or .75, the working factor, as stated in Step 2. Convert new amounts back to pounds and ounces.

Example: A standardized recipe yields 75 portions. A large party is booked, and 225 portions are required.

First, you must find the working factor by following the formula given in Step 1:

$$\frac{225 \text{ New yield}}{75 \text{ Old yield}} = 3 \text{ Working factor}$$

Next, convert the quantity of each ingredient in the original recipe to ounces and multiply each ingredient by 3, the working factor, as stated in Step 2. Convert new amounts back to pounds and ounces.

T I P S . . . . To Insure Perfect Solutions

When converting recipes to **more portions,** realize that the working factor will be **greater than one.**
When converting recipes to **fewer portions,** realize that the working factor will be **less than one.**

SUMMARY REVIEW 8-1

Find the working factor for each problem.

1. The standardized recipe is for 40 portions. The party is for 250 guests.

   _____

2. The standardized recipe is for 50 portions. The party is for 35 guests.

   _____

3. The standardized recipe is for 75 portions. The party is for 185 guests.

   _____

4. The standardized recipe is for 10 portions. The party is for 193 guests.

   _____

5. The standardized recipe is for 50 portions. The party is for 15 guests.

   _____

6. The standardized recipe is for 30 portions. The party is for 350 guests.

   _____

7. The standardized recipe is for 90 portions. The party is for 25 guests.

   _____

8. The standardized recipe is for 65 portions. The party is for 185 guests.

   _____

9. The standardized recipe is for 25 portions. The party is for 4 guests.

   _____

10. The standardized recipe is for 4 portions. The party is for 160 guests.

   _____

When working a recipe after a conversion has taken place, some common sense must also be applied. You might think of this common sense or judgment as an extra ingredient. For instance, the recipe may not account for how fresh or old the spices or herbs are, or how hot the kitchen or bakeshop is when mixing a yeast dough. Common sense or judgment must be applied when converting any recipe because it may not be practical to increase or decrease the quantity of each ingredient by the exact same rate. Many spices and herbs cannot be increased or decreased at the same rate as other ingredients. This may also be true of salt, garlic, and sugar in certain situations. Use good judgment in these situations and carry out tests before deciding on amounts.

Example: The following recipe yields 12 dozen hard rolls. It must be converted to yield 9 dozen rolls.

Ingredients for 12 dozen rolls	Amount of conversion	Amount needed to yield 9 dozen rolls
7 lb. 8 oz. bread flour	$\frac{3}{4}$	5 lb. 10 oz.
3 oz. salt		$2\frac{1}{4}$ oz.
$3\frac{1}{2}$ oz. granulated sugar		$2\frac{5}{8}$ oz.
3 oz. shortening		$2\frac{1}{4}$ oz.
3 oz. egg whites		$2\frac{1}{4}$ oz.
4 lb. 8 oz. water (variable)		3 lb. 6 oz.
$4\frac{1}{2}$ oz. yeast, compressed		$3\frac{3}{8}$ oz.

Step 1: Find the working factor.

$$\frac{9 \text{ dozen new yield}}{12 \text{ dozen old yield}} = \frac{3}{4} \text{ Is the working factor}$$

The quantity of each ingredient in the original recipe is multiplied by $\frac{3}{4}$ (working factor).

Step 2: Convert all ingredients.

Example: 7 pounds 8 ounces of bread flour
$(7 \times 16) + 8 = 120$ ounces

Example: $3\frac{1}{2}$ ounces of granulated sugar $= \frac{7}{2}$ ounces

Step 3: Multiply all ingredients by the working factor $\left(\frac{3}{4}\right)$.

Example: bread flour $\left(120 \text{ ounces} \times \frac{3}{4} = 90 \text{ ounces}\right)$

Example: granulated sugar $\left(\frac{7}{2} \text{ ounces} \times \frac{3}{4} = \frac{21}{8}\right)$

Step 4: Convert new amounts back to pounds and ounces.

Example: bread flour (90 ounces divided by 16 = 5 pounds and 10 ounces)

Example: granulated sugar $\left(\frac{21}{8} = 2\frac{5}{8} \text{ ounces}\right)$

Step 5: Continue converting all ingredients in 9 dozen rolls recipe.

SUMMARY REVIEW 8-2

1. The following recipe yields 50 portions of curried lamb. Convert it to yield 150 portions.

Ingredients for 50 Portions	Amount of Conversion	Amount Needed to Yield 150 Portions
18 lb. lamb shoulder; boneless, cut into 1-inch cubes E.P.		
$2\frac{1}{2}$ gallons water		
2 lb. butter or shortening		
1 lb. 8 oz. flour		
$\frac{1}{3}$ cup curry powder		
2 qt. tart apples, diced		
2 lb. onions, diced		
$\frac{1}{2}$ tsp. ground cloves		
2 bay leaves		
1 tsp. marjoram		
salt and pepper to taste		

2. The following recipe yields 100 portions of Hungarian goulash. Convert it to yield 75 portions.

Ingredients for 100 Portions	Amount of Conversion	Amount Needed to Yield 75 Portions
36 lb. beef chuck or shoulder, diced 1-inch cubes E.P.		
$1\frac{1}{4}$ oz. garlic, minced		
1 lb. 4 oz. flour		
$1\frac{1}{4}$ oz. chili powder		
10 oz. paprika		
2 lb. tomato puree		
2 gal. brown stock		
4 bay leaves		
$\frac{3}{4}$ oz. caraway seeds		
3 lb. 8 oz. onions, minced		
salt and pepper to taste		

3. The following recipe yields nine 8-inch lemon pies. Convert it to yield six 8-inch pies.

Ingredients for 9 Pies	Amount of Conversion	Amount Needed to Yield 6 Pies
4 lb. flour		
3 lb. 6 oz. granulated sugar		
$\frac{1}{2}$ oz. salt		
3 oz. lemon gratings		

Chef Sez...

"If you are the chef owner of a restaurant, you must have a knowledge of math and how to use it or else you will go under (bankrupt). When you are the head chef, if you are not good at math you lose your job."

Andre Soltner
Founder and former owner of Lutece
Master Chef, Senior Lecturer
The French Culinary Institute
New York City

To fully understand Chef Soltner's remarks and to discover why Lutece has been called the finest French restaurant in America, the authors recommend the book, *Lutece, A Day in the Life of America's Greatest Restaurant,* by Irene Daria. The book is published by Random House, copyright 1993.

1 lb. water

8 oz. corn starch

12 oz. egg yolks

1 lb. 6 oz. lemon juice

4 oz. butter, melted

yellow color, as needed

4. The following recipe yields 12 dozen hard rolls. Convert it to yield 48 dozen rolls.

Ingredients for 12 Dozen Rolls	Amount of Conversion	Amount Needed to Yield 48 Dozen Rolls
7 lb. 8 oz. bread flour		
3 oz. salt		
$3\frac{1}{2}$ oz. granulated sugar		
3 oz. shortening		
3 oz. egg whites		
4 lb. 8 oz. water (variable)		
$4\frac{1}{2}$ oz. yeast, compressed		

5. The following recipe yields 8 dozen soft dinner rolls. Convert it to yield 5 dozen rolls.

Ingredients for 8 Dozen Rolls	Amount of Conversion	Amount Needed to Yield 5 Dozen Rolls
10 oz. granulated sugar		
10 oz. hydrogenated shortening		
1 oz. salt		
3 oz. dry milk		
4 oz. whole eggs		
3 lb. 12 oz. bread flour		
2 lb. water		
5 oz. yeast, compressed		

FINDING APPROXIMATE RECIPE YIELD

Yield is defined as the amount of portions, servings, or units a particular recipe or formula will produce. It is one of the most important features of a recipe or formula. Yield is probably one of the first items a cook will look at when selecting a certain recipe for preparation. Observing a recipe or formula yield provides the preparer with an approximate guide to the numbers the recipe or formula will produce. The yield must also be known before conversion can take place.

Most recipes provide an approximate guide as to the number or amounts the recipe will produce. However, occasions arise when you will want to determine your own yield because the suggested recipe or formula portion size is too large or small for your need.

You may also wish to work out your own recipe for a preparation—a recipe you have used many times but for which you have never determined an approximate yield.

Suggested recipe or formula yields will fluctuate if you determine a larger or smaller portion is required. To show how this situation could happen, let us assume a yellow cake batter is prepared from a recipe that states the approximate yield is twenty 14-ounce cakes (14 ounces of batter used in each cake). You wish to use a smaller pan that will only hold 10 ounces. The yield will, of course, fluctuate and produce a larger amount of yellow cakes.

It is for these reasons that the student cook or baker must understand how a yield can be determined by applying some simple mathematics. The chef can approximate the serving size by determining a formula yield (see Figure 8–2).

The yield for some recipes or formulas is found by preparing a certain amount, determining a serving portion, and measuring it to see what it

Figure 8–2 *By determining a formula yield, the chef can approximate the serving size.*

will produce. The yield for other recipes—such as cake or muffin batters, roll or sweet doughs, pie filling and some cookie doughs—can be determined by taking the total weight of all ingredients used in the preparation and dividing that figure by the weight of an individual portion or unit. Let us take the formula of a white cake and of a roll dough to show how an approximate yield can be obtained by this method.

The formula is:

Total weight of preparation ÷ weight of portion = recipe yield.

Example:

White Cake

Ingredients: Find the approximate yield ___?___

2 lb. 8 oz. cake flour (40 oz.)

1 lb. 12 oz. shortening (28 oz.)

3 lb. 2 oz. granulated sugar (50 oz.)

$1\frac{1}{2}$ oz. salt (1.5 oz.)

$2\frac{1}{2}$ oz. baking powder (2.5 oz.)

14 oz. water (14 oz.)

$2\frac{1}{2}$ oz. dry milk (2.5 oz.)

10 oz. whole eggs (10 oz.)

1 lb. egg whites (16 oz.)

1 lb. water (16 oz.)

vanilla to taste (to taste)

total ounces = 180.5 oz.

The total weight of all ingredients is 11 pounds $4\frac{1}{2}$ ounces. Each cake is to contain 14 ounces of batter. The first step is to convert the weight of all ingredients to ounces, since only like things can be divided: 11 pounds $4\frac{1}{2}$ ounces contains $180\frac{1}{2}$ ounces. The second step is to divide the weight of one cake (14 ounces) into the total weight of all ingredients:

$$
\begin{array}{r}
12 \text{ cakes} \\
14\overline{)180.5} \\
\underline{14} \\
40 \\
\underline{28} \\
12
\end{array}
$$

When preparing a cake from scratch—that is, step-by-step preparation—the baker must first determine the size of each pan to be used and the amount of batter each pan is to contain. He or she may determine an 8-inch cake pan will be used and each pan is to contain 14 ounces of batter to produce the size of cake desired. Many times the cake recipe will state, in the method of preparation, the amount of batter to place in a certain size pan. Usually the type of cake prepared will have a bearing on the amount of batter placed in each pan. For example, light semi-sponge cake batters will not require as much batter as a pound cake.

There is no reason to carry the division any further because only figures on the left side of the decimal point are whole numbers. So 12 cakes, each containing 14 ounces of batter, were realized from this recipe.

When preparing a roll dough, the baker must determine how much each roll will weigh. Some bakers like a larger roll than others. The usual size is $1\frac{1}{4}$ to 2 ounces. Once the size is determined, an approximate yield is easy to find.

Example:

Soft Dinner Roll Dough

Ingredients: Find the approximate yield ___?___

1 lb. 4 oz. granulated sugar

1 lb. 4 oz. shortening

2 oz. salt

6 oz. dry milk

6 oz. whole eggs

7 lb. 8 oz. bread flour

4 lb. water

10 oz. compressed yeast

The total weight of all ingredients is 15 pounds 8 ounces. Each roll is to weigh $1\frac{1}{2}$ ounces. The first step is to convert the weight of all ingredients to ounces, since only like things can be divided; 15 pounds 8 ounces contain 248 ounces. Now, dividing the total weight by the weight of one roll gives the recipe yield:

$$
\begin{array}{r}
165. \\
1.5\,\overline{)248.0.} \\
15 \\
\hline
98 \\
90 \\
\hline
80 \\
75 \\
\hline
5
\end{array}
$$

Thus, the yield is 165 rolls or $13\frac{3}{4}$ dozen rolls, or 13 dozen and 9 rolls, when yielding a 1.5-ounce roll.

Most recipes used in the commercial kitchen will be stated in weights, and an approximate yield is easier to determine when ingredients are listed in weights. Weights will also produce a more accurate preparation. There are occasions when recipes will be stated in measures. In this case, the formula used to determine a yield will be the same, but the measuring units in finding an approximate yield will differ.

Example:

Honey Cream Dressing

Ingredients: Find the approximate yield ___?___

3 cups cream cheese

2 cups honey

$\frac{1}{2}$ cup pineapple juice (variable)

$\frac{1}{4}$ tsp. salt

$2\frac{1}{2}$ qt. mayonnaise

In this example, total cups must be determined. There are $15\frac{1}{2}$ cups in the preparation. A 2-ounce ladle is used to portion. A 2-ounce ladle contains $\frac{1}{4}$ cup, so, following the formula given to determine an approximate yield, the math involved would be as follows:

$15\frac{1}{2}$ cups (total measure of preparation) $\div$ $\frac{1}{4}$ cup (portion measure)

$$= \frac{31}{2} \times \frac{4}{1} = 62 \text{ portions (yield)}.$$

SUMMARY REVIEW 8–3

1. Determine the approximate yield of the following formula if **each** coffee cake is to contain a 12-ounce unit of sweet dough.

Coffee Cake Ingredients   Find the approximate yield __?__

1 lb. granulated sugar

1 lb. golden shortening

1 oz. salt

3 lb. bread flour

1 lb. 8 oz. pastry flour

12 oz. whole eggs

4 oz. dry milk

2 lb. water

8 oz. compressed yeast

mace to taste

vanilla to taste

2. Determine the approximate yield of the following formula if **each** cookie is to contain $1\frac{1}{2}$ ounces of dough.

Fruit Tea Cookies   Find the approximate yield __?__

1 lb. 6 oz. shortening

1 lb. 6 oz. powdered sugar

2 lb. 8 oz. pastry flour

2 oz. liquid milk

6 oz. raisins, chopped

2 oz. pecans, chopped

3 oz. pineapple, chopped

2 oz. peaches, chopped

8 oz. whole eggs

$\frac{1}{4}$ oz. baking soda

$\frac{1}{4}$ oz. vanilla

$\frac{1}{2}$ oz. salt

3. Determine the approximate yield of the following formula if each cake is to contain 11 ounces of batter.

Yellow Cake Ingredients   Find the approximate yield ___?___

2 lb. 8 oz. cake flour

1 lb. 6 oz. shortening

3 lb. 2 oz. granulated sugar

1 oz. salt

$1\frac{3}{4}$ oz. baking powder

4 oz. dry milk

1 lb. 4 oz. water

1 lb. 10 oz. whole eggs

12 oz. water

$\frac{1}{4}$ oz. vanilla

4. Determine the approximate yield of the following recipe if each gelatin mold is to hold $\frac{3}{4}$ cup of liquid gelatin mix.

Sunshine Salad   Find the approximate yield ___?___

1 pt. lemon-flavored gelatin

1 qt. hot water

1 qt. cold water

$\frac{1}{4}$ cup cider vinegar

1 qt. grated carrots

1 pt. pineapple, crushed

5. Determine the approximate yield of the following recipe if a 6-ounce ladle ($\frac{3}{4}$ cup) is used to portion.

Beef Stroganoff   Find the approximate yield ___?___

2 gal. beef tenderloin, cut into thin strips E.P.

1 cup flour

$\frac{1}{2}$ cup shortening

3 qt. water

$\frac{1}{2}$ cup tomato puree

$\frac{1}{2}$ cup cider vinegar

1 lb. onions, minced

1 qt. mushrooms, sliced

1 qt. sour cream

1 tbsp. salt

3 bay leaves

Practical Use of Ratios and Proportions

Ratios and proportions were covered in Chapter 4. This chapter requires the student to use them in solving problems. The term *ratio* is used to express a comparison between two numbers. A **ratio** between two quantities is the number of times one contains the other. For example, to prepare pie dough, the baker must use 1 quart of liquid to every 4 pounds of flour. Therefore, the ratio is 1 to 4.

Mathematical or word problems that include ratios may be solved by using proportions. A **proportion** is defined as a relation in size, number, amount, or degree of one thing compared to another. For example, when preparing the pie dough, the ratio is 1 to 4—that is, 1 quart of liquid to 4 pounds of flour. It is important to realize that the order in which the numbers are placed when expressing a ratio is crucial, as was explained in Chapter 4.

Using the ratio from above, we will illustrate how to solve the following word problem using a proportion. Your chef tells you to make 10 pounds of pie dough. You must find out how much liquid is required.

As a review from Chapter 4, this is the information about proportions that you must know.

> The unknown is represented by an x, since that is the answer to be determined.
> "Is to" in a mathematical equation is represented by a full colon (:).
> The numbers on the outside of the equation are called extremes.
> The numbers on the inside of the equation are called means.

Step 1: Set up a proportion.
How much liquid is required to make 10 pounds of pie dough? You know that when preparing pie dough, the ratio is 1 to 4—that is, 1 quart of liquid to 4 pounds of flour.

Step 2: Set up a mathematical equation.
How much liquid is required is represented by the x, which is the unknown factor.
The pie dough is represented by the 10, the pounds of pie dough that have to be made.
The 1 is equal to 1 quart of liquid.
The 4 is equal to 4 pounds of flour.

So, the equation reads: The unknown amount of liquid to 10 pounds of pie dough is equal to 1 quart of liquid to 4 pounds of flour.

$$x : 10 = 1 : 4$$

Step 3: Multiply the means together (1 times 10), which is equal to 10. Multiply the extremes together (x times 4), which is equal to 4x.

The formula now reads:
$$4x = 10$$

Step 4: Divide both sides of the equation by the number next to the x.

$$\frac{4x}{4} = \frac{10}{4}$$

(The fours on the left side of the = sign cancel each other out.)
You are left with x = 10 divided by (÷) 4 = 2.5

Step 5: The cook needs 2.5 quarts of liquid to make 10 pounds of pie dough.

SUMMARY REVIEW 8–4

Use proportions to solve the following problems. Before setting up the proportion, convert all amounts to like amounts. For example, if the ratio is stated as a quart and the problem is stated as gallons, convert all gallons to quarts before attempting to solve the problem.

1. Determine the amounts of liquid required if a pie dough formula contains the following amounts of flour. The ratio is 1 part liquid to 4 parts flour.

   a. 20 pounds   _____

   b. 12 pounds   _____

   c. 16 pounds   _____

   d. 18 pounds   _____

2. Determine the amount of dry milk required to produce the following amounts of liquid milk. The ratio is 4 ounces of dry milk to 1 quart of water.

   a. $1\frac{1}{2}$ gallons liquid milk   _____

   b. 3 gallons liquid milk   _____

   c. $3\frac{1}{2}$ quarts liquid milk   _____

   d. $4\frac{3}{4}$ gallons liquid milk   _____

3. Determine the amount of unflavored gelatin required to jell the following amounts of aspic. The ratio is 6 ounces of unflavored gelatin to each gallon of water.

   a. 6 quarts aspic   _____

   b. $1\frac{3}{4}$ gallons aspic   _____

   c. $3\frac{1}{2}$ gallons aspic   _____

   d. $2\frac{1}{2}$ gallons aspic   _____

4. Determine the amount of liquid needed to prepare the following amounts of raw barley. The ratio calls for 4 parts of liquid to every 1 part of raw barley.

   a. 1 pint raw barley   _____

   b. 3 pints raw barley   _____

   c. 3 quarts raw barley   _____

   d. 1 cup raw barley   _____

5. Determine the amount of pudding powder needed to prepare the following amounts of pudding. The ratio is 3.25 ounces of pudding powder to every pint of milk.

   a. 3 quarts pudding   _____

   b. $2\frac{1}{2}$ quarts pudding   _____

   c. 6 quarts pudding   _____

   d. $1\frac{1}{2}$ quarts pudding   _____

6. Determine the amount of dry nondairy creamer required to produce the following amounts of liquid cream. To convert dry nondairy creamer to liquid, mix 1 pint of dry creamer with 1 quart of hot water.

   a. 2 gallons liquid cream   _____

   b. $1\frac{1}{2}$ gallons liquid cream   _____

   c. $\frac{1}{2}$ gallon liquid cream   _____

   d. $3\frac{1}{2}$ gallons liquid cream   _____

7. Determine the amount of dry instant potato powder needed to prepare the following amounts of mashed potatoes. To prepare mashed potatoes using the dry instant potato powder, use 1 pound 13 ounces of the powder to each gallon of water or milk.

   a. 2 gallons mashed potatoes   _____

   b. 6 gallons mashed potatoes   _____

   c. $2\frac{1}{2}$ gallons mashed potatoes   _____

   d. $4\frac{1}{2}$ gallons mashed potatoes   _____

8. When preparing pasta or egg noodles, use 1 gallon of boiling water to every pound of pasta. Determine the amount of liquid required to cook the pasta.

   a. 3.5 pounds pasta   _____

   b. 5 pounds pasta   _____

   c. 6.5 pounds pasta   _____

   d. 7 pounds pasta   _____

9. When preparing egg wash, how many eggs will be needed when preparing the following amounts? To prepare a fairly rich egg wash, mix together 4 whole eggs to every quart of milk.

   a. 1 cup milk   _____

   b. 1 pint milk   _____

   c. 2 quarts milk   _____

   d. 3 quarts milk   _____

10. Determine the amount of flour needed if the following amounts of shortening are used when preparing pan grease. To prepare pan

grease, thoroughly mix together 8 ounces of flour to every pound of shortening.

a. $1\frac{1}{2}$ pounds of shortening   _____

b. 8 ounces of shortening   _____

c. 12 ounces of shortening   _____

d. $2\frac{3}{4}$ pounds of shortening   _____

BAKER'S PERCENTAGE

In cooking, if a recipe or formula should become unbalanced or if a mistake should occur when adding ingredients, the situation might easily be corrected by making a few adjustments. This is not the case when working with baking formulas. Bakers use a simple yet versatile system designed to balance all formulas with flour as the main ingredient. Each minor ingredient is a percentage of the main (flour) ingredient. Industry standards determine the percentages of each ingredient in most of the popular formulas to ensure that the formula is balanced.

The ingredients in baking formulas must be balanced if the finished product is to possess all the qualities necessary to please the customer and to warrant return sales. Most formulas used in bakeshops today have been developed in research laboratories operated by the companies that manufacture the products bakers use. The formulas are used to test the manufacturer's products and are passed on to bakers in the hope that they will use the manufacturer's products.

Keeping in mind that flour is the main ingredient, bakers' percentages designate the amount of each ingredient that would be required if 100 pounds of flour were used. Thus, flour is always 100 percent. If, for instance, two kinds of flour were used in a preparation, the total amounts of the two would represent 100 percent and any other ingredient that weighs the same as the flour is also listed at 100 percent. To find ingredient percentages, divide the total weight of the ingredient by the weight of the flour, then multiply by 100 percent.

Example:

The following ingredients for a yellow pound cake illustrate how these percentages are found.

Yellow Pound Cake Recipe		
Ingredients	Weights	Baker's percentage
Cake flour	2 lb. 8 oz., or 40 ounces	100%
Vegetable shortening	1 lb. 12 oz., or 28 ounces	
Granulated sugar	2 lb. 8 oz., or 40 ounces	
Salt	1.5 ounces	
Water	1 lb. 4 oz., or 20 ounces	
Dry milk	2.5 ounces	
Whole eggs	1 lb. 12 oz., or 28 ounces	
Vanilla to taste	-------	
Total Weight	160 ounces	

In the above chart, all ingredients have been converted to ounces so we can calculate like amounts.

To determine the percentage of each item, take the weight of each ingredient and divide by the weight of the flour (since the flour represents 100%), and then multiply by 100%.

Weight of each ingredient ÷ total weight of the flour times (×) 100 % = percentage of each item.

Here is how we determine the percentage of vegetable shortening:

Vegetable shortening (28 ounces) is divided by the flour (40 ounces) = .7 × 100% = 70%

$$
\begin{array}{r}
.70 \\
40\overline{)28.0} \\
28\ 0 \\
\end{array}
$$

.70 × 100% = 70%

After doing the math, the chart looks as follows. Please check our figures in the chart to practice obtaining the baker's percentage.

Yellow Pound Cake Recipe		
Ingredients	**Weights**	**Baker's percentage**
Cake flour	2 lb. 8 oz., or 40 ounces	100%
Vegetable shortening	1 lb. 12 oz., or 28 ounces	70%
Granulated sugar	2 lb. 8 oz., or 40 ounces	100%
Salt	1.5 ounces	3.75%
Water	1 lb. 4 oz., or 20 ounces	50%
Dry milk	2.5 ounces	6.25%
Whole eggs	1 lb. 12 oz., or 28 ounces	70%
Vanilla to taste	-------	---------
Total Weight	160 ounces	400%

The advantage of finding and using these percentages, when flour is the main ingredient, is that the formula can be changed easily to any yield and, if a single ingredient needs to be altered, it can be done without changing the complete formula.

Why Are Baker's Percentages Used?

One advantage occurs when new items are added to the recipe, in order to enhance the recipe. For example, the authors would like to add chocolate chips to the recipe to make it a yellow chocolate chip pound cake. If they add 8 oz. of chocolate chips, they figure out the baker's percentage of chocolate chips based upon the weight of the flour. They do not have to change all the ingredients and all the percentages. In this example, 8 (the ounces of chocolate chips) is divided by 40 (the ounces of the flour). The chocolate chip percentage is 20%. Notice that the sum of the total weight and the sum of the baker's percentage have also been increased.

Yellow Pound Cake Recipe Modified with Chocolate Chips		
Ingredients	Weights	Baker's percentage
Cake flour	2 lb. 8 oz., or 40 ounces	100%
Vegetable shortening	1 lb. 12 oz., or 28 ounces	70%
Granulated sugar	2 lb. 8 oz., or 40 ounces	100%
Salt	1.5 ounces	3.75%
Water	1 lb. 4 oz., or 20 ounces	50%
Dry milk	2.5 ounces	6.25%
Chocolate chips	8 ounces	20%
Whole eggs	1 lb. 12 oz., or 28 ounces	70%
Vanilla to taste	-------	------
Total Weight	168 ounces	420%

The second advantage occurs when the amount of flour is changed. If the baker has a 5-pound bag of flour left over and wants to use it, the baker can make up another batch of yellow chocolate chip pound cake by using the baker's percentage. The baker first changes the weight of the flour to 80 ounces. The remaining ingredients are calculated by multiplying the baker's percentages from the original recipe. The amount of the vegetable shortening is now increased to 56 ounces (70% × 80) or $3\frac{1}{2}$ pounds (56 divided by 16 is equal to 3 pounds and 8 ounces). The baker continues to convert all ingredients using the baker's percentage method for each ingredient. This will keep the recipe in balance and assure consistency for each cake.

The third advantage occurs when the total formula weight for the recipe is known and your head baker tells you to make up a certain amount of dough. As an example, your head baker tells you to make up 50 pounds of batter for our yellow chocolate chip pound cake. You know that for one cake, you must use 168 ounces total weight for the recipe. How much of each ingredient will be used for 50 pounds (16 × 50 = 800 ounces)? This is how you solve the problem using the baker's percentage.

Step 1: Add up the total baker's percentage formula. The answer comes to 420%.

Step 2: Calculate the total flour weight using this formula:

$$\frac{\text{Total formula weight} = 800 \text{ ounces}}{\text{Total formula percentage} = 420\%}$$

Or

$$\frac{800 \text{ ounces}}{4.20} = 190.47619 \text{ total ounces of flour}$$

Step 3: The total flour weight is 190.47619 ounces of flour needed to make 50 pounds of batter. Mathematically, this is the correct answer. Realistically, we would increase this to 191 ounces.

Step 4: Convert each ingredient using the flour as the base.

In the original recipe, our chocolate chips weighed 8 ounces, or 20% of the recipe.

Using the baker's percentage of 20%, multiply the .20 × 191, which equals 38 ounces.

The end result is the recipe shown in the following chart, with a yield of 50 pounds of batter.

Yellow Pound Cake Recipe Modified with Chocolate Chips (Yield: 50 Pounds of Batter)		
Ingredients	**Weights**	**Baker's percentage**
Cake flour	11 lb. 15 oz., or 191 ounces	100%
Vegetable shortening	8 lb. 6 oz., or 134 ounces	70%
Granulated sugar	11 lb. 15 oz., or 191 ounces	100%
Salt	7.16 ounces	3.75%
Water	5 lb. 15 oz., or 95 ounces	50%
Dry milk	12 ounces	6.25%
Chocolate chips	2 lb. 6 oz., or 38 ounces	20%
Whole eggs	8 lb. 6 oz., or 134 ounces	70%
Vanilla to taste	-------	------
Total Weight	50 lb. 2.12 oz., or 802.16 ounces	420%

Notice that the total amount of the batter is not exactly 50 pounds. This allows for losses in preparing the batter. Rounding up using the baker's percentage does not affect the proportion of the recipe.

What if I want to increase the yield from 1 cake to 20 cakes; do I have to use the baker's percentage?

You may go through all the steps, but, realistically, it would be better to use the working factor method that was covered earlier in this chapter.

$$\frac{\text{New recipe}}{\text{Old recipe}} = \text{Working factor}$$

$$\frac{20}{1} = 20$$

In this example, all of the ingredients will be multiplied by the working factor of 20. As an example, the chocolate chips will be multiplied by 20. This results in 160 ounces of chocolate chips, or 10 pounds.

SUMMARY REVIEW 8-5

Find the percent of each ingredient used in the following formulas. Remember that flour is always 100%. Round to the tenth place.

1. **Pie dough**

   (a)

Ingredients	Weight	Percentage
Pastry flour	10 lb.	_____
Shortening	7 lb. 8 oz.	_____
Salt	5 oz.	_____
Sugar	3 oz.	_____
Cold water	2 lb. 8 oz.	_____
Dry milk	3 oz.	_____

   Using the percentage found for each ingredient, determine the amount of each ingredient if the flour amount is changed to 12 pounds.

   (b)

Ingredients	Weight
Pastry flour	12 lb.
Shortening	_____
Salt	_____
Sugar	_____
Cold water	_____
Dry milk	_____

2. **Golden Dinner Roll Dough**

   (a)

Ingredients	Weight	Percentage
Bread flour	9 lb.	_____
Pastry flour	1 lb.	_____
Shortening	1 lb.	_____
Sugar	18 oz.	_____
Eggs	13 oz.	_____
Salt	5 oz.	_____
Dry milk	8 oz.	_____
Compressed yeast	10 oz	_____
Cold water	5 lb.	_____

   Using the percentage found for each ingredient, determine the amount of each ingredient if the flour amount is changed to: bread flour 10 lb., pastry flour 2 lb.

   (b)

Ingredients	Weight
Bread flour	_____
Pastry flour	_____
Shortening	_____
Sugar	_____

Eggs   _____

Salt   _____

Dry milk   _____

Compressed yeast   _____

Cold water   _____

3. **Brown Sugar Cookies**

   (a)

Ingredients	Weight	Percentage
Pastry flour	4 lb. 8 oz.	_____
Hydrogenated shortening	2 lb. 4 oz.	_____
Whole eggs	1 lb.	_____
Brown sugar	3 lb. 2 oz.	_____
Salt	1 oz.	_____
Baking soda	$\frac{1}{2}$ oz.	_____
Vanilla	to taste	_____

   Using the percentage found for each ingredient, determine the amount of each ingredient if the flour amount is changed to 6 lb. 10 oz. Round to the nearest tenth.

   (b)

Ingredients	Weight
Pastry flour	_____
Hydrogenated shortening	_____
Whole eggs	_____
Brown sugar	_____
Salt	_____
Baking soda	_____
Vanilla	_____

DISCUSSION QUESTION 8-A

What is the purpose of using the working factor? What happens if the formula is figured incorrectly?

CHAPTER
9

Food, Recipe, and Labor Costing

OBJECTIVES

At the completion of this chapter, the student should be able to:

1. Define food costs.
2. Define labor costs.
3. Calculate the unit costs of individual items.
4. Define standard recipe.
5. Recognize the importance of A.P. versus E.P. in determining cost per ounce.
6. Calculate recipe cost charts to determine the extension costs of recipes.
7. Calculate recipe costs charts to determine the yield costs of recipes.
8. Identify and calculate the costs of labor.
9. Calculate gross and overtime wages.
10. Calculate payroll.

KEY WORDS

food costs	gross wages
labor costs	payroll
costed out	wages
shrinkage	salary
standard recipe	overtime
unit cost	hourly rate
total cost	hours worked
yield	

The price of food fluctuates, making it difficult for the food service operator to maintain a selling price for his or her food that will continue to show a profit. If a profit is not maintained, it means the owner is working for nothing and has no reason to stay in business. Ways must be found to keep up with changing prices. The answer to this problem could be to standardize and cost all recipes used in food service operations. This means staying current with the changing market prices so management will continually know the cost of the items to be sold. It is important in any business venture to *know your cost* before establishing a selling price.

In most food service operations, the two areas that incur the greatest costs are food and labor. **Food costs** are moneys spent to prepare any and all products used in an individual recipe or an entire meal. **Labor costs** are defined as the total moneys needed to pay all the employees who create, make, and serve food to the guests. The purpose of this chapter is to teach the food service professional how to recognize and calculate both food and labor costs. It is essential that the food service professional knows how to calculate the individual cost of every item that is served to guests. This is one of the most important steps to obtaining profitability in the food service business.

Andre Halston, the chief culinary officer of the 62-unit, French-themed la Madeleine restaurants, was quoted in an October 2003 interview in *Chef* magazine. Melanie Wolkoff (2003) wrote that Mr. Halston said, "You have to be great in math outside of measurements. You must be able to justify percentages, know cost, understand profit and loss, and basically all aspects of financial math" (p. 28). George Tice (2005), writing in the June 2005 *Santé* magazine, stated that "All restaurateurs would agree that controlling food costs is a primary constituent of any winning operating formula" (p. 36). At his restaurants Toulouse and Portofino, in Atlanta, Georgia, Tice has developed a method of costing out each menu item that they serve. His key to his winning formula is that he knows the exact food cost of *every item* that is served in the restaurants. He further states that, once a system is set in place to figure out food costs, menu prices can be set or adjusted.

HOW TO CALCULATE THE INDIVIDUAL OR UNIT COST OF FOOD

This is a simple mathematical operation, if two facts are known. First, the food service professional must know the size of the portion of food or beverage that will be served to the guest. Second, the cost that the establishment paid for all of the raw ingredients that are used to create the menu item has to be known. As an example, our restaurant will serve our guests an 8-ounce glass of milk (this is the first known fact). Our restaurant buys milk in half-gallon containers that cost $1.49 each (this is the second known fact). By using division and multiplication, the cost of a glass of milk in our restaurant can be determined.

Step 1: Divide the amount of ounces in the half-gallon (64) into the cost of the milk ($1.49).

$$64 \div \$1.49 = .023 \text{ cents per ounce for the milk}$$

Step 2: Multiply the size of the portion (8 ounces) by the cost per ounce of milk (0.023 cents).

$$8 \times .023 = .184$$

Each 8-ounce glass of milk that is consumed (whether it is sold or given away) costs our restaurant $0.184 cents.

For our restaurant's breakfast menu, each and every menu item would be calculated in the same manner as above. If a guest ordered a bagel, not only the cost of the bagel would have to be included, but also the cost of butter and/or cream cheese that the guest may use must be included. If a guest has a breakfast that consists of two eggs, three slices of bacon, an 8-ounce glass of milk, and the bagel, each item must be calculated (or, in the language of food service, **costed out**) individually, and then all items are added up to obtain the total raw food cost for the restaurant to serve the above breakfast.

T I P S . . .   **To Insure Perfect Solutions**

Remember that, when calculating costs, all figures should represent the same quantity; that is, pounds multiplied or divided by price per pound, ounces multiplied or divided by price per ounce, and so on.

SUMMARY REVIEW 9-1

Find the food costs of each item. The student may use knowledge learned from information in Chapters 1 to 8 in order to solve the problems. Round off each answer to the hundredth place (e.g., $0.235).

1. Two limes were purchased for $0.98. How much does one lime cost?

   _____

2. One dozen eggs were purchased for $0.89 cents. How much do three eggs cost?

   _____

3. Six baked potatoes were purchased for $3.15. How much does one potato cost?

   _____

4. Sour cream was purchased for $1.14 per pint. How much does 1 ounce cost?

   _____

5. Using the answers from questions 3 and 4, what is the cost of the baked potato if each guest is served a baked potato and 2 ounces of sour cream?

   _____

6. From your invoice, you have purchased 2.60 lbs of red grapes. The cost is $5.15. If each guest is served a garnish consisting of three grapes that weigh 2 ounces each, what is the cost of the garnish?

   _____

7. One loaf of bread was purchased for $2.89. There are 20 slices of bread in the package, but the 2 end pieces cannot be used? What is the cost of two slices of bread for an order of toast?

_____

8. The butter for the toast is purchased at $2.99 per pound. If your restaurant serves 2 ounces of butter with the toast, what is the cost of the butter?

_____

9. A package of sausage was purchased for $2.99. There are 10 links of sausage in each package. How much does one link of sausage cost?

_____

10. Using the information from questions, 2, 6, 7, 8, and 9, figure out the total cost of our gigantic breakfast if each guest receives three eggs, three pieces of sausage, four pieces of toast with 3 ounces of butter, and the plate is garnished with 8 ounces of grapes. How much is the total cost of the food for the breakfast that will be served to each guest?

_____

COSTING MEAT AND FISH PORTIONS

Meat and fish items are popular on a food service menu. They are also the most expensive. In fact, many food service establishments estimate that 25 to 35% of their food dollar goes for these two items. Therefore, the portion cost of these items must be controlled and reviewed from time to time because of fluctuating prices.

To find the cost of a portion, the total cost of the amount purchased must first be established. This is accomplished by multiplying the price per pound by the number of pounds purchased.

Price per pound × A.P. (as purchased) amount purchased = Total cost.

The amount purchased is then converted into ounces by multiplying the number of pounds purchased by 16 (16 ounces to one pound).

A.P. amount purchased × 16 = Total ounces.

The amount lost through boning, trimming, or **shrinkage** is converted into ounces and subtracted from the original amount.

Amount lost × 16 = Total ounces lost.
Total ounces purchased − total ounces lost =
E.P. (edible portion) ounces.

The actual usable amount (E.P.) is divided into the total cost (carry the division three places to the right of the decimal). This gives the cost of 1 ounce of cooked meat.

Total cost ÷ E.P. amount = Cost of 1 ounce.

The cost of 1 ounce is multiplied by the number of ounces contained in one portion.

Cost of 1 ounce × serving portion = cost of one portion.

Example: A 9-pound leg of lamb costs $4.85 per pound. A total of 15 ounces is lost in boning and trimming, and 1 pound 8 ounces through shrinkage, during the roasting period. How much does a 3-ounce serving cost?

$ 4.85	Price per pound
× 9	Pounds purchased (A.P.)
$43.65	Total cost

16	Ounces in 1 pound
× 9	Number of pounds purchased
144	Number of ounces purchased

144	Number of ounces purchased
− 39	Number of ounces lost
105	Number of E.P. ounces

$$\begin{array}{r} 0.415 \\ \text{E.P. ounces } 105\overline{)43.650} \\ 420 \\ \hline 165 \\ 105 \\ \hline 600 \\ 525 \\ \hline \end{array}$$

Cost of 1 ounce of cooked meat
Total cost

$0.415	Cost of 1 ounce
× 3	Ounce serving portion
$1.245	Cost of each 3-ounce serving of roast lamb
$ 1.25	Cost of each 3-ounce serving of roast lamb

Once the actual cost of a serving is established, it is easy to determine a selling price by adding on the amount of markup.

T I P S . . . .   To Insure Perfect Solutions

It would be profitable for the chef or manager to round up when calculating food cost.

SUMMARY REVIEW 9–2

Round up to the higher cent, if the answer is not exact.

1. If a 24-pound (A.P.) leg of veal costs $8.50 per pound, and 5 pounds 6 ounces are lost through trimming and boning, how much does a 5-ounce veal cutlet cost?

2. A 24-pound (A.P.) rib of beef costs $2.85 per pound. Four pounds are lost through trimming, and $\frac{1}{4}$ of the remaining weight is lost through shrinkage when it is roasted. How much does a 6-ounce serving cost?

_____

3. A 50-pound (A.P.) round roast costs $92.50. Five pounds are lost through trimming, and 5 pounds through shrinkage, when it is roasted. How much does 1 pound of cooked meat cost?

_____

4. A 6-pound 6-ounce (A.P.) beef tenderloin costs $90.00. One pound 5 ounces are lost through trimming. How much does an 8-ounce filet mignon cost?

_____

5. If a 20-pound (E.P.) rib of beef costing $45.00 is purchased oven-ready, and $\frac{1}{4}$ of it is lost during roasting, how much does a 6-ounce serving cost?

_____

6. A 9-pound (E.P.) leg of lamb costing $4.85 per pound is roasted. When the roast is removed from the oven, only $\frac{2}{3}$ of the original amount is left. How much does a $3\frac{1}{2}$-ounce serving cost?

_____

7. Roast sirloin of beef is served to a party. Each sirloin weighs 16 pounds (E.P.) and costs $5.90 per pound. If 17 portions are cut from each sirloin, what is the cost per serving?

_____

8. A 10-pound (E.P.) box of halibut steaks is ordered costing $4.65 per pound. If each steak weighs 5 ounces, what is the cost of each steak?

_____

9. A 13-pound pork loin costs $2.92 per pound. A 10-ounce tenderloin is removed from the loin, and 2 pounds 2 ounces are lost through boning and trimming. How much does a 4-ounce chop cost?

_____

10. A 9-pound (A.P.) saddle of lamb costs $5.62 per pound. Twelve ounces are lost through trimming. How much does a 4-ounce chop cost?

_____

DISCUSSION QUESTION 9–A

The Importance of Determining and Using E.P Versus A.P. to Cost Out Recipes Many food service professionals do not take the time to do a butcher test or a yield test to determine the amount of ounces that are lost to boning and shrinkage. Both of these tests take time and accuracy to complete and record the results. Those food service operations that conduct and record the results of the tests and then figure out the actual cost of the portion size will be able to price their menu items accurately and make money, instead of losing money because a step was skipped and E.P was not figured. The following example will illustrate this point.

A restaurant buys a 24-pound (A.P.) rib of beef. The price per pound of the beef is $9.50. The total cost of this piece of meat is $228.00 (24 × 9.50). If our lazy food service professional figured out the cost of 1 ounce of beef, he would arrive at a cost of $0.59375. He determined, in this manner, that 24 pounds times 16 ounces results in 384 ounces of beef. The 384 ounces of beef are divided into the $228 cost of the rib of beef.

In reality, when the cook prepares the beef, 4 pounds (or 64 ounces) are lost through boning and trimming (determined by a butcher test). This leaves the rib weighing 320 ounces. The cook seasons and puts the roast into the oven, and when it is done cooking, it is weighed. During the cooking process, the roast loses 25% of its weight (320 ounces minus 25% of 320), or another 80 ounces. Now the cooked rib weighs 240 ounces (320 − 80). The math is calculated by the food service professional, and it is determined that 1 ounce of beef costs $0.95.

Our lazy food service professional serves three hundred 8-ounce portions of beef each night. He thinks that it costs him $4.75 (8 × 0.59375). Actually, it costs him $7.60 (8 × 0.95). What may happen to the lazy food service professional's business?

THE STANDARD RECIPE

A **standard recipe** is one that will produce the same amount, quality, and taste of each menu item each time it is prepared. If consistency is a factor in the recipe, that too will be the same. The standard recipe provides assurance that the preparation will not fluctuate from one day to the next, regardless of who is preparing the food. If the recipe is followed correctly, quality is maintained. This type of recipe is ideal for food preparation in schools, hospitals, nursing homes, retirement villages, in-plant food service, and other similar institutions, as well as in restaurants.

Figuring the Cost of the Standard Recipe

When figuring the cost of a standard recipe, the cost of each ingredient that goes into the preparation is totaled and a per-unit cost is calculated. (See Figure 9–1.) For example, when preparing a recipe that yields 50 servings, the cost of all the ingredients used in making these 50 servings are added together to obtain the complete cost of the preparation. The total cost of the preparation is then divided by 50 (the yield) to find the unit cost. The **unit cost** represents what one serving of this particular item costs to prepare. With this knowledge, the manager or food and beverage controller can establish a menu price. The formula for finding the unit cost is:

Total Cost ÷ Yield = Unit Cost.

Hungarian Beef Goulash		Approximate Yield: 50–6-ounce servings	
Ingredients	Amount	Market Price	Extension Cost
Beef Chuck E.P.	18 lb.	$2.25 per lb.	$40.50
Garlic, Minced	1 oz.	$2.52 per lb.	0.158
Flour	8 oz.	0.18 per lb.	0.09
Chili Powder	$\frac{3}{4}$ oz.	3.65 per lb.	0.171
Paprika	5 oz.	4.50 per lb.	1.406
Tomato Puree	1 qt.	1.88 per gal.	0.47
Water	8 lb.	—	—
Bay Leaves	2	—	—
Caraway Seeds	$\frac{1}{2}$ oz.	5.72 per lb.	0.179
Onions, Minced	2 lb.	0.75 per lb.	1.50
Salt	1 oz.	0.42 per lb.	0.026
Pepper	$\frac{1}{4}$ oz.	5.18 per lb.	0.081
		Total Cost	$44.581
		Cost Per Serving	.892

Figure 9–1 *Standardized recipe—costs included*

The form used to record the cost of a certain recipe may differ, depending on the food service establishment. However, they all usually supply the same information: the exact cost to produce one serving. Of course, in order to obtain the proper yield and determine the correct unit cost, all servings must be uniform. (See Figure 9–2.)

A typical standardized recipe showing the market price of each ingredient, the extension cost, total cost, and unit cost per serving is provided in Figure 9–1. An explanation of the standardized recipe shown in this figure follows.

The first column in Figure 9–1 lists all the ingredients used in the preparation of this dish—in this case, Hungarian beef goulash.

The second column lists the amount of each ingredient needed to prepare fifty 6-ounce servings.

The third column lists the current market price of each ingredient. These prices must be watched carefully because they fluctuate (go up and down) from time to time. The price is listed in quantities that are usually quoted by the vendor. For example, meat is always purchased by the pound, eggs by the dozen, milk by the gallon, and so forth.

The fourth column in Figure 9–1 is the extension cost of the quantity listed. This figure is found by multiplying the amount of the ingredient by the market price. Remember that when multiplying, both figures should represent the same quantity. That is, pounds multiplied by price per pound, ounces multiplied by price per ounce, and so on.

The following information explains how the cost was determined for one serving of Hungarian beef goulash.

The market price of beef chuck is $2.25 per lb. (pound) E.P. The amount is also in pounds (18). Since both the amount and market price are represented by the same quantity (in this case, pounds), the extension cost of $40.50 was determined by multiplying the amount (18) by the market price ($2.25).

The next ingredient, minced garlic, shows the amount and market price represented by different quantities—the amount in ounces and the market price in pounds. To determine the extension cost, a series of small

Figure 9–2 *Uniform size allows the food service employee to determine the proper yield and unit costs.*

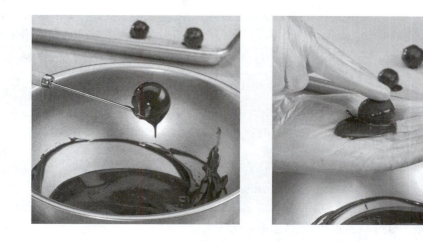

steps must be performed. First, convert the market price to a cost per ounce. The garlic costs $2.52 per pound. Divide $2.52 by 16 (the number of ounces in a pound), which equals $0.1575. This is the cost of 1 ounce of garlic. (Note: the answer has *not been* rounded off.) Since both the amount and market price are in like quantities (ounces), the extension cost can be figured out. The next step is to multiply the $0.1575 (cost of 1 ounce) by 1 (amount of ounces that the recipe requires), which equals $0.1575. Because we round off to the mill, the extension cost of 1 ounce of garlic is $0.158.

Flour, chili powder, paprika, tomato puree, caraway seeds, onions, salt, and pepper also have the amount and market price represented by different quantities. Before extension costs can be calculated for these ingredients, the amount and market price have to be converted to the same quantities (ounces). All of the extension costs for these ingredients, except for the tomato puree, can be calculated by following the steps in the previous paragraph.

Tomato puree is slightly different. The amount is represented in quarts and the market price is represented in gallons; therefore, both must be converted into like amounts. There are three quantities that gallons and quarts can be converted into: quarts, gallons, or ounces.

For example, the market price can be converted into a price per quart. There are 4 quarts in a gallon. Therefore, the market price of $1.88 per gallon is divided by the amount of quarts in a gallon (4). This equals $0.47 per quart.

Or, one quart is equal to a $\frac{1}{4}$ (.25) of a gallon. To determine the cost of the tomato puree, 0.25 is multiplied by $1.88, which equals $0.47.

Finally, both the market price and the amount can be converted to ounces. There are 128 ounces in a gallon. The cost of a gallon, $1.88, is

		YIELD		Fruit Sauce (Hot)			
	Port	Oz.	Port	Oz.	Port	Oz.	
Ingredients	**25**	**2**	**100**	**2**			**Method**
Orange Juice	2 cups		2 qts.				1. Combine first eight ingredients. Bring to a boil.
Pineapple Juice	2 cups		2 qts.				
Water	$\frac{3}{4}$ cup		3 cups				2. Dissolve cornstarch in cold water.
Cloves, whole	2 ea.		4 ea.				
Lemon Juice	1 Tbsp.		$\frac{1}{4}$ cup				3. Add to hot mixture, cook over low heat until thick and clear. Hold hot in bain-marie. Taste.
Salt	$\frac{1}{2}$ tsp.		2 tsp.				
Granulated Sugar	12 oz.		3 lbs.				
Fruit Cocktail (drained)	8 oz.		2 lbs.				
Cold Water	$\frac{3}{4}$ cup		3 cups				*Note: Serve with Baked Ham, Canadian Bacon, Chicken*
Cornstarch	$2\frac{1}{2}$ oz.		10 oz.				
Yield:	$1\frac{3}{4}$ qt.		$1\frac{3}{4}$ gal.				

Cooking Equipment: Sauce pan, stock pot	**Service Equipment:** 2 oz. ladle	**Garnish:**
Temperature: 160°F	**Color:** Multicolor	**Date:**

Figure 9–3 *Standardized recipe—costs not included*

divided by 128 (amount of ounces in a gallon), which equals $0.0146875. This is the cost of 1 ounce of tomato puree. That cost of $0.0146875 is multiplied by the ounces in a quart (32). This results in a cost of $0.47.

In calculating costs, the authors have demonstrated that the three methods used above all result in the same answer. We used different methods to determine the correct answer. The one constant was that the amount and market price were represented in like quantities.

Once all of the extension costs have been calculated, the column is added to determine the total cost of the recipe.

To find the cost per serving, divide the total cost by the number of servings the recipe will yield. In this case, the yield is 50, so 50 is divided into $44.581 to get $0.892, which is the cost of each serving. (Note: prices have been carried to the mill, three places to the right of the decimal.)

In this type of standard recipe, where market price and extension cost are stated, the procedure or method of preparation is listed on the back of the card. This is done so that the card can be kept to a size that is easy to file. Other standard recipes that do not list market price and extension cost (the total cost of each ingredient used in the preparation) have the procedure or method of preparation listed on the face of the recipe. (See Figure 9–3.) In some kitchens, standardized recipes are stored and printed from software on a computer.

SUMMARY REVIEW 9-3

Complete the following recipe cost charts to determine the extension costs. When calculating the cost per ounce, per pound, etc., do not round off at this point. Carry the price three places to the right of the decimal when calculating the extension cost, the total cost, and the cost per serving.

1. **Braised Swiss Steak**   Yield 50 servings

Ingredients	Amount	Price	Extension Cost
6 oz. Round Steak E.P.	50 ea.	2.25 per lb.	_____
Onions	12 oz.	0.75 per lb.	_____
Garlic	1 oz.	2.52 per lb.	_____
Tomato Puree	1 pt.	1.88 per gal.	_____
Brown Stock	6 qt.	1.25 per gal.	_____
Salad Oil	3 cups	6.57 per gal.	_____
Bread Flour	12 oz.	0.18 per lb.	_____
Salt	$\frac{3}{4}$ oz.	0.42 per lb.	_____
		Total Cost	_____
		Cost per Serving	_____

2. **Salisbury Steak**   Yield 50 servings

Ingredients	Amount	Price	Extension Cost
Beef Chuck E.P.	14 lb.	$2.25 per lb.	_____
Onions	3 lb.	0.75 per lb.	_____
Garlic	$\frac{1}{2}$ oz.	2.52 per lb.	_____
Salad Oil	$\frac{1}{2}$ cup	6.57 per gal.	_____
Bread Cubes	2 lb.	0.65 per lb.	_____
Milk	$1\frac{1}{2}$ pt.	2.18 per gal.	_____
Whole Eggs	8	0.89 per doz.	_____
Pepper	$\frac{1}{4}$ oz.	5.18 per lb.	_____
Salt	1 oz.	0.42 per lb.	_____
		Total Cost	_____
		Cost per Serving	_____

3. **Buttermilk Biscuits**   Yield
                                        6 dozen = 72 biscuits

Ingredients	Amount	Price	Extension Cost
Cake Flour	1 lb. 8 oz.	0.25 per lb.	_____
Bread Flour	1 lb. 8 oz.	0.18 per lb.	_____
Baking Powder	$3\frac{1}{2}$ oz.	1.68 per lb.	_____
Salt	$\frac{1}{2}$ oz.	0.42 per lb.	_____
Sugar	4 oz.	0.36 per lb.	_____
Butter	12 oz.	1.26 per lb.	_____
Buttermilk	2 lb. 4 oz.	1.23 per qt.	_____
		Total Cost	_____
		Cost per Dozen	_____
		Cost per Biscuit	_____

4. **Brown Sugar Cookie**

Yield
14 dozen = 168 cookies

Ingredients	Amount	Price	Extension Cost
Brown Sugar	3 lb. 2 oz.	0.38 per lb.	_____
Shortening	2 lb. 4 oz.	0.48 per lb.	_____
Salt	1 oz.	0.42 per lb.	_____
Baking Soda	$\frac{1}{2}$ oz.	0.44 per lb.	_____
Pastry Flour	4 lb. 8 oz.	0.20 per lb.	_____
Whole Eggs	9	0.89 per doz.	_____
Vanilla	$\frac{1}{4}$ oz.	1.77 per qt.	_____
		Total Cost	_____
		Cost per Dozen	_____
		Cost per Cookie	_____

5. **Soft Dinner Rolls**

Yield
16 dozen = 192 rolls

Ingredients	Amount	Price	Extension Cost
Sugar	1 lb.	$0.36 per lb.	_____
Shortening	1 lb. 4 oz.	0.48 per lb.	_____
Dry Milk	8 oz.	1.93 per lb.	_____
Salt	2 oz.	0.42 per lb.	_____
Whole Eggs	3	0.98 per doz.	_____
Yeast	6 oz.	3.27 per lb.	_____
Water	4 lb.	—	_____
Bread Flour	7 lb.	0.18 per lb.	_____
		Total Cost	_____
		Cost per Dozen	_____
		Cost per Roll	_____

Chef Sez...

"Precost every penny before it goes on the menu."

Fritz Sonnenschmidt
Certified Master Chef, Past Chairman of the American Academy of Chefs Ambassador, Culinary Institute of America Hyde Park, NY

Fritz Sonnenschmidt is one of less than 60 certified master chefs in the United States. In order to become certified, an individual must pass a complicated test of both practical and written work. Also, Chef Sonnenschmidt was the American Culinary Federation 1994 Chef of the Year. This award was created in 1963 to pay tribute to that active member whose culinary expertise and exemplary dedication have enhanced the image of the chef and his or her professional association; who commands the respect of his or her own peers because of character and performance; and whose accomplishments have been of benefit to the American Culinary Federation.

The Cost of Labor and Types of Payment

Food service establishments must pay employees for the work that is done to do business with the goal of making a profit. The cost of labor has to be controlled, just as food costs are controlled. Management must have enough staff to meet the demands of the business, but not too much staff as to create a situation where money is being paid to employees when there is no work for them to do. Employees are paid in a variety of ways. One method is by paying them an hourly wage. Another method is to pay them a salary. Some establishments pay a salary plus a commission. Some businesses pay an employee a flat rate for a day or a party. As long as laws or union contracts are not broken, any method of paying employees is acceptable. In some food service establishments, overtime is paid at the rate of one and a half times the hourly rate. Other businesses pay a bonus for working holidays. Some establishments pay double the hourly rate for certain events. Whatever method is used, the **gross wages** (pay before any deductions are taken from the employee's wages) should be used to figure out the labor cost of the establishment. This labor cost is calculated in every pay period and recorded as **payroll.**

Payroll

A **payroll** is a record of earnings kept by the employer on all persons classified as employees. The employer is required by law to record and maintain complete, up-to-date, accurate records on all employees. How this information is recorded and maintained is up to the employer. In a small operation, they may be kept up to date by an individual bookkeeper, controller, or accountant using customary office machines. Or the operation may hire a bank or company that offers a payroll service for a fee that is based on the number of employees on the payroll. In a large or chain operation, a computer would be used. Forms and methods used in compiling a payroll will vary from company to company and even from state to state. State laws and company policy differ in certain areas.

Wages refer to a payment made for a service rendered, usually referring to payment for total hours of work at a designated hourly rate. When a person accepts employment by a company, an agreement is made on wages. The wages will be based on a specific amount for each hour worked.

When the term **salary** is used, it usually refers to payment set for a week, month, or year. When payment is based on salary, the work may exceed 8 hours a day or 40 hours a week.

When an employee is paid on an hourly basis, a definite amount of money is paid for each hour worked. The total number of hours scheduled to work each day may be 8, or 40 for a week. These are called regular hours. Hours worked over these regular hours are called **overtime** hours. In accordance with federal wage and hour laws, companies that engage in interstate commerce or companies that have union contracts with an overtime clause must pay overtime at a rate of time and a half for work over 8 hours a day or 40 hours a week. Some union contracts specify that when an employee works on certain days, such as Sundays and holidays, they receive *double time.* That is, the employee is paid two times his or her regular rate of pay for each hour worked.

Figure 9–4 *Time card*

```
 5 MALTSEV, SERGEY
 TIMECARD # 2                    PAGE  1
 - - - - - - - - - - - - - - - - - - - - - - - -
 IN/OUT   TIME    #HRS DAY/PERIOD

 1 IN  MON FEB21 10:26AM
        5/1 SERVER
 1 OUT MON FEB21 02:32PM
        5                 4.10/4.10
```

The hours that an employee works are usually recorded on a *time card,* which is punched on a *time clock* when the employee reports to work, and again when he or she leaves for the day. (See Figure 9–4.) When a time clock is used, the company will have a set policy on time limits for punching in and out before a penalty is imposed. Another method of recording employees' hours worked is by computer. The employee punches a certain number assigned to him or her when arriving and leaving work, and the computer records the time.

Calculating Gross Wages

To compute an employee's wage, the hourly rate of pay is multiplied by the number of hours worked.

Hourly rate × hours worked = Gross pay.

For example:

Thomas Payne is paid $9.75 per hour. He works a regular 40-hour week. To calculate his gross pay for one week:

$$40 \times \$9.75 = \$390.00$$

$$\begin{array}{rl} \$9.75 & \text{per hour worked} \\ \times\ 40 & \text{hours worked} \\ \hline \$390.00 & \text{Gross pay} \end{array}$$

When overtime is involved, gross pay can be calculated in two ways but with the same results:

1. Multiply the number of hours over the regular work time of 40 hours by $1\frac{1}{2}$ (for time and a half) or by 2 (for double time). Multiply this result by the hourly rate. Add the overtime pay to regular pay.

   Overtime hours $\times 1\frac{1}{2}$ = Total regular hours
   Total regular hours $\times$ hourly rate = Overtime pay
   Overtime pay + regular 40 hours pay = Gross wages

For example:

Tim Macke earns $9.00 per hour for a regular work week of 40 hours with overtime pay at time and a half. To calculate his gross wages for a week in which he worked 48 hours:

Overtime hours $8 \times 1\frac{1}{2} = 12$ regular hours
$12 \times \$9.00$ hourly rate $= \$108$ overtime pay

Overtime pay	$108.00
Regular pay (40 × $9.00)	+ 360.00
Gross wages	$468.00

or

2. Multiply the hourly rate by $1\frac{1}{2}$ or 2 = overtime rate. Then multiply the number of hours over 40 (regular time) by the overtime rate = overtime pay. Add overtime pay to regular pay = gross pay.

Hourly rate × 1.5 = Overtime rate
Overtime rate × overtime hours = Overtime pay
Overtime pay + regular pay = Gross pay

For example (using the same problem as example number 1):

$9.00 hours rate × 1.5 = $13.50 overtime rate
$13.50 × 8 overtime hours = $108.00 overtime pay

Overtime wages	$108.00
Regular wages (40 × $9)	+ 360.00
Gross wages	$468.00

In comparing the two methods of calculating overtime pay, you will notice that the results are the same and that only the method used differs.

Calculating the Daily and/or Weekly Payroll

To control the cost of labor, food service managers would be wise to know exactly how much they are paying the employees on an hourly, daily, and weekly basis. Just as the food service manager calculates the cost of food, the labor cost is calculated with basic mathematical operations: multiplication, division, and addition.

If an employee is receiving $11.00 per hour, to find the total daily cost the manager multiples the amount of hours times the rate per hour. The hourly cost for this employee is $11.00. During the week, the employee worked 40 hours. The amount of money paid to the employee would be calculated as: the number of hours worked (40) times the rate of pay ($11.00). This employee would cost the establishment $440 for the week.

Our chef receives a salary of $75,000 a year. To determine the cost of a salaried employee, the food service manager divides the salary by the number of weeks in the year. This problem is calculated in the following manner: $75,000 ÷ 52 = $1,442.3076 cents per week.

To determine the cost of our weekly payroll, the amount paid for all employees is added together. In this example, the $440 and the $1,442.3076 results in a total of $1,882.3076 that the establishment had to pay out in wages this week. Depending on the size of the staff, the food service manager would calculate the wages paid to all employees for the day and the week. This step is basic and must be done to control the cost of labor.

SUMMARY REVIEW 9–4

1. Bill Miller, a cook at the Blue Boar Restaurant, earns $9.50 per hour for a 40-hour week, with time and a half for all hours worked over 40 hours per week. This past week he worked a total of 46 hours. What was his gross wage for the week?

_____

2. Faiza Khan, a fry cook at the Conservatory Restaurant, works on a 40-hour-a-week basis, with time and a half for all overtime. Her regular hourly rate of pay is $8.75. Last week, she worked a total of 49 hours. What was her gross wage for the week?

_____

3. Gloria Luran, a salad person at Lang's Cafeteria, works on an eight-hour-per-day basis, plus time and a half for time worked over eight hours in any one day. Her regular hourly rate of pay is $6.50 per hour. This past week, her time card recorded the following hours:

S	M	T	W	TH	F	S
12	9	8.5	8	10		

What was her gross wage for the week?

_____

4. Mario Astor, the sauce cook at the Metropole Hotel, worked a total of $49\frac{1}{2}$ hours during a recent week. He is paid $12.25 per hour, plus time and a half for all hours over 40 hours per week. What was his gross wage for the week?

_____

5. Jacob Rowe, a salad person at the Gibson Hotel, worked seven consecutive days, eight hours a day, from Monday through Sunday. His regular pay rate is $7.25 per hour. The hotel pays time and a half for all hours worked on Saturday, and double time for all hours worked on Sunday. What was his gross wage for this period of work?

_____

6. Chef Monique Estranza receives a salary of $90,000 annually. What is her weekly gross pay?

_____

7. The Chardonnay Café employs 12 waitstaff who each earn $6.50 per hour. During the week, they each work five 6-hour shifts. What is the cost of labor for the waitstaff?

_____

8. The Chardonnay Café employs 6 culinary staff who each earn $10.50 per hour. During the week, they each work five 8-hour shifts. What is the cost of labor for the culinary staff?

_____

9. The Chardonnay Café employs 4 dishwashers who each earn $6.50 per hour. During the week, they each work five 8-hour shifts. What is the cost of labor for the dishwashers?

_____

10. Using questions 1 to 9, determine the total payroll that was paid.

_____

REFERENCES

Tice, George. (2005, June). Plate cost analysis. _Santé,_ 9(4), 36.

Wolkoff, Melanie. (2003, October). Corporate calling. _Chef,_ 13(10), 28.

PART IV

MATH ESSENTIALS IN FOOD SERVICE RECORD KEEPING

CHAPTER 10 • Determining Cost Percentages and Pricing the Menu

CHAPTER 11 • Inventory Procedures

CHAPTER 12 • Purchasing and Receiving

CHAPTER 13 • Daily Production Reports

Chapters 10 through 13 will focus on controlling costs for the purpose of making a profit. Food service operations that are successful develop and use formulas and different types of reports to control food costs. The information and problems presented in all four chapters are essential for the food service professional to understand and know how to use in order to have a successful business.

Chapter 10 explains how a food service professional determines food cost percentages and what they mean. This chapter also gives strategies for pricing the menu. Chapter 11 explains the importance of keeping track of inventory; failure to do so can mean the loss of revenue and customers. In Chapter 12, the authors emphasize the importance of proper purchasing and receiving techniques. Chapter 13 highlights the ways food service establishments determine how to produce the correct amount of food and track what food has been sold.

Most of the information that will be learned in Part IV is now entered and controlled using computer software programs. The material is presented in the simplest form to convey how this information is acquired and recorded. Once students master Part IV, they can transfer this knowledge of record keeping to computer software. This book does not teach the student how to use any computer software; the authors recommend that students learn about computer software after mastering these basic skills of food service record keeping.

The chapters in this part of the book explain how and why functions such as determining cost percentages, pricing the menu, inventory, purchasing, and keeping accurate records are vital to the success of a food service operation.

Part V of this text will consist of more managerial tasks for determining the profitability of a food service operation.

CHAPTER 10

Determining Cost Percentages and Pricing the Menu

OBJECTIVES

At the completion of this chapter, the student should be able to:

1. Define food cost.
2. Define labor cost.
3. Explain the purpose of food cost percentages.
4. Explain the purpose of labor cost percentages.
5. Calculate food cost percentages.
6. Calculate labor cost percentages.
7. Calculate the daily sales of an establishment.
8. Calculate the daily food cost of an establishment.
9. Calculate the daily labor cost of an establishment.
10. Identify the strategies to determine menu prices.
11. Find the menu price using the markup strategy.
12. Find the menu price using the food cost percent method.
13. Find the food cost, food cost percent, or sales price using the Chef's Magic Circle.

KEY WORDS

daily food cost report	labor cost percentages
storeroom requisition	menu
direct purchases	markup
total sales	raw food cost
customer count	food cost percent
amount of average sales	menu or selling price
food cost percentages	multiplier effect

Purpose of Food and Labor Cost Percentages

As was stated in the last chapter, the two areas that incur the most costs are food and labor in most food service establishments. **Food costs** are the moneys spent to prepare any and all products used in an individual recipe or an entire meal. **Labor costs** are defined as the total moneys needed to pay all the required employees to create, make, and serve food to the guests. The purpose of this chapter will be to teach the food service professional how to recognize and calculate both food and

179

	June	July
Total Sales for the month	$40,000	$55,000
Raw Cost of food for the month	$11,000	$11,000
Food Cost Percentage for the month	27.5%	20%
Raw Cost of labor for the month	$14,000	$14,000
Labor Cost Percentage for the month	35%	25.5%

Figure 10–1 *Illustration of food and labor cost percentages for the months of June and July*

labor cost percentages. It is essential that the food service professional know how to calculate the food and labor cost percentages and know how to calculate the individual cost of every item that is served to guests.

Every food service operation should set a goal to determine how much money should be spent on buying food and providing labor for the food service establishment. Because of the great fluctuation in the volume of food sales, it is impractical to state this goal in a dollar amount, such as $6,000 each month. One month the sales could be $40,000, while another month they may be only $3,000. Therefore, it is impractical to use a dollar figure because food service professionals would have a hard time understanding whether $10,800, $9,000, or $910.00 is a reasonable amount to spend on buying food. Instead, food service professionals use percentages to help them control and understand food costs. For example, a pizza operation sets a monthly food cost percentage goal of 27%. Regardless of how many pizzas are sold in that month, the raw cost of the food to prepare all the pizzas sold should be 27% of the amount of money received in sales dollars. If the number is lower than 27%, it could be that the cost of cheese has gone down. If the number is higher than the goal, it could be that an employee is giving away free pizzas to friends. There can be many reasons for the fluctuation in the food cost percentage. A manager knows that if the cost does not equal the goal, then an investigation must take place to determine why the cost is different from the goal. The manager can use the same concept in determining the ideal labor cost percentage needed to provide staff to operate the business.

To explain and illustrate the value of the concept of food and labor cost percentages, the following example is given. The manager receives a monthly printout stating the amount of raw food and raw labor cost. The cost of food was $11,000 and the cost of labor was $14,000. Do these numbers mean anything to the food service professional? Yes, they are numbers, and yes, a lot of money was spent. The food service operation's goal is to have a raw food cost of 27% and a labor cost of 30% at the end of the month. Figure 10–1 illustrates the value of using food and labor cost percentages for the months of June and July.

From the chart, the food service professional can see that using percentages for food and labor costs gives meaningful figures. In June, the cost of food was 27.5%, or 27 and a half cents of each dollar earned in sales. In July, our sales went up, and the costs of both food and labor were reduced. In other words, the food service manager observes that, in July, only 45.5 cents were spent on food and labor, compared to 62.5 cents in June, making July a more profitable month.

Meaning of Food and Labor Cost Percentages

Food cost percentage is the cost of the food as it relates to the amount of dollars received in sales. **Labor cost percentage** is the cost of labor as it relates to the amount of dollars received in sales. In the previous section, we stated that our goals for our pizza shop were to have a food cost percentage of 27% and a labor cost percentage of 30%. This means that for every $1.00 charged for a cheese pizza, it costs $0.27 for the food to make that cheese pizza. So if our pizza shop sells the pizza to the customer for $5.00, we should pay 27% of $5.00, or $1.35, for the cost of food.

To further explain this, refer back to Figure 10–1. These percentage figures represent numbers that are now quickly understood by the food service professional. In the month of June, for every $1.00 that was collected in sales, $0.275 were used to pay for food and $0.35 were paid for labor, totaling $0.625. There will still be money leftover to pay other bills and make a profit. In July, because sales were higher, our costs dropped and the business was more profitable.

Using and understanding percentages assists food service professionals in setting menu prices and managing their businesses. If the price of cheese rises and the pizza shop owner gives the staff a raise, the percentages of both food and labor will go up, leaving less money for profit.

FOOD AND LABOR COSTING

As stated previously, in any food service operation, the two biggest expenditures are the cost of food and labor. If the operation is to have any chance for success, these two items must be controlled. It is not an easy task, because it seems that both are constantly rising. One of the tools that is used to control the cost and use of food is the **daily food cost report**, the purpose of which is to show management the exact cost and amount of food used on any given day. This report is a guide that keeps the manager aware of costs, thus helping to control the cost of food being used in the establishment. The high cost of food, waste, and theft by employees make it essential that tight controls be maintained on the items that can lead a food service operation to bankruptcy. The same process should be used to keep track of the daily cost of labor. A **daily labor cost report** should be generated each day for the manager's review.

The daily food cost report also helps to provide a more accurate picture of the food service operation's monthly food cost pattern. That is, if the planned monthly food cost percent is set at a certain rate to ensure a profitable operation, and each day this rate is exceeded, something is not right. It would therefore be apparent to management that all factors, such as portion size, waste, theft, and food production, must be investigated to find the cause.

There are several kinds of food cost reports in use. The simplified type is made up from the totals of storeroom requisitions and direct purchases for the day. (See Figure 10–2.)

A **storeroom requisition** is a list of food items issued from the storeroom upon the request of the production crew. These may be requests for certain meats, other groceries, canned foods, or frozen foods. The requisitions are priced and extended at the end of each day. The unit prices are usually marked on all storeroom items as they are received, or they may be stored on a computer. This way, the requisitioned foods can be priced immediately. **Direct purchases** are those foods that are usually purchased each day or every other day. They include produce, dairy products, fresh seafood, bread, rolls, and any other items that are considered perishable. The total for direct purchases can be obtained from the **invoice** (a list of goods sent to the purchaser with their prices and quantities listed), which is sent with each order.

| Customer Count | 300 | | Date | January 15, 20 |
| Average Sale | $1.20 | | Day | Thursday |

Issues	Today	To Date	Last Month To Date
Storeroom			
Canned Goods	$ 25.50	$ 100.50	$ 95.25
Other Groceries	15.60	46.25	43.50
Meat	35.25	225.50	222.30
Frozen Foods	10.60	30.40	25.50
Direct Purchases			
Poultry, fresh	20.15	75.30	74.35
Seafood, fresh	21.30	58.60	57.60
Produce	8.00	39.25	35.20
Dairy Products	6.00	25.00	20.70
Bread and Rolls	5.00	20.35	18.40
Miscellaneous	4.00	10.50	10.45
Total Cost	$151.40	$ 631.65	$ 603.25
Total Sales	$360.00	$1,500.00	$1,400.00
Food Cost Percent	42.1%	42.1%	43.1%

Figure 10–2 *Daily food cost report*

A raw labor cost report is generated daily using the same method as the daily food cost report. The manager is given a report that shows how much is spent on wages each day for all employees. The report can be set up in categories of management, waitstaff, cooks, dishwashers' and so forth. Each operation should set up its own type of report, but the key fact that must be known is how much money was paid in wages daily.

Finding the Total Sales

In Figure 10–2, the total sales for the day is $360. This figure is found by totaling the register sales for the day. The figure can be checked by multiplying the average sales by the customer count.

Average Sales × Customer Count = Total Sales.

$$\begin{array}{rl} \$1.20 & \text{Average Sales} \\ \underline{\times 300} & \text{Customer Count} \\ \$360.00 & \text{Total Sales} \end{array}$$

Finding the Amount of Average Sale

The customer count is obtained by checking the register, which records the total number of customers as sales are rung up. The amount of average sales for the day is found by dividing the customer count into the total sales.

Total Sales ÷ Customer Count = Amount of Average Sales.

$$\begin{array}{r} \$1.20 \quad \text{Average Sales} \\ \text{Customer Count} \quad 300)\overline{\$360.00} \quad \text{Total Sales} \\ \underline{300} \\ 600 \\ \underline{600} \end{array}$$

Finding the Food and Labor Cost Percent

To find the food cost for a restaurant. The manager must add together the cost of all items issued for the day's food production (see Figure 10–2). If the total cost of food for the day is $151.40 and the sales for the day is $360, the food cost percentage is 42.1%.

$$\text{Cost of Food} \div \text{Total Sales} = \text{Food Cost Percent}$$

<pre>
                   .4205 equals 42.1%   Food Cost Percentage
Total Sales $360)151.4000   Cost of Food
               144 0
                 7 40
                 7 20
                  2000
                  1800
                   200
</pre>

To calculate the labor cost for a food service operation. The manager must add together the cost of all wages paid for the day. If the total cost of the wages is $90 and the sales for the day is $360, the labor cost percentage is 25%.

$$\text{Cost of Labor} \div \text{Total Sales} = \text{Labor Cost Percent}$$

<pre>
                   .25 equals 25%   Labor Cost Percentage
Total Sales $360)90.00   Daily Cost of Labor
               −720
               1800
              −1800
                000
</pre>

To find the individual menu item's food cost percentage. The food service professional must know the exact cost of the food needed to produce the menu item and the price of the menu item. The Scrimshaw Restaurant at the Desmond Hotel (see Figure 10–4) lists the price of New England clam chowder as $4.00. The Desmond's chef calculates the exact cost of the recipe for the chowder, and it comes to $0.50 for one portion. To calculate the individual clam chowder's food cost, the following is done: divide the menu price by the cost of the food to prepare the clam chowder.

<pre>
                      .125 = 12.5%   Food Cost Percentage
Menu price $4.00).50.000   Cost of the clam
                     −40 0   chowder ingredients
                     10 00
                     −8 00
                     2 000
                    −2 000
</pre>

It is recommended that all menu items be calculated to determine the individual food cost. This will greatly assist management to determine what items should be on the menu and what items should be removed, or if prices of the items should be increased or decreased.

In addition to the daily food and labor cost percents, some daily reports also show the increasing totals for the month and the totals of the previous month to date. By including this information, the owner or manager has a clearer picture of the food cost pattern.

SUMMARY REVIEW 10–1

For the following daily food cost reports, find:

- Total cost of food for today, to date, and last month to date.
- Total sales for today.
- Food cost percent today, to date, and last month to date.

1.

Customer Count	390	Date	July 15, 20
Average Sale	$1.45	Day	Monday

Issues	Today	To Date	Last Month To Date
Storeroom			
Canned Goods	$24.30	$ 106.55	$ 98.40
Other Groceries	17.80	40.50	42.20
Meat	47.25	325.50	312.30
Frozen Foods	9.50	25.22	23.60
Direct Purchases			
Poultry, fresh	18.15	75.45	72.53
Seafood, fresh	20.35	52.60	48.22
Produce	10.56	37.65	34.25
Dairy Products	6.90	23.75	19.85
Bread and Rolls	5.85	24.43	23.46
Miscellaneous	6.20	12.24	11.47
Total Cost	—	—	—
Total Sales	—	$1,650.00	$1,560.00
Food Cost Percent	—	—	—

2.

Customer Count	290	Date	August 3, 20
Average Sale	$1.50	Day	Tuesday

Issues	Today	To Date	Last Month To Date
Storeroom			
Canned Goods	$30.24	$ 110.50	$ 112.25
Other Groceries	15.20	40.65	45.50
Meat	58.65	228.60	248.40
Frozen Foods	10.90	30.75	25.95
Direct Purchases			
Poultry, fresh	17.55	68.30	75.35
Seafood, fresh	25.40	59.42	65.75
Produce	15.50	49.25	52.20
Dairy Products	8.22	22.00	20.80
Bread and Rolls	8.45	18.80	21.50
Miscellaneous	6.30	12.43	13.65
Total Cost	—	—	—
Total Sales	—	$1,600.00	$1,700.00
Food Cost Percent	—	—	—

3.

Customer Count	380		Date	September 8, 20
Average Sale	$1.35		Day	Wednesday

Issues	Today	To Date	Last Month To Date
Storeroom			
Canned Goods	$36.75	$ 115.25	$ 116.35
Other Groceries	16.26	42.75	43.85
Meat	68.40	245.30	240.75
Frozen Foods	12.65	28.80	27.60
Direct Purchases			
Poultry, fresh	18.95	58.35	85.62
Seafood, fresh	24.15	46.12	58.14
Produce	18.85	39.25	48.20
Dairy Products	9.95	20.90	21.76
Bread and Rolls	10.22	18.80	22.87
Miscellaneous	7.50	9.20	13.70
Total Cost	—	—	—
Total Sales	—	$1,550.00	$1,590.00
Food Cost Percent	—	—	—

4. The menu price of a turkey sandwich is $5.95. The raw cost of food is $1.50. Find the food cost percentage.

_____

5. A chicken marsala dinner has a menu price of $15.95. The raw cost of food is $3.89. Find the food cost percentage.

_____

6. A lazy man's lobster dinner has a menu price of $19.95. The raw cost of food is $6.89. Find the food cost percentage.

_____

7. A fajita platter has a menu price of $12.95. The raw cost of food is $2.22. Find the food cost percentage.

_____

8. The total cost of all food purchased for the day is $1,020. Total sales for the day is $350. Find the daily food cost percentage.

_____

9. The total cost of all food purchased for the day is $367. Total sales for the day is $989.50. Find the daily food cost percentage.

_____

10. The total cost of all food purchased for the day is $20. Total sales for the day is $1,642.78. Find the daily food cost percentage.

_____

11. Chef Monique Estranza receives a salary of $90,000 annually. What is her daily gross pay, figuring she works five days a week for 52 weeks of the year?

_____

12. The Chardonnay Café employs 12 waitstaff who each earn $6.50 per hour. They each work an eight-hour shift. What is the cost of labor for the waitstaff?

_____

13. The Chardonnay Café employs six culinary staff who each earn $10.50 per hour. They each work an eight-hour shift. What is the cost of labor for the culinary staff?

_____

14. The Chardonnay Café employs four dishwashers who each earn $6.50 per hour. They each work an eight-hour shift. What is the cost of labor for the dishwashers?

_____

15. Using questions 11 to 14, determine the daily payroll.

_____

Determine the daily labor cost percentage for questions 11 to 15 if the daily sales were $5,000.

16. Chef Monique   _____%

17. Waitstaff   _____%

18. Culinary staff   _____%

19. Dishwashers   _____%

20. Daily labor cost   _____%

DISCUSSION QUESTION 10-A

What reasons can be given to justify that the answers from questions 8 and 10 are correct?

The **menu** is a detailed list of food served in a food service establishment. It should be organized in such a way that selections can be made in a short period of time. For example, the Desmond Hotel in Albany, New York offers their guests two restaurants for dining. (See Figures 10–3 and 10–4.) Each item listed on a menu is priced for sale to customers, and in this chapter we will show how prices are determined.

PRICING THE MENU

In the past, pricing the menu was often done in a random fashion. Arriving at a selling price per item was based on your competition rather than your cost. If your competition charged $22.95 for prime rib of beef au jus, you would charge the same. Although there is still no one standard method of pricing items on a menu, food service operators must now determine their cost before deciding how much should be charged to make a profit. Many elements must be considered before a menu price is determined. The cost of all items purchased, rent, labor costs, equipment, taxes, and so forth must be considered before establishing a price.

Large food service operations and chain operations doing a significant volume of business usually have accountants and computers to supply an accurate picture of the overall cost of maintaining a food service business. This makes pricing decisions easier for those involved. In smaller operations, however, the overall cost is more difficult to compute because controls are not always as tight as they should be and records are not always as accurate because of the time and cost involved.

Determining the menu price per item is one of the most challenging and difficult tasks a food service professional will have to accomplish. As the previous paragraph states, large food service operations and chain operations have an easier time setting menu prices than smaller operations. One of the first questions asked by small operators, caterers, and students is, "How do I price my menu?"

Ideally, the food service professional should *figure out and know all the costs before* setting the menu price. Then the menu price can be determined based on costs, type of service, location, and other factors. The final question that has to be answered concerns the amount of profit that is desired. Small operators may not have this information available before the restaurant is opened.

However, there is one thing a restaurant owner *can and must* do before setting the menu price of an individual entree or sandwich. Taking Chef Sonnenschmidt's advice from Chapter 9 (Chef Sez), the price of the raw food cost for each menu item *must* be determined. In other words, each food service business should know *exactly* how much it costs to place one meal in front of one guest. Once that is determined, the menu price can be calculated. This food cost must include the entree, starch, vegetable, and whatever else is included. For example, if a restaurant is serving a lobster roll, the cost of the lobster meat, roll, and butter has to be included. A 3-ounce portion of lobster meat costs $2.50, the roll costs $0.10, and the butter costs $0.10. Therefore, it costs the restaurant $2.70 to serve one lobster roll to a guest.

The restaurant owner must also include all of the costs involved in serving one lobster roll to one guest. The cost of people to prepare the food (labor cost), paper plates, garbage removal, snow plowing, and so on must be figured into the equation before establishing a price for the lobster roll. Then an amount of money (the profit) must be added to the costs, and a final menu determination can be made.

SIMPSON'S

Appetizers

Desmond Shrimp $7.95
Horseradish stuffed jumbo shrimp, wrapped in pancetta and broiled

New England Clam Chowder $4.00	Maryland Crab Cakes $6.95
A rich and creamy Desmond specialty	Served with a spicy remoulade sauce
French Onion Soup $4.25	Clams or Oysters on the Half Shell $6.95
You will love this traditional cheesy soup	Shrimp Cocktail $7.95
Soup of the Day $2.75	Spinach Salad $3.95

Eggplant Panini $6.95
Medallions of eggplant lightly sautéed and layered with smoked
mozzarella, topped with herbed tomato concasse

Salads

Cobb Salad $12.95
Field greens tossed with Dijon vinaigrette topped with turkey breast, proscuitto, avocado, cheddar cheese,
hard boiled egg and crumbled bleu cheese. Garnished with grilled scallions.

Drunken Goat Cheese Salad $13.95
A char-grilled boneless breast of chicken served over mesclun greens, accompanied by
red wine soaked goat cheese, pecans, cranberry vinaigrette and garnished with strawberry halves

Low-Carb Lifestyle

Chicken Breast Tequila $15.95
Boneless breast of chicken rubbed with fresh herbs, sautéed and finished with a tequila butter sauce,
accompanied by fresh asparagus spears

Spaghetti Squash Alfredo $13.95
Fresh spaghetti squash served with a rich parmesan alfredo sauce, garnished with plum tomatoes

Save Room For Dessert, We now have Atkins Endulge Ice Cream
Chocolate Peanut Butter Swirl or Vanilla

Selections From The Sea

Seafood Pasta Alfredo $17.95
A combination of Alaskan crabmeat, Jumbo Gulf shrimp and Georges Bank sea scallops,
served in a garlic cream sauce over mini penne,
topped with grated parmesan cheese

Char-grilled Swordfish $19.95
Center cut Block Island swordfish, char-grilled and served with a
roasted red pepper caper relish

Citrus Grilled Shrimp $18.95
Marinated Jumbo Gulf shrimp, char-grilled and
accompanied by a tropical fruit salsa

Fillet of Sole $15.95
Fresh Atlantic sole, broiled with crushed herbs and drizzled with a
sun dried tomato infused olive oil

Pesto Herb Crusted Sea Scallops $17.95
Georges Bank sea scallops encrusted with fresh herbs and pesto, broiled and
served with tomato-caper vinaigrette

Grilled Salmon $17.95
Fresh Atlantic salmon fillet basted with dill butter,
char-grilled and served with dill hollandaise on the side

Figure 10–3 *Simpson menu*

SIMPSON'S

Simpson's English Style Carvery

In the English tradition we slowly roast whole, the finest quality meats available
and slice it to order. While quantities last.

Prime Rib
Choose your portion of this succulent
aged prime rib, cooked as you like it, served with a tangy horseradish sauce on the side
12-ounce $18.95   16-ounce $22.95   24-ounce $27.95

Fresh Roasted Turkey Breast $15.95
Tender sliced turkey, served with home style giblet gravy

Roasted Sliced Pork loin $17.95
Center cut whole pork loin slowly roasted with fresh herbs, sliced and served with sauce robert

Each entrée includes your choice of Simpson's house or Caesar salad,
choice of potato (garlic mashed, au gratin, baked or french fries),
and fresh vegetables of the day.

Traditional Fare

Chicken Marsala $17.95
Boneless breast of chicken sautéed with wild mushrooms and finished with a rich
marsala wine demi glace

New York Sirloin Steak $19.95
A thick 14-ounce tender aged New York sirloin char-grilled to your
liking, topped with crispy fried onions and a side of Sauce Béarnaise
add fresh Atlantic salmon for just $4.00 more

Filet Mignon $24.95
10-ounce center-cut, char-grilled Filet Mignon, topped with crispy
fried onions and a side of Sauce Béarnaise

Veal Saltimbocca $17.95
Tender veal cutlet lightly breaded and sautéed, layered with plum tomatoes,
proscuitto, leaf spinach, and topped with smoked mozzarella, served with
sun dried tomato orzo

Chicken Teriyaki $15.95
Tender boneless breast of chicken marinated in teriyaki sauce and char-grilled

Char ~grilled Ribeye Steak $17.95
14 ounce tender ribeye grilled to your liking

Each entrée includes your choice of Simpson's house or Caesar salad,
choice of potato (au gratin, baked or french fries) or rice pilaf
and fresh vegetables of the day.

Vegetarian Stuffed Peppers $15.95
A duet of chevre cheese and seasonal squash stuffed peppers, oven roasted and garnished with a
traditional béchamel sauce

Bow-Tie Primavera $12.95
An array of fresh vegetables tossed with bow-tie pasta, garlic and olive oil

Vegetarian selections served with your choice of Simpson's house or Caesar salad

Figure 10–3 *Simpson menu (continued)*

Appetizers

Zinfandel Glazed Pork Tenderloin	*$8.50*
Center cut pork tenderloin, roasted and glazed with a rich Zinfandel demi, sliced and served with a whole grain mustard butter	
Scallops Vol-au-vent	*$7.95*
Atlantic Georges Bank sea scallops sauteed in a lemon tarragon cream served in a crispy puff pastry shell	
Jumbo Shrimp Cocktail	*$8.50*
Lobster Ravioli	*$6.50*
Fresh Maine lobster meat folded with drawn butter and lobster mousse, encased in fresh parsley and squid ink pasta.	
Caramelized Pear Beggar's Purse	*$8.50*
Local Anjou pears caramelized with maple sugar and baked in a phyllo purse with Mascarpone cheese, served with a honey-lime drizzle	
Chilled Seafood Trio	*$8.50*
For the seafood lover, a selection of jumbo shrimp, oysters and clams on the half shell.	
Escargot	*$7.50*
Large snails simmered in a white wine, garlic, tarragon butter sauce.	
Desmond's Shrimp Specialty	*$7.95*
Horseradish stuffed jumbo shrimp wrapped in pancetta and broiled	
Soup du Jour	*$2.95*
New England Clam Chowder	*$4.00*
A rich and creamy Desmond specialty	
Smoked Norwegian Salmon	*$7.95*
Clams on the Half Shell	*$6.95*
Oysters on the Half Shell	*$6.95*

All Entrees Served with Salad, Sorbet, Vegetable of the day & Potato

SCRIMSHAW POTATO
A flaky puff pastry shell filled with caramelized onions, topped with duchess whipped potatoes and baked to a golden brown.
Or
Baked potato, French fries, au gratin or rice

Salads

Scrimshaw Salad
Radicchio, romaine, Boston bibb and red leaf lettuce topped with sliced mushrooms, Mandarin oranges, sliced almonds, cheddar cheese and our own creamy garlic dressing.

Caesar Salad
Chilled romaine served with the traditional accompaniments

Figure 10–4 *Scrimshaw menu*

Traditional Entrees

Rack of Lamb $27.95
Wild mushroom dusted, oven seared and served with roasted garlic demi glace

➤   **Suggested Wine: Hanwood Estate, Shiraz, Australia**
*This wine is vibrant crimson in color, with layers
of plum and raspberry fruit flavors.*

Veal Marsala $22.95
*Tender scallops of veal sauteed with wild mushrooms in a delicate
marsala wine sauce*

Filet Mignon $29.95
*A 12-ounce center cut tournado of our finest aged tenderloin, accompanied
by a wild mushroom confit*

➤   **Suggested Wine: Blackstone, Cabernet Sauvignon, California**
Well rounded with strong cherry and plum flavors.

New York Sirloin $23.95
*A 16-ounce dry-aged center cut sirloin char-grilled and topped
with a maitre d' butter and wild mushroom confit*

Prime Rib
*Coated with our house blend of herbs and spices, then slow roasted
to achieve optimum flavor*
Petite 12 ounce cut $21.95   *Gentlemen's 16 ounce cut $25.95*

➤   **Suggested Wine: Pindar, Mythology, North Fork, Long Island, NY**
A wine of complexity and grand elegance.

Chicken Francaise $18.95
*Boneless breast of chicken dredged in a parmesan cheese batter, sauteed
and finished with a chardonnay lemon butter sauce*

Veal Oscar $22.95
*Tender veal cutlet batter dipped, sauteed and topped with king crab,
white asparagus, hollandaise sauce and served over a rich demi glace*

➤   **Suggested wine: Chateau Ste. Michelle, Johannisberg Riesling, Washington**
A beautiful nectarine-like aroma and flavors of grapefruit and lime.

Steak Au Poivre $24.95
*A 12 oz center cut trimmed sirloin dredged in a three pepper mélange,
pan seared and topped with a mushroom cognac cream sauce*

Figure 10–4 *Scrimshaw menu (continued)*

Desmond Specialties

Lobster Tail Thermidor $33.95
A prized cold water lobster tail stuffed with a King crabmeat thermidor
dressing, baked and garnished with a classic aioli and grilled Georges
Bank sea scallops

➢   Suggested wine: MezzaCorona, Pinot Grigio, Trentino
Elegant, dry and fruity

Cedar Planked Salmon $22.95
Our most popular entrée, Fresh Atlantic salmon broiled on a cedar plank and
served with a lingonberry port sauce. You will enjoy the unique flavor the cedar
plank imparts..

➢   **Suggested wine:** Columbia Crest, Merlot, California
Complex fruit flavors with a smooth and silky finish.

Shrimp Scampi $22.95
Jumbo gulf shrimp sautéed in a chardonnay lemon garlic butter until
golden brown, and served with wild mushroom basmati rice

Georges Bank Sea Scallops $21.95
Taste the difference in these unique Scallops from the best fishing grounds in
the world. Dusted with black and white sesame seeds and pan seared, served
over a fresh herb sherry beurre blanc

➢   Suggested wine: Kendall Jackson, Chardonnay, California
Beautifully balanced fruit flavors with a rich mouth feel.

Lobster Tails $29.95
Succulent lobster meat marinated in a fresh herbed citrus vinaigrette,
chargrilled and served with clarified butter

➢   **Suggested Wine:** Kunde Estate Sauvignon Blanc, California
Flavors of ripe peaches or melons contrast with green herbal
notes of spearmint and lime. Bright acidity balances with a
finish reminiscent of ripe peaches and sweet vanilla..

Roasted Vegetable Strudel $19.95
Marinated seasonal vegetables, oven roasted and wrapped in flaky phyllo dough.
Baked to a golden brown and drizzled with pesto sauce.

Traditional Surf and Turf $34.95
A center cut filet mignon char grilled to you liking accompanied by
a broiled cold water lobster tail

Shrimp Scampi or broiled scallops may be substituted

Scrimshaw is the proud recipient of the prestigious
Wine Spectator Award of Excellence since 1997

Michael St. John, C.E.C., Executive Chef
2003 Restaurateur of the Year, New York State Restaurant Association

Figure 10–4 *Scrimshaw menu (continued)*

When pricing the menu, food service professionals use three methods that take into account all of the factors listed above. They are *amount of markup using a percent, food cost percent, and multiplier effect.*

MARKUP

In menu pricing, the only standard is that cost must be established before a markup can be added to determine an item's selling price. **Markup** is the money added to raw food cost to obtain a menu price. The amount of markup usually varies depending on the type of establishment. A cafeteria might mark up all its items by one-half the cost to obtain a menu price; a gourmet restaurant might mark up all its items by two or three times the cost to obtain a menu price. The markup is not always figured using fractions. In many cases, percents are used because they are easier to work with and less mistakes are made.

Amount of Markup Using a Fraction

If the price of a raw food is \$1.95 and the markup rate is $\frac{2}{3}$, markup is obtained by multiplying the cost by the markup rate. The formula for this is:

> **Step 1:** Raw food cost × markup rate = markup amount
> **Step 2:** Raw food cost + markup amount = menu or selling price

For example:

$$\frac{\$1.95}{1} \times \frac{2}{3} = \frac{\$3.90}{3} = \$1.30 \text{ markup amount}$$

$$\$1.95 \text{ raw food cost} + \$1.30 \text{ markup amount}$$

$$= \$3.25 \text{ menu or selling price}$$

Amount of Markup Using a Percent

If the markup is figured by using percent, the menu or selling price of an item is determined by multiplying the raw food cost by the percent and adding the markup to the raw food cost. The formula for this is:

> **Step 1:** Raw food cost × percent = markup amount
> **Step 2:** Raw food cost + markup amount = menu or selling price

When multiplying or dividing with percents, it is best to convert the percent to its decimal equivalent. This is done by removing the percent sign (%) and moving the decimal point two places to the left. For instance:

$$60\% = 0.60$$

$$75\% = 0.75$$

$$25.5\% = 0.255$$

$$50.5\% = 0.505$$

For example: if the raw food cost is $1.95 and the markup rate is 45 percent, convert 45 percent to 0.45 and multiply.

$$
\begin{array}{rl}
\$1.95 & \text{Raw food cost} \\
\underline{\times 0.45} & \text{Markup percent} \\
975 & \\
\underline{780} & \\
\$0.8775 = & \$0.88 \text{ markup amount}
\end{array}
$$

Then add the markup ($0.88) to the raw food cost to determine the selling cost or menu price.

$$
\begin{array}{rl}
\$1.95 & \text{Raw food cost} \\
\underline{+\ 0.88} & \text{Markup amount} \\
\$2.83 & \text{Menu or selling price}
\end{array}
$$

Food Cost Percent

Another method of menu pricing is to determine the monthly food cost percent and divide the food cost percent into the raw food cost. The formula for this is:

> **Raw food cost ÷ food cost percent = menu or selling price.**

For example: if the raw food cost is $2.90 and the monthly food cost percent is 35%, the menu price is determined by dividing 35% (or 0.35) into $2.90.

$$
\begin{array}{r}
8.285 \quad = \$8.29 \text{ menu or selling price} \\
\text{Food cost percent } 0.35\overline{)2.90000} \quad \text{ Raw food cost} \\
\underline{2\ 80} \\
100 \\
\underline{70} \\
300 \\
\underline{280} \\
200 \\
\underline{175} \\
25
\end{array}
$$

Many operators rely on the food cost percentage method of pricing the menu. In the example, our restaurant has set a goal of 25% for food cost for the lobster roll. That will leave 75% of the menu price to pay for all the expenses (plates, snow plowing, etc.) as well as make a profit.

$2.70 raw food cost ÷ .25 food cost percent
= $10.80 menu price

Our menu price of one lobster roll will be $10.80.

Multiplier Effect

Many restaurant owners do not take the time or effort to figure out their exact costs before they price the menu. An easier and quicker system has been developed to price the menu, called the **multiplier effect.** It works on the principle of food cost percentage, but instead of dividing, the restaurant owner multiplies the cost of the raw food by a number that corresponds to the food cost percentage goal. Therefore, to obtain a food cost percentage, the restaurant owner takes the cost of the raw food and multiplies that number by the multiplier. In our example with the lobster roll, if we desire a food cost percentage of 25%, we take the cost of the raw food ($2.70) and multiply by 4 (dividing the desired food cost percent of 25 into 100 arrived at the multiplier number of 4).

$$\begin{array}{ll} \$2.70 & \text{Cost of the lobster roll} \\ \underline{\times\ 4} & \text{Multiplier} \\ \$10.80 & \text{Menu price} \end{array}$$

This is the same menu price that was obtained by dividing the raw cost of food by the food cost percentage.

$2.70 raw food cost ÷ .25 food cost percent = $10.80 menu price

This method of pricing is used to quickly figure out desired food cost percentages. If a chef desires a food cost percentage of 50%, the raw food cost will be multiplied by 2; 40% by 2.5; 33.3% by 3; 25% by 4; and 20% by 5, as illustrated in Figure 10–5. Using this method is quick, with less figuring involved.

For example: if the raw food cost is $2.90 and the desired food cost is 40% ($2\frac{1}{2}$ times the raw food cost), the price is determined by multiplying $2\frac{1}{2} \times \$2.90$.

$$2\frac{1}{2} \times \$2.90 = \frac{5}{2} \times \frac{2.90}{1} = \$7.25 \text{ menu or selling price}$$

This problem can also be done by first converting $2\frac{1}{2}$ to the decimal 2.5 before multiplying.

$$\begin{array}{r} \$2.90 \\ \underline{\times\ 2.5} \\ 1450 \\ \underline{580\ \ } \\ \$7.250 \end{array} = \$7.25 \text{ menu or selling price}$$

In addition to using mathematical formulas to set prices, chefs and food service managers also take into account psychological factors. Look at the Desmond's two menus in Figures 10–3 and 10–4. Notice how many menu items end with $0.95. Most likely, very few (if any) of the menu items, when costed out, resulted in the exact ending price of

Raw food cost	Percent using a markup	Food cost percent	Multiplier effect	Menu price
$3.00	100%	50%	2	$ 6.00
$3.00	150%	40%	2.5	$ 7.50
$3.00	200%	33.3%	3	$ 9.00
$3.00	300%	25%	4	$12.00
$3.00	400%	20%	5	$15.00

Figure 10–5 *Pricing the menu*

Chef Sez...

"Chefs need to learn the books, the profit and loss statement. You might be very talented, but if you can't control the numbers, you can't make any money. You've got to know the cost of food, when products are out of season and costly, and when they are in season and are a good buy. So, you see, you can be talented, but you also need to think like a business owner."

Rodney Renshaw
Executive Chef
The Savoy
Washington, DC

Chef Renshaw was featured in the May 10, 1999, Culinary Currents of *Nation's Restaurant News,* written by Milford Prewitt. Besides the above quote, Prewitt also writes that "Renshaw is one of a growing number of black chefs, striving to catapult African-American cuisine into the realm of fine dining." The Savoy is a supper club that features live jazz and true Southern fine dining in Washington, D.C.

$0.95. As was stated previously, it is always a great idea to cost up. Examples of this idea are listed below.

Determined Price	Menu Price
$11.15	$11.95
$13.35	$13.95
$15.60	$15.95
$18.90	$18.95

Remember that prices are important in a customer's appraisal of a food service operation. It is essential that a price level be established that appeals to all types of potential customers. It must not only be a price customers can afford, but one that they feel is closely related to the quality of food and service they receive.

Remember, too, that the food service operator is in business to make a profit and that profits will usually result if an establishment is built on a solid foundation of quality food, attractive decor, fair prices, and good service.

Pricing the Menu

The three methods that can be used to price the menu—amount of markup using a percent, food cost percent, and multiplier effect—will all yield the same final menu price. Figure 10–5 illustrates how each method is to be used.

For example: the cost of the raw food is $3.00. To find the menu price of the item with a markup of 100%, the $3.00 is multiplied by 100%, which equals $3.00. This product of $3.00 is added to the original raw food cost to arrive at a menu cost of $6.00.

To find the menu price of the item using a 50% food cost, the 50%, or .50, is divided into the raw cost of food ($3.00). The menu price with a 50% food cost is $6.00.

The easiest way to obtain the answer to the above questions is to use the multiplier. From the chart, the student can see that a markup of 100% or a food cost of 50% is arrived at by multiplying the raw food cost by 2. The menu price using 2 as a multiplier is $6.00.

The Method—Food Cost The Chef's Magic Circle is a paper calculator that allows for the easy calculation of Food Cost, Food Cost Percentage, and Sales Price. The method involves covering up what it is you want to find. Place your thumb over what you want to calculate on the circle, for instance Food Cost, and see what is left. Notice that Food Cost Percentage and Sales Price remain, separated by a vertical line. When calculating Food Cost, multiply Food Cost Percentage by Sales Price, with Food Cost Percentage expressed as a decimal. The vertical line indicates multiplication. In algebraic terminology, this calculation would be expressed as FC = SP*FC%, but who wants, or needs, to remember formulae when you have the Chef's Magic Circle? Just plug in the numbers and perform the calculation indicated.

The Method—Sales Price (or Menu Price) To calculate Sales Price, cover Sales Price on the circle and notice that Food Cost and Food Cost Percentage are divided by the horizontal line. When calculating Sales Price, divide Food Cost by Food Cost Percentage, which is expressed as a decimal. The horizontal line indicates division. In algebraic terminology, this calculation would be expressed as SP = FC/FC%, but who wants, or needs, to remember formulae when you have the Chef's Magic Circle? Just plug in the numbers and perform the calculation indicated.

Figure 10–6 *The Chef's Magic Circle*

The Method—Food Cost Percentage To calculate Food Cost Percentage, cover Food Cost Percentage on the circle and notice that Food Cost and Sales Price are divided by the horizontal line. Again, the horizontal line indicates division. In algebraic terminology, this calculation would be expressed as FC% = FC/SP, but who wants, or needs, to remember formulae when you have the Chef's Magic Circle? Just plug in the numbers and perform the calculation indicated.

SUMMARY REVIEW 10–2

Determine the menu price if:

1. The raw food cost is $4.20 and the markup rate is $\frac{2}{3}$.

   _____

2. The raw food cost is $6.60 and the markup rate is $\frac{5}{8}$.

   _____

3. The raw food cost is $3.25 and the markup rate is 43%.

   _____

4. The raw food cost is $5.55 and the markup rate is 60.5%.

   _____

5. The raw food cost is $4.96 and the markup rate is 38%.

   _____

6. The raw food cost is $3.72 and a 25% food cost is desired.

   _____

7. The raw food cost is $4.29 and a 59% food cost is desired.

   _____

8. The raw food cost is $12.72 and a 100% food cost is desired.

   _____

9. The raw food cost is $1.57 and a 43% food cost is desired.

   _____

10. The raw food cost is $5.63 and a 17% food cost is desired.

_____

11. The raw food cost is $4.25 and a 25% food cost is desired.

_____

12. The raw food cost is $4.25 and a 20% food cost is desired.

_____

13. The raw food cost is $4.25 and a 40% food cost is desired.

_____

14. The raw food cost is $4.25 and a 50% food cost is desired.

_____

15. The raw food cost is $4.25 and a 33.3% food cost is desired.

_____

16. The raw food cost is $4.25 and a 200% markup is desired.

_____

17. What is the menu price using the multiplier of 3 if the raw food cost is $4.25?

_____

18. What is the menu price using the multiplier of 2.5 if the raw food cost is $4.25?

_____

19. What is the menu price using the multiplier of 2 if the raw food cost is $4.25?

_____

20. What is the menu price using the multiplier of 5 if the raw food cost is $4.25?

_____

SUMMARY 10-3

Using the Chef's Magic Circle, complete the following chart:

Question	Food Cost	Food Cost Percentage	Sales Price
21	$ 2.79	31.4%	$———
22	$ 3.97	39.8%	$———
23	$———	24.9%	$ 7.35
24	$———	19.4%	$24.95
25	$ 2.48	———%	$11.95
26	$ 6.93	———%	$19.95
27	$11.99	———%	$49.95

28. In our restaurant we used a total of $43,189 in food last month. We earned revenue of $99,687. What was our food cost percentage for the month?

_____

29. In May we spent $51,292 for food. Revenue for May was $109,213 and we have projected a 32.8% food cost percentage for the month. What was our food cost percentage for the month?

_____

30. Next month we have forecasted a revenue of $61,484 and want a food cost percentage of 33.3%. What should our total expenditure of food dollars be for the month to achieve the desired food cost percentage?

DISCUSSION QUESTION 10–B

Referring to question 29, if you were the chef, what would you look for to figure out why the food cost percentage was not 32.8%? What would make it higher than the ideal food cost?

Inventory Procedures

OBJECTIVES

At the completion of this chapter, the student should be able to:

1. Identify perpetual inventory.
2. Identify physical inventory.
3. Find the cost of food sold.
4. Find the monthly food cost percent.
5. Identify computer applications for inventory procedures.
6. Explain the purpose of taking both a perpetual and a physical inventory.
7. Calculate physical inventory.
8. Identify and explain the concept of food in production.

KEY WORDS

inventory	purchases
perpetual inventory	beginning inventory
physical inventory	cost of food sold
food in production	monthly food cost percent
transfers	weekly or period inventory
final inventory	recapitulation

In the previous two chapters, the importance of determining food and labor costs was explained, along with how to determine food and labor cost percentages. The purpose of this chapter is to explain the importance of determining the amount of inventory in a food service operation and the role inventory plays in determining food cost percentages. Both the actual taking of inventory and the costing out of inventory can be tedious and time-consuming jobs. However, for a food service operation to obtain an accurate monthly and yearly food cost percentage, they must be done.

Inventory is a well-known business term because it is an activity that takes place in many business operations at least once a year. In a food service operation, it can be a continuous activity. An **inventory** is a catalog or itemized list of stock and its estimated value. An inventory of food service equipment may be taken from time to time, but the most important inventory concerns food. There are two kinds of inventories pertaining to food that are of major importance: the perpetual inventory and the physical inventory.

PERPETUAL INVENTORY

A **perpetual inventory** is a continuous or endless inventory. It is a record that is taken in the storeroom to show the balance on hand for each storeroom item. (See Figure 11–1.) As a requisition from the production

Chef Sez...

"We have three and a half hours to feed a small city; potentially 78,000 guests. When a popular team or a popular player is scheduled, we have a capacity crowd. The next day we may only have 11,000 fans. A chef or food service manager needs to use math to figure out how much food to order and how much to cook in order to have enough food for our guests, but not too much where we have waste."

Matthew J. Kaperka
General Manager, The Mark of
the Quad Cities
Sports & Entertainment,
ARAMARK Corporation

Matt Kaperka is the general manager for food and beverage at The Mark of the Quad Cities on the banks of the Mississippi. The quad cities are Davenport and Bettendorf in Iowa and Moline/East Moline and Rock Island in Illinois. He has used knowledge gained from both Shea Stadium and the Houston Astrodome to manage the food for the 12,000 seat arena in the Quad Cities that holds events such as rock shows, hockey, and arena 2 football. Formerly Matt was the concessions manager at Shea Stadium in New York, home of the New York Mets professional baseball team. He has had a wealth of experience in sports and entertainment food service. Previously, he worked in Houston, Texas, at the Astrodome. The tenants at the Astrodome included the Houston Astros baseball team and the Houston Oilers football team. In addition, there were many special events such as the rodeo, for which ARAMARK and Mr. Kaperka had to provide the concessions. He must use his math skills daily to accomplish his goals.

crew is received and the items are issued, the amounts are subtracted from the inventory balance. When new shipments of each item arrive and are placed on the shelves, they are added to the inventory balance.

If the food service operation does a large volume of business, a computer would probably be placed in the storeroom to handle these functions. If a

Figure 11–1 *Formal storeroom operation.*

computer is not available, the functions are done manually. At the end of each month, when the physical inventory of each item is taken, the physical inventory should match the perpetual inventory. If the two do not match, a problem exists. The problem may be poor bookkeeping, negligence in checking incoming orders, theft, or a similar situation. Keep in mind that, in a business operation, control is a key word. The more departments, functions, or activities that can be controlled by management, the more profits will show up on the P&L sheet (profit and loss sheet).

PHYSICAL INVENTORY

The **physical inventory** may be taken at the end of each month or as frequently as needed, in order to determine the accurate cost of food consumed during that period. When doing a physical inventory, an actual count is taken of all stock on hand. The physical inventory figures are most important when making out the profit and loss sheet.

The inventory sheet should be prepared in advance using a standard form. This form should contain the name of each item, the quantity, size or bulk, unit price, and total price of items on hand. Two people usually take the inventory, one calling out the items on hand and the other recording the items and quantities. (See Figure 11–2.) While this task can be done by one person, it would be time consuming. Two people ensure accuracy and make it more difficult to steal inventory. Of course, if they work together, it will be easy for them to steal. That is why it is beneficial for the food service operator to have different individuals take the physical inventory from time to time. The unit price for each item listed can be obtained from invoices and purchase records. When setting up an inventory sheet, most establishments classify the food and supply items into common groups such as:

- canned foods
- other groceries
- butter, eggs, and cheese
- coffee and tea
- fruits and vegetables
- meat, poultry, and fish
- supplies

Figure 11–2 *Two employees conducting an inventory of the storeroom*

When the total inventory value is found, this figure represents the cost of food still on hand or in storage. It is food that has not been sold during this inventory period. The inventory value is then used to find the monthly food cost percent. When computing the monthly food cost percent, this figure is referred to as the **final inventory.**

FOOD IN PRODUCTION AND OTHER TRANSFERS

In order to obtain an accurate food cost percentage, the amount of food that has been prepared, but not served, must be included. This figure also includes the food that is in the refrigerators or freezers on the cooking and dessert lines. The amount of food can equal a large amount of dollars, and, if not calculated in the food cost percentage, the percentage will not be accurate. The authors know of a chef who lowered his food cost by including the food in production. Before he did this, his food costs were just a bit too high. By including the food in production when calculating his monthly food cost, he achieved his desired food cost percentage.

Other transfers also affect food cost percentage. For example, if all of the fruits and vegetables that are used to garnish alcoholic beverages at the bar are not transferred to the bar costs, the food cost percentage will increase. In our examples in this textbook, the authors will not use any transfers. However, the student should be aware that if transfers are used in the operation where he or she is employed, the transfers should be included when calculating costs.

CALCULATING THE MONTHLY FOOD COST PERCENTAGE

To find the monthly food cost percent, the purchases for the month are added to the inventory at the beginning of the month, and the final inventory plus the amount of food in production is subtracted to give the cost of food sold for the month. The food cost percent is then found by dividing the total sales for the month into the cost of food sold. The division should be carried four places to the right of the decimal to give the percent. (See Figure 11–3.)

Purchases + beginning inventory − (food in production + final
inventory) = (equals)
Cost of food sold.

Cost of food sold ÷ total sales
= (equals)
Food cost percent.

The amount of sales is the total food sold during that particular month. It is the total of all sales made during that period. The purchases for the month represent the total of all the food purchased during that month. This is found by adding the totals of all invoices sent with each food purchase. The inventory at the beginning of the month is the final inventory from the previous month. (For an example of a physical inventory recapitulation see Figure 11–4.)

Sales for the Month	$2,550.00
Inventory at the Beginning of the Month	$300.00
Purchases for the Month	$895.00
Food in Production	$150.00
Final Inventory	$250.00

Step 1 — **Step 1**

To find the **Cost of Food Sold,** first add:
Inventory at the Beginning of the Month $ 300.00
To Purchases for the Month   + 895.00
Sum for the Beginning Inventory and Purchases for the Month $ 1,195.00

Step 2 — **Step 2**

Add the Food in Production $ 150.00
To the Final Inventory   + 250.00
Sum for the Food in Production and the Final Inventory $ 400.00

Step 3 — **Step 3**

Take the Sum of the Beginning Inventory and Purchases for the Month $ 1,195.00
And subtract the Sum for the Food in Production and the Final Inventory   − 400.00

Cost of Food Sold is   **$795.00**

Step 4 — **Step 4**

To find the **Monthly Food Cost Percent**
Divide the Sales for the Month $ 2,550.00
into the **Cost of Food Sold** $795.00

Monthly Food Cost Percent

$$\begin{array}{r} .31176 \\ 2550\overline{)795000000} \\ -7650 \\ \hline 3000 \\ -2550 \\ \hline 4500 \\ -2550 \\ \hline 19500 \\ -17850 \\ \hline 16500 \end{array}$$

Monthly Food Cost Percent is   **31.18%**

Figure 11–3 *How to find cost of food sold and monthly food cost percent*

Example of a Physical Inventory
(Prices are not current)
Weekly or Period Inventory Recapitulation

Week Ending August 9, 20___		Period Ending August 31, 20___
Item No.	**Item**	**Amount**
1.	Canned Goods	$ 628.59
2.	Other Groceries	779.48
3.	Butter, Eggs, Cheese	42.44
4.	Coffee and Tea	45.69
5.	Fruits and Vegetables	294.12
6.	Meat, Poultry, and Fish	1140.14
	TOTAL FOOD	$2930.46
7.	Supplies	$ 590.77
	Total Inventory Value	$3,521.23
Called By_____	Extended by _____	
	Manager _____	

Figure 11–4 *Example of a physical inventory*

SUMMARY REVIEW 11–1

Calculate the extension prices for Items 1–7 on the following pages.

Canned Goods			
Quantity/Size	**Item**	**Unit Price**	**Extension**
8-#10	Apples	$ 3.52	$ ———
6-#10	Apricots	5.29	———
9-#10	Beans, Green	2.61	———
10-#10	Beans, Kidney	1.84	———
12-#10	Beans, Wax	2.07	———
14-#10	Bean Sprouts	2.79	———
4-#10	Beets, Whole	3.03	———
3-#10	Carrots, Whole	3.44	———
8-#10	Cherries	7.31	———
2-#10	Fruit Cocktail	4.10	———
3-#10	Noodles (Chow Mein)	2.74	———
6-#10	Peach Halves	3.71	———
5-#10	Peaches, Pie	3.60	———
5-#10	Pears	3.51	———
4-#10	Pineapple Tidbits	3.79	———
10-#10	Pineapple Slices	3.84	———
4-#10	Plums	3.24	———
6-#10	Pumpkin	3.85	———
7-#10	Sweet Potatoes	3.26	———
9-#10	Tomato Catsup	2.12	———
8-#10	Tomato Puree	3.67	———
3-#10	Tomatoes	3.41	———
6-#10	Asparagus Spears	6.50	———
8-#10	Cream Style Corn	2.08	———
12-#10	Whole Kernel Corn	2.15	———
24-#2	Salmon	2.30	———
		Canned Goods Total	$ ———

Item No. 1 *Canned goods*

Groceries — Dry Bulk Goods			
Quantity/Size	**Item**	**Unit Price**	**Extension**
8 lb.	Baking Soda	$0.22	$ ——
9 lb.	Baking Powder	8.40	——
8 lb.	Cocoa	5.90	——
6 lb.	Coconut Shred	1.12	——
10 lb.	Cracker Meal	0.18	——
4 lb.	Chicken Base	1.12	——
7 lb.	Beef Base	1.15	——
6 lb.	Raisins	1.19	——
9 lb.	Cornmeal	0.15	——
12 lb.	Cornstarch	0.46	——
20 lb.	Tapioca Flour	0.22	——
63 lb.	Bread Flour	0.20	——
53 lb.	Cake Flour	0.25	——
74 lb.	Pastry Flour	0.22	——
15 lb.	Elbow Macaroni	0.49	——
18 lb.	Spaghetti	0.52	——
6 lb.	Rice	0.45	——
12 lb.	Noodles	1.13	——
		Subtotal	$ ——

Item No. 2 *Other groceries*

Groceries — Oils and Fats			
Quantity/Size	**Item**	**Unit Price**	**Extension**
12 cases	Margarine	$50.52	$ ——
$1\frac{1}{2}$ tin	Shortening, 50-lb. tin	26.00	——
2 cans	Salad Oil, 5-gal. can	22.10	——
		Subtotal	$ ——

Item No. 2 *Other groceries*

Groceries — Spices			
Quantity/Size	**Item**	**Unit Price**	**Extension**
$1\frac{1}{2}$ lb.	Allspice, Ground	$ 7.02	$ ——
$1\frac{3}{4}$ lb.	Bay Leaves	4.20	——
2 lb.	Chili Powder	4.35	——
3 lb.	Cinnamon	6.20	——
4 lb.	Cloves, Ground	6.95	——
$1\frac{1}{4}$ lb.	Ginger, Ground	4.50	——
$1\frac{1}{2}$ lb.	Cumin Seed	3.82	——
$2\frac{1}{2}$ lb.	Celery Seed	5.10	——
$2\frac{1}{4}$ lb.	Caraway Seed	2.90	——
$1\frac{3}{4}$ lb.	Mace	12.50	——
$2\frac{3}{4}$ lb.	Mustard, Dry	2.80	——
$1\frac{1}{2}$ lb.	Marjoram, Dry	3.50	——
3 lb.	Nutmeg	8.50	——
4 lb.	Oregano	4.25	——
5 lb.	Pepper, White	6.00	——
3 lb.	Pepper, Black	5.00	——
2 lb.	Pickling Spice	4.18	——
$1\frac{1}{2}$ lb.	Rosemary Leaves	8.12	——
$1\frac{1}{4}$ lb.	Sage	10.82	——
$1\frac{3}{4}$ lb.	Thyme	5.89	——
		Subtotal	$ ——

Item No. 2 *Other groceries*

Groceries — Dressing and Condiments			
Quantity/Size	**Item**	**Unit Price**	**Extension**
3 gal.	Mayonnaise	$ 8.44	$ ——
2 gal.	Dill Pickles	3.22	——
$1\frac{1}{2}$ gal.	Sweet Relish	4.60	——
4 gal.	Salad Dressing	3.88	——
$6\frac{1}{2}$ gal.	Vinegar	1.20	——
$1\frac{1}{4}$ gal.	Soy Sauce	6.48	——
4 gal.	Worcestershire Sauce	3.73	——
5 gal.	French Dressing	4.54	——
		Subtotal	$ ——

Item No. 2 *Other groceries*

Groceries — Coloring and Extracts			
Quantity/Size	**Item**	**Unit Price**	**Extension**
$1\frac{1}{2}$ qt.	Caramel Color	$ 5.95	$ ———
$1\frac{1}{4}$ pt.	Yellow	3.12	———
$1\frac{3}{4}$ pt.	Red	2.82	———
2 pt.	Green	3.16	———
1 pt.	Lemon Extract	6.99	———
3 pt.	Vanilla Extract	11.89	———
$1\frac{1}{2}$ pt.	Maple Extract	4.09	———
		Subtotal	$ ———
		Other Groceries Total	$ ———

Item No. 2 *Other groceries*

Butter, Eggs, and Cheese			
Quantity/Size	**Item**	**Unit Price**	**Extension**
8 lb.	American Cheese	$ 1.70	———
15 lb.	Chip Butter	1.12	———
14 doz.	Eggs	0.86	———
	Butter, Eggs, and Cheese Total		———

Item No. 3 *Butter, eggs, and cheese*

Coffee and Tea			
Quantity/Size	**Item**	**Unit Price**	**Extension**
16 lb.	Coffee	$ 2.68	$ ———
$\frac{1}{2}$ pkg.	Tea — indiv. (100)	2.50	———
$\frac{1}{4}$ pkg.	Tea — iced (48)	6.24	———
	Coffee and Tea Total		$ ———

Item No. 4 *Coffee and tea*

Fruits and Vegetables — Fresh			
Quantity/Size	Item	Unit Price	Extension
4 bu.	Carrots	$ 0.89	$ ———
3 lb.	Endive	1.45	———
7 head	Head Lettuce	0.89	———
8 lb.	Leaf Lettuce	1.25	———
20 lb.	Dry Onions	0.46	———
54 lb.	Red Potatoes	0.53	———
44 lb.	Idaho Potatoes	0.51	———
6 lb.	Tomatoes	0.88	———
3 bu.	Parsley	0.45	———
5 lb.	Green Peppers	0.48	———
8 lb.	Apples	0.83	———
7 lb.	Bananas	0.35	———
4 doz.	Lemons	2.25	———
5 doz.	Oranges	2.25	———
5 bu.	Radishes	0.35	———
3 bu.	Celery	0.89	———
		Subtotal	$ ———

Item No. 5 *Fruits and vegetables—fresh*

Fruits and Vegetables — Frozen			
Quantity/Size	Item	Unit Price	Extension
9 lb.	Strawberries	$ 1.06	$ ———
12 lb.	Peaches	1.17	———
16 lb.	Blueberries	1.52	———
34 lb.	Lima Beans	1.23	———
25 lb.	Corn	0.63	———
18 lb.	Broccoli	0.78	———
12 lb.	Brussels Sprouts	0.87	———
18 lb.	Mixed Vegetables	0.57	———
22 lb.	Peas	0.56	———
16 lb.	Cauliflower	0.90	———
		Subtotal	$ ———
		Fruits and Vegetables Total	$ ———

Item No. 5 *Fruits and vegetables—frozen*

Meat, Poultry, and Fish			
Quantity/Size	**Item**	**Unit Price**	**Extension**
15 lb.	Beef Ground	$ 1.72	$ ———
21 lb.	Beef Round	2.25	———
30 lb.	Beef Ribs	2.95	———
22 lb.	Beef Rib Eyes	3.20	———
19 lb.	Beef Chuck	1.95	———
15 lb.	Club Steak	3.58	———
14 lb.	Beef Tenderloin	6.20	———
28 lb.	Pork Loin	5.40	———
22 lb.	Boston Butt	2.20	———
36 lb.	Veal Leg	7.40	———
12 lb.	Veal Shoulder	6.22	———
14 lb.	Veal Loin	8.20	———
32 lb.	Ham	2.35	———
		Subtotal	$ ———
	Meat, Poultry, and Fish Total		

Item No. 6 *Meat, poultry, and fish*

Supplies			
Quantity/Size	**Item**	**Unit Price**	**Extension**
4	Napkins	$ 41.00	$ ———
8	Butter Chips	5.48	———
22	Souffle Cups	7.80	———
15	Paper Bags	7.95	———
12 gal.	Bleach	1.24	———
13 gal.	Dish	3.89	———
21 lb.	Salute	0.58	———
5 ea.	Pot Brushes	2.89	———
		Supplies Total	$ ———

Item No. 7 *Supplies*

SUMMARY REVIEW 11–2

From Summary Review 11–1, fill in the totals for all the categories.

Example of a Physical Inventory (Prices are not current) **Weekly or Period Inventory Recapitulation**		
Week Ending August 9, 20___		Period Ending August 31, 20___
Item No.	**Item**	**Amount**
1.	Canned Goods	$ ———
2.	Other Groceries	———
3.	Butter, Eggs, Cheese	———
4.	Coffee and Tea	———
5.	Fruits and Vegetables	———
6.	Meat, Poultry, and Fish	———
	TOTAL FOOD	$ ———
7.	Supplies	$ ———
	Total Inventory Value	$ ———
Called By_____		Extended by _____ Manager _____

SUMMARY REVIEW 11–3

Find the monthly food cost percent and the cost of food sold using the following information. Calculate the food cost percentage two places to the right of the decimal.

Sales for the Month	$54,000.00
Beginning Inventory	6,780.50
Purchases for the Month	15,890.00
Food in Production	2,005.10
Final Inventory will be the answer from Summary Review 11–2	

The cost of food sold is _____?
The monthly food cost percentage is _____?

Identifying Beginning and Final Inventory

To explain the beginning inventory further and to clarify a point that can be confusing, let us use the months of October and November as examples. The final inventory for the month of October becomes the beginning inventory for the month of November. The final inventory, as stated before, is found from the physical inventory taken at the end of each month. To carry this point further, the final inventory for the month of November becomes the beginning inventory for the month of December.

The **monthly food cost percent** tells the food service operator what percentage of the total sales for that period was used to purchase food for the operation. This is a very important figure and one that must be controlled because the cost of food and labor are the highest costs in any food service operation.

SUMMARY REVIEW 11–4

In problems 1 through 5, find the cost of food sold and the monthly food cost percent. Carry percents two places to the right of the decimal.

1. Food in Production $5,025.00
   Sales $48,500.00
   Inventory at Beginning of Month   4,890.00
   Purchases for the Month   41,465.00
   Final Inventory   3,682.00
   Cost of Food Sold   _____
   Monthly Food Cost Percent   _____

2. Food in Production $2,017.25
   Sales $76,585.54
   Inventory at Beginning of Month   8,296.25
   Purchases for the Month   18,440.25
   Final Inventory   4,635.65
   Cost of Food Sold   _____
   Monthly Food Cost Percent   _____

3. Food in Production $1,025.00
   Sales $29,760.00
   Inventory at Beginning of Month   1,495.00
   Purchases for the Month   12,025.00
   Final Inventory   675.00
   Cost of Food Sold   _____
   Monthly Food Cost Percent   _____

4. Food in Production $895.00
   Sales $125,545.00
   Inventory at Beginning of Month   6,264.36
   Purchases for the Month   28,418.00
   Final Inventory   3,268.45
   Cost of Food Sold   _____
   Monthly Food Cost Percent   _____

5. Food in Production $1,395.00
   Sales $66,342.50
   Inventory at Beginning of Month   4,615.15
   Purchases for the Month   22,728.00
   Final Inventory   3,785.00
   Cost of Food Sold   _____
   Monthly Food Cost Percent   _____

Case Study In this exercise, your instructor calls out the quantity and unit price of each item listed. Quantity and unit price may be true and current or hypothetical. The instructor should also give the figures of sales, inventory at the beginning of month, purchases for the month, and food in production.

The student is asked to find the extension price, subtotals, totals, total food (on front of inventory), total inventory value (on front of inventory), and the monthly food cost percent.

<table>
<tr><td colspan="3">Form to Use for Part B.
Weekly or Period
Inventory Recapitulation</td></tr>
<tr><td colspan="2">Week Ending
_____</td><td>Period Ending
_____</td></tr>
<tr><td>Item No.</td><td>Item</td><td>Amount</td></tr>
<tr><td>1.
2.
3.
4.
5.
6.</td><td>Canned Goods
Other Groceries
Butter, Eggs, Cheese
Coffee and Tea
Fruits and Vegetables
Meat, Poultry, and Fish</td><td></td></tr>
<tr><td></td><td colspan="2">TOTAL FOOD</td></tr>
<tr><td>7.</td><td>Supplies</td><td></td></tr>
<tr><td colspan="3">Total Inventory Value</td></tr>
<tr><td colspan="2">Called By_____</td><td>Extended by _____
Manager _____</td></tr>
</table>

<table>
<tr><td colspan="4">Groceries — Dry Bulk Goods</td></tr>
<tr><td>Quantity/Size</td><td>Item</td><td>Unit Price</td><td>Extension</td></tr>
<tr><td>lb.</td><td>Baking Soda</td><td></td><td></td></tr>
<tr><td>lb.</td><td>Baking Powder</td><td></td><td></td></tr>
<tr><td>lb.</td><td>Cocoa</td><td></td><td></td></tr>
<tr><td>lb.</td><td>Coconut Shred</td><td></td><td></td></tr>
<tr><td>lb.</td><td>Cracker Meal</td><td></td><td></td></tr>
<tr><td>lb.</td><td>Chicken Base</td><td></td><td></td></tr>
<tr><td>lb.</td><td>Beef Base</td><td></td><td></td></tr>
<tr><td>lb.</td><td>Raisins</td><td></td><td></td></tr>
<tr><td>lb.</td><td>Cornmeal</td><td></td><td></td></tr>
<tr><td>lb.</td><td>Cornstarch</td><td></td><td></td></tr>
<tr><td>lb.</td><td>Tapioca Flour</td><td></td><td></td></tr>
<tr><td>lb.</td><td>Bread Flour</td><td></td><td></td></tr>
<tr><td>lb.</td><td>Cake Flour</td><td></td><td></td></tr>
<tr><td>lb.</td><td>Pastry Flour</td><td></td><td></td></tr>
<tr><td>lb.</td><td>Elbow Macaroni</td><td></td><td></td></tr>
<tr><td>lb.</td><td>Spaghetti</td><td></td><td></td></tr>
<tr><td>lb.</td><td>Rice</td><td></td><td></td></tr>
<tr><td>lb.</td><td>Noodles</td><td></td><td></td></tr>
<tr><td colspan="4">Subtotal</td></tr>
</table>

Groceries — Oils and Fats			
Quantity/Size	**Item**	**Unit Price**	**Extension**
lb.	Margarine		
lb.	Shortening		
lb.	Salad Oil		
		Subtotal	

Groceries — Dressing and Condiments			
Quantity/Size	**Item**	**Unit Price**	**Extension**
gal.	Mayonnaise		
gal.	Dill Pickles		
gal.	Sweet Relish		
gal.	Salad Dressing		
gal.	Vinegar		
gal.	Soy Sauce		
gal.	Worcestershire Sauce		
gal.	French Dressing		
		Subtotal	

Groceries — Coloring and Extracts			
Quantity/Size	**Item**	**Unit Price**	**Extension**
qt.	Caramel Color		
pt.	Yellow		
pt.	Red		
pt.	Green		
pt.	Lemon Extract		
pt.	Vanilla Extract		
pt.	Maple Extract		
		Subtotal	
		Other Groceries Total	

Butter, Eggs, and Cheese			
Quantity/Size	**Item**	**Unit Price**	**Extension**
lb.	American Cheese		
lb.	Chip Butter		
doz.	Eggs		
	Butter, Eggs, and Cheese Total		

Fruits and Vegetables — Frozen			
Quantity/Size	**Item**	**Unit Price**	**Extension**
lb.	Strawberries		
lb.	Peaches		
lb.	Blueberries		
lb.	Lima Beans		
lb.	Corn		
lb.	Broccoli		
lb.	Brussels Sprouts		
lb.	Mixed Vegetables		
lb.	Peas		
lb.	Cauliflower		
		Subtotal	
		Fruits and Vegetables Total	

Meat, Poultry, and Fish			
Quantity/Size	**Item**	**Unit Price**	**Extension**
lb.	Beef Ground		
lb.	Beef Round		
lb.	Beef Ribs		
lb.	Beef Rib Eyes		
lb.	Beef Chuck		
lb.	Club Steak		
lb.	Beef Tenderloin		
lb.	Pork Loin		
lb.	Boston Butt		
lb.	Veal Leg		
lb.	Veal Shoulder		
lb.	Veal Loin		
lb.	Ham		
		Subtotal	
		Meat, Poultry, and Fish Total	

Supplies			
Quantity/Size	**Item**	**Unit Price**	**Extension**
	Napkins		
	Butter Chips		
	Souffle Cups		
	Paper Bags		
gal.	Bleach		
gal.	Dish		
lb.	Salute		
ea.	Pot Brushes		
		Supplies Total	

Sales . . . . _____
Inventory at Beginning of Month . . . . _____
Purchases for the Month . . . . _____
Food in Production . . . . _____
Final Inventory . . . . _____
Cost of Food Sold . . . . _____
Food Cost Percent . . . . _____

COMPUTER APPLICATIONS

An important application of the computer involves the recording of the food service establishment's inventory. The calculations involved in completing an inventory sheet are very time consuming. The computer inventory sheet will eliminate most of the mathematical calculations, saving the establishment both time and money.

There are many types of software available to complete this task. Some chefs and managers use "canned programs," while others set up their own spreadsheets using programs like Microsoft Excel.

The format of the computer inventory sheet varies from the form used when taking inventory by hand. (See Figure 11–5.)

You will be responsible for entering the quantity. What is entered into the quantity column is determined by how much you have in stock, and by how the product is packaged. It is important that the quantity entered is in terms of the unit. For example, suppose you have 16 pounds of margarine in inventory, and the cost of the margarine is $16.64 for a 32-pound case. The amount you enter into the quantity column is 0.5, since the 16 pounds you have in inventory is one-half of the 32 pounds that is in one case.

Example: the following has been found in inventory:

- 8 lb. of margarine at $16.63 for a 32-lb. case
- 20 lb. of shortening at $26.00 for a 50-lb. tin
- 3 lb. of salad oil at $22.00 for a 5-gal. can

Figure 11–6 shows how the computer inventory sheet would look.

Groceries — Oils and Fats				
Quantity	Item	Size	Unit Price	Extension
	Margarine	32-lb. case	$ 16.64	
	Shortening	50-lb. tin	26.00	
	Salad Oil	5-gal. can	22.00	
			Subtotal	

Figure 11–5 *Computer inventory sheet*

Groceries — Oils and Fats				
Quantity	Item	Size	Unit Price	Extension
0.25	Margarine	32-lb. case	$ 16.64	$ 4.16
0.4	Shortening	50-lb. tin	26.00	10.40
0.075	Salad Oil	5-gal. can	22.20	1.67
			Subtotal	$16.23

Figure 11–6 *Computer inventory sheet, completed*

SUMMARY REVIEW 11–5

Calculate the extension prices for Items 1–7 on the following pages using either a computer or calculator.

Canned Goods				
Quantity	Item	Size	Unit Price	Extension
6	Apples	#10	$ 3.52	$ ———
7	Apricots	#10	5.29	———
10	Beans, Green	#10	2.61	———
7	Beans, Kidney	#10	1.84	———
12	Beans, Wax	#10	2.07	———
13	Bean Sprouts	#10	2.79	———
5	Beets, Whole	#10	3.03	———
6	Carrots, Whole	#10	3.44	———
7	Cherries	#10	7.31	———
2	Fruit Cocktail	#10	4.10	———
1	Noodles (Chow Mein)	#10	2.74	———
4	Peach Halves	#10	3.71	———
6	Peaches, Pie	#10	3.60	———
5	Pears	#10	3.51	———
3	Pineapple Tidbits	#10	3.79	———
8	Pineapple Slices	#10	3.84	———
3	Plums	#10	3.24	———
5	Pumpkin	#10	3.85	———
7	Sweet Potatoes	#10	3.26	———
8	Tomato Catsup	#10	2.12	———
7	Tomato Puree	#10	3.67	———
4	Tomatoes	#10	3.41	———
6	Asparagus Spears	#2	6.50	———
10	Cream Style Corn	#22	2.08	———
8	Whole Kernel Corn	#2	2.15	———
16	Salmon	#2	2.30	———
			Canned Goods Total	$ ———

Item No. 1 *Canned goods*

Groceries — Spices				
Quantity	**Item**	**Size**	**Unit Price**	**Extension**
1.25	Allspice, Ground	lb.	$ 7.02	$ ———
2.5	Bay Leaves	lb.	7.20	———
1	Chili Powder	lb.	4.35	———
3	Cinnamon	lb.	6.20	———
2.5	Cloves, Ground	lb.	6.95	———
1.75	Ginger, Ground	lb.	4.50	———
2.25	Cumin Seed	lb.	3.82	———
1.5	Celery Seed	lb.	5.10	———
3.25	Caraway Seed	lb.	2.90	———
0.25	Mace	lb.	12.50	———
1.25	Mustard, Dry	lb.	2.80	———
2.75	Marjoram, Dry	lb.	3.50	———
2	Nutmeg	lb.	8.50	———
3.5	Oregano	lb.	4.25	———
2	Pepper, White	lb.	6.00	———
4	Pepper, Black	lb.	5.00	———
3	Pickling Spice	lb.	4.18	———
2	Rosemary Leaves	lb.	8.12	———
1.74	Sage	lb.	10.82	———
2.25	Thyme	lb.	5.89	———
			Subtotal	$ ———

Item No. 2 *Other groceries*

Groceries — Dressing and Condiments				
Quantity	**Item**	**Size**	**Unit Price**	**Extension**
4	Mayonnaise	gal.	$ 8.44	$ ———
2	Dill Pickles	gal.	3.22	———
3	Sweet Relish	gal.	4.60	———
3.5	Salad Dressing	gal.	3.88	———
7	Vinegar	gal.	1.20	———
2.75	Soy Sauce	gal.	6.48	———
5	Worcestershire Sauce	gal.	3.73	———
6.25	French Dressing	gal.	4.54	———
			Subtotal	$ ———

Item No. 2 *Other groceries*

Groceries — Oils and Fats				
Quantity	**Item**	**Size**	**Unit Price**	**Extension**
0.43	Margarine	3-lb. case	$ 7.28	$ ———
1.5	Shortening	50-lb. tin	20.80	———
0.8	Salad Oil	5-gal. can	6.60	———
			Subtotal	$ ———

Item No. 2 *Other groceries*

Groceries — Dry Bulk Goods				
Quantity	Item	Size	Unit Price	Extension
7	Baking Soda	lb.	$ 0.22	$ ———
1.6	Baking Powder	5-lb. box	8.40	———
1.6	Cocoa	5-lb. box	5.90	———
5	Coconut Shred	lb.	1.12	———
9	Cracker Meal	lb.	0.18	———
3	Chicken Base	lb.	1.12	———
8	Beef Base	lb.	1.15	———
5	Raisins	lb.	1.19	———
8	Cornmeal	lb.	0.15	———
13	Cornstarch	lb.	0.46	———
18	Tapioca Flour	lb.	0.22	———
0.58	Bread Flour	100-lb. bag	20.00	———
0.61	Cake Flour	100-lb. bag	25.00	———
0.75	Pastry Flour	100-lb. bag	22.00	———
13	Elbow Macaroni	lb.	0.49	———
16	Spaghetti	lb.	0.52	———
7	Rice	lb.	0.45	———
10	Noodles	lb.	1.13	———
			Subtotal	$ ———

Item No. 2 *Other groceries*

Groceries — Coloring and Extracts				
Quantity	Item	Size	Unit Price	Extension
2	Caramel Color	qt.	$ 5.95	$ ———
1.5	Yellow	pt.	3.12	———
2.25	Red	pt.	2.82	———
3	Green	pt.	3.16	———
2	Lemon Extract	pt.	6.99	———
2	Vanilla Extract	pt.	11.89	———
2.5	Maple Extract	pt.	4.09	———
			Subtotal	$ ———
			Other Groceries Total	$ ———

Item No. 2 *Other groceries*

Butter, Eggs, and Cheese				
Quantity	Item	Size	Unit Price	Extension
6	American Cheese	lb.	$ 1.70	$ ———
12	Chip Butter	lb.	1.12	———
18	Eggs	doz.	0.86	———
	Butter, Eggs, and Cheese Total			$ ———

Item No. 3 *Butter, eggs, and cheese*

Coffee and Tea				
Quantity	**Item**	**Size**	**Unit Price**	**Extension**
18	Coffee	lb.	$ 2.68	$ ———
$\frac{1}{4}$	Tea — indiv. (100)	pkg.	2.50	———
$\frac{1}{2}$	Tea — iced (48)	pkg.	6.24	———
			Coffee and Tea Total	$ ———

Item No. 4 *Coffee and tea*

Fruits and Vegetables — Fresh				
Quantity	**Item**	**Size**	**Unit Price**	**Extension**
3	Carrots	bu.	$ 0.89	$ ———
2	Endive	lb.	1.45	———
8	Head Lettuce	head	0.89	———
9	Leaf Lettuce	lb.	1.25	———
18	Dry Onions	lb.	0.46	———
50	Red Potatoes	lb.	0.53	———
46	Idaho Potatoes	lb.	0.51	———
4	Tomatoes	lb.	0.88	———
2	Parsley	bu.	0.45	———
6	Green Peppers	lb.	0.48	———
9	Apples	lb.	0.83	———
8	Bananas	lb.	0.35	———
6	Lemons	doz.	2.25	———
4	Oranges	doz.	2.25	———
6	Radishes	bu.	0.35	———
4	Celery	bu.	0.89	———
			Subtotal	$ ———

Item No. 5 *Fruits and vegetables—fresh*

Fruits and Vegetables — Frozen				
Quantity	**Item**	**Size**	**Unit Price**	**Extension**
8	Strawberries	lb.	$ 1.06	$ ———
10	Peaches	lb.	1.17	———
18	Blueberries	lb.	1.52	———
27	Lima Beans	lb.	1.23	———
30	Corn	lb.	0.63	———
17	Broccoli	lb.	0.78	———
11	Brussels Sprouts	lb.	0.87	———
19	Mixed Vegetables	lb.	0.57	———
23	Peas	lb.	0.56	———
18	Cauliflower	lb.	0.90	———
			Subtotal	$ ———
			Fruits and Vegetables Total	$ ———

Item No. 5 *Fruits and vegetables—frozen*

Meat, Poultry, and Fish				
Quantity	Item	Size	Unit Price	Extension
16	Beef Ground	lb.	$ 1.72	$ ———
20	Beef Round	lb.	2.25	———
25	Beef Ribs	lb.	2.95	———
23	Beef Rib Eyes	lb.	3.20	———
20	Beef Chuck	lb.	1.95	———
16	Club Steak	lb.	3.58	———
15	Beef Tenderloin	lb.	6.20	———
27	Pork Loin	lb.	5.40	———
19	Boston Butt	lb.	2.20	———
33	Veal Leg	lb.	7.40	———
10	Veal Shoulder	lb.	6.22	———
13	Veal Loin	lb.	8.20	———
30	Ham	lb.	2.35	———
			Meat, Poultry, and Fish Total	$ ———

Item No. 6 *Meat, poultry, and fish*

Supplies				
Quantity	Item	Size	Unit Price	Extension
6	Napkins		$ 41.00	$ ———
9	Butter Chips		5.48	———
20	Souffle Cups		7.80	———
17	Paper Bags		7.95	———
6	Bleach	gal.	1.24	———
9	Dish	gal.	3.89	———
20	Salute	lb.	0.58	———
6	Pot Brushes	ea.	2.89	———
			Supplies Total	$ ———

Item No. 7 *Supplies*

SUMMARY REVIEW 11–6

From Summary Review 11–5, fill in the totals for all the categories.

Weekly or Period Inventory Recapitulation		
Week Ending September 12, 20___		Period Ending September 30, 20___
Item No.	**Item**	**Amount**
1.	Canned Goods	$ ———
2.	Other Groceries	———
3.	Butter, Eggs, Cheese	———
4.	Coffee and Tea	———
5.	Fruits and Vegetables	———
6.	Meat, Poultry, and Fish	———
	TOTAL FOOD	$ ———
7.	Supplies	$ ———
	Total Inventory Value	$ ———
Called By_____		Extended by _____ Manager _____

SUMMARY REVIEW 11–7

Calculate the monthly food cost using the final inventory from Summary Review 11–6. The amount of food in production is $15,020.

Total Sales $53,265.00
Inventory at the Beginning of the Month 6,525.35
Purchases for the Month 16,001.19
Final Inventory . . . . ———
Cost of Food Sold . . . . ———
Food Cost Percent . . . . ———

DISCUSSION QUESTIONS

Based upon your answer in Summary Review 11–7, does this establishment have problems with their monthly food cost? What will happen to the food cost if no one counts the amount of food in production?

CHAPTER
12
Purchasing and Receiving

OBJECTIVES

At the completion of this chapter, the student should be able to:

1. Prepare requisitions.
2. Prepare invoice forms and find extension prices.
3. Prepare purchase specifications and purchase orders.
4. Identify the computer as a means of communication.

KEY WORDS

requisition
invoice
purchase specifications

purchase order
point-of-sale computers
purveyors

In order to run a successful food service operation it is essential that the chef, manager, or food service professional keep accurate, up-to-date, and detailed records. Records must be kept of all business transactions that are carried on within an organization. In this chapter, we will discuss three vital business forms that are used in the food service industry. Invoices, requisitions, and purchase orders are familiar forms to managers that buy and sell products.

VITAL BUSINESS FORMS

Business forms used in food service operations vary depending on the accounting system. The accountant may be a full-time employee or hired on a part-time basis. He or she provides the operation with forms that must be kept up to date and that reflect the daily business operation. It is important to keep a daily record of such items as the cash register readings, cash on hand, bank deposits, cash paid out, checks issued, invoices, requisitions, and purchase orders.

It can be said, without hesitation, that behind every successful business is usually a good record keeper. In a food service operation, that person might be the manager, assistant manager, or someone designated for this specific duty, such as the food and beverage controller.

Requisitions

In a food service operation, all supplies (food, cleaning products, paper products, etc.) are kept in the storage area. The storage area may be located on the same floor as the kitchen for easy access, or on another floor or basement area, making it a little difficult to reach. A cook in the

Storeroom Requisition

Date: October 23, 20 ____   Charge to Kitchen

Quantity	Unit	Item	Unit Price	Extension Price
6	#10 cans	Sliced Apples	$3.55	$21.30
4	#10 cans	Tomato Juice	1.97	7.88
1	lb.	Fresh Mushrooms	1.55	1.55
2	lb.	Beef Base	5.21	10.42
4	lb.	Cornstarch	0.46	1.84

TOTAL $42.99

Approved by _____

Signed _____

Figure 12–1 *Storeroom requisition form*

kitchen needs certain supplies from the storage area to carry out the day's production. To obtain these supplies, the cook fills out a storage area **requisition.** (See Figure 12–1.) A requisition is a demand made, usually in written form, for something that is required. On the form, the cook states the quantity needed, the unit, and a description or name of each item. The requisition may be approved by a superior. The cook who is going to use the items must also sign the requisition. This requisition is then taken to the storage area and the supplies are issued. If the storage area is a distance from the cook's station, the requisition may be given to a runner who acquires the supplies for the cook. The person in charge of the storage area, usually referred to as the steward, marks the unit price and extension price on each item. The steward also finds the total price of the food items issued. The requisition is then filed and used for the following purposes:

1. Accounts for all items issued from the storage area each day.

2. Controls theft and waste.

3. Provides the figures necessary for the daily food cost report.

4. Ensures that all items are issued only to the proper personnel.

5. Assists in controlling purchasing and eliminating large inventories.

T I P S . . .   **To Insure Perfect Solutions**

Multiply the quantity times the unit price to find the extension price.

President Sez...

"Knowing and learning how to use math is essential for a chef or manager or anyone involved in a food service operation. Math is the building block for everything you do in business and in life. It is the logic of the thought process. It allows you to plan and forecast for future business when you have to purchase foods and supplies. Simply put, it means that by knowing how to use math and using it correctly, you will have enough steaks available for your guests who want to order them on a Saturday evening."

Gail Allen
President
SYSCO Foods
Albany, New York

Gail Allen is the president of SYSCO Foods in Albany, New York. SYSCO is a full-service distributor of perishable and nonperishable supplies. SYSCO's number one goal is to work in partnership with food service operators and provide them with quality products. SYSCO of Albany provides their customers with convenient service and the customer satisfaction that they demand and deserve in today's competitive marketplace. President Allen oversees a company that provides products to food service operators in a large geographical area that includes the state of Vermont and Berkshire County in Massachusetts. In New York State, SYSCO of Albany provides food and supplies to operators reaching south to the Bronx, north to the Canadian border, and west to Oneonta and Herkimer, New York.

SUMMARY REVIEW 12–1

Prepare four storage area requisition forms using the example shown in this section. Work the following problems by finding the extension price and the total.

1. 8—#10 cans sliced peaches @ $3.71 per can
   7—#10 cans whole tomatoes @ $2.83 per can
   12 heads iceberg lettuce @ $0.79 per head
   3 dozen eating apples @ $3.50 per dozen
   5 pounds corn starch @ $.56 per pound
   4 pounds margarine @ 4.76 per pound

2. 5—#10 cans sliced pineapple @ $3.50 per can
   4—#10 cans cherries @ $7.21 per can
   3 bunches celery @ $0.89 per bunch
   6 pounds tomatoes @ $0.76 per pound
   2 bunches carrots @ $0.59 per bunch
   9 dozen eggs @ $0.92 per dozen

3. 8—13-ounce cans tuna fish @ $1.79 per can
   5 dozen eggs @ $0.92 per dozen
   9—1-pound cans salmon @ $2.25 per can
   6—$2\frac{1}{2}$-pound boxes frozen peas @ $0.56 per pound
   8—$2\frac{1}{2}$-pound boxes frozen corn @ $0.58 per pound
   7 heads iceberg lettuce @ $0.79 per head

Distributor:	Haines Foods, Inc.		Phone: _____
			Date: October 20, 20___
Address:	70 Greenbrier Avenue Ft. Mitchell, KY 41017		

Distributors of Fine Food Products — Wholesale Only

| No. of Pieces 5 | Salesperson Joe Jones | | Order No. 2860 | Invoice # J 2479 |

| Packed by: G.C. City State: | Sold To: Street: Covington, KY | Mr. John Doe 120 Elm Avenue | | |

Case	Pack	Size	Canned Foods	Price	Amount
4	6	#10 can	Sliced Apples	20.87	83.48
3	6	#10 can	Pitted Cherries	43.85	131.55
2	12	#5 can	Apple Juice	11.97	23.94
1	24	1 lb.	Cornstarch	11.04	11.04
2	24	#2$\frac{1}{2}$ can	Asparagus	25.73	51.46
				Total Amount	$301.47

Figure 12–2 *Invoice form*

4. 3—#10 cans tomato puree @ $2.65 per can

    4—1-pound boxes cornstarch @ $0.56 per pound

    $2\frac{1}{2}$ pounds leaf lettuce @ $0.89 per pound

    5—$2\frac{1}{2}$-pound boxes lima beans @ $1.23 per pound

    $2\frac{1}{2}$ pounds fresh mushrooms @ $1.26 per pound

    4 bunches green onions @ $0.95 per bunch

    3 bunches parsley @ $0.49 per bunch

    5 heads iceberg lettuce @ $0.79 per head

Invoices

An **invoice** is a written document listing goods sent to a purchaser by a vendor with their prices, quantity, and charges. (See Figure 12–2.) Individual companies have their own types of invoices depending upon what they feel is necessary to list. Some invoices are simple, while others are more complex. Most invoices today, in our computerized world, are computer printouts. An invoice accompanies each shipment or delivery of food brought into a food service operation. Before signing for a shipment, the person receiving the delivery must check the items delivered with those listed on the invoice to ensure all items listed have been received. This person also checks for sanitation and quality of the purchased items.

The invoice is important to the food service operator or manager because it provides the figures for the food purchased. These figures are necessary when computing the food cost percent. The invoice is also important when checking the charges listed on the bill or statement sent by the vendor. Some business people opt to pay cash for the delivery or must pay cash on delivery because of a poor credit rating. Most wait for a bill or statement and check all charges against the invoices received with each delivery. This is a good business practice.

If an establishment has a policy of using purchase orders, then the invoice can be used by the bookkeeper to check against a copy of the purchase order before the bill is paid.

T I P S . . . .   **To Insure Perfect Solutions**

To find the amount column, multiply the number of cases times the price.

SUMMARY REVIEW 12–2

Prepare four invoice forms using the example shown in this section. Work the following problems by finding the extension price and the total. Assume that you work for Curran Foods, Inc. Use today's date and your own name as salesperson.

1. Order No. 2861; Invoice No. J2480; packed by R.G.;
   sold to Manor Restaurant, 590 Walnut Street,
   Cincinnati, Ohio 45202.
   4 cases 6—#10 cans whole tomatoes @ $16.98 per case
   6 cases 12—50-ounce cans tomato soup @ $16.40 per case
   2 cases 20 pounds spaghetti @ $9.77 per case
   $4\frac{1}{2}$ cases 4—1-gallon jars mayonnaise @ $14.84 per case
   2 boxes—15 pounds sliced bacon @ $24.30 per box
   2 cases 24—1-pound cans coffee @ $68.17 per case

2. Order No. 2862; Invoice No. J2481; packed by R.H.;
   sold to Sinton Hotel, 278 Vine Street,
   Cincinnati, Ohio 45202.
   3 cases 4—1-gallon whole dill pickles @ $16.10 per case
   6 cases 12—15-ounce chicken rice soup @ $27.37 per case
   4 cases 4—1-gallon sweet pickle relish @ $18.40 per case
   6 cases 6—#10 cans tomatoes diced @ $13.97 per case
   5 cases 6—#10 cans sliced pineapple @ $22.70 per case
   3 cases 4—5-pound American cheese, sliced @ $33.98 per case

3. Order No. 2863; Invoice No. J2482; packed by B.B.;
   sold to Cincinnati Businessmen's Club, 529 Plum Street,
   Cincinnati, Ohio 45202.
   3 cases 6—#10 cans catsup @ $19.51 per case
   2 cases 6—#10 cans chili sauce @ $22.49 per case
   1 case 6—1-gallon cider vinegar @ $10.41 per case
   3 boxes 10 pounds lasagna @ $6.84 per box
   9 cases 6—#10 cans sliced peaches @ $22.26 per case
   2 pack 16-ounce cracked black pepper @ $5.30 per pack

4. Order No. 2864; Invoice No. J2482; packed by J.M.;
   sold to Norwood High School Cafeteria,
   2078 Elm Avenue, Norwood, Ohio 45212.

   7 cases 6—#10 cans sliced apples @ $20.87 per case

   6 boxes 10 pounds medium egg noodles @ $8.86 per box

   2 cases 6—#10 cans bean sprouts @ $16.72 per case

   3 bags 50 pounds granulated sugar @ $16.70 per bag

   2 cases 12—2-pound brown sugar @ $12.67 per case

   2 cases 30—1-pound margarine @ $10.77 per case

PURCHASE SPECIFICATIONS

Purchase specifications are an important part of a successful food service operation. They provide a detailed description of the items being purchased.

Most restaurants use purchase specifications when purchasing meat, seafood, and produce (fruit and vegetables). For example, when purchasing ribs of beef, the specifications may be:

1. Grade—choice.

2. Weight—20 to 22 pounds.

3. Short ribs removed after measuring $1\frac{1}{2}$ inches from the "eye" of the rib.

4. The back should not have a heavy covering of fat.

5. Ribs should be aged 15 to 20 days.

6. Back bones should be separated from the seven rib bones.

7. Rib tied—Oven ready.

When purchasing fruit, the specifications usually list the size, weight, softness, brand, number desired, and, when appropriate, the color. A copy of purchase specifications is mailed, given, or faxed to the vendor before the food service establishment begins buying.

Purchase Orders

Purchase orders are used often in certain business operations, but only occasionally in the food service business. Large restaurant chains are more likely to use them than small or independent operators.

A **purchase order** is a written form that indicates to the vendor how many items are to be delivered to an establishment, and lists the prices for each item. (See Figure 12–3.) Two individual employees of the food service operation, such as the manager and purchasing agent, should sign the order. This step is necessary for control purposes. With two signatures, there is less chance for collusion between the purveyor and the person who buys the products. This form tells the vendor that if the items delivered compare favorably with the items and prices listed on the order, then payment will be made.

In most food service operations, one person is designated to do the purchasing. This person is usually called the *purchasing agent*. In small operations, this duty is often performed by the manager, assistant

Hasenours Restaurant Barret and Oak Streets Louisville, KY 40222			Purchase Order No. 1492 Date: October 20, 20___	

To: Jefferson Meat Co.
2868 Baster Avenue
Louisville, KY 40222

Ship To: Hasenours Restaurant
Barrett and Oak Streets
Louisville, KY 40222

Date of Delivery: January 10, 20___
Deliver the items listed below, which are being purchased in accordance with descriptions and prices stated.

Description	Unit	Quantity	Unit Price	Amount
Ribs of Beef — choice 20 to 22 lbs. Aged 15 to 20 days Short ribs removed	lb.	132 lb.	$2.95	$389.40
12 oz. Sirloin Steaks — choice $1\frac{1}{2}$-inch thick Packed for storage	lb.	288 lb.	$3.75	$1,080.00
Beef Chuck for Stew Cut into 1-inch cubes Grade Choice	lb.	40 lb.	$2.28	$91.20
			Total Cost	$1,560.60

Purchasing Agent

Figure 12–3 *Purchase order form*

manager, or chef. In any case, the person doing the buying checks prices and quality with different vendors before the purchase order is sent to the one offering the best deal. Recently, the trend has been to compare vendor prices at the beginning of the year and purchase from one vendor throughout the year. This vendor is referred to as the primary vendor.

The purchase order is usually made out in triplicate (three copies). An original copy is sent to the vendor or, if both have fax (facsimile) machines, it is faxed to them. Copies are kept by the steward and the bookkeeper. The steward uses a copy of the purchase order to check the merchandise when it is delivered by the vendor. A bookkeeper uses a copy to check what was ordered against invoices and statements. Purchase orders eliminate controversy over what was ordered, how much was ordered, who ordered it, and when it was ordered. It is another tool used to exercise good business practices. The memory sometimes fails, which is why records are essential.

T I P S . . . To Insure Perfect Solutions

To find the amount on the purchase order form, multiply the quantity times the unit price.

DISCUSSION QUESTION

What are the benefits of having written purchase specifications as they relate to the financial implications of running a food service establishment? Give at least three examples of why a business should have these specifications.

SUMMARY REVIEW 12–3

Prepare four purchase order forms as shown in this section. Work the following problems by finding the amount and total cost for all items. Assume that you are purchasing for Scarlet Oaks Vocational School, 3254 East Kemper Road, Cincinnati, Ohio. Use today's date and show the date of delivery as one week from that date.

1. Purchase Order No. 1493; To: Hands Packing Co., 8567 Spring Grove Avenue, Cincinnati, Ohio.

Description:	Ground Beef—Chuck 85% lean 15% suet Medium grind
Quantity:	165 pounds
Unit Price:	$2.10 per pound
Description:	10-ounce Sirloin Steaks—Choice $1\frac{1}{2}$-inch tail Frozen
Quantity:	260 pounds
Unit Price:	$3.96 per pound
Description:	14 pounds pork loins—spine bones removed; rib and loin end are separated leaving 2 ribs on loin end. Tenderloin left on loin end.
Quantity:	84 pounds
Unit Price:	$2.85 per pound

2. Purchase Order No. 1494; To: Ideal Bakers Supply, 458 Ross Avenue, Cincinnati, Ohio.

Description:	Cake Flour, 100 pounds
Quantity:	9
Unit Price:	$24.58 per 100 pounds
Description:	Pastry flour, 100 pounds
Quantity:	9
Unit Price:	$17.52 per 100 pounds
Description:	Powdered sugar, 10X, 25-pound bag
Quantity:	5
Unit Price:	$9.01 per bag

Description: Meringue powder, 10-pound box
Quantity: 3
Unit Price: $21.20 per box

3. Purchase Order No. 1495; To: Deluxe Foods,
   6870 High Street, Hamilton, Ohio.

Description: Tuna fish, light meat, chunk 24—13-ounce cans
Quantity: 12 cases
Unit Price: $42.89 per case

Description: Coffee, drip grind, 12—2-pound cans
Quantity: 5 cases
Unit Price: $32.16 per case

Description: Sliced pineapple, 50 count, 6—#10 cans
Quantity: 13 cases
Unit Price: $22.70 per case

Description: Pear halves, 50 count, 6—#10 cans
Quantity: 7 cases
Unit Price: $21.50 per case

4. Purchase Order No. 1496; To: Surk's Meat Packing Co.,
   1520 Eastern Avenue, Covington, Kentucky.

Description: Boston Butt, average, 4 pounds, cottage butt and
                blade bone removed.
Quantity: 48 pounds
Unit Price: $1.92 per pound

Description: Ham, average, 12 pounds, shank bone removed
Quantity: 36 pounds
Unit Price: $2.12 per pound

Description: Sausage, 6 to 1 pound
Quantity: 26 pounds
Unit Price: $1.79 per pound

Description: Bacon, lean, 28 slices to 1 pound
Quantity: 28 pounds
Unit Price: $1.82 per pound

POINT OF SALE COMPUTERS

Computers have also revolutionized the dining experience. In many restaurants, the waitstaff enters the order of the guest into a computer called **point of sales (POS)** either via a touch screen or a handheld terminal. The order is then transmitted to printers in the kitchen. The culinary staff prepares the orders as they are printed in the kitchen. These computerized POS systems save time for food service professionals in many ways—in taking inventory, making reports, handling accounting, and so forth. The systems will calculate the total amount of meals served, the individual items ordered, and numerous other reports that enable a chef to manage the kitchen effectively. Some point-of-sale computers are integrated with inventory programs; when an item is ordered, the inventory is updated instantaneously. The computer has been programmed to know the ingredients in each item ordered. Every time an item is ordered, the computer program subtracts the amount from its inventory database. The chef must know math basics in order to eyeball the reports and determine if the computer is programmed incorrectly.

PURCHASING FOOD USING THE COMPUTER

Most major food **purveyors** have a software program that enables a food service professional to place orders using the computer. This allows information to be transmitted directly.

Each purveyor has developed a software program that lists all of their products offered for sale. The products are categorized (e.g., fish, meat, poultry), or they may be looked up alphabetically. Each product lists information concerning quality, pack, size, and pricing. Many programs also give the buyer nutritional information about the product. Once the purchaser decides how much food to order, the food order is entered into the computer and transmitted to the purveyor. The food company delivers the order at the next scheduled delivery. The food service professional can print the order, invoice, and the receiver's copy with or without prices before it arrives at the establishment. The purveyor can also give the food service professional a list of products and amounts purchased during a specific time period.

CHAPTER 13

Daily Production Reports

OBJECTIVES

At the completion of this chapter, the student should be able to:

1. Complete the cook's production report.
2. Complete the baker's production report.
3. Complete the salad production report.
4. Complete the counter production report.

KEY WORDS

forecasting
food production report
daily production report
cook's production report

baker's production report
salad production report
counter production report

There are a number of production departments in a commercial kitchen. The number and size depends on the size of the food service operation. Each department produces its own special kind of food to meet the needs required for serving breakfast, luncheon, and dinner menus. The production departments will include *cooking, salad, pastry, baking,* and *butchering.* The production that goes on in these departments must be *controlled.* The device used is called a **food production report.** These reports are probably more important in large operations because they help the chef or manager control production situations that can become out of control. (See Figure 13–1.) In small operations, with a smaller production

Chef Sez...

Chef Greg has a lot of sayings:

"Little things mean a lot."

"Being organized and accurate are two of the most important keys to a successful operation."

"In higher volume establishments, even items dropped or damaged should be counted."

"When calculating food wastage (or food harvest that goes to a shelter, which is common now) everything should be accounted for, because it is here where your profits and losses will occur."

"In accordance with daily reports, accuracy is essential in completing food production sheets and annual forecasts."

Greg Benamati
Sous Chef
Whispering Canyon Café & Artist Point
Disney's Wilderness Lodge
Lake Buena Vista, Florida

Whispering Canyon Café is open for breakfast, lunch, and dinner, while Artist Point is a four-star, dinner-only restaurant. Chef Greg supervises 45 cast members (Walt Disney World's name for employees).

Figure 13–1 *A cook counting sausage to complete a daily production report*

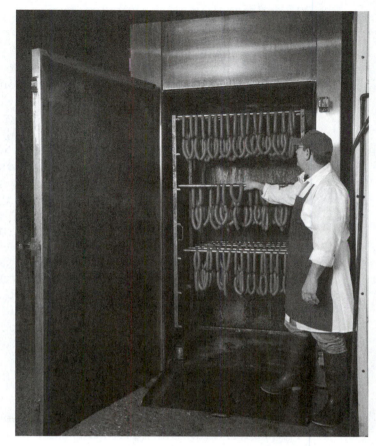

crew and work areas, it is easier to observe all that is taking place; however, production reports are still a necessity to control food cost.

USES OF DAILY PRODUCTION REPORTS

Production reports help to control such essentials as:

- Over or under production
- Leftovers
- Purchasing
- Labor cost
- Waste
- Theft

They will also inform the manager of popular preparations that are selling out, menu items that are not selling, and, to a degree, whether portion sizes should be adjusted. In addition, the report is used in predicting future sales, referred to as **forecasting.** Predicting future sales assists management in the purchasing of food and hiring of future food service employees. If a rotating menu is being used (for example, in retirement communities or senior living centers) on a monthly, biannual, or annual basis, these reports become even more valuable. Management can check back and see which items sold best and how many of each item were sold the last time the menu was used. If these reports are used properly, management can improve the food cost percentage.

FOOD PRODUCTION REPORTS

The forms used in compiling the daily food production reports vary depending on the individual food service operation. Each establishment has its own ideas about control and the information it would like to have listed on the report. Most establishments do, however, request reports from cooks, pastry cooks, bakers, and the salad and counter service departments. The report forms are usually quite simple to fill out so they do not take up too much of an employee's time to complete. Some forms, such as the one used in the counter report, show unit price, total price, and total sales.

Examples of four different daily food production reports are shown in Figures 13–2 through 13–6. These forms are typical of those used in the food service industry. Although these examples are easy to follow, a few comments on each can help you to become more competent when filling them out. The math involved in completing all of these reports is counting and subtraction. The person who plans the size of the portion, the quantity required, and the amount of portions to prepare has to use additional math skills such as yield tests, proportions and ratios, and so forth. For the purpose of this chapter, the student should concentrate on learning how to accurately complete the reports, because food cost and food cost percentages depend upon their accuracy.

Cook's Production Report (See Figure 13–2)

Recipe File Number. This number is placed on the recipe for easy access when it is filed. Standard recipes are used in many food service establishments to control the cost, taste, texture, quality, and amount of food being prepared.

Size of Portion. The manager or chef fills in this column to let the cook and the waitperson know the portion size they are serving or dishing up. In most establishments, the portion size is a set policy and is indicated on the portion charts on display in the production area.

Raw Quantity Required. This is usually designated by the chef or cook. Sometimes the manager lists this figure, but it must be done by a person familiar with production and with the policy of the establishment. The chef, manager, or purchasing agent is responsible for ordering the raw

Unit: First National Bank Day: Thursday		Meal: Luncheon Date: June 23, 20___				Customers: 150
Item	Recipe File Number	Size of Portion	Raw Quantity Required	Portions to Prepare	Portions Left or Time Out	Portions Served
Roast Round of Beef	15	3 oz.	25 lb.	80	out 8:15	80
Roast Loin of Pork	20	$4\frac{1}{2}$ oz.	12 lb.	30	8	22
Filet of Sole	8	5 oz.	14 lb.	42	2	40
Veal Goulash	18	6 oz.	10 lb.	24	9	15
Swiss Steak	14	5 oz.	15 lb.	48	12	36
Mashed Potatoes	42	4 oz.	20 lb.	60	5	55
Peas and Carrots	51	3 oz.	9 lb.	48	18	30
Succotash	52	3 oz.	5 lb.	26	1	25

Figure 13–2 *Cook's production report*

quantity required from a vendor and seeing that it is on hand when needed.

Portions to Prepare. This decision is made by the manager or chef and is based on previous production reports and sales history. It is important to know how much of a particular item was sold the last time it appeared on the menu. Also, consideration must be given to other external factors. For example, cold weather could have resulted in an increase of soup sales. This is called **forecasting.**

Portions Left or Time Out. This figure is recorded by the cook and is found by counting the number of portions left after the meal is over. Time out is recorded when the number of a certain item is completely sold out. The time an item sold out is important because it affects the number of items prepared the next time the item appears on the menu.

Portions Served. This is recorded by the cook and is found by subtracting the number left from the number prepared. It is an important figure because this number influences the number of portions prepared when the item appears again on the menu.

SUMMARY REVIEW 13-1

Complete the following cook's production reports to find the amount of portions served. To complete the production report, use today's day and date.

1. Unit: Mason Art Co.

   Day: _____

   Date: _____

   Meal: Luncheon

   Customers: 50

Item	Recipe Number	Size of Portion	Raw Quantity Required	Portions to Prepare	Portions Left or Time Out	Portions Served
Spanish Steak	18	5 oz.	8 lb.	25	7	_____
Salisbury Steak	19	5 oz.	7 lb.	22	9	_____
Beef Pot Roast	20	3 oz.	8 lb.	32	13	_____
Au Gratin Potatoes	2	4 oz.	10 lb.	35	6	_____
KY Succotash	10	3 oz.	5 lb.	30	4	_____
Mashed Potatoes	3	4 oz.	20 lb.	60	13	_____
Lima Beans	12	3 oz.	$2\frac{1}{2}$ lb.	15	2	_____

2. Unit: 2nd National Bank

Day: _____

Date: _____

Meal: Luncheon

Customers: 131

Item	Recipe Number	Size of Portion	Raw Quantity Required	Portions to Prepare	Portions Left or Time Out	Portions Served
Sautéed Pork Chop	32	4 oz.	6 lb.	22	8	_____
Turkey Steaks	45	4 oz.	12 lb.	45	7	_____
Baked Halibut	54	5 oz.	10 lb.	32	12	_____
Roast Veal	30	3 oz.	10 lb.	38	13	_____
Parsley Potatoes	4	4 oz.	15 lb.	50	6	_____
Hash in Cream Potatoes	5	4 oz.	14 lb.	45	11	_____
Peas and Celery	13	3 oz.	$7\frac{1}{2}$ lb.	44	9	_____
Cut Green Beans	16	3 oz.	5 lb.	30	5	_____

3. Unit: Chase Machine Tool Co.

Day: _____

Date: _____

Meal: Luncheon

Customers: 155

Item	Recipe Number	Size of Portion	Raw Quantity Required	Portions to Prepare	Portions Left or Time Out	Portions Served
Sautéed Veal Steak	31	4 oz.	5 lb.	26	3	_____
Beef Sauerbraten	21	3 oz.	8 lb.	32	6	_____
Beef Goulash	26	6 oz.	15 lb.	54	2	_____
Swiss Steak	22	5 oz.	20 lb.	62	8	_____
Rissel Potatoes	1	4 oz.	12 lb.	36	9	_____
Escallop Potatoes	6	4 oz.	8 lb.	26	11	_____
Stewed Tomatoes	14	3 oz.	1 #10 can	22	5	_____
Corn	15	3 oz.	$7\frac{1}{2}$ lb.	44	12	_____

4. Unit: Norwood High School

Day: _____

Date: _____

Meal: Luncheon

Customers: 100

Item	Recipe Number	Size of Portion	Raw Quantity Required	Portions to Prepare	Portions Left or Time Out	Portions Served
Ham Steak	34	4 oz.	7 lb.	28	6	_____
Roast Turkey	37	3 oz.	15 lb.	36	8	_____
Hamburger Steak	23	5 oz.	13 lb.	42	7	_____
Beef Stroganoff	25	6 oz.	7 lb.	20	5	_____
Macaroni Au Gratin	74	4 oz.	4 lb.	45	11	_____
Mashed Potatoes	3	4 oz.	12 lb.	40	9	_____
Mixed Greens	9	3 oz.	10 lb.	58	13	_____
Carrots Vichy	17	3 oz.	5 lb.	29	16	_____

Baker's Production Report (See Figure 13–3)

Order. The order is recorded by the manager, chef, or pastry chef, and this represents the amount of bakery and pastry items needed for service throughout the day in all departments of the food service operation. If the operation is a catering company, it represents the amount needed in all units served.

On Hand. This figure is recorded by the baker and represents the amount of each item that was left by the previous shift or from the previous day and is still in a usable condition. It may be in a raw or cooked state, frozen or unfrozen.

Prepare. The number to prepare is found by subtracting the amount on hand from the amount ordered. The remainder is the amount to prepare and is recorded by the baker or pastry chef.

Left. The number left is found by counting the number of pieces remaining after the day's service is over. This figure is recorded by the baker or pastry chef.

Sold. The number sold is found by subtracting the number left from the number ordered. This figure is recorded by the cook or pastry chef.

Comments. This space is provided for any information that may be valuable to management. Examples: the time a product is sold out, and the selling of the leftover baked products at a reduced cost or their donation to a charity.

Day: Monday		Date: June 27, 20___				Unit: Leo's Cafeteria
Item	**Order**	**On Hand**	**Prepare**	**Left**	**Sold**	**Comment**
Rolls						
Soft Rye	20 doz.	3 doz.	17 doz.	2 doz.	18 doz.	
Soft White	35 doz.	4 doz.	31 doz.	6 doz.	29 doz.	
Hard White	26 doz.	5 doz.	21 doz.	4 doz.	22 doz.	
Cinnamon	18 doz.	2 doz.	16 doz.	1 doz.	17 doz.	
Rye Sticks	15 doz.	6 doz.	9 doz.	0	15 doz.	Out 7 p.m.
Quick Breads						
Biscuits	12 doz.	1 doz.	11 doz.	3 doz.	9 doz.	Biscuits
Raisin Muffins	24 doz.	5 doz.	19 doz.	5 doz.	19 doz.	left unbaked
						in freezer
Pies						
Cherry	22	6	16	0	22	Out 8 p.m.
Apple	25	4	21	2	23	
Chocolate	15	3	12	0	15	Out
Banana	12	1	11	8	4	7:30 p.m.
Cakes						
Bar	6	2	4	3	3	These left
899 White	10	4	6	6	4	in freezer
Mocha	8	1	7	0	8	Out 7 p.m.

Figure 13–3 *Baker's production report*

Figure 13–4 *Baker completing a production report*

SUMMARY REVIEW 13-2

Complete the following baker's production reports. Find the portions to prepare and how many items were sold. To complete the production report, use today's day and date.

1. Unit: Norwood High School

   Day: _____

   Date: _____

Item	Order	On Hand	Prepare	Left	Sold
Seed Rolls	25 doz.	6 doz.	_____	4 doz.	_____
Rye Rolls	36 doz.	3 doz.	_____	5 doz.	_____
Hard Rolls	28 doz.	6 doz.	_____	2 doz.	_____
Rye Sticks	22 doz.	4 doz.	_____	3 doz.	_____
Biscuits	12 doz.	0	_____	3 doz.	_____
Banana Muffins	10 doz.	0	_____	$1\frac{1}{2}$ doz.	_____
Cherry Pies	18	5	_____	2	_____
Banana Pies	16	2	_____	4	_____
Boston Cream Pies	22	7	_____	6	_____
Devil's Food Cake	13	5	_____	2	_____

2. Unit: Deluxe Shoe Co.

   Day: _____

   Date: _____

Item	Order	On Hand	Prepare	Left	Sold
Soft Rolls	30 doz.	4 doz.	_____	2 doz.	_____
Hard Rolls	28 doz.	6 doz.	_____	5 doz.	_____
Rye Sticks	22 doz.	4 doz.	_____	1 doz.	_____
Pecan Rolls	16 doz.	2 doz.	_____	$\frac{1}{2}$ doz.	_____
Raisin Muffins	9 doz.	1 doz.	_____	$\frac{3}{4}$ doz.	_____
Apple Pies	18	3	_____	1	_____
Peach Pies	14	2	_____	2	_____
Chocolate Pies	22	4	_____	3	_____
Lemon Cake	9	2	_____	4	_____
Chocolate Bar Cake	12	5	_____	3	_____
Fudge Cake	14	1	_____	5	_____

3. Unit: Joe's Cafeteria

Day: _____

Date: _____

Item	Order	On Hand	Prepare	Left	Sold
Cloverleaf Rolls	40 doz.	7 doz.	_____	3 doz.	_____
Caramel Rolls	26 doz.	3 doz.	_____	1 doz.	_____
Seed Rolls	35 doz.	4 doz.	_____	2 doz.	_____
Biscuits	22 doz.	5 doz.	_____	$\frac{1}{2}$ doz.	_____
Corn Muffins	18 doz.	2 doz.	_____	$\frac{3}{4}$ doz.	_____
Pecan Pie	12	3	_____	5	_____
Pumpkin Pie	15	2	_____	4	_____
Custard Pie	10	4	_____	3	_____
Éclair	48	0	_____	8	_____
Cherry Tarts	54	5	_____	7	_____

4. Unit: Wine & Dine Restaurant

Day: _____

Date: _____

Item	Order	On Hand	Prepare	Left	Sold
Soft Rolls	68 doz.	9 doz.	_____	$4\frac{3}{4}$ doz.	_____
Rye Rolls	38 doz.	4 doz.	_____	$5\frac{1}{2}$ doz.	_____
Split Rolls	26 doz.	7 doz.	_____	$2\frac{1}{4}$ doz.	_____
Cinnamon Rolls	32 doz.	6 doz.	_____	$7\frac{3}{4}$ doz.	_____
Apple Muffins	18 doz.	4 doz.	_____	$4\frac{1}{2}$ doz.	_____
Corn Sticks	16 doz.	3 doz.	_____	$2\frac{1}{4}$ doz.	_____
Blueberry Pie	12	4	_____	2	_____
Coconut Cream Pie	14	3	_____	4	_____
White Cake, 8"	9	2	_____	1	_____
Apple Cake, 8"	8	1	_____	0	_____
Yellow Cake, 8"	6	0	_____	3	_____

Salad Production Report (See Figure 13–5)

Order. The order is recorded by the manager, chef, or head salad person, and this represents the amount of each salad to be prepared. It is an estimate of the number or kind of salad needed for serving one meal or for the complete day. Cafeterias and buffet-style restaurants provide an array of assorted salads. The order is very helpful in this type of operation.

On Hand. This figure is recorded by the salad person and represents the amount of each salad that was left by the previous shift or from the previous day and is still in a usable condition.

Day: Tuesday	Date: June 29, 20___		Unit: First National Bank		
Item	**Order**	**On Hand**	**Prepare**	**Left**	**Sold**
Toss	23	8	15	3	20
Italian	12	0	12	0	12
Garden	22	9	13	7	15
Waldorf	16	2	14	6	10
Potato	25	10	15	6	19
Cole Slaw	32	8	24	1	31
Sliced Tomato	26	0	26	3	23
Fruited Gelatin	28	12	16	2	26
Sunshine	14	3	11	4	10
Green Island	25	5	20	5	20
Mixed Fruit	35	6	29	3	32
Chef	46	7	39	12	34
Cucumber	12	1	11	10	2

Figure 13–5 *Salad production report*

Prepare. The number to prepare is found by subtracting the amount on hand from the amount ordered. This figure is recorded by the salad person.

Left. The number left is found by counting the number of each kind of salad remaining after the meal or day's service is concluded. The salad person records this figure.

Sold. The number sold is found by subtracting the number left from the number ordered. This figure is recorded by the salad person.

Comments. This space is provided for information that may be valuable to the head salad person or management. Examples: weather conditions that day, the time a certain salad is sold out, production information or mistakes, and the disposition of leftover salads.

SUMMARY REVIEW 13-3

Complete the following salad production reports. Find the portions to prepare and how many items were sold. To complete the production report, use today's day and date.

1. Unit: 1st Federal Bank

Day: _____

Date: _____

Item	Order	On Hand	Prepare	Left	Sold
Toss	24	4	_____	4	_____
Chef	20	3	_____	2	_____
Garden	16	6	_____	6	_____
Slaw	12	2	_____	3	_____
Gelatin	9	1	_____	7	_____
Fruit	15	9	_____	5	_____
Sliced Tomato	18	4	_____	1	_____
Waldorf	8	5	_____	0	_____

2. Unit: 2nd Federal Bank

Day: _____

Date: _____

Item	Order	On Hand	Prepare	Left	Sold
Italian	22	5	_____	1	_____
Cucumber	24	4	_____	4	_____
Jellied Slaw	18	2	_____	5	_____
Green Island	16	1	_____	2	_____
Macaroni	12	3	_____	6	_____
Carrots	15	6	_____	3	_____
Mixed Greens	14	4	_____	0	_____
Sunshine	26	2	_____	1	_____

3. Unit: Western Insurance Co.

Day: _____

Date: _____

Item	Order	On Hand	Prepare	Left	Sold
Chef	32	6	_____	7	_____
Waldorf	18	7	_____	6	_____
Fruited Slaw	14	8	_____	5	_____
Fruited Gelatin	16	4	_____	1	_____
Sliced Tomato	25	3	_____	0	_____
Garden	28	2	_____	2	_____
Italian	35	0	_____	3	_____
Mixed Green	40	1	_____	4	_____

4. Unit: Garrison Greeting Card Co.

Day: _____

Date: _____

Item	Order	On Hand	Prepare	Left	Sold
Toss	35	4	_____	0	_____
Mixed Green	25	8	_____	2	_____
Garden	20	6	_____	4	_____
Spring	22	2	_____	7	_____
Cottage Cheese	18	0	_____	6	_____
Waldorf	16	3	_____	3	_____
Sunshine	14	0	_____	2	_____
Hawaiian	12	1	_____	0	_____
Macaroni	10	7	_____	1	_____

Counter Production Report (See Figure 13–6)

Number of Portions for Sale. This figure may be recorded by management or the person working the counter. It represents the number of on-hand items that are for sale.

Number of Portions Not Sold. This figure is recorded by the person working the counter. It is found by counting the remaining pieces of each item left after the day's service is concluded.

Number of Portions Sold. This is found by subtracting the number of portions not sold from the number of portions for sale. It is recorded by the person working the counter.

Value Sold. This is found by multiplying the number of portions sold by the unit price. It is found and recorded by the person working the counter.

Total. This is found by adding the figures in the value sold column. It is found and recorded by the person working the counter.

Customer Count. This figure is recorded on the register.

Unit: Latonia Racetrack			Customer Count: 405	
Day: Tuesday			Date: June 28, 20___	

Item	Number of Portions for Sale	Number of Portions Not Sold	Number of Portions Sold	Unit Price	Value Sold
Hot Dogs	135	26	109	$3.25	$354.25
Chicken Patty	75	15	60	4.75	285.00
Hamburgers	150	23	127	4.75	603.25
Barbecue	50	5	45	4.75	213.75
Cube Steaks	70	6	64	5.25	336.00
Milk	125	18	107	1.00	107.00
Shakes	80	7	73	2.50	182.50
Soda	225	28	197	2.00	394.00
Cake	15	2	13	2.75	35.75
Pie	35	8	27	2.75	74.25
Ice Cream	65	9	56	2.25	126.00
Potato Chips	85	13	72	1.50	108.00
Pretzels	45	11	34	1.50	51.00
Name: Bill Thompson				Total	$2870.75

Figure 13–6 *Counter production report*

SUMMARY REVIEW 13-4

Complete the following counter production reports. Find the number of portions not sold, the value of the amount that was sold, and the total value sold. To complete the production report, use today's day and date.

1. Unit: Stevens Processing Co.

   Customer Count: 305

   Day: _____

   Date: _____

Item	Number of Portions for Sale	Number of Portions Not Sold	Number of Portions Sold	Unit Price	Value Sold
Hot Dogs	85	6		3.25	
Hamburgers	95	7		4.75	
Chicken Patty	65	19		4.75	
Barbecue	55	2		5.50	
Cube Steak	40	5		5.75	
Soda	120	21		1.75	
Shakes	60	8		3.25	
Milk	110	7		1.25	
Pie	48	12		3.50	
Ice Cream	60	5		3.75	
			Total Value Sold		

2. Unit: Wall Manufacturing Plant

Customer Count: 435

Day: _____

Date: _____

Item	Number of Portions for Sale	Number of Portions Not Sold	Number of Portions Sold	Unit Price	Value Sold
Hot Dogs	120	6		3.25	
Hamburgers	115	7		4.75	
Chicken Patty	651	19		4.75	
Barbecue	557	2		5.50	
Cube Steak	408	5		5.75	
Soda	1201	21		1.75	
Shakes	6090	8		3.25	
Milk	1101	7		1.25	
Pie	4890	12		3.50	
Ice Cream	6090	5		3.75	
			Total Value Sold		

3. Unit: Deluxe Playing Card Co.

Customer Count: 308

Day: _____

Date: _____

Item	Number of Portions for Sale	Number of Portions Not Sold	Number of Portions Sold	Unit Price	Value Sold
Hot Dogs	120	19		3.25	
Hamburgers	115	24		4.75	
Chicken Patty	651	38		4.75	
Barbecue	557	5		5.50	
Cube Steak	408	17		5.75	
Soda	1201	42		1.75	
Shakes	6090	5		3.25	
Milk	1101	23		1.25	
Pie	4890	16		3.50	
Ice Cream	6090	125		3.75	
			Total Value Sold		

4. Unit: United Shoe Co.

   Customer Count: 390

   Day: _____

   Date: _____

Item	Number of Portions for Sale	Number of Portions Not Sold	Number of Portions Sold	Unit Price	Value Sold
Hot Dogs	175	19		3.25	
Hamburgers	195	24		4.75	
Chicken Patty	751	38		4.75	
Barbecue	587	5		5.50	
Cube Steak	427	17		5.75	
Soda	1238	42		1.75	
Shakes	6290	5		3.25	
Milk	1025	23		1.25	
Pie	4792	16		3.50	
Ice Cream	6193	125		3.75	
			Total Value Sold		

PART V

ESSENTIALS OF MANAGERIAL MATH

CHAPTER 14 • Front of the House and Managerial Mathematical Operations

CHAPTER 15 • Personal Taxes, Payroll, and Financial Statements

People are attracted to a food service establishment because they have heard it has excellent food, competent, friendly service and positive price value relationship, and, perhaps, an attractive decor and atmosphere. The customers may keep coming, but this does not necessarily ensure a successful operation. Behind these necessary elements must be skilled management—an individual or team that can direct people, provide efficient service, and control both money and material so a profit can be made. In this section of the text, the emphasis is on the math functions that help management control money and material and at the same time provide the records necessary for a good accounting system. In addition, information will be presented concerning personal taxes, payroll, and financial reports.

Not all food service students have the desire or ability to manage a food service establishment. However, it is helpful to learn management procedures to better understand the functions of management and to know what makes a successful operation. With this knowledge you can become a better food service employee, which may lead to a more responsible position.

CHAPTER 14

Front of the House and Managerial Mathematical Operations

OBJECTIVES

At the completion of this chapter, the student should be able to:

1. Identify how guest checks are controlled.
2. Compare and contrast old method versus new method in guest check writing.
3. Calculate guest checks.
4. Calculate **sales tax** and **gratuity.**
5. Back out **sales tax** and **gratuity.**
6. Identify the terms **minimum** and **cover charge.**
7. Identify items on the daily cash report.
8. Complete and calculate a daily cash report.
9. Identify and fill out a deposit slip.
10. Write a check.
11. Identify the items on a bank statement.
12. Identify and balance a check register.

KEY WORDS

guest check
POS
cover charge
minimum charge
tipping
sales tax
gratuity
cashier's daily report
expenditures
receipts
gross receipts
bank
total cash

cash paid outs
cash in drawer
actual cash
over or short
record of cash paid outs
all-inclusive
savings or checking account
deposit slip
interest
check
check register
sales tax

As creatively as the culinary staff prepares the food and as good as it tastes, someone has to serve the food, collect the guest check, and account for the amount of money paid for the superb culinary creations. There has to be a partnership between the culinary staff, the front of the house (waitstaff, counter people, cashiers, etc.), and managerial employees in order to collect and account for the revenue received from the guests. This is necessary to exceed the costs of doing business and to make a profit. There are many different types of operations in the food service business. The procedures discussed in this chapter are used in traditional, quick, or casual service restaurants, banquet facilities, city or country clubs, business and industry accounts, or hospital and sports venues. The list can be expanded to any operation that serves and charges guests for food and beverages. The purpose of this chapter is to explain the importance of mathematical skills to the front of the house and managerial employees. These skills will enable employees to calculate and account for money earned by the waitstaff, as well as the business.

WAITSTAFF MATHEMATICAL OPERATIONS

Most food service operations have point-of-sales (POS) computers, used by the waitstaff to calculate the amount of the guest checks. Some establishments still prefer the system of handwritten checks. Regardless of the methods used to keep track and calculate the guests' orders, the waitstaff may use all four basic mathematical operations (addition, subtraction, multiplication, and division) to perform their jobs effectively. In addition, the knowledge of percentage calculation is of utmost importance, since most waitstaffs' pay is dependent on receiving a percentage of the guest or banquet check. Some individuals argue that knowledge of math is not needed because of modern technology (POS), but the authors believe that all waitstaff should know how to do these mathematical operations. This knowledge is required when the waitperson has to calculate guest checks in the event of a power failure or a computer crash. More important to the waitperson, however, is knowing how to determine how much money is owed to him or her when a gratuity is automatically added onto the check.

Guest Check

In the food service industry, the bill or bill of sale is called a **guest check.** It is a list of items ordered and the cost of those items tallied when dining in a food service establishment. (See Figure 14–1.) In addition, a guest check will have other information listed on it. This information will be pointed out when explaining the types of checks usually used in the industry. The appearance of a guest check will vary from simple to elaborate depending on the type and kind of operation. From the roadside truck stop to the gourmet restaurant, guest checks are in use and presented at the conclusion of the meal. There are exceptions, however, such as quick and casual service restaurants and buffet-type restaurants, where the guest has to pay for the food and beverages before they are received.

Guest Check Responsibility

Whether the food service operation is using a POS or a guest check that is written and totaled by the waitperson, controls must be in place to eliminate theft by members of the waitstaff and cashiers.

```
            Pavilion
          The Sagamore

1283 DEVIN
--------------------------------
TBL 4/1      CHK 9834  GST 2
    JUL12    12:44PM
--------------------------------

1 CHARD PRIVATE         7.00
1 HONIG SAUV BLANC      7.50
1 COCONUT SHRIMP        8.25
2 TURK/BACON  WRAP     16.50

  Food                 24.75
  Wine                 14.50
  18% Service Chg       7.07
  7% Tax                2.75
  Total Due     $49.07

  Automatic 18% gratuity
  is included.  Additional
  tip is at your discretion.

Add'l Tip:  $_____

  Room Number: _____

Print Name: _____

Signature : _____
```

Figure 14–1 *Point-of-sale guest check*

Date	**Server**	**Table No.**	**No. Persons**	**No. 487176**
1				
2				
3				
4				
5				
6				
7				
8				
9				
10				
11				
12				
13				
14				
15				
16				
17				
18				
19				
20				
21				
22		SUBTOTAL		
23		TAX		
24		TOTAL		
—				No. 487176

Date	Guest Receipt	Persons	Amount of Check	

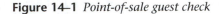

LaRosa's

Figure 14–2 *Blank check*

Guest checks are the responsibility of the waitperson. Although other employees are guided by the information listed on the check during and after the dining period, the waitperson is held responsible for its safekeeping. If a guest walks out without paying or if a check is misplaced or lost, the waitperson may be required to pay the amount due.

At the beginning of the dining period, the waitperson is issued a book or stack of blank checks with serial numbers on them. (See Figure 14–2.) Each individual check is numbered consecutively. The waitperson should sign for each book or stack of checks received. In this way, management can account for each check issued. If a check is missing, it will indicate which person is responsible. At the end of the day or at the end of a service period, the checks are reviewed to determine whether any are missing or contain any errors. Numbering checks and being able to identify the person responsible for each check are also important in checking the daily receipts and assisting the accounting department or accountant in finding and correcting any errors. With a POS system, each waitperson is assigned a personal number or code that identifies him or her, which makes the waitperson accountable for each electronic guest check. This code must be entered into the POS in order to process a guest check. The waitperson must enter all vital information, such as the table number and the guests' order. Figure 14–1 shows that Devin (server number 1283) was the waitperson, and the check was numbered 9834. The POS will keep track of the status of the guest checks, whether they are closed or open. In simple terms, a closed check means that the bill has been paid; an open check means that the guest has not yet paid the bill. It is easy for managers to see which waitperson has not turned in their (still opened) guest checks. Regardless of the system being used, a waitperson should never destroy or discard a check without receiving permission from the supervisor. The authors emphasize that controls are necessary in any business operation. Accounting for guest checks, whether written or computer generated, is essential in order to have a successful business.

Minimum Charge

Establishments featuring live music, a floor show, or some special type of entertainment usually add a **cover charge** to the check. The cover charge is a form of admission fee charged to each person to help pay for the cost of the entertainment. Another method of collecting for entertainment or service is by having a **minimum charge.** This means that a guest is required to spend a certain amount of money, once seated, even if the total check amounts to less. For example, if the minimum charge is $15.00, but the check amounts to only $4.25, the guest is still required to pay the $15.00 minimum charge.

Calculating Guest Checks

In calculating guest checks, two mathematical operations are normally used: multiplication and addition. Figure 14–3 illustrates a bill that shows the operations of multiplication and addition. The first ordered item on the guest check is for "3 Clos Du Bois Merlot" that cost $103.50. The POS is programmed to multiply the quantity by the cost of the individual bottle of wine. The cost of each item has been put into the POS (programmed) by management. In our example, the cost of one bottle was $34.50, so the total was calculated by multiplying $34.50 by 3. As each new item was added to the guest bill, the total amount of that item or items was multiplied to arrive at the subtotal. When the guests had completed their meal, the bill was added to obtain a subtotal. In Figure 14–3, the tax was added to the guest check, and a final total was printed.

There are times when a waitperson will also have to use the mathematical operation of subtraction. Subtraction will occur when an establishment offers a discount, coupon, or some type of reduction on the guest check. In this instance, the discount amount has to be subtracted from the original total.

Figure 14–3 *Printed check used for computerized cash register*

```
TRELLIS RESTAURANT
   MERCHANT'S SQUARE

0383    Table 42  #Party 8
BRYAN S     SvrCk: 19 18:58 12/30

3 CLOS DU BOIS MERLOT         103.50
3 LENTIL APPETIZER             23.85
1 CHOWDER                       4.95
2 SAUSAGE APPETIZER            17.50
1 SHRIMP APPETIZER              9.50
1 TROUT APPETIZER               8.95
6 PORK ENTREE                 112.50
1 DUCK ENTREE, med well        24.50
1 WINTER SUPPER                20.00
2 ICE CREAM                     7.90
1 BALLOON                       4.95
1 PASTRY 5.95                   5.95
4 DEATH BY CHOCOLATE           22.00
5 COFFEE                        9.75
1 hot tea                       1.95
1 GL/SUDUIRAUT                 11.50
1 GALLIANO, rocks               5.00

               Sub Total: 394.25
                    TX1:   37.45
12/30 20:29   TOTAL: 431.70

DESSERTS TO GO
DAZZLING CAKES BY THE SLICE
COLOSSAL COOKIES, ONE OR A DOZEN
ICE CREAM AND SORBETS BY THE CUP OR PINT

CHECK NUMBER:   383
```

SUMMARY REVIEW 14–1

Calculate and total the following guest checks.

1. Three guests had lunch at the Lake Resort. They had two orders of coconut shrimp @ $8.25 each for appetizers; two glasses of Sauvignon Blanc @ $7.50 each; and three glasses of private Chardonnay @ $7.00 each. For their main courses, they had a turkey bacon wrap @ $8.25, a club sandwich @ $9.95, and a chicken wrap @ $8.50.

_____

2. Two guests ordered a $\frac{1}{2}$ bottle of Chianti at $21.00; a bruchetta @ $6.95; an entrée portion of sausage con verde @ $11.95, and a lunch portion of sausage con verde @ $8.95.

_____

3. Four guests dined at a golf club for lunch. They had three pints of Saranac Pale Ale, which cost $3.50 each; one iced tea @ $2.00; two Birdies @ $8.95 each; and two Bunkers @ $9.50 each.

_____

4. Two guests had dinner, and they had an entertainment card that qualified them for a discount. The guests had three glasses of Camelot Pinot Noir @ $6.25 each; a veal artichoke entrée @ $16.95; and a pork tenderloin entrée @ $18.95. The entertainment card discount was $14.00.

_____

5. Four guests went to a buffet show at a casino. The cost of the buffet was $21.95 each. The minimum charge was $30.00 for each person.

_____

Sales Tax

Most states and many municipalities have passed laws that mandate that the food service establishment collect a percentage of the guest bill in the form of **sales taxes.** The percentage amount is not the same in each municipality; even the items that have to be taxed are different. The food service professional must know what is taxed and what is exempt from tax in the municipality in which his or her business is being conducted. Knowing how to multiply using percentages is essential in determining the amount of tax that must be added to the subtotal of the guest check. For example:

Bob and Dolores received a dinner check at the Blue Star Restaurant for $30.75. The sales tax for that particular state is 6%. How much tax did they pay? What was the total bill?

$$
\begin{array}{ll}
\$30.75 & \text{Cost of two dinners} \\
\underline{\times\ .06} & \text{6\% sales tax} \\
\$1.8450 & = \$1.85 \text{ amount of tax}
\end{array}
$$

$$
\begin{array}{ll}
\$30.75 & \text{Cost of two dinners} \\
\underline{+\ 1.85} & \text{Amount of tax} \\
\$32.60 & \text{Total bill}
\end{array}
$$

Amount purchased + amount of tax = Total bill

SUMMARY REVIEW 14–2

Calculate the sales tax and compute the total amount of the guest check for each problem in Summary Review 14–1.

1. Sales tax of 6.5%. Sales tax amount _____ Guest check total _____

2. Sales tax of 8.25%. Sales tax amount _____ Guest check total _____

3. Sales tax of 5.5%. Sales tax amount _____ Guest check total _____

4. Sales tax of 7.125%. Sales tax amount _____ Guest check total _____

5. Sales tax of 6.75%. Sales tax amount _____ Guest check total _____

TIPPING OR GRATUITY

Tipping, also referred to as a **gratuity,** is the giving of a fee for a service rendered. It is sometimes voluntarily given by customers to the waitperson for waiting on them. In banquet service, a gratuity is almost always added automatically onto the bill. Many a la carte restaurants also add the gratuity onto the guest check automatically. Even restaurants that have a voluntary gratuity have modified their practice. In many restaurants, a statement like the following will be on the menu: "A gratuity of 18% will be automatically added to your check for parties of six guests or more."

Most people tip at a percentage of the total check. The accepted practice used to be 15%, but in recent years inflation has even found its way into this old custom. Now the accepted practice is 15 to 20%. Some establishments automatically add 15 to 20% of the check amount to the bill. If this is done, guests should be made aware of this policy before they are served. Often, when the tip is added to the check, the guest is unaware of this policy and still leaves a tip at the table. If the gratuity is added automatically to the check, the gratuity can only be calculated on the amount of food and beverage, not including the tax.

For the guest who wishes to tip 15 or 20% of the amount of the check, or for the waitperson who is asked to figure the amount, there is an easy way to do this mentally. First, find 10% of the bill by moving the decimal point in the total bill one place to the left. Next, take half of the figure just found and add the two figures together if the tip is to be 15%. If the tip is to be 20%, just double the 10% amount.

For example: The total bill is $18.00. To find 10%, move the decimal one place to the left, yielding $1.80. Half of $1.80 is $0.90. Add the two together, $1.80 + 0.90 = $2.70, the amount of the tip at 15%. If tipping 20%, take the amount found for 10%, $1.80, and double it. $1.80 + $1.80 = $3.60, the amount of the tip at 20%.

Computerized registers may be programmed to print out suggested amounts of tips at the bottom of the receipt. (See Figure 14–4.)

SERVICE AMERICA CORP

BEL AQU SAR RACTRACK 34

300 UNION AVE

SARATOGA SPRINGS, NY 12866

AMOUNT: $47.88

TIP TABLE PROVIDED FOR YOUR

CONVENIENCE

15%=$7.18   20%=$9.58   25%=$11.97

Figure 14–4 *Computerized register recipe with suggested tips*

T I P S . . . To Insure Perfect Solutions

To quickly figure out a 15% tip:

1. Use the cost of the food and beverage on the guest check (example $240.00).

2. Take a look at the first two numbers, which equal 24.

3. Divide by 2, which equals 12.

4. Add the 12 to the 24; the 15% tip is $36.00.

5. If you get great service and want to leave a 20% tip, just take the first two numbers and multiply them by 2.

SUMMARY REVIEW 14–3

Find the amount of tip for each of the following bills if the tip equals 15% of the bill.

1. $12.00 _____	6. $52.85 _____
2. $20.00 _____	7. $70.65 _____
3. $24.25 _____	8. $82.60 _____
4. $30.25 _____	9. $105.40 _____
5. $32.50 _____	10. $125.50 _____

Guests, for the most part, generally tip 15 to 20% regardless of the service they receive. Some guests will tip more for exceptional service, some less for poor service. If a waitstaff's gratuity depends on the amount of the guest check, then they should be encouraged to sell more items in order to increase their income (which will also increase the establishment's income)! This is another reason for the food service professional to understand and use math. It can serve as a motivational tool. For example, if one additional $30.00 bottle of wine is sold and the guest leaves an 18% tip, the waitperson will make an additional $5.40. To understand this concept, complete Summary Review 14–4.

SUMMARY REVIEW 14–4

Calculate the additional tip for each server using logic and multiplication to solve the problems. Question 4 also requires addition.

1. Marisa works three shifts a week. If she sells nine additional $30.00 bottles of wine a night and the gratuity is 18%, what is her additional income?

   Each shift _____ Weekly total _____

2. Joe works five shifts a week. He sells 10 additional $7.00 desserts each shift. If the gratuity is 15%, what is his additional income?

   Each shift _____ Weekly total _____

3. Valerie works four shifts a week. She sells 20 additional $6.00 appetizers each shift. If the gratuity is 16%, what is her additional income?

Each shift _____ Weekly total _____

4. Antonio works seven shifts a week. He sells 20 additional $45.00 bottles of wine during the week. He also sells 12 additional $8.50 desserts each shift and 15 additional $9.50 appetizers each shift. If the gratuity is 20%, what is his additional income?

Wine_____ Desserts _____ Appetizers _____Weekly income _____

DISCUSSION QUESTION 14-A

You are a waitperson at a restaurant with a check average of $60.00 per person. A gratuity of 18% is automatically added onto each check. You worked five shifts and served a total 168 guests during the week. Your paycheck summary states that the gratuity is $814.40. What would you do?

Checking the Amount of the Gratuity

If your income depends upon receiving gratuities and the gratuity is automatically added to the check, you should know how to calculate the gratuity and determine if you have been paid the correct amount by the establishment. When waitstaff receive their total gratuity at the end of the pay period, they should check to make certain they've received all the gratuities coming to them. Using a percent to find the total amount of the checks, when only the tip is known, is one way for the waitperson to check that the gratuity is correct.

This is the formula you will use when you know the percent and the amount of the gratuity:

Amount of tip ÷ percent = amount of check.

For example:

A gratuity of 15% is automatically added onto all guest checks. The amount of the tip was $2.00. How much was the check?

Solution:

Change 15 percent to 0.15. Divide 0.15 into the amount of the tip which was $2.00.

$$
\begin{array}{r}
\$13.333 \\
0.15{\overline{\smash{\big)}\,2.000}} \\
\underline{-1\,5} \\
50 \\
\underline{-45} \\
50 \\
\underline{-45}
\end{array}
$$

This procedure will be the quotient, which is the total amount of the check: $13.33.

SUMMARY REVIEW 14–5

Find the total amount of each check.

1. The amount of gratuity received was $18.25. How much was the check if the gratuity was 15%?

_____

2. The amount of gratuity received was $16.50. How much was the check if the gratuity was 18%?

_____

3. The amount of gratuity received was $12.26. How much was the check if the gratuity was 20%?

_____

4. The amount of gratuity received was $29.17. How much was the check if the gratuity was 18%?

_____

5. The amount of gratuity received was $218.25. How much was the check if the gratuity was 18%?

_____

Cashier's Mathematical Operations

A t the end of each day or each service period, the cashier is required to fill out a **cashier's daily report.** The report is a tool used by management to keep track of cash and charge sales. Its purpose is to determine whether the actual amount of cash in the register drawer equals the total amount of cash sales made during a specific time period, as well as whether all sales (cash and charges) show the same total that the register prints out. In the past, the largest percentage of sales was cash. Today, credit card sales may exceed cash sales.

The cashier's daily report may show a very small amount of cash over or under what should be in the cash register. With the constant exchange of cash between the guests and the cashier, small mistakes may occur. Management should become concerned when amounts exceed a couple of dollars. The report is designed not only to protect the business operator from theft, but also the cashier. If the cashier makes a costly mistake, the error can usually be found by checking the daily report. The cashier's daily report shows information that will assist the accountant or accounting department when filling out financial statements at the end of a financial period.

Vice-President Sez...

"Math is at the core of all successful businesses. We make decisions based on financial performance, which is predicated ultimately on daily cash sales reports. We add, subtract, multiply, and divide to obtain food, labor, and controllable percentages. These percentages are the basis of decisions that will affect the bottom line of your operation. It makes sense—we must do the math and do it correctly.

All the hard work in both the front and the back of the house would be for naught without current, accurate, and verified bank deposits from the daily cash register tapes. If you are the owner, manager, or the chef manager, insist on accurate daily cash reports. Anything less, and the integrity of your operation will be compromised. As managers, we are paid to make decisions. Without accurate, daily verified bank deposits, these decisions are jeopardized.

In this age of ultimate technological devices, it remains imperative for us to utilize these tools to our advantage. Whether it is a POS system or an Excel spreadsheet, we need to ensure that the fundamental business math rule that 'our revenues exceed our expenses' is constantly monitored. Invest the time . . . it may be your employment career that is in the balance."

James V. Bigley
Vice President
HMB Consultants
Voorheesville, NY

HMB Consultants assists self-operated school districts (college and K–12) in assessing and fine-tuning their food service operations. This company analyzes and makes recommendations to the school districts, both for financial and operational success. HMB Consultants assists school districts from Washington D.C. to the Canadian border.

THE DAILY CASH REPORT

There are many different types of cashier's daily reports in use, since most establishments create their own form that is best suited for their particular operation. For example, some operations may keep charge sales separate from the cash sales so that the actual cash in the register drawer can be determined more easily. In general, however, all forms will contain the same information. An example of a typical report is given in Figure 14–5. Students should be knowledgeable about accounting for credit card sales. Credit card receipts represent money taken in by the establishment in place of cash. On the daily cash report there should be a place to enter all credit card receipts. They should be broken down by companies—for example, American Express, MasterCard, and so forth. The total of each company's receipts should be listed on a separate line on the daily cash receipt form. When the food service establishment pays out tips in cash to the waitstaff, the cash amount should be recorded as cash paid outs.

```
Today's date
                 POS Register Readings or Total of Guest Check Sales

    Food Sales                                             $2,035.78
    Beverage Sales                                          3,015.95
    Miscellaneous Sales                                       257.00
       Total Sales                                          5,308.73
    Add the amount of Sales Tax                               451.24

                          Gross Receipts                    5,759.97

Add—Start of Shift Money (Bank)                               200.00
Total of Gross Receipts and Money Started With (Bank)       5,959.97

    Cash Collected from Guest Checks During the Shift         689.25
    Less Total Cash Paid Out                                  157.00
    Total Cash in Drawer                                      532.25

                        Credit Card Receipts

    American Express                                         2270.72
    Discover                                                  450.00
    MasterCard                                                 25.00
    Visa                                                    1,750.00
    House Accounts                                            732.00
Total Charge & House Receipts                                5227.72
    Add Cash in Drawer                                        532.25
Total Cash and Charges (Should Equal
    the Amount of Gross Receipts)                            5,759.97
Over or (Short)                                                 0.00

                      Record of Cash Paid Out

City Ice Company                                               25.00
Tips                                                          132.00
Arkay Florist                                                  0.00
Other                                                          0.00
                        Total Cash Paid Out                  157.00

Signed by: Thomas Kearney
```

Figure 14–5 *Cashier's daily report*

Items on the Daily Cash Report

The items listed on the daily cash report example are those most important to the food service operator. (See Figure 14–5.) These items will appear on most reports. An explanation of each is given.

Explanation of Items on Report
POS Register Readings or Total of Guest Check Sales. Receipts are taken from the register. With the versatile and sometimes computerized registers in use today, items can be categorized, rung up, and totaled separately or together. For operations that do not have a computerized register, the guest checks have to be totaled.

Gross Receipts. Gross receipts are a total of all separate register readings. The gross is the total before any deductions are made. In our example, gross receipts are a total of the amounts collected for food, beverages, miscellaneous items, and sales taxes. (See Figure 14–5.) Examples of miscellaneous items are gift certificates and clothing.

Add—Start of Shift Money (Bank). Starting change is added to the gross receipts. This money is placed in the register before any sales are made. It consists of both paper currency and coins. Its purpose is to assist the cashier in making change at the start of, and during, the dining period.

Cash Collected During the Shift. This amount represents the cash that should be in the cash register drawer after adding the of cash received from guests to the bank before any paid outs are made.

Less—Cash Paid Outs. This figure is acquired by totaling the amounts of money paid out of the register during the day. When a paid out occurs, a record must be made of the transaction by recording it on a report in the section headed "Record of Cash Paid Outs." For each cash paid out, the cashier should have a receipted bill, invoice, or cash payment voucher. Most registers have a key for recording paid outs. The total amount of paid outs on the report should equal the total amount of paid outs recorded by the register. Paid outs are subtracted from the total cash because this money was taken out of the register drawer.

Total Cash in Drawer. Total cash, less paid outs, gives the amount of cash that should be in the register at the end of the day or whenever the totals are taken.

House Accounts. The total amount of money that has been collected through direct charges that are billed directly to the guest or charged back to the room in a hotel.

Total Charge and House Receipts. The total amount of money that has been collected in credit card charges from American Express, Visa, and so forth, as well as house accounts.

Total Cash and Charges. The total amount of money collected by adding the cash and charge receipts together.

Over/Short. If the amount in the Total Cash and Charges line is not equal to the Gross Receipts line, the cashier is either over or short of money. If the amount shown in the Gross Receipts line is more than the Total Cash and Charges line, there is not enough money collected (a shortage). If the cashier has more money and credit card receipts than guest charges, there is an overage. In either case, the cashier must determine where the error has occurred before turning in the daily cashier report.

Record of Cash Paid Outs. All money paid out of the register drawer is recorded here with the name of the person or company to whom it was paid. Items paid out of the cash register are usually small items that are needed in a hurry and picked up, such as flowers, ice, candy, candles, tips paid to the waitperson, and so forth.

Signed. The cashier checks all the figures and is then required to sign the report.

SUMMARY REVIEW 14–6

Complete the following cashier's daily reports, using Figure 14–5 as an example.

1.

Today's date	
POS Register Readings or Total of Guest Check Sales	
Food Sales	$2,856.63
Beverage Sales	1,474.68
Miscellaneous Sales	191.21
Total Sales	
Add the amount of Sales Tax	316.58
Gross Receipts	
Add—Start of Shift Money (Bank)	150.00
Total of Gross Receipts and Money Started With (Bank)	
Cash Collected from Guest Checks During the Shift	625.75
Less Total Cash Paid Out	
Total Cash in Drawer	
Credit Card Receipts	
American Express	1,550.56
Discover	315.45
MasterCard	900.37
Visa	975.25
House Accounts	528.82
Total Charge & House Receipts	
Add Cash in Drawer	
Total Cash and Charges (Should Equal the Amount of Gross Receipts)	
Over or (Short)	
Record of Cash Paid Out	
City Ice Company	21.50
Tips	16.85
Arkay Florist	18.75
Other	0.00
Total Cash Paid Out	
Signed by:	

2.

Today's date	
POS Register Readings or Total of Guest Check Sales	
Food Sales	$1,275.65
Beverage Sales	824.30
Miscellaneous Sales	116.45
Total Sales	
Add the amount of Sales Tax	155.15
Gross Receipts	
Add—Start of Shift Money (Bank)	225.00
Total of Gross Receipts and Money Started With (Bank)	
Cash Collected from Guest Checks During the Shift	625.75
Less Total Cash Paid Out	
Total Cash in Drawer	
Credit Card Receipts	
American Express	550.56
Discover	260.00
MasterCard	450.37
Visa	9.50
House Accounts	528.82
Total Charge & House Receipts	
Add Cash in Drawer	
Total Cash and Charges (Should Equal the Amount of Gross Receipts)	
Over or (Short)	
Record of Cash Paid Out	
City Ice Company	13.92
Tips	15.73
Arkay Florist	8.76
Other	12.95
Total Cash Paid Out	
Signed by:	

3.

Today's date	
POS Register Readings or Total of Guest Check Sales	
Food Sales	$3,675.00
Beverage Sales	785.90
Miscellaneous Sales	96.48
Total Sales	
Add the amount of Sales Tax	319.02
Gross Receipts	
Add—Start of Shift Money (Bank)	250.00
Total of Gross Receipts and Money Started With (Bank)	
Cash Collected from Guest Checks During the Shift	625.75
Less Total Cash Paid Out	
Total Cash in Drawer	
Credit Card Receipts	
American Express	2500.92
Discover	260.00
MasterCard	450.37
Visa	89.50
House Accounts	1028.00
Total Charge & House Receipts	
Add Cash in Drawer	
Total Cash and Charges (Should Equal the Amount of Gross Receipts)	
Over or (Short)	
Record of Cash Paid Out	
City Ice Company	20.50
Tips	25.80
Arkay Florist	10.40
Other	22.95
Total Cash Paid Out	
Signed by:	

4.

Today's date	
POS Register Readings or Total of Guest Check Sales	
Food Sales	$6,296.50
Beverage Sales	1,457.95
Miscellaneous Sales	117.86
Total Sales	
Add the amount of Sales Tax	551.06
Gross Receipts	
Add—Start of Shift Money (Bank)	125.00
Total of Gross Receipts and Money Started With (Bank)	
Cash Collected from Guest Checks During the Shift	930.85
Less Total Cash Paid Out	
Total Cash in Drawer	
Credit Card Receipts	
American Express	3750.25
Discover	260.00
MasterCard	450.37
Visa	2,085.25
House Accounts	1,028.00
Total Charge & House Receipts	
Add Cash in Drawer	
Total Cash and Charges (Should Equal the Amount of Gross Receipts)	
Over or (Short)	
Record of Cash Paid Out	
City Ice Company	20.65
Tips	15.75
Arkay Florist	11.75
Other	32.95
Total Cash Paid Out	
Signed by:	

5.

Today's date	
POS Register Readings or Total of Guest Check Sales	
Food Sales	$10,650.00
Beverage Sales	2,460.55
Miscellaneous Sales	127.25
Total Sales	
Add the amount of Sales Tax	926.65
Gross Receipts	
Add—Start of Shift Money (Bank)	75.00
Total of Gross Receipts and Money Started With (Bank)	
Cash Collected from Guest Checks During the Shift	930.85
Less Total Cash Paid Out	
Total Cash in Drawer	
Credit Card Receipts	
American Express	5,750.75
Discover	625.50
MasterCard	1,430.25
Visa	3,175.95
House Accounts	2,408.60
Total Charge & House Receipts	
Add Cash in Drawer	
Total Cash and Charges (Should Equal the Amount of Gross Receipts)	
Over or (Short)	
Record of Cash Paid Out	
City Ice Company	15.40
Tips	220.35
Arkay Florist	9.70
Other	12.00
Total Cash Paid Out	
Signed by:	

DISCUSSION QUESTION 14–B

After completing the Summary Review 14–6, number 5, what might have happened to cause the report to be short?

T I P S . . . To Insure Perfect Solutions

Don't ask a guest if they need change, assume they do! Learn how to count up change for great customer service.

Returning Change to the Guest

Cashiers and waitstaff should know how to verbally state and count the amount of change that a guest receives after that guest pays the bill

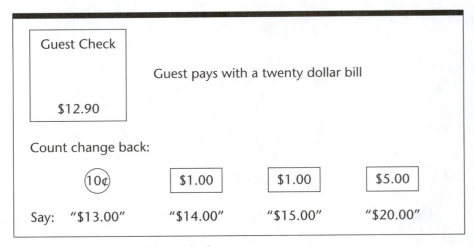

Figure 14–6 *Diagram of change back*

with cash. Figure 14–6 illustrates how to count up change. For example, the guest check is for the amount of $12.90. The guest gives a $20.00 bill to whoever (waitperson or cashier) collects the money. Start by handing the guest a dime and say $13.00. Next, hand them a dollar bill and say $14, and then another dollar bill and say $15. Finally hand them a $5 dollar bill and say $20.00. Remember to thank them for their business.

Managerial Mathematical Functions

A manager of a food service operation has to be aware of the amount of money that is being received and the amount of money that has to be paid out in order to make a profit. Simply put, the manager must use math and common sense to control the profitability of a food service operation.

DISCUSSION QUESTION 14–C

You are the manager of a food service operation. As you are checking over the POS register tapes and the cashier's report for the previous day, you discover that a check for $97.20 is missing. What may have happened to the check, and what would you do?

All-Inclusive Pricing

Some food service operators find it advantageous to set their prices in a manner that is called **all-inclusive pricing.** This means that all charges (cost of food, beverages, tax, gratuity, etc.) are stated as one price, usually on a per-person basis. The guest will know the exact amount of money that he or she will spend for the meal or event. In order to compute and set the price, food service operators must know:

1. The raw cost of the meal and beverages

2. The goods and services that are subject to taxes in the municipality in which they conduct their food service business

3. The percentage amount of taxes that they must charge by law

4. The percentage of gratuity that they are charging the guest

Backing Out the Sales Tax and Gratuity

The business owner who utilizes all-inclusive pricing will need to determine how much money will be credited for each item included in the price. This is necessary for accounting purposes to make proper allocation to food and beverage costs, gratuity, and taxes. How will the owner figure out these amounts? He or she will have to use a mathematical process called backing out the sales tax and gratuity from the all-inclusive price.

It is a common practice for operators that serve alcoholic and nonalcoholic beverages to guests at a stand-up bar to include the sales tax in the cost of the beverage. In this instance, only the sales tax will be backed out, because the gratuity is an additional amount that will be voluntarily added by the guest. For example, if a guest orders two glasses of wine at a bar, the price is $7.50 per glass and the tax is included. The guest then leaves a separate gratuity on the bar for the bartender.

How to Back Out the Sales Tax

Our guest has spent $15.00 on two glasses of wine. Included in the $15.00 price for both glasses of wine is the sales tax of 7.5%. It must first be determined how much money is collected for sales tax. It can then be determined how much money is left for the price of the wine, minus the sales tax. The procedure to back out the sales tax is done in the following way:

Step 1: Convert 7.5% to a decimal.

$$7.5\% = 0.075$$

Step 2: Add 100%, or 1, to the decimal of .075.

$$1 + 0.075 = 1.075 \text{ (divisor) sales tax rate}$$

Step 3: Divide the wine price by the (divisor) sales tax rate.

$15.00 divided by 1.075 = $13.95 (which equals the price without the tax)

Step 4: Subtract the results from the original wine price, which equals the sales tax owed.

$$\$15.00 - \$13.95 = \$1.05 \text{ (sales tax owed)}$$

To prove the formula:

Step 1: Multiply the price obtained, $13.95, by the sales tax rate of 7.5%.

$$
\begin{array}{r}
\$\ 13.95 \quad \text{price} \\
\times\ .075 \quad \text{sales tax rate} \\
\hline
6975 \\
+9765 \\
\hline
104625 = 1.04625 = \$1.05
\end{array}
$$

Step 2: Add the sales tax amount to the price of the food.

$$
\begin{array}{rl}
\$\ 1.05 & \text{Sales tax} \\
+\ \$13.95 & \text{Price} \\
\hline
\$15.00 & \text{Original price for 2 glasses} \\
& \text{of wine}
\end{array}
$$

Backing Out Gratuity

Another example of backing out the amount of money from all-inclusive pricing occurs when the owner or manager includes the price of the gratuity with the meal. For example, a guest states that her tax-exempt group (they have obtained a form from the government stating that they do not have to pay taxes) would like to have an end-of-the year banquet. They tell the manager that their budget only allows them to pay $25.00 per person. The manager agrees to the $25.00 price, which includes the meal and the gratuity. In this instance, the percentage rate of the gratuity is backed out in the exact manner that the sales tax was backed out in the previous section. In addition to managers and cashiers knowing how to do this mathematical problem, waitstaff should also know how to back out the gratuity so they will be able to calculate the amount of gratuity owed to them. In our example, the cost of a meal is $25.00, which includes the 15% gratuity. The problem is solved as follows:

Step 1: Convert 15% to a decimal.

$$15\% = 0.15$$

Step 2: Add 100%, or 1, to the decimal of 0.15.

$$1 + 0.15 = 1.15 \text{ (divisor) gratuity rate}$$

Step 3: Divide the menu price by the (divisor) gratuity rate.

$25.00 divided by 1.15 = 21.74 (which equals the price without the tax)

Step 4: Subtract the results from the original menu price, which equals the gratuity owed.

$$\$25.00 - 21.74 = \$3.26 \text{ (gratuity owed)}$$

To prove the formula:

Step 1: Multiply the menu price obtained, $21.74, by the gratuity rate of 15%.

$$
\begin{array}{rl}
\$\ 21.74 & \text{Price of meal} \\
\times\ .15 & \text{Gratuity percentage} \\
\hline
10870 & \\
+2174 & \\
\hline
32610 = \$3.26 & \text{Amount of gratuity}
\end{array}
$$

Step 2: Add the gratuity to the price of the food to obtain the original menu price.

$$
\begin{array}{rl}
\$\ 3.26 & \text{Amount of gratuity} \\
+\$21.74 & \text{Price of meal} \\
\hline
\$25.00 & \text{Original all-inclusive price}
\end{array}
$$

SUMMARY REVIEW 14–7

Back out the sales tax or gratuity from the following problems. Show the sales tax owed and the amount of money that the business or waitperson will receive.

1. John Curry purchased a new combination oven for $12,500, tax included. The sales tax was 7.25%.

   Sales tax owed_____ Amount of money for the oven
   _____

2. The Paridiso Restaurant charges $125.00 for its chef's seven-course meal, inclusive. The gratuity of 20% is included in the price. There is no sales tax.

   Gratuity owed_____ Amount of money for the restaurant
   _____

3. For a banquet, each guest pays $95.00, inclusive. A gratuity of 19% will have to be backed out.

   Gratuity owed_____ Amount of money for the restaurant
   _____

4. For a tax-exempt banquet, each guest pays $75.00, inclusive. A gratuity of 18% will have to be backed out.

   Gratuity owed_____ Amount of money for the restaurant
   _____

5. Judy Brown's wedding cost her $35,500, with the sales tax of 8% included.

   Sales tax owed_____ Amount of money for the restaurant
   _____

Backing Out Both the Sales Tax and Gratuity or All–Inclusive Pricing

Whenever the owner or a manager decides to engage in all-inclusive pricing, the backing out process has to be exact for accounting and record-keeping purposes. In the following example, our restaurant charged each guest a price of $40.00, all-inclusive. This price was for the food, gratuity of 15%, and sales tax of 7%. It must be determined how much of the $40.00 will be allocated for food, how much for the gratuity, and how much for the sales tax.

T I P S . . . To Insure Perfect Solutions

Back out sales tax first, because a gratuity is not paid on the sales tax.

Step 1: Back out the sales tax.

Convert 7% to a decimal

7% = 0.07

Step 2: Add 100%, or 1, to the decimal of 0.07.

1 + 0.07 = 1.07 (divisor) sales tax

Step 3: Divide the all-inclusive price by the (divisor) sales tax.

$40.00 divided by 1.07 = $37.383 (which equals food and gratuity)

Step 4: Subtract the results from the original all-inclusive price, which equals the sales tax owed.

$40.00 − $37.383 = $2.617 (sales tax owed)

Step 5: Back out the 15% gratuity from the remaining all-inclusive price of food and gratuity.

$37.383 is the amount of money left after sales tax has been removed.

Step 6: Convert 15% to a decimal.

15% = 0.15

Step 7: Add 100%, or 1, to the decimal of 0.15.

1 + 0.15 = 1.15 (divisor) gratuity rate

Step 8: Divide the remaining all-inclusive price by the (divisor) gratuity rate.

$37.383 divided by 1.15 = $32.507 (which equals the food amount)

Step 9: Subtract the results from the all-inclusive price (without the tax), which equals the gratuity owed.

$37.383 − $32.507 = $4.876 (gratuity owed)

To prove the formula:

Add the food, gratuity, and tax to obtain the all-inclusive price.
$32.507 + $4.876 + $2.617 = $40.00

SUMMARY REVIEW 14–8

Back out the sales tax and gratuity from the following problems. Show the sales tax owed, the gratuity owed, and the amount of money that the business will receive.

1. An all-inclusive banquet was held that cost $52,100. The sales tax was 6.25% and the gratuity was 18%.

   Sales tax owed_____ Amount of money for the restaurant _____

   Gratuity owed_____

2. Mr. Toby's restaurant charges $20.00 for an all-inclusive, complete meal. The sales tax is 8.25% and the gratuity is 15%.

Sales tax owed_____ Amount of money for the restaurant _____

Gratuity amount_____

3. A guest has to pay $20.00 for a meal. Both the gratuity of 15% and the sales tax of 5% have to be backed out.

Sales tax owed_____ Amount of money for the restaurant _____

Gratuity amount_____

4. An all-inclusive banquet was held that cost $72,100. The sales tax was 8.25% and the gratuity was 18%.

Sales tax owed_____ Amount of money for the restaurant _____

Gratuity owed_____

5. An all-inclusive banquet was held that cost $152,100. The sales tax was 7.25% and the gratuity was 20%.

Sales tax owed_____ Amount of money for the restaurant _____

Gratuity owed_____

BANK DEPOSITS

Bank deposits are a system used to entrust accumulated money for safekeeping in a bank. It is a system used by both individuals and businesses. It is unwise to store money at home or on the premise of a business. This can be an invitation to theft, or loss by a disaster. After opening an account, a deposit can be transacted in person—by taking a completed deposit slip and money to the bank—or the deposit can be made automatically. These two methods will be discussed further in this section. Depositing money in an account is a way of holding money in reserve for future **expenditures.**

When a bank deposit is made, the money deposited is placed in a **savings** or **checking account.** If the deposit is made in person at a bank, the money being deposited is accompanied by a **deposit slip,** which provides the depositor and the bank with a record of the transaction. (See Figure 14–7.) If the deposit is made electronically, the transfer of funds is made through special communication lines set up between the depositor and the banking institution.

If the money deposited is placed in a savings account, it is held by the banking institution until the depositor wishes to withdraw some or all of the funds. While the money is in the savings account, the bank uses the money to make loans to customers for home or business improvements, the purchasing of new or existing homes, and so forth. At the same time, the bank pays you **interest** (the sum paid for the use of money) at a certain percent annually. This means that while your money is in the banking institution, it is earning money. This money can be withdrawn at any time without a penalty.

CHECKING ACCOUNT DEPOSIT TICKET	CASH →	201	50	
1852064 8 8 63631	C H E C K S	20	40	
ACCOUNT NUMBER			8	10
Robert Smith				
NAME				29-8 / 213
DATE *November 8* 20 *01*				
CHECKS AND OTHER ITEMS ARE RECEIVED FOR DEPOSIT SUBJECT TO THE TERMS AND CONDITIONS OF THIS BANK'S COLLECTION AGREEMENT.	TOTAL FROM OTHER SIDE			USE OTHER SIDE FOR ADDITIONAL LISTING ◆ ENTER TOTAL HERE
DEPOSITED IN	TOTAL ITEMS TOTAL	230	00	BE SURE EACH ITEM IS PROPERLY ENDORSED

⊕⑆0 2 13⑈0008⑆

Figure 14–7 *Deposit slip*

If the money is deposited in a checking account, it is held in reserve to cover any check amount written by the depositor. A **check** is a written order directing the bank to make a payment for the depositor. The bank honors the check and makes the payment, providing the depositor has enough money in the checking account. A checking account is more active than a savings account because the money is usually on the move. That is, deposits are made, checks are written, and money is withdrawn.

Bills are usually paid by check whether they are for business, or personal and household expenses. Therefore, you should have some knowledge of how a checking account works. There are four important steps involved in using a checking account.

1. Filling out the deposit slip

2. Balancing the check register

3. Writing a check

4. Checking the bank statement

If these steps are not completed properly, problems result for both the depositor and the banking institution. These problems can sometimes result in *a* fine for the depositor, especially if the account is **overdrawn** (to write checks upon an account for a greater amount than the money in the account).

The Deposit Slip

The **deposit slip** provides the depositor and the banking institution with a record of the transaction when money is deposited in the checking account. (See Figure 14–7.) When filling out the deposit slip, cash and checks are listed separately. After this is done, they are added to find a *subtotal*. ("Sub" means under; therefore, this is a part of the total.) If cash is received when the deposit is made, the amount is subtracted from the subtotal, giving the net deposit, or the amount you wish to place in the checking account. When receiving cash, some institutions require your signature on the deposit slips. In the upper left-hand corner of the slip your name and address usually appear, and in the bottom left-hand corner two groups of numbers appear. The first group is a routing number for the purpose of routing automatic deposits and checks to the correct institution. The second group is the customer's checking account number. (These numbers are not shown on Figure 14–7.) When deposits are made electronically, a deposit slip is not required, but the depositor would be required to know the proper route number. All deposit slips are not the same. Each institution has its own idea of arrangement and information desired. However, you will find that most are very similar. The banking institution supplies the deposit slips to the customer.

The Check Register

The **check register** is given to the depositor by the banking institution, so the depositor can record deposits and checks, knowing the balance of money on hand. (See Figure 14–8.) In this way, the depositor always knows the largest amount for which a check can be written and is less likely to overdraw the account.

CHECK NO.	CHECKS DRAWN IN FAVOR OF	DATE	BAL. BRT. FRD.	√	∅ 283	00
111	TO *Cinti Bell* FOR *Telephone Service*	8/10	AMOUNT OF CHECK OR DEPOSIT BALANCE		18 265	00 00
112	TO *Allstate Insurance* FOR *Car Insurance*	8/13	AMOUNT OF CHECK OR DEPOSIT BALANCE		175 90	00 00
	TO *Deposit* FOR	8/16	AMOUNT OF CHECK OR DEPOSIT BALANCE		250 340	00 00
113	TO *Shilliton Dept. Store* FOR *Charge Account*	8/18	AMOUNT OF CHECK OR DEPOSIT BALANCE		75 265	00 00
114	TO *Norwood Building & Loan* FOR *House Payment*	8/20	AMOUNT OF CHECK OR DEPOSIT BALANCE		135 130	00 00
	TO FOR		AMOUNT OF CHECK OR DEPOSIT BALANCE			
	TO FOR		AMOUNT OF CHECK OR DEPOSIT BALANCE			
	TO FOR		AMOUNT OF CHECK OR DEPOSIT BALANCE			
	TO FOR		AMOUNT OF CHECK OR DEPOSIT BALANCE			
	TO FOR		AMOUNT OF CHECK OR DEPOSIT BALANCE			
	TO FOR		AMOUNT OF CHECK OR DEPOSIT BALANCE			
	TO FOR		AMOUNT OF CHECK OR DEPOSIT BALANCE			

Figure 14–8 *Check register*

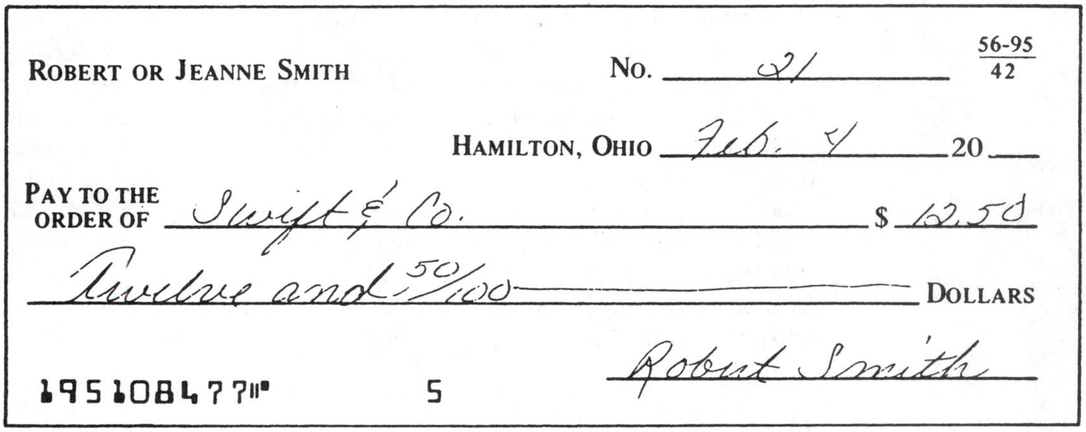

ROBERT OR JEANNE SMITH   NO. _____ *21* _____   56-95⁄42

                    HAMILTON, OHIO _____ *Feb. 4* _____ 20 __

PAY TO THE
ORDER OF *Swift & Co.* _____ $ *12.50*

Twelve and 50⁄100 _____ DOLLARS

                                        Robert Smith

⑆195108477⑈   5

Figure 14–9 *Writing a check*

The balance brought forward (shown at the top in Figure 14–8), is the balance from the previous page in the register. It shows a total of $283.00. On August 10, a check was drawn for $18.00, leaving a balance of $265.00. On August 13, another check was drawn for $175.00, leaving a balance of $90.00. On August 16, a deposit of $250.00 was made. This amount was added to the previous balance, creating a new balance of $340.00. On August 18, a check for $75.00 was drawn, leaving a balance of $265.00, and on August 20, another check for $135.00 was drawn. The remaining balance, $130.00, is the net amount against which future checks may be drawn.

Writing a Check

The check, as pointed out previously, is a written order directing the bank to make a payment for the depositor out of the money the depositor has in his or her checking account. The banking institution issues checks to the depositor. The depositor may be required to pay for the checks, or the bank may deduct the cost from the balance in the checking account. Sometimes the checks are free, if the depositor has a savings account or C.D. (certificate of deposit) at the same banking institution.

When writing a check, always write neatly and clearly, using ink. (See Figure 14–9.) Be sure that all of the information listed on the check is complete and correct, such as amount, date, check number, account number, and so forth. Do not forget to sign the check. Without your signature, the payment will not be made.

T I P S . . . . **To Insure Perfect Solutions**

When writing a check, never use a pen with erasable ink. Anyone can change the information that you write on the check.

The Bank Statement

At the end of a certain period of time (for example, one month, three months, etc., each banking institution has its own regulations), the bank provides the depositor with a statement showing the activity of the account during that time period. In Figure 14–10 (time period of three

486-174-8		John or Jane Doe
Account Number		9464 Stone Hill Dr.
		Westchester, Ohio 45070

BALANCE FORWARD		DEPOSITS & CREDITS		CHECKS & DEBITS			CURRENT BALANCE	
AS OF	05/20	NO.	AMOUNT	NO.	AMOUNT	SER. CHG.	AS OF	07/15
	$0.00	8	$1,710.32	25	$1,435.25			$275.07

DATE	CHECK NO. OR CODE	AMOUNT	DATE	CHECK NO. OR CODE	AMOUNT	DATE	CHECK NO. OR CODE	AMOUNT
05|20	DP	200|00	07|05		50|00			
06|03	DP	200|00	07|05		139|88			
06|05		100|00	07|08		14|47			
06|07		132|00	07|09		10|50			
06|10	DP	500|00	07|10		14|44			
06|13		105|00	07|10		16|56			
06|13		110|35	07|10		18|40			
06|17	DP	200|00	07|11		50|00			
06|18		20|00	07|11		50|00			
06|19		255|92	07|15	DP	200|00			
06|24		10|00						
06|24		30|00						
06|24		50|00						
06|24		97|00						
06|27	DP	200|00						
06|28		25|16						
07|01	DP	200|00						
07|01		4|13						
07|01		7|00						
07|01		13|25						
07|01		100|00						
07|03	DP	10|32						
07|05		11|19						

Figure 14–10 *Bank statement*

months), the statement shows the checks drawn and deposits made during that period of time. The bank also returns all checks (canceled checks), or a copy of the checks issued during that period. The canceled checks are the depositor's receipts if proof is needed that payment was made. The bank statement is used to check the bank's figures against those recorded in the depositor's check register. In this way, mistakes can be detected before a problem arises or a fine is imposed.

The top left corner of Figure 14–10 shows the depositor's account number. In the center, the depositor's name and address are given. The balance brought forward shows that, as of May 20, there was no money in this account. This was probably when the account was opened at the bank. Deposits and credits show that during this period (May 20 to July 15), eight deposits were made totalling $1,710.32. This figure can be checked by finding the sum of all the amounts listed with a DP (deposit) before them. Checks and debits (a charge against the account) show that 25 checks were drawn on the account, and the amount of those checks totaled $1,435.25. There is no service charge indicated by the bank during this period, which shows that the depositor received this service free of charge or paid for the checks when they were received. The current balance shows that as of July 15, $275.07 remained in the account. Other figures shown on this statement include the complete checking activity during this period of time, and the dates and amounts of all checks written. The bank statement shown in Figure 14–10 is a simplified one so that you can follow it without becoming confused. Most statements issued by banking institutions today are computer printouts and can be a little more confusing, because they combine statements for both the checking and savings accounts and show a service charge for regular account maintenance.

DISCUSSION QUESTION 14–D

The bank statement for the checking account does not balance with your checkbook. The bank statement shows that your restaurant has $10,500. Your checkbook shows that you have $11,462. Give five possible reasons why the checkbook is out of balance with the bank statement.

SUMMARY REVIEW 14–9

1. Prepare deposit slips for problems a through c. Follow the example given in Figure 14–7. If deposit slips are not available, make some by listing the necessary information on blank paper.

   a. On August 18, Duane Johnstone deposited the following in his checking account.

      2 twenty-dollar bills

      4 ten-dollar bills

      6 five-dollar bills

      5 one-dollar bills

      2 checks: $12.75 and $22.25

      2 half dollars

      8 quarters

      6 dimes

      7 nickels

   b. On October 6, Carmen Santi-Roberts deposited the following in her checking account.

      4 twenty-dollar bills

      8 ten-dollar bills

      7 five-dollar bills

      4 two-dollar bills

      9 one-dollar bills

      1 check for $53.40

      6 half dollars

      3 quarters

      7 dimes

      9 nickels

c. On November 10, Sonna Kozlowski, treasurer of the Cuisine Club, deposited in their checking account the following checks and money collected for dues.

2 twenty-dollar bills

2 ten-dollar bills

8 five-dollar bills

6 one-dollar bills

3 checks: $10.40, $8.50, and $6.75

5 half dollars

5 quarters

4 dimes

2. Prepare check registers for problems a through c. Follow the example given in Figure 14–8. If a check register is not available, make one by listing the necessary information on a sheet of paper.

a. Balance brought forward $520.65

October 2	Check No. 6 $43.50 Gas and Electric Co.
October 5	Check No. 7 $25.80 Best State Insurance Co.
October 10	Deposit $165.50
October 15	Check No. 8 $35.80 Albers Meat Market
October 20	Check No. 9 $265.00 Bill's Service Station

b. Balance brought forward $680.48

December 3	Check No. 15 $63.45 Swallen's Dept. Store
December 5	Deposit $183.20
December 8	Check No. 16 $158.00
	Evanston Building and Loan Co.
December 9	Check No. 17 $178.25
	Bay State Insurance Co.
December 12	Deposit $98.75
December 15	Check No. 18 $62.78 G.M.A.C.

c. Balance brought forward $728.60

January 4	Check No. 19 $15.34 Webster Insurance Co.
January 6	Check No. 20 $187.00
	Home Savings and Loan Co.
January 9	Deposit $223.50
January 12	Check No. 21 $208.60 Joe's Service Station
January 14	Deposit $197.60
January 17	Check No. 22 $179.79
	McMillians Dept. Store
January 20	Deposit $368.75
January 25	Check No. 23 $76.45 Metropolitan Hospital

CHAPTER 15

Personal Taxes, Payroll, and Financial Statements

OBJECTIVES

At the completion of this chapter, the student should be able to:

1. Identify and understand the concept of employee's withholding tax (federal, state, local).

2. Identify and understand the concept of employee's income tax (federal, state, local).

3. Identify and understand the concept of FICA (Social Security) tax.

4. Calculate gross wages.

5. Calculate net pay.

6. Calculate salary plus commission.

7. Identify listings on the profit and loss statement.

8. Find the cost of food sold, gross margin, total operating expenses, net profit, and the percent of sales.

9. Identify listings on the balance sheet.

10. Find total assets, total liabilities, net worth and total liabilities, and net worth-proprietorship.

11. Identify and calculate the break-even point for a business using contribution rate and contribution rate percentages.

12. Identify items that are budgeted.

13. Find the amount or percent of items budgeted.

KEY WORDS

federal taxes	depreciation
local taxes	balance sheet
income tax	net worth
Social Security tax	capital
payroll or labor cost	break-even analysis
gross wages	break-even point
overtime	serving expenses
salary plus commission	sales revenue
profit and loss statement	variable cost
cost of food sold	cost of goods sold
total operating expenses	certificates of deposit
income book	budgeting
inventory at the beginning of the month	expenditures
	state taxes
cost of food in production	employee's withholding tax

FICA	gross profit
wages	straight line method
deductions	assets
net pay	liabilities
commission	proprietorship
financial statements	fiscal year
sales	contribution rate and percentage
gross margin	fixed cost
net profit	total variable profit
total sales	charge accounts
purchases for the month	income
final inventory	menu price

There is a lot of truth to the old saying, "The only sure things in this life are death and taxes." People pay taxes to operate our federal, state, and local governments as well as our school districts and other services necessary to our daily lives.

In general, we are faced with the obligation of paying taxes to the three levels of government mentioned above: federal, state, and local (city and county). The following is a list of the taxes that food service operators and their employees are required to pay or the employer is required to collect by deductions from the employee's paycheck:

Federal Taxes

Employee's Withholding Tax

Income Tax

Social Security

State Taxes

Employee's Withholding Tax

Income Tax

Sales Tax

Various Licenses

Local Taxes

Employee's Withholding Tax

Income Tax

Personal Property Tax

Occupational Tax

Various Licenses

Real Estate Tax

Since these taxes affect you, the employee, as they show up in the form of deductions on your paychecks, it is important to learn as much as possible about them. Many people do not understand why all this money is taken out of their paychecks. Our goal is to acquaint you with these taxes and provide enough information to help you understand their importance.

FEDERAL TAXES

These are taxes collected by the federal government. They are established and enforced by federal law so that each individual citizen pays what he or she properly owes to support the functions financed by the federal government.

Employee's Withholding Tax

Employee's withholding tax is money withheld from each employee's paycheck during the year to pay for the income tax that he or she owes the federal government at the end of the year. The money withheld is sent to the government by the employer and is credited to the employee's account. Paying the tax as the money is earned, called "pay as you go," is a system devised by the federal government to ensure that your tax money is available when your taxes are due. At the end of the calendar year (December 31) and before January 31 of the following year, the employer sends each employee a W-2 form (wage and tax statement) indicating the total amount of money earned during the year, as well as how much money was withheld for taxes, Social Security payments, and any other money withheld, such as state and city income taxes. (See Figure 15–1.)

Sometimes the employer deducts too little or too much money from the employee's paychecks during the year. If too little money was deducted and money is owed the government, a check for the amount owed must be sent to the Internal Revenue Service (IRS) with the employee's federal tax return. If the amount owed is less than the amount deducted from the paychecks, the government sends the individual a check for the amount overpaid after the return is processed.

a Control number 5621	Void ☐	OMB No. 1545-0008		
b Employer's identification number 138-71-8521			1 Wages, tips, other compensation 72,665.88	2 Federal income tax withheld 16,828.15
c Employer's name, address, and ZIP code John Phillips Restaurant 3567 Meadowcreek Drive Albany, NY 12203			3 Social security wages 7,260.00	4 Social security tax withheld 4,501.20
			5 Medicare wages and tips 72,665.88	6 Medicare tax withheld 1,053.66
			7 Social security tips	8 Allocated tips
d Employee's social security number 022-35-6241			9 Advance EIC payment	10 Dependent care benefits
e Employee's name, address, and ZIP code Carlita Alverez 287 Third Avenue Albany, NY 12203			11 Nonqualified plans	12 Benefits included in Box 1
			13 See Instrs. for Form W-2	14 Other
			15 Statutory employee Deceased Pension plan Legal rep. Deferred compensation	
16 State NY	Employer's state I.D. No. 138-71-8521	17 State wages, tips, etc. 72,665.88	18 State income tax 4,114.53	19 Locality name 20 Local wages, tips, etc. 21 Local income tax

Department of the Treasury—Internal Revenue Service

Form **W-2** Wage and Tax Statement
Copy D For Employer

For Privacy Act and Paperwork Reduction Act Notice, see separate instructions.

Figure 15–1 Form W-2 wage and tax statement

The W-2 form annually received from the employer usually comes in four parts. One copy is to be filed with the employee's federal return, one with the state return, one for local use, and one for the individual's personal files.

Income Tax

The main source of income for operating the federal government is obtained from taxes levied on the income of individuals and corporations. Income tax returns must be filed by all people who earn over a specified amount of money. These individuals are required by law to file a federal income tax return with the Internal Revenue Service on or before each April 15th. If an employee does not earn enough money to pay taxes, he or she must file an income tax return to get the money back that was withheld by his or her employer for taxes.

Depending upon the income earned, tax forms can be submitted electronically, by using the telephone, or by sending the forms through the mail. Many individuals with limited income file simple forms, which are fairly easy to prepare and submit. For individuals with a high amount of income and deductions, tax forms can be confusing and difficult to complete. For those individuals, the authors recommend that an accountant or qualified person be hired to prepare the taxes.

A major concern for food service employees is that income tax must be paid on all tips received. The employee must give to the employer a written statement declaring how much money was received in tips during the pay period. The employer deducts from the employee's paycheck the proper amount of withholding tax for these tips, or the employee pays the employer the amount of tax due out of the tips collected.

The cost of meals furnished to the employee by the employer is also considered part of the employee's income. It is, therefore, subject to income tax unless it can be shown that the employee was given the meals for the convenience of the employer.

The authors advise all employees to consult the current tax code concerning tips, as well as any other questions that employees may have, in order to be in compliance with the tax laws. This is because the law may (and usually does) change from year to year.

FICA (Social Security) Tax

The letters FICA stand for the Federal Insurance Contributions Act, which became law in 1935. This act established the Social Security system and tax. The Social Security system provides for the payment of retirement, survivor, and disability insurance benefits. It also provides hospital insurance benefits for persons age 65 and over who meet its eligibility requirements. This insurance, commonly known as Medicare, provides coverage for both hospital and doctor visits. Funds for payment of these benefits are provided by taxes levied on employees and their employers as well as self-employed persons.

Under the terms of the Social Security Act, the employer is required by law to deduct a certain percentage of the employee's wages each payday and remit the amount deducted to the federal government. For a self-employed person, the percentage is doubled. Each self-employed person has to pay the FICA rate as an employer and an equal amount as an employee.

The term **wages** means "that which is paid or received for services" and includes salaries, commissions, fees, bonuses, tips, and so forth. For example:

Bill Clark, manager of the Red Gate Restaurant, is paid a salary of $550 per week, plus a 2% commission on the private party business in excess of $6,000 per week. During the first week of June, the restaurant's private party business was $10,500. Assume that the Social Security tax rate is 7.65%. How much FICA tax was deducted from Bill's earnings for that week?

Salary	$550.00	
Commission	90.00	(2% of 4,500)
Total Earnings	$640.00	
7.65% of $640.00 =	$ 48.96	FICA tax

The amount of Social Security tax deducted from Bill's earnings that week was $48.96.

Besides the money deducted each payday from the employee's paycheck, a tax equal to that amount is levied on the employer. The tax is computed at the same rate as the employee's tax and is based on the total taxable wages paid by the employer. For example:

During the month of June, the Red Gate Restaurant paid out $10,650 in taxable wages. If the Social Security rate is 7.65%, the owner must pay the federal government $814.73.

$$\$10,650 \times 0.0765 = \$814.73$$

Self-employed persons must also pay Social Security taxes on income, but as pointed out previously, at double the rate.

In the food service industry, once a knowledge of food preparation and managing is acquired it is a fairly easy step to go from employee to employer. However, with tax obligations such as these, much thought must go into taking that big step.

SUMMARY REVIEW 15–1

Calculate the following problems concerning Social Security tax. Round answers to the nearest cent.

1. The cook at the Sea Shore Restaurant is paid a salary of $395 per week, plus 2% commission on all food sales for the week in excess of $20,000. During the second week of March, the food sales amounted to $25,000. If the Social Security tax rate is 7.30%, how much Social Security tax was deducted from his earnings for that week?

2. Bill Walters, a waiter at the Red Gate Restaurant, is paid a salary of $150 per week, plus tips. During the first week of July his tips amounted to $220. Assuming that the Social Security tax rate is 7.30%, how much FICA tax was deducted from Bill's earnings for that week?

3. Jean Curran, a hostess at the Red Gate Restaurant, is paid a salary of $120 per week, plus tips. During the first week of May her tips amounted to $155. Assuming that the Social Security tax rate is 7.30%, how much tax was deducted from Jean's earnings for that week?

_____

4. Fred Hartzel, manager of the Kentucky Inn, is paid a salary of $525 per week, plus 2.5% commission on the food and beverage business in excess of $12,500 per week. During the second week of November, the business amounted to $24,600. Assuming that the Social Security tax rate is 7.30%, how much tax was deducted from Fred's earnings for that week?

_____

5. The catering manager of the Gourmet Catering Company works on a 3% commission of total sales for each week. During the first week in June total sales were $24,000. What were her total earnings?

_____

How much Social Security tax did she pay if the rate is 7.30%?

_____

STATE TAXES

These are taxes collected by the state government. The taxes collected are for the purpose of operating all the state functions and agencies. Each agency submits a budget outlining how their money will be spent. Each state government operates independently from others. The state governing body (generally the governor and state legislature) determines the amount of tax revenue required to operate and how those taxes will be imposed upon its citizens.

Employee's Withholding Tax

Employee's withholding tax is money withheld from each employee's paycheck by the employer during the year for the purpose of paying the employee's state income tax at the end of the calendar year. It is done for the same purpose as the employee's federal withholding tax. The amount of money withheld from each individual's paycheck is determined by the amount of income earned and the percentage set by the state. The tax is always lower than the amount withheld for federal tax.

Income Tax

Most states have an income tax. The income tax laws in most states are patterned after the federal income tax laws. The percentage of tax collected on each individual's adjusted gross income varies from state to state, but it is usually a percentage that graduates with the increase of income and it is always less than the amount paid to the federal government. Your state income tax is paid to the state in which you live even though the money may be earned in another state.

SUMMARY REVIEW 15–2

For the following problems, compute the state income tax due on net income. Use statements (a) through (e) as a guide in solving these problems.

(a)   Net income is $3,000 or less; your tax is 2%.

(b)   Net income is over $3,000, but not over $4,000; your tax is $60, plus 3% of excess over $3,000.

(c)   Net income is over $4,000, but not over $5,000; your tax is $90, plus 4% of excess over $4,000.

(d)   Net income is over $5,000, but not over $8,000; your tax is $130, plus 5% of excess over $5,000.

(e)   Net income is over $8,000; your tax is $280, plus 6% of the excess over $8,000.

State Taxes Due

1.   Net income $12,990.   _____

2.   Net income $7,950.   _____

3.   Net income $19,589.   _____

4.   Net income $7,460.   _____

5.   Net income $45,980.   _____

Calculating Net Pay

Gross wages are the amount of money you earn before any deductions (the amount taken away) are made. After deductions are made, the result is called **net pay** (net meaning free of all deductions). An employer is required by law, or in some cases by clauses in a union contract, to make certain required deductions. Any deductions beyond those required must be authorized by the employee. Some of the required deductions are FICA (Social Security) taxes, federal withholding taxes (income tax), state income tax, city income tax, health insurance, and retirement fund. Some of the deductions that you may authorize include union dues, contributions to charitable organizations, credit unions, and company stock purchases.

To calculate net pay, all deductions are subtracted from gross wages. Net pay is the figure that will appear on your weekly, semimonthly, or monthly paycheck. The formula for calculating net pay is as follows:

Gross wages − deductions = Net pay.

For example:

Jerry Roth, an employee of the Terrace Plaza Hotel, receives $7.45 an hour for a regular 40-hour workweek, with time and a half for overtime. Last week Jerry worked 52 hours. Deducted from his gross wages were: $31.54 FICA (Social Security) taxes, $64.81 federal withholding taxes, $21.65 health insurance, and $25.93 state income tax.

To determine Jerry's gross wage and net pay, follow Step 1 and Step 2.

Step 1:

52	Total hours worked
− 40	Regular hours
12	Overtime hours
12	Overtime hours
×1.5	Time and a half
60	
12	
18.0	Overtime hours converted to regular hours
18	Overtime hours converted to regular hours
+ 40	Regular hours
58	Total regular hours to be paid for working
$7.45	Per hour
× 58	Total regular hours
5960	
3725	
$432.10	Gross wages

Step 2:

$ 31.54	FICA tax
$ 64.81	Federal withholding tax
$ 21.65	Health insurance
+ $ 25.93	State income tax
$143.93	Total deductions
$432.10	Gross wages
− 143.93	Total deductions
$288.17	Net pay (take-home pay)

As you can see by comparing the two steps to solving this problem, there is a great deal of difference between gross wages and net or take-home pay.

Sometimes the payroll department may not have all the proper schedules, tax guides, and tables put out by the various tax agencies of the federal and state governments. In such cases, they may be required to calculate deductible dollar amounts using percentages.

For example:

Jerry Roth, an employee of the Terrace Plaza Hotel, receives $7.45 an hour for a regular 40-hour workweek, with time and a half for overtime. Last week, Jerry worked 52 hours. Deducted from his gross wages were: 7.30% for FICA (Social Security) taxes, 15% for federal withholding taxes, 5% for state income tax, and 1.5% for city income tax.

To determine Jerry's gross wage and net pay, follow Step 1 and Step 2.

Step 1:

52	Total hours worked
− 40	Regular hours
12	Overtime hours

12	Overtime hours
× 1.5	Time and a half
60	
12	
18.0	Overtime hours converted to regular hours
18	Overtime hours converted to regular hours
+ 40	Regular hours
58	Total regular hours to be paid for working
$7.45	Per hour
× 58	Total regular hours
5960	
3725	
$432.10	Gross wages

Up to this point, the calculations are the same as in the previous example. The difference lies in calculating the deductions, because dollar amounts must be found when deductions are given in percents.

Step 2:

FICA 7.30% × 432.10 gross wages	$ 31.54
Federal withholding tax 15% × 432.10	$ 64.82
State income tax 5% × 432.10	$ 21.61
City income tax 1.5% × 432.10	+ $ 6.48
Sum of deductions	= $124.45

$432.10	Gross wages
− 124.45	Sum of deductions
$307.65	Net pay (take-home pay)

SUMMARY REVIEW 15–3

1. The chef at the Metropole Hotel is paid a salary of $3,500 per month and receives a paycheck twice a month. On a recent paycheck, the deductions from his total earnings were as follows: $127.75 FICA tax, $350.00 federal withholding tax, $87.50 state income tax, and $26.25 city income tax.

   What was his gross wage for this pay period? _____

   What was his net pay? _____

2. For each of the following, find gross wages and amount of net pay based on a 40-hour workweek, with time and a half for all hours worked over 40.

Name	Total Hours Worked	Hourly Rate	Gross Wages	Total Deductions	Net Pay
Tisha Adams	46	$ 5.95	$	$ 79.95	$
Rafael Romero	56	$ 7.50	$	$120.10	$
Rose Fahery	45.5	$ 9.25	$	$126.90	$
Paul Brown	49.5	$10.75	$	$137.50	$
Kim Lee	57	$12.25	$	$142.60	$

3. The head salad person at the Kemper Lane Hotel is employed on the basis of eight hours per day, with time and a half for all overtime hours. Her regular hourly pay rate is $9.50. In a recent week, she

worked the following hours:

S	M	T	W	TH	F	S
—	9.5	9	10.5	8	12	—

Deducted from her gross wages were: FICA tax $21.00, federal withholding tax $76.70, state income tax $10.95, and health insurance $16.90.

What was her gross wage?   _____

What was her net pay?   _____

4. John Linsdale, a waiter at the Sands Hotel, receives a base salary of $125.00 per week, plus tips. Last week, his tips amounted to $260.00. From his gross wages the following deductions were made: FICA tax 7.30%, federal withholding tax 15%, state income tax 4%, and $20.45 for health insurance.

What was his gross wage?   _____

What was his net pay?   _____

5. Elsa Suarez, a baker at the Chesapeake Hotel, works on a 40-hour-per-week basis, with time and a half for all overtime. During this past week, she worked 49 hours. Her regular pay rate is $12.95 per hour. The following deductions were taken from her gross pay: federal withholding tax $65.60, FICA $27.14, health insurance $12.95, and union dues $7.00.

What was her gross wage?   _____

What was her net pay?   _____

Calculating Salary Plus Commission

There are situations in the food service industry where an employee is paid a salary plus a commission (generally a percentage of sales for a given period). These situations usually occur to motivate supervisors and managers to increase production and sales. Commissions are calculated by the financial officers usually referred to as controllers in the hospitality industry (see Figure 15–2).

Figure 15–2 *Controller computing salary with commission information for a food service employee*

To calculate a gross wage when a commission is involved, the amount of the commission is added to the basic salary. To find the amount of the commission, sales are multiplied by the percent of commission. The formula for calculating gross wages involving commission is as follows:

> **Amount of sales × percent of commission =
> Amount of commission.**

> **Amount of commission + salary = Gross wages.**

For example:

The banquet manager at the Alms Hotel is paid a salary of $590 per week, plus a 1.5% commission on the private party business in excess of $5,000 per week. In a recent week, the party business amounted to $12,000. To determine the gross pay, refer to the following example.

$12,000	Total sales
− 5,000	Amount deducted
$7,000	Amount on which commission is paid
× .015	Percent of commission
35000	
7000	
$105.00	Amount of commission
$590.00	Weekly salary
+ 105.00	Amount of commission
$695.00	Gross pay

SUMMARY REVIEW 15–4

1. The catering manager at Elegant Fare Catering Company receives a basic salary of $950 per month, plus a 2% commission on all the catered business. Last month, the catered business amounted to $35,000. What was her gross wage?

2. The manager of a local fast-food restaurant receives a monthly salary of $1,600, plus a commission of $0.12 for every sandwich sold during the month. Last month, 1,200 sandwiches were sold. What was his gross wage for the month?

3. The manager of the food concession at the local swimming club receives a small weekly salary of $125, plus a commission of 6% on all food sales for the week. Last week, the food sales amounted to $7,550. What was her gross wage for the week?

4. The preparation cook at Bob's Catering Company receives a salary of $350 per week, plus a commission of 1.5% on all the catered party business. In a recent week, the catered party business amounted to $15,000. Deducted from her gross wages were the following: FICA tax $41.98, federal withholding tax $126.50, and city income tax $8.63.

What was her gross wage?

_____

What was her net pay?

_____

5. The food and beverage manager at the Fountain Square Hotel receives a salary of $2,800 per month, plus a commission of 0.5% on all food and beverage business for the month. Last month, the food business amounted to $24,500. The beverage business was $8,600. What was her gross wage for the month?

_____

FINANCIAL STATEMENTS

Financial statements are the instrument used in a business operation to let management know its exact financial position. The figures tell a story of success or failure. There are two major financial statements that must be prepared and are essential to the operation of a business: the profit and loss (income) statement, sometimes referred to as the P&L sheet, and the balance sheet. These financial statements are especially important to the food service operation because of high labor cost and food prices that fluctuate quite rapidly.

THE PROFIT AND LOSS STATEMENT

The **profit and loss statement** is a summary or report of the business operation for a given period of time. The purpose of the statement is to determine how much money the business is making or losing. In the profit and loss statement, all income from sales is set off against expenses to determine the profit or loss. The following formula summarizes the profit and loss statement of a food service operation:

> **Sales − cost of food sold = Gross margin.**
> **Gross margin − total operating expenses = Net profit or loss.**

The net profit or loss is the figure that is of greater concern to the food service operator because it determines the success or failure of the business.

Most of the figures used to compile a profit and loss statement are taken from the daily records that are recorded and made available by the bookkeeper. The daily records of the food service operation are kept in a book called the **income book.** The income book contains a record of all income and expenses. It is a means of keeping track of every sales dollar. The income book is also important for securing the figures needed for tax purposes and other financial obligations. Many food service operations have a computer available, and these income book records can be kept on a disk. The availability of a computer simplifies the task of record keeping. It can produce the most complicated figures immediately.

A profit and loss statement can be made up whenever the food service operator wants to know the business' financial situation or feels it necessary to review the financial situation. It can be done every month, every three months, every six months, or even once a year. However, for control purposes, it is recommended that the profit and loss statement be completed each month. When the statement is completed, the food service operator analyzes all the figures and compares the dollar amounts in each category with those of previous months or years, looking for ways to cut costs for a more efficient operation. The operator may also wish to make a percent comparison of all figures with total sales, which represents 100%. The example of a profit and loss statement shows dollar amounts and percentages of the total sales. (See Figure 15–3.) As explained previously, percents are usually the language spoken by the food service operator. Percents, rather than dollar amounts, give a clearer picture of the overall operation. It is suggested within the food service industry that a successful operation must hold its food and labor cost below 70%.

Figure 15–3 shows that the cost of food sold is 42.3% and the labor cost is 32%, totaling 74.3%. This suggests that this business may be in trouble. The food service professional will have to either increase the volume of sales or cut costs. The Crossgates Restaurant is still showing a profit of 6%, but a higher profit would be desired. As you review the profit and loss statement in Figure 15–3, notice that the cost of food sold (42.3%) and the gross margin (57.7%), when added together, add up to 100%. The total

Chef Sez…

"Remember, we are banking dollars, not percentages."

Robert S. Faller
Director of Sales and Marketing
The Otesaga Resort Hotel
Cooperstown, New York

The Otesaga Resort Hotel of Cooperstown is one of New York State's most distinctive resorts. Since 1909, the Otesaga has offered distinguished service, dining, and memorable experiences to guests from around the world. With only a short walk or trolley ride from the Otesaga one can relive the memories of America's national pastime at the National Baseball Hall of Fame and Museum. The word *Otesaga* is derived from the Iroquois phrase for "the meeting place," which is consistent with the Otesaga Resort experience. The resort has 136 rooms, a golf course, a bar and grill, a lounge, a lakeside patio, and a dining room, as well as space for meetings and conferences.

Figure 15–3 *Profit and loss statement*

Crossgates Restaurant Profit and Loss Statement For the month of September, 20__			
Category	Dollars	Summary	% of Sales
Total Sales	$96,000	$96,000	100.0%
Food Cost			
Inventory, beginning of month	$9,680		
Purchases for the month	$37,600		
Subtotal	$47,280		
Less Food in Production	$650		
Less Final Inventory	$6,000		
Cost of Food Sold		$40,630	42.3%
Gross Margin		$55,370	57.7%
Expenses			
Payroll/Labor Cost	$30,720		32%
Social Security Taxes	$1,920		2%
Rent	$4,800		5%
Laundry and Linens	$672		0.7%
Repairs and Maintenance	$2,688		2.8%
Advertising	$480		0.5%
Taxes and Insurance	$1,440		1.5%
Supplies	$672		0.7%
Depreciation	$1,920		2%
Utilities	$2,880		3%
Miscellaneous Expenses	$1,440		1.5%
Total Operating Expenses		$49,632	51.7%
Net Profit		$5,738	6%

operating expenses add up to 51.7%. When the total operating expenses are subtracted from the gross margin, the results show a net profit of 6%.

Listings on the Profit and Loss Statement

Each item listed and explained below is an indispensable part of most food service profit and loss statements. Each item must be thoroughly understood, whether it represents income or expense. Knowledge of these items will give you a better understanding of the importance of a profit and loss statement.

Total sales. Total sales are the income for that particular month. After business is completed each day, a total is taken of all sales. These totals are kept on file in the computer, on a disk, or in the income book.

Inventory at the beginning of the month. Inventory at the beginning of the month is acquired from the final inventory from the previous month. For example, the final inventory for the month of August is the beginning inventory for the month of September.

Purchases for the month. The total of all food purchased during the month is the purchases for the month. Total all invoices sent with each order.

Cost of food in production. This is the amount of food that has been cooked, is being cooked, or is in refrigerators waiting to be served. For example, a food service operation may be having a banquet, and 10 prime ribs have been cooked or are being cooked. The prime ribs would not be counted as inventory in the meat cooler, so they must be considered food in production in order to achieve an accurate financial picture.

Total. The sum of the inventory at the beginning of the month and the purchases of the month is the total. It is a total of all food that was available during that month.

Final inventory. Final inventory is acquired from the physical inventory taken at the end of each month's operation. It represents the cost of food that is still in stock and was not sold. Since it represents food that was not sold, it is subtracted from the total cost of food available during the month.

Cost of food sold. When the final inventory is subtracted from the cost of food on hand, the result is the cost of food sold that month.

Gross margin. The gross margin or gross profit is found by subtracting the cost of food sold from the total sales. Gross means the total value before deductions are made. Margin is the difference between the cost and the selling price, so sales minus cost of food gives gross margin.

Payroll/labor cost. Payroll or labor cost consists of all wages paid to all employees, including the owner's salary. You will notice it is the largest figure listed under expenses. Except for the cost of food, this is the most important item to control.

Social Security Taxes. Social Security taxes are paid to the federal government for the purpose of retirement benefits. The employer must deduct a certain percent of the employee's salary for Social Security taxes and, at the same time, must match the amount the employee pays. The amount shown on the profit and loss statement represents only the amount the employer must pay.

Rent. Rent is a fixed amount paid at a certain time of each month to the owner of a property for the use of that property. If a food service operator owns the building in which the operation is located, this particular expense is not incurred. However, there may be a similar expense if the building is not paid for (for example, paying off the mortgage to a financial institution).

Laundry and linens. These items include the cost of cleaning or renting all uniforms, napkins, tablecloths, towels, and so forth.

Repairs and maintenance. These are expenses that result from equipment failure or building repairs. If the property is rented, the owner may assume the responsibility for all repairs. This item is an essential part of any food service operation because equipment must be kept in good working condition at all times for an efficient operation.

Advertising. Advertising is an expense that is incurred when notifying the public about a place of business. The advertising may be done through the newspaper, television, radio, entertainment book, billboards, periodicals, Internet, or other media.

Taxes and insurance. These may be paid on an annual basis. If these are listed on the monthly statement, as shown in Figure 15–3, the monthly cost is found by taking one-twelfth of the yearly payment.

Supplies. Supplies are the cost of those items used other than food. These include janitorial supplies, paper products, and similar expenses.

Depreciation. Depreciation is the act of lessening the value of an item as it wears out. For example, if a new slicing machine is bought for

$2,700.00, and is used constantly for one year, at the end of that year it is worth less than $2,700.00. It has been worn out slightly through use, and therefore has less value. There are several methods used for figuring depreciation, but the simplest and most practical is the straight line method.

In the **straight line method,** estimate the length of time a piece of equipment is expected to last, and the trade-in value it should possess at the end of its estimated life. The difference between the original cost of the equipment and its estimated trade-in value gives the total amount of allowable depreciation. For example: the slicing machine that was purchased for $2,700.00 is expected to last 15 years, at which time it will probably have a trade-in value of $600.00.

Original cost	$2,700.00
Estimate trade-in	− 600.00
Allowable depreciation	$2,100.00

The allowable depreciation, $2,100, is divided by the number of years the item is expected to last (15).

140.00 Amount that can be deducted each of 15 years

Some food service operators estimate that all of their major pieces of equipment must be replaced every 10 or 12 years; instead of figuring depreciation on individual pieces of equipment, they figure it on the group. Thus, each year they charge off one-tenth or one-twelfth of the allowable depreciation. If a depreciation figure for a month is needed, find the depreciation figure for one year and take one-twelfth of that amount.

Utilities. Utilities include the cost incurred through the supply of gas, sewer, electricity, and water. These bills are usually based on monthly use and are presented to the customer on a monthly basis.

Miscellaneous expenses. These are usually smaller amounts than the others listed. They include licenses, organization dues, charitable contributions, and so forth. These amounts vary with the size and policy of the operation.

Total operating expenses. Total operating expenses are the sum of all the expenses incurred during the period or month that the P&L statement covered.

Net profit. The most important figure on the profit and loss statement, and probably the one first observed by the owner or manager, is the net profit. This figure is found by subtracting total operating expenses from gross margin. In Figure 15–3, the profit is not a large one, but at least it shows that the business is heading in the right direction. Concern occurs when that figure shows a net loss.

T I P S . . . *To Insure Perfect Solutions*

Percentage of cost of food sold plus percentage of gross margin will equal 100%.

SUMMARY REVIEW 15–5

Prepare profit and loss statements using the amounts given in problems 1–3. Use the same form as shown in the example in Figure 15–3. Find the cost of food sold, gross margin, total operating expenses, net profit, and the percent of sales for each problem listed. Round percentages to the tenth.

1. The Manor Restaurant had total sales for the month of November of $15,500. Their inventory at the beginning of the month was $5,280. During the month, they made purchases that totaled $8,200. Food in production = $225. The final inventory at the end of the month was $4,690.

   The Manor Restaurant had the following expenses during the month: salaries $3,220, Social Security taxes $115, rent $460, laundry $95, repairs and maintenance $421, advertising $75, taxes and insurance $195, supplies $120, depreciation $540, utilities $380, and miscellaneous expenses $210.

2. Connie's Cafeteria had total sales for the month of March of $25,830. Their inventory at the beginning of the month was $7,275. During the month, they made purchases that totaled $10,900. Food in production = $975. The final inventory at the end of the month was $6,870.

   Connie's Cafeteria had the following expenses during the month: salaries $5,225, Social Security taxes $313.50, rent $540, laundry and linens $98, repairs and maintenance $268, advertising $78, taxes and insurance $218, supplies $120, depreciation $395, utilities $270, and miscellaneous expenses $168.

3. The Golden Goose Restaurant had total sales for the month of April of $75,300. Their inventory at the beginning of the month was $8,880. During the month, they made purchases that totaled $25,500. Food in production = $1,250. The final inventory at the end of the month was $8,440.

   The Golden Goose Restaurant had the following expenses during the month: salaries $14,350, Social Security taxes $875, rent $650, laundry $225, repairs and maintenance $563, advertising $156, taxes and insurance $419, supplies $280, depreciation $690, utilities $345, and miscellaneous expenses $242.

THE BALANCE SHEET

The **balance sheet** is a necessary part of any business operation, almost as important as the profit and loss statement. It is a statement listing all the company's **assets** (what they own) and **liabilities** (what they owe) to determine **net worth, proprietorship** (ownership), or **capital** (money). It is a dollar-and-cents picture of a company's financial status at a given time. The given time is usually December 31 if based on the calendar year, or another date if based on the fiscal year. A **fiscal year** is defined as the time between one yearly settlement of financial accounts and another.

A balance sheet can be prepared by a company at any time they wish to know their net worth. The balance sheet is not restricted for use in the business community; it can also be used by individuals. It serves many purposes: to provide necessary information in reporting financial matters to the state and federal governments for income taxes, to secure loans from financial institutions, and in the case of many business operations, to provide the information stockholders and partners want to see or hear in the annual report.

The balance sheet is another financial report that can be simplified by using a computer and storing the information on a disk. Since every food service operation does not have a computer, it is to your advantage to learn how to perform the functions manually.

The formula for preparing a balance sheet can be expressed by the following equation:

> **Assets − Liabilities = Net Worth or Proprietorship.**

As the equation points out, a company totals all the money it owes and subtracts that amount from the total value of all it owns to find out its total worth.

To prove that the balance sheet has been prepared correctly, the liabilities are added to the net worth. The sum should equal the total assets. The relationship may be expressed by this equation:

> **Assets = Liabilities + Proprietorship.**

Two examples of balance sheets are shown in Figure 15–4. Example A is for an individual, and Example B is for a food service operation.

Listings on the Balance Sheet

The amounts shown on Example A, the William Jones balance sheet of Figure 15–4, come from various sources, as indicated in the following sections. (See Figure 15–4, Example A.)

Home. What a home is worth on the current market can be determined by a real estate appraisal.

Home furnishings. This amount is more difficult to figure. The best method may be to list the original cost and deduct a certain percentage for age and wear.

Certificates of deposit. Certificates of deposit are easy to total since the amounts are stated on each certificate. If the amount is difficult to find, just call your bank.

Cash in savings account. This figure is listed in the passbook or on your monthly statement received from the bank.

Automobile, houseboat. The current worth of an automobile or houseboat may be found by checking with the company from which they were purchased. There is a book available that will list the value of an automobile, called the blue book.

Liabilities. Liabilities are available by checking with the institution that made the loan.

Charge accounts. Statements of amounts owed are sent each month. If still in doubt, check with the company who issued the card.

The figures shown on the balance sheet for the Charcoal King Restaurant come from many sources, but can be obtained from records kept on file by the food service establishment in the computer, on a disk

---

Example A

William Jones
Balance Sheet, December 31, 20___

Assets		Liabilities	
Home	$165,000	Home mortgage	$ 66,000
Home furnishings	19,470	Houseboat loan	13,500
Certificates of deposit	30,000	Auto loan	4,500
Cash in savings account	13,500	Charge accounts (retail)	2,070
Cash in checking account	885	Total Liabilities	$ 86,070
Automobile	13,950	Net Worth-	
Houseboat	26,325	Proprietorship	183,060
Total Assets	$269,130	Total Liabilities and Net Worth- Proprietorship	$269,130

Example B

Charcoal King Restaurant
Balance Sheet, June 30, 20___

Assets (Current)		Liabilities (Current)	
Cash in bank and on hand	$ 21,800	Accounts payable	$ 14,716
Accounts receivable	6,700	Installment accounts or bank notes payable	48,624
Food and beverage inventory	10,340	Payroll and taxes payable	3,956
Supplies	1,680		
Total Current Assets	$ 40,520	Total Current Liabilities	67,296
Assets (Fixed)		Net Worth- Proprietorship	49,024
Stationary kitchen equipment	$ 41,288	Total Liabilities and	
Hand kitchen equipment	9,824	Net Worth- Proprietorship	$116,320
Dining room furniture and fixtures	13,548		
China glassware, silver, and linen	11,140		
Total Fixed Assets	$ 75,800		
Total Assets (Current and Fixed)	$116,320		

Figure 15–4 *(A) Balance sheet for an individual (B) Balance sheet for a company*

---

or in the income book. (See Figure 15–4, Example B.) The bookkeeper will keep these figures, discussed in the following sections, current.

Cash. The cash amount is found in the income book, in the computer, or on a disk. This figure is kept up to date by the bookkeeper.

Accounts receivable. Accounts receivable refers to money that is owed to the company by various people or companies for various reasons.

Food and beverage inventory. This figure is taken from the profit and loss statement.

Assets (fixed). The value of the fixed assets listed (which, in this case, are for various kinds of equipment) can be acquired by referring to purchase contracts or equipment records.

Accounts payable. Accounts payable refers to money the food service operation owes for purchases made. (In other words, bills that have not been paid.) The amounts may be found by referring to the unpaid bill or invoice file.

Installment accounts or bank notes payable. These figures are found by referring to sales contracts or equipment records. Another possible source is the bank or company to whom the money is owed.

Payroll and taxes payable. These figures are found by checking with the bookkeeper or accountant who keeps these figures up to date.

SUMMARY REVIEW 15–6

Prepare balance sheets for problems 1–5, using the figures listed. Find total assets, total liabilities, net worth and total liabilities, and net worth-proprietorship.

1. Tim Wu had the following assets as of May 15 this year: home $138,000, home furnishings $26,085, automobile $12,750, speedboat $6,450, cash in savings accounts $38,670, cash in checking account $5,034, and stocks $4,825. His liabilities were as follows: home mortgage $85,500, auto loan $7,200, boat loan $3,900, note payable to loan company $4,500, and charge accounts $2,682.

2. Joe and Mary Hernandez had the following assets as of July 15 this year: home $157,500, house trailer $11,100, home furnishings $23,325, automobile $11,580, cash in savings account $18,795, cash in checking account $759, U.S. savings bonds $2,500, and certificates of deposit $15,000. Their liabilities were as follows: home mortgage $85,500, loan on house trailer $6,600, automobile loan $6,900, and charge accounts $2,691.

3. Robert and Dolores O'Shaunessey had the following assets as of December 31 this year: local home $116,250, vacation home $45,840, motor-boat $8,400, automobile $19,650, home furnishings $17,970, certificates of deposit $20,000, cash in savings account $3,500, cash in checking account $1,695, and U.S. savings bonds $1,275. Their liabilities were as follows: local home mortgage $66,700, vacation home mortgage $31,650, motorboat loan $3,900, automobile loan $10,350, loan on home furnishings $5,400, and charge accounts $2,700.

4. Jim's Hamburger Palace had the following assets as of December 31 this year: cash $5,956, food and beverage inventory $4,800, supplies $392, equipment (stationary, hand, and serving equipment) $14,140, and furniture and fixtures $5,000. The restaurant's liabilities were as follows: accounts payable $344.80, notes payable to First National Bank $3,900, note payable to Mike Bryce $1,120, sales tax payable $278, and taxes payable $1,040.

5. Bill's Oyster House had the following assets as of December 31 this year: cash $18,770, accounts receivable $2,186.32, food and

beverage inventory $5,982, supplies $1,559.60, stationary kitchen equipment $21,797.40, hand equipment $1,714.20, dining room furniture and fixtures $14,453, and serving equipment and dishes $11,507. The liabilities were as follows: accounts payable $25,191.20, installment accounts payable $10,682, bank notes payable to First National Bank $30,100, sales tax payable $1,061.60, payroll tax payable $1,112, and taxes payable $243.80.

BREAK-EVEN ANALYSIS

Break-even analysis is a mathematical method for finding the dollar amount needed for a food service operation to break even.

Break-even analysis calculates the level of economic activity where the operation neither makes a profit nor incurs a loss. It is based on a certain amount that must be achieved through total sales before a profit can be realized and below which a loss is incurred. This method is beneficial to the food service operator for planning profits. Planning profits is extremely important to any business operation when financial planning decisions must be made. In the food service industry, where bankruptcy may occur, the break-even figure could be a key to survival.

Every business has peaks and valleys. These terms relate to the amount of sales for a business. The peaks represent the great business days when there is an abundance of sales. The valleys are the bad days when hardly anyone comes into the business and the owner loses money. Each food service operator must know how to determine the amount of sales dollars needed to show a profit or a loss. This is referred to as the **break-even point.** The food service operator must know how to calculate and understand the meaning of the break-even point. Simply put, the break-even point occurs when sales volume covers all of the costs related to doing business. The operator should know the amount of sales that has to be generated in order to pay all of the bills. Once that point has been reached, the additional sales will create a profit. Another term for the break-even point is "cracking the nut."

In order to calculate the break-even point and understand the concept of break-even analysis, the food service operator must know and understand the meaning of some specific terms that are used in this mathematical process.

Mathematical problems are expressed by formulas. If the formula is followed, a solution can be found. It is important to be able to identify, understand, and be familiar with each part of the break-even formula.

Sales revenue is the money received from the sale of all products, food, beverages, and so forth. It represents all of the money received over a certain period of time through sales.

Variable cost is the changeable cost or expenses that will increase or decrease with the level of sales volume. The greater the number of people served and meals produced, the greater the variable cost. Variable cost may be divided into two categories: cost of goods sold and serving expenses.

Cost of goods sold is the amount it costs the operator to provide food, beverages, and so forth, to serve customers. It is the operator's cost of goods to be sold.

Serving expenses are additional expenses incurred as a result of serving customers. These include:

- Laundry—tablecloths, napkins, kitchen towels, uniforms
- Paper supplies—guest checks, report forms, register tapes
- Payroll—labor cost
- Tableware replacement—glassware, china, silverware

Gross profit is the sales revenue minus variable costs. This is the total value before deducting fixed cost.

Fixed cost is the expenses that remain constant regardless of the level of sales volume. They may be divided into two categories: occupational expenses and primary expenses.

Occupational expenses, also called the cost of ownership, are those that continue whether or not the restaurant is operating. They include such expenses as property tax, insurance, interest on the mortgage, and depreciation of equipment, furniture, and building. There may be others, depending on the local situation.

Primary expenses are those that result from being open for business. These expenses are constant, whether serving a few customers or many. They include such expenses as utilities, basic staff (preparation, service, etc.), telephone service, repairs and maintenance, licenses, and exterminating costs.

The authors will explain this concept by using the following example. This example, although not logical, will help to illustrate the concept of the break-even point.

Example:

Janet Downs has developed a great-tasting vegetable onion burger. Janet is a sharp businesswoman and has figured out that each burger she serves will cost her $0.75 to produce. This price takes into account all the ingredients needed to make one 6-ounce burger. The price also includes the cost of the roll, salt and pepper, condiments, a napkin, and a paper plate on which to serve the burger. Janet has been offered a location to sell her burgers that will cost her $250 a week in rent. This cost of rent includes all refrigeration and cooking equipment, and the energy needed to produce the product. This rent will be her only other expense, in addition to the cost to produce the burger. Before Janet decides to open up her business, she has to determine how many vegetable onion burgers she must sell each week in order to "crack the nut," or reach the break-even point. Since Janet will do all the work herself, she will have no labor cost and will only get paid when she makes a profit.

Before this problem can be solved, the following terms must be defined and explained. In the food service profession, the vegetable onion burger is referred to as **cost of goods sold.** This is the amount of money it costs the operator to provide food, beverages, condiments, and so forth to customers.

Janet has also included in her price for the vegetable onion burger the serving expenses of the napkin and paper plate. **Serving expenses** are the costs incurred as a result of serving customers. Other examples of serving expenses are replacement costs for china, laundry, paper supplies, and payroll or labor costs.

Because Janet may sell 1 burger or 100 burgers a day, the cost of goods sold for the onion vegetable burgers will increase or decrease depending on the amount of burgers she makes. The amount of burgers sold will also reflect the cost of the serving expenses. Adding together the **cost of goods sold** and the **serving expenses** results in the **variable cost.**

Variable cost = Cost of goods sold + serving expenses.

As stated previously, Janet has calculated her variable cost (of one burger and serving expenses) to be $0.75. Obviously, the amount of burgers made will cause her costs to vary; if she has to make more burgers, her variable cost will increase, and if she has a bad business day, her variable costs will decrease. If she must make 100 burgers, her cost will be $75.00 ($0.75 \times 100$). If she only has to make 25 burgers, the cost will be $18.75 ($0.75 \times 25$).

Janet has determined that she wants to have a 25% food cost. As you have learned previously, in order to obtain a 25% food cost you must multiply the variable cost by four. Thus, she multiplies the variable cost of $0.75 by four. This results in a menu price of $3.00 for each burger.

She now wants to determine how many burgers she must sell each week to reach her break-even point, or "crack the nut." But before she can make this calculation, she must determine exactly how much of the $3.00 (the menu price) that she receives in payment for her vegetable onion burger she will actually keep. This is calculated by subtracting the **variable cost** from her **menu price,** resulting in her **total variable profit.**

Menu price − variable cost = Total variable profit.
$3.00 − $0.75 = $2.25

Her variable cost is $0.75 cents, and her menu price for one burger is $3.00. She receives a total variable profit of $2.25 for each burger sold.

The rent charged to Janet is called **fixed cost.** This is the expense that remains constant, regardless of the amount of burgers that are sold. Janet has to pay $250 in rent each week whether she sells 1, 25, or 100 burgers. Janet can now determine how many burgers she needs to sell each week to "crack the nut" by using the following formula.

Break-even point = Fixed cost ÷ (total variable profit)
Break-even point = $250 ÷ 2.25
Break-even point = 111.111 burgers

Using the above formula, Janet's fixed costs are $250 a week. Her total variable profit is $2.25 for each burger sold.

Since it is unrealistic to expect someone to buy 0.111 of a burger, Janet has to round up to reach her break-even point. She has to sell 112 vegetable onion burgers a week to break even or "crack the nut."

In order to prove this formula, multiply 112 by $3.00, which results in total sales or income of $336. Since each burger costs Janet $0.75, multiply the cost (0.75) by the amount of burgers sold (112). Janet's variable cost to make the burgers is (112×0.75) $84. The fixed rent of $250 is added to the $84, which equals $334. Once Janet sells 112 burgers, she will have covered all of her costs and reached the break-even point. There is an additional $2.00 leftover because Janet had to sell an additional burger; she could not have sold 0.111 of a burger.

The previous example of Janet's burger business illustrated how to determine the break-even point for a business that sells only one item, has no employees, and has only one fixed cost. All food service operations are more complicated than the previous example. Most of them don't have the time to break down each item, as was done in the first example. Instead, they use a method called the contribution rate and contribution rate percentage to determine the break-even point. The authors will continue illustrating the break-even point by using Janet's business. This next section will illustrate how the monthly break-even point is determined using the contribution rate.

CONTRIBUTION RATE AND CONTRIBUTION RATE PERCENTAGE

The **contribution rate** is the amount of money that is left after the variable costs are subtracted from the sales.

$$\text{Contribution rate} = \text{Sales} - \text{variable costs.}$$

The **contribution rate percentage** is calculated by dividing the contribution rate by the sales.

$$\text{Contribution rate percentage} = \frac{\text{Contribution rate}}{\text{Sales}}$$

Janet's business is doing well. She has added more items onto the menu, increased her sales, and, as a result, increased her staff to meet the demand of the business. Her landlord has kept her rent at $250 a week, or $1,000 a month, but she now has to pay $2,000 in additional fixed costs. At the end of the month, Janet's profit and loss statement has been condensed into a document that will allow her to figure out her break-even point using the contribution rate percentage. She has determined which of her expenses are variable costs and which are fixed costs. Her April condensed profit and loss statement is shown in Figure 15–5.

Janet's Famous Vegetable Onion Burgers
Condensed Profit and Loss Statement for the Month of April

Categories	Amount of Money	Percentage
Sales	$25,000	100%
– Variable Costs	$10,000	40%
Contribution rate	$15,000	60%
– Fixed Costs	$3,000	
Profit before taxes	$12,000	

Figure 15–5 *Condensed profit and loss statement showing contribution rate*

Janet may now determine how many sales must be generated each month in order to reach her break-even point by using the contribution rate percentage. The formula to determine her break-even point is to take her fixed costs and divide them by her contribution rate percentage.

$$\text{Break-even point} = \frac{\text{Fixed costs}}{\text{Contribution rate percentage}}$$

Using all the information from Janet's condensed profit and loss statement, the authors will illustrate how Janet determines her break-even point in sales.

Step 1: Determine the amount of the contribution rate.

Contribution rate = Sales − variable costs.		
	Sales	$25,000
Minus	Variable Costs	$10,000
Equals	Contribution Rate	$15,000

The contribution rate is $15,000.

Step 2: Determine the contribution rate percentage.

$$\text{Contribution rate percentage} = \frac{\text{Contribution rate}}{\text{Sales}}$$

	Contribution Rate	$15,000
Divided by	Sales	$25,000
Equals	Contribution Rate %	0.6, or 60%

The contribution rate percentage is 60%.

Step 3: Determine Janet's Famous Vegetable Onion Burgers break-even point.

$$\text{Break-even point} = \frac{\text{Fixed costs}}{\text{Contribution rate percentage}}$$

	Fixed Costs	$3,000
Divided by	Contribution Rate %	60%
Equals	Break-even Point	$5,000

Janet's Famous Vegetable Onion Burgers has to generate $5,000 a month in sales to break even.

Janet, being the sharp businesswoman that she is, keeps meticulous records. She knows that the check average (how much a guest spends at each transaction) is $5.25. She would now like to determine how many guests she needs to purchase food and beverages each day to "crack the nut." Janet is open for 20 days each month. Her first step is to divide the break-even sales amount of $5,000 by the check average of $5.25. This equals 952.38095 transactions a month that must occur. Janet then takes her 20 days and divides that into the 953 (she rounds up from 952.38095) transactions, and determines that she must have 47.65 customers a day to break even. Janet has used mathematics for the food service industry to determine her break-even point and analyze her business. Janet determines that this is a great business and starts looking for new sites to expand her famous Vegetable Onion Burger Empire!

T I P S . . .   To Insure Perfect Solutions

When a profit occurs, the accounting profession writes the number in black ink . . . thus, the business is "in the black." If a loss occurs, the number is written in red ink . . . thus, the business is "in the red." With computer-generated profit and loss statements, when a loss occurs, the dollar amount is written inside parentheses.

SUMMARY REVIEW 15–7

For each problem determine the contribution rate, contribution rate percentage, and break-even point. Identify whether the business made or lost money. If the business lost money, what possible steps could be taken to put the business "in the black"?

1. The Blue Bird Cafeteria did $80,000 in sales. Their variable cost was 40% of the total sales and the fixed costs were $24,000.

2. The Castle Restaurant did $120,000 in sales. Their variable cost was 36% of the total sales and the fixed costs were $32,000.

3. The Blue Angel Restaurant did $32,000 in sales. Their variable cost was 40% of the total sales and the fixed costs were $24,000.

4. The Red Gate Cafeteria did $96,000 in sales. Their variable cost was 43% of the total sales and the fixed costs were $63,600.

5. The Old Mill Restaurant did $72,500 in sales. Their variable cost was 44% of the total sales and the fixed costs were $28,112.

BUDGETING

Budgeting is a plan for adjusting expenditures to probable income for a calendar or fiscal year. It is a plan that works equally well for individuals, small businesses, and large corporations, for maintaining a fairly equal balance between income and expenses. Businesses use the budget not only to gauge expenses and income for the year, but also to keep all departments within the company on the proper financial track. Some companies even require department heads to submit a written report showing why they have exceeded their budget. The budget is just a plan, and, like most plans, if followed, good results often happen. If one goes astray, problems will probably develop.

In a budget, the areas listed under the two major components, **income** and **expenditures,** will vary, depending on the size of the overall operation. Generally included under income are the total of register receipts and income from sales that would not pass through the register, such as payment for a catered affair. These figures can be obtained from income records of the previous year.

Expenditures might include:

- labor cost
- total supplies (food, paper goods, cleaning supplies, etc.)
- telephone service
- new equipment
- service calls on equipment
- workmen's compensation
- utilities (gas and electric)
- printing service for menus
- fringe benefits (dental plan, hospitalization, etc.)

Many of the estimated figures required for these items can again be obtained from the records of the previous year. If, after checking the figures from the previous year, you are aware of or believe that an increase or decrease of funds will be required for the coming year, then adjustments are in order. Remember, the purpose of a budget is to give a general idea of what will happen. The budget is very seldom exact.

Using hypothetical figures, let us set up a budget as if it were a pie. The whole pie would be the food service operation's total income for a year. Two examples will be given.

Example 1: A food service budget (break-even budget) is shown in Figure 15–6. The yearly income from register and supplemental sales is $300,000. The total dollar amounts budgeted for each item are listed.

Food and Supplies (30%)	= $90,000
Labor (25%)	= $75,000
Workmen's Compensation (3%)	= $ 9,000
Fringe Benefits (8%)	= $24,000
Utilities (9%)	= $27,000
Printing Service (5%)	= $15,000
New Equipment (10%)	= $30,000
Equipment Service (6%)	= $18,000
Telephone (4%)	= $12,000

Figure 15–6 *Sample food service budget, Example 1*

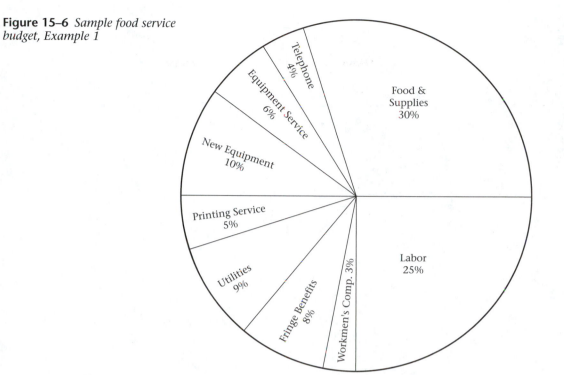

When taking a percent of a whole number, in this case $300,000, we must multiply. For example:

$$\begin{array}{rl} \$\;300,000 & \text{Yearly income} \\ \underline{\times\;0.30} & \text{Food \& supplies} \\ \$90,000.00 & \text{Amount budgeted for food \& supplies} \end{array}$$

$$\begin{array}{rl} \$\;300,000 & \text{Yearly income} \\ \underline{\times\;.25} & \text{Labor} \\ 1500000 & \\ \underline{600000} & \\ \$75,000.00 & \text{Amount budgeted for labor} \end{array}$$

The other amounts shown in the budget are found by the same procedure.

Example 2: Another sample food service budget (break-even budget) is shown in Figure 15–7. The yearly income from register and supplemental sales is $300,000. The percentage of the total income that was budgeted for each item is listed. The sum of the completed percentages should equal 100%.

Food and Supplies ($75,000)	=	25%
Labor ($69,000)	=	23%
Workmen's Compensation ($24,000)	=	8%
Fringe Benefits ($27,000)	=	9%
Utilities ($33,000)	=	11%
Printing Service ($9,000)	=	3%
New Equipment ($45,000)	=	15%
Equipment Service ($12,000)	=	4%
Telephone ($6,000)	=	2%

Figure 15–7 *Sample food service budget, Example 2*

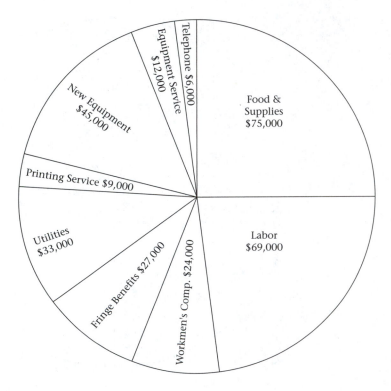

To find what percent one number is of another number, divide the number that represents the part by the number that represents the whole. For example:

$$\begin{array}{r} 0.25 \;\; = 25\% \\ \text{Represents the whole} \;\; \$300,000\overline{)\$75,000.00} \;\; \text{Food \& supplies} \\ \underline{60,000.00} \;\; \text{represent the part} \\ 15,000.00 \\ \underline{15,000.00} \end{array}$$

Thus, 25% is the percentage of the $300,000 yearly income set aside for the cost of food and supplies. The other percentages shown in the budget are found by the same procedure.

Budgeting is also an important step in the proper management of personal affairs. The family income certainly should be budgeted so that money will be on hand when the bills are due. The family budget may be set up on a monthly or yearly basis, with a percentage of income or a dollar amount set aside for each important family expense.

Example: For a monthly income of $2,000, the budget might be as follows:

Item	Percent	Dollar Amount
Food	25%	$ 500
Clothing	15%	$ 300
Mortgage Payment	35%	$ 700
Recreation	9%	$ 180
Benevolences	5%	$ 100
Savings	11%	$ 220
	100%	$2,000

SUMMARY REVIEW 15–8

1. For a food service budget, the yearly income from register and supplemental sales is $550,000. Find the dollar amount that was budgeted for each item listed.

   a. Food and Supplies   26% $_____

   b. Labor   24% $_____

   c. Workmen's Compensation   4% $_____

   d. Fringe Benefits   8% $_____

   e. Utilities   11% $_____

   f. Printing Service   2% $_____

   g. New Equipment   10% $_____

   h. Equipment Service   5% $_____

   i. Telephone   3% $_____

   j. Profit   7% $_____

2. For a food service budget, the yearly income from register and supplemental sales is $725,000. Find the percentage of total income that was budgeted for each item listed.

   a. Food and Supplies $188,500   _____%

   b. Labor $166,750   _____%

   c. Workmen's Compensation $ 21,750   _____%

   d. Fringe Benefits $ 65,250   _____%

   e. Utilities $ 72,500   _____%

   f. Printing Service $ 29,000   _____%

   g. New Equipment $ 79,750   _____%

   h. Equipment Service $ 43,500   _____%

   i. Telephone $ 14,500   _____%

   j. Profit $ 43,500   _____%

3. The Piazza family has a monthly income of $2,400. What percentage of the monthly income was budgeted for each item? Prove that your percentages are correct by adding the results. The sum should be 100%. Their monthly budget is as follows:

   a. Food $ 600.00   _____%

   b. Clothing $ 432.00   _____%

   c. Charities $ 144.00   _____%

   d. Savings $ 192.00   _____%

   e. Mortgage Payment $ 648.00   _____%

   f. Recreation $ 216.00   _____%

   g. Utilities $ 168.00   _____%

4. The Fahy family has a yearly income of $28,975. Find the dollar amount that was budgeted for each item listed. The sum of the completed budget should equal the yearly income of $28,975. Their budget for the year is as follows:

a. Food   23% $_____

b. Mortgage Payment   27% $_____

c. Utilities   8% $_____

d. Clothing   13% $_____

e. Recreation   7% $_____

f. Family Welfare   6% $_____

g. Benevolences   3% $_____

h. Savings   9% $_____

i. Other Items   4% $_____

5. The Curran family has a monthly income of $2,260. What percentage of the monthly income was budgeted for each item? Prove that your percentages are correct by adding the results. The sum should be 100%. Their monthly budget is as follows:

a. Rent $ 565.00   _____%

b. Food $ 519.80   _____%

c. Clothing $ 429.40   _____%

d. Utilities $ 180.80   _____%

e. Entertainment $ 248.60   _____%

f. Insurance $ 67.80   _____%

g. Doctors' Fees $ 90.40   _____%

h. Savings $ 158.20   _____%

SOURCES CITED

Case Western Reserve University Weatherhead School of Management. (2001). *The break-even calculator*. Retrieved November 2, 2005, from Case Western Reserve University Web site at http://connection.cwru.edu/mbac424/breakeven/breakeven.html

Miller, J. E., Hayes, D. K., & Dopson, L. R. (2002). *Food and beverage cost control* (2nd ed). New York: John Wiley & Sons, Inc.

Posttest

The posttest evaluates a student's math skills after the student completes the food service math course. This posttest identifies the competency in mathematics in food service for both the student and the instructor.

The instructor will determine the percentage of questions that must be answered correctly to show competency in mathematics in the food service industry.

Addition

1. 36.9 + 626.42 + 2,430.07 + 14.03 = _____

Subtraction

2. $7,669.75 − $5,248.46 = _____

Multiplication

3. 47.8 × 8 × 13.3 × 15.2 = _____

Division

4. 9,245.25 ÷ 182 = _____

Compute the following chain calculation.

5. $43,687.50 − $31,628.75 + $.05 = _____

Using a sales tax percentage of 8.50%, what is the amount of sales tax?

6. $8,169.43 _____

Using 25% as the desired food cost percentage, find the menu price based upon the raw food cost of the following questions. Round answers to the nearest cent.

7. $2.22 _____

8. $0.75 _____

Multiply the following problem.

9. $996.30 × 8.5% _____

Division problem

10. $2890.00 ÷ 14.2% _____

Figure out the total cost of the following problems.

11. $5892.15 + 17.8% gratuity _____

12. $5192.14 − 12.6% discount _____

Case	Size	Product	Unit	Price	Amount
9	#10	Sliced apples	Case	20.87	_____
5	#10	Sliced pineapples	Case	17.27	_____
9	#10	Tomato puree	Case	13.85	_____
8	#10	Green beans, cut	Case	11.58	_____
4	#10	Tomatoes, whole pealed	Case	16.98	_____
3	10 lbs.	Fettuccine, long	Lbs.	6.56	_____
5	10 lbs.	Vermicelli, cut	Lbs.	4.20	_____
3	13 oz.	Pickling spices	Oz.	4.18	_____
4	6 oz.	Rubbed sage	Oz.	5.42	_____
3	11 oz.	Thyme, ground	Oz.	5.89	_____
4	46 oz.	Cranberry juice cocktail	Case	22.66	_____
5	50 lbs.	Granulated sugar	Bag	16.70	_____
		Total			

13. Complete the following invoice, showing the extension amount of all items.

14. What is the total cost of the invoice? _____

15. Fifteen items were purchased at $13.60 each and 6 items at $9.95 each. If the sales tax on the total purchase was 8.25%, what was the total cost? _____

16. A dessert cart was purchased for $2,880. A discount of 8.5% was given. What is the total cost if a sales tax of 7.5% is added to the purchase? _____

Rewrite the following number by adding commas in the correct place.

17. 235620425 _____

Write out the words for the following dollar amount. For example, $195.23 would be written as "One hundred ninety five and 23/100 dollars."

18. $21,495.25 _____

Change the following amount to the nearest cent using the mill.

19. $55,678.526 _____

Find the sum in the following addition problem. Simplify the answer to lowest terms.

20. $20\frac{3}{5} + 16\frac{3}{15} + 20\frac{3}{10} =$ _____

Find the difference in the following subtraction problem. Simplify the answer to lowest terms.

21. $29\frac{4}{5} - 16\frac{3}{15} =$ _____

Find the product in the following multiplication problem.

22. $30\frac{4}{5} \times 16\frac{6}{15} =$ _____

Find the quotient in the following division problem.

23. $27\frac{4}{5} \div 2\frac{6}{15} =$ _____

Change the following fractions to decimals

24. $\frac{7}{10}$ = _____

25. $\frac{5}{100}$ = _____

Write the following decimals and mixed decimal fractions in words.

26. 0.7 = _____

27. 9.5 = _____

Write each of the following numbers as decimals.

28. Six tenths _____

29. Fifty-three ten thousandths _____

Compute the following problems.

30. 0.146 + 0.002 + 643 + 6.2675 = _____

31. 149.371 − 121.218 = _____

32. 8.323 × 5.324 = _____

33. 64.25 ÷ 3.8 = _____

34. How much water should be used to cook 4 pints of barley using a ratio of 4 to 1 water to barley? _____

35. The Bears Restaurant sells 15 times as many orders of chateaubriand as chicken breasts. How many orders of chateaubriand were sold if 12 orders of chicken breasts were sold? _____

Express the following common fraction as a percent

36. $\frac{7}{12}$ = _____

Express the following percent as a common fraction. Reduce the answer to the lowest common denominator

37. 22% = _____

38. A 628-pound side of beef is ordered. The chuck cut weighs 76 pounds and the round cut weighs 58 pounds. What percent of the side is the chuck? _____

39. What percent is the round cut? _____

40. The food cost percentage for the month is 38%. If $25,485 was taken in on sales that month, how much of that amount went for the cost of food? _____

41. How many tablespoons are there in 12 teaspoons?

_____

42. One hundred and ten quarts equals how many gallons?

_____

43. A recipe calls for 4 pounds of apple juice. How much liquid would you use? _____

44. What is the range of ounces in a #10 can?

_____

45. Determine the cost of hamburger if the dial pointer on the portion scale points to the third mark beyond the 5 and the cost of 1 pound of ground beef is $4.99. _____

Find the amount of ounces in the following problems.

46. 18.23 pounds   _____

47. 11.25 gallons   _____

48. The Merlot Restaurant receives 10 ribs of beef weighing 22.45 pounds each. How many ounces of beef does this represent?

Convert the following Fahrenheit temperature to Celsius. Round off the answer to two places to the right of the decimal point.

49. 212   _____

Convert the following Celsius temperature to Fahrenheit. Round off the answer to two places to the right of the decimal point.

50. 100   _____

Convert the following recipe from the American customary system to the metric system.

51. 2 lb. 6 oz. shortening   _____g

52. 9 pounds of powdered sugar   _____kg

Convert the following recipe from the metric system to the American customary system. Answer should be carried out three places to the right of the decimal point.

53. 1 liter of mayonnaise   _____qt.

54. 5 milliliters of lemon juice   _____tsp.

55. A 2.5 pound box of frozen corn costs $3.55. How much does a 4-ounce serving cost?   _____

56. How many servings can be obtained from 25 gallons of soup if a $\frac{1}{2}$ -cup ladle is used?

_____

57. A 4-ounce serving of wax beans is served to each of 255 people. How many cans of wax beans are needed if each can weighs 14 ounces?   _____

58. A 19-pound A.P. beef tenderloin is trimmed; 8 ounces are lost. How many E.P 6-ounce filets mignons can be cut from the tenderloin?

_____

59. For a wedding of 470 guests, an E.P. 8-ounce sirloin steak will be served. If each fabricated sirloin weighs 16 pounds, how many sirloins must be ordered?   _____

60. How many pounds of drawn fish should be ordered when preparing for a party of 288 guests?   _____

61. What is the yield percentage of a 24-pound turkey? The turkey lost 8 pounds and 5 ounces after fabrication and shrinkage.

_____

Find the working factor for the next two problems

62. The standardized recipe is for 35 portions. The party is for 350 guests.   _____

63. The standardized recipe is for 50 portions. The party is for 20 guests.

_____

64. The following recipe yields nine 8-inch pies. Convert each ingredient to yield thirty-six 8-inch pies.

Amount of conversion   _____

4 lbs. flour   _____

3 lbs. 6 oz. granulated sugar _____

½ oz. salt   _____

3 oz. lemon gratings   _____

1 lb. water   _____

8 oz. corn starch   _____

12 oz. egg yolks   _____

1 lb. 6 oz. lemon juice   _____

4 oz. butter, melted   _____

65. Determine the approximate yield of the following formula if each cookie is to contain 1½ ounces of dough.

1 lb. 6 oz. shortening   _____

1 lb. 6 oz. powdered sugar   _____

2 lb. 8 oz. pastry flour   _____

2 oz. liquid milk   _____

6 oz. raisins, chopped   _____

2 oz. pecans, chopped   _____

3 oz. pineapple, chopped   _____

2 oz. peaches, chopped   _____

8 oz. whole eggs   _____

1/4 oz. baking soda   _____

1/4 oz. vanilla   _____

1/2 oz. salt   _____

Find the approximate yield.   _____

66. Determine the amount of dry instant potato powder needed to prepare 6.5 gallons of mashed potatoes if the ratio calls for 1 lb. 13 oz. of powder for each gallon of milk. _____

67. Find the baker's percentage of each ingredient used in the following formula. Round to the tenth place.

9 lbs. bread flour   _____

1 lb. pastry flour   _____

2 lbs. shortening   _____

18 oz. sugar   _____

13 oz. eggs   _____

5 oz. salt   _____

8 oz. dry milk   _____

10 oz. compressed yeast   _____

5 lbs. cold water   _____

68. One loaf of bread was purchased for $1.89. There are 20 slices of bread in the package, but the 2 end pieces cannot be used. What is the cost of 2 slices of bread for an order of toast?

_____

69. A 9-pound (E.P.) leg of lamb costing $3.85 per pound is roasted. When the roast is removed from the oven, only 2/3 of the original amount is left. How much does an 8-ounce serving cost?

_____

70. Find the cost of the following recipe for soft dinner rolls. Recipe yields 15 dozen rolls.

Ingredients	Amount	Price	Cost
Sugar	1 lb.	$0.36 per pound	_____
Shortening	1 lb. 4 oz.	$0.48 per pound	_____
Dry milk	8 oz.	$1.93 per pound	_____
Salt	2 oz.	$0.42 per pound	_____
Eggs	3	$0.95 per doz.	_____
Yeast	6 oz.	$3.50 per pound	_____
Water	4 lbs.	$1.25 per gallon	_____
Bread flour	7 lbs.	$0.20 per pound	_____

71. Total cost of the recipe   _____

72. Cost of one dozen   _____

73. Cost of one roll   _____

74. The Chardonnay Café employees eight culinary staff who each earn $11.50 per hour. During the week, they each work five 8-hour shifts. What is the cost of labor for the culinary staff?

_____

75. A fajita platter has a menu price of $13.95. The raw cost of food is $3.24. What is the food cost percentage?

_____

76. Determine the menu price if the raw food cost is $5.75 and the markup rate is $\frac{5}{8}$.   _____

77. Determine the menu price if the raw food cost is $3.75 and a 38% food cost is desired.   _____

78. What was our food cost percentage for the month if we had sales of $211,213.25 and our purchases totaled $53,292?

_____

Find the monthly food cost percentage and the cost of food sold using the following information. Carry the food cost percentage two places to the right of the decimal.

Sales for the Month	$64,000.00
Beginning Inventory	$6,780.50
Purchases for the Month	$15,890.00
Food in Production	$2,005.10
Final Inventory	$4,852.27

79. The cost of food sold is   _____

80. Monthly food cost percentage   _____

81. Prepare a storeroom requisition form. Find the extension price and the total.

    Ten #10 cans peaches @ $4.71 per can   _____

    Seven #10 cans tomatoes @ $2.83 per can   _____

    12 heads lettuce @ $0.99 per head   _____

    3 dozen apples @ $4.50 per dozen   _____

    6 pounds of corn starch @ $0.56 per pound   _____

    4 pounds of margarine @ $4.76 per pound   _____

82. Total cost of this requisition   _____

83. Complete the following counter production reports.

Item	Number of Portions For Sale	Number of Portions Not Sold	Number of Portions Sold	Unit Price	Value Sold
Hot Dogs	95	5		3.25	
Hamburgers	95	7		4.75	
Chicken Patty	65	18		4.75	
Barbecue	55	2		5.50	
Cube Steak	40	5		5.75	
Soda	120	21		1.75	
Shakes	60	8		3.25	
Milk	110	7		1.25	
Pie	48	12		3.50	
Ice Cream	60	15		3.75	
			Total Value Sold		

84. Calculate and total the following guest check. Three guests had lunch at the Lake Resort. They had two orders of coconut shrimp @ $7.25 each for appetizers; two glasses of Sauvignon Blanc @ $7.50 each; and three glasses of private Chardonnay @ $7.00 each. For their main courses, they had a turkey bacon wrap @ $8.25, a club sandwich @ $9.95, and a chicken wrap @ $9.50.

  _____

85. What is the sales tax amount if the sales tax is 6.5%?

  _____

86. What is the guest check total?   _____

87. What will the tip be on the guest check if the tip is 15%?

  _____

88. Marisa works three shifts a week. If she sells nine additional $35.00 bottles of wine a night and the gratuity is 15%, what is her additional income?

Each shift   _____

Weekly total   _____

89. Complete the following cashier's daily report.

Today's date	
POS Register Readings or Total of Guest Check Sales	
Food Sales	$3,856.63
Beverage Sales	1,474.68
Miscellaneous Sales	191.21
Total Sales	
Add the Amount of Sales Tax	316.58
Gross Receipts	
Add—Start of Shift Money (Bank)	150.00
Total of Gross Receipts and Money Started With (Bank)	
Cash Collected from Guest Checks During the Shift	625.75
Less Total Cash Paid Out	
Total Cash in Drawer	
Credit Card Receipts	
American Express	1,550.56
Discover	315.45
MasterCard	900.37
Visa	975.25
House Accounts	528.82
Total Charge & House Receipts	
Add Cash in Drawer	
Total Cash and Charges (Should Equal the Amount of Gross Receipts)	
Over or (Short)	
Record of Cash Paid Out	
City Ice Company	31.50
Tips	16.85
Arkay Florist	18.75
Other	0.00
Total Cash Paid Out	
Signed by:	

90. Mr. Toby's restaurant charges $175 for an all-inclusive meal. The sales tax is 8.25% and the gratuity is 15%.

What is the sales tax owed?   _____

Amount of money for the restaurant?   _____

Gratuity amount?   _____

91. A cook is paid a salary of $595 per week, plus a 2% commission on all food sales for the week in excess of $20,000. During the second week of March, the food sales amounted to $30,000. If the Social Security tax is 7.30%, how much Social Security tax was deducted from his earnings for that week? _____

92. How much tax would be paid if your net income is $55,880, and your tax is $380 plus 6% of the excess over $8,000?

_____

93. The food and beverage manager is paid a salary of $9,000 a month and receives two paychecks each month. On a recent paycheck, the deductions from his total earnings were as follows: $135.87 FICA tax; $450.00 federal withholding tax; $97.50 state income tax; and $36.50 city income tax.

What was his gross wage for this pay period?

_____

What was his net pay? _____

Prepare a profit and loss statement. Find the cost of food sold, gross margin, total operating expenses, net profit, and the percent of sales. Round percentages to the tenth.

The Manor Restaurant had total sales for the month of November of $35,500. Their inventory at the beginning of the month was $6,280. During the month, they made purchases that totaled $8,200. The food in production cost was $225. The final inventory at the end of the month was $4,690.

Their expenses: salaries $3,220; Social Security taxes $115; rent $460; laundry $95; repairs and maintenance $421; advertising $75; taxes and insurance $195; supplies $120; depreciation $540; utilities $380; and miscellaneous expenses $210.

94. Cost of food sold _____ % _____

95. Gross margin _____ % _____

96. Total operating expenses _____ % _____

97. Net profit _____ % _____

98. Prepare a balance sheet. Find the total assets, total liabilities, and net worth.

Assets of May 15 : Home $238,000, home furnishings $26,085, automobile $22,750; speedboat $6,540, cash in savings accounts $38,670, cash in checking account $5,034, and stocks $4,824. Liabilities: home mortgage $85,500, auto loan $7,200, boat loan $3,900, note payable to loan company $4,500, and charge accounts $2,682.

Total assets _____

Total liabilities _____

Net worth _____

99. Determine the contribution rate, contribution rate percentage, and break-even point.

The Blue Bird Cafeteria did $120,000 in sales. Their variable costs were 40% of the total sales and the fixed costs were $54,000.

Contribution rate _____

Contribution rate percentage   _____

Break-even point   _____

100. For a food service budget, the yearly income is $650,000. Find the dollar amount that was budgeted for each item listed.

     a. Food and Supplies   26%   _____

     b. Labor   24%   _____

     c. Workman's Compensation   4%   _____

     d. Fringe Benefits   8%   _____

     e. Utilities   11%   _____

     f. Printing Service   2%   _____

     g. New Equipment   10%   _____

     h. Equipment Service   5%   _____

     i. Telephone   3%   _____

     j. Profit   7%   _____

APPENDIX

A

FORMULAS

addition—Addend plus addend = Sum

assets—Liabilities plus proprietorship

break-even analysis—Sales revenue minus variable costs = Gross profit. Gross profit minus fixed costs = Break-even point

check amount based on tip—Money amount of tip divided by percent of tip

containers needed—Ounces needed divided by ounces in one container

converting Celsius temperature to degrees Fahrenheit—Multiply the Celsius temperature by $\frac{9}{5}$ and add 32 to the result.

converting Fahrenheit temperature to degrees Celsius—Subtract 32 from the given Fahrenheit temperature and multiply the result by $\frac{5}{9}$.

converting standard recipes—Multiply each ingredient in the original recipe by the working factor to find the new desired quantity.

cost of food sold—Beginning inventory plus purchases minus final inventory

cost, ounce—Total cost divided by total ounces

cost per serving—Cost of 1 ounce times number of ounces served

cost, total (per pound)—Number of pounds times cost per pound

division—Dividend divided by divisor = Quotient

edible portion (E.P.)—Weight of product after trimming or processing

food cost—Sales (or menu) price times food cost percentage

food cost percentage—Food cost divided by sales or menu price

gross pay—Hourly rate times hours worked

gross profit percent—Sales minus variable cost

interest—Principal times rate times time

interest paid—Interest per day times number of days of loan

interest per day—Amount of interest for one year divided by ordinary or exact days per year

menu pricing using the food cost percent method—Raw food cost divided by food cost percent

menu pricing using the markup amount method—Raw food cost times markup rate. To obtain menu price: add the markup amount to the raw food cost.

Multiplication—Multiplier times multiplicand = Product

net pay—Gross pay or wages minus deductions

net worth or proprietorship—Assets minus liabilities

number of ounces required—Amount of portion times number of people served

number of servings—Total weight of all ingredients used divided by serving portion size

number to order—Number of ounces required divided by ounces in container

ounces in one container—Pounds in container times 16

ounces needed—Number of people to be served times portion size

ounces, total—Total weight times 16

percent of ingredient—Weight of ingredient divided by weight of flour

pounds needed—Number of ounces needed divided by 16

price, extension—Quantity of items multiplied by the unit price

recipe yield—Total weight of preparation divided by weight of portion

salary plus commission—Amount of sales times percent of commission = Amount of commission. Salary plus amount of commission = Gross wages.

sales, average—Total sales divided by customer count

sales price or menu price—Food cost divided by food cost percentage

sales, total—Average sales multiplied by customer count

subtraction—Minuend minus subtrahend = Difference

unit Cost—Total cost divided by yield

working factor—New yield divided by old yield

Glossary

A

abbreviation—The shortened form of a word or phrase.

account, checking or savings—A record in which an individual's or a business's money is deposited or withdrawn, usually in a financial institution.

accountant—A person skilled in keeping, examination of, and adjustment of financial records.

accounts payable—Money owed by the business operator for purchases made.

accounts receivable—Money owed to the business operator by customers.

addressing (in data communication)—A computer term by which you are selecting another computer to send data via modem.

adhere—To stick fast; to become attached or cling to.

a la carte—Foods ordered and paid for separately; usually prepared to order.

analysis—The division or separation of a thing into the parts that compose it.

annual—Pertaining to a year; happening once in 12 months.

A.P. weight—As purchased weight. The weight of an item before processing.

approximate—To come near to, nearly correct.

aspic—A clear meat, fish, or poultry jelly.

assess—To fix or determine the amount of a tax, fine, or damage; to rate or set a certain charge upon, as for taxation.

assessor—A person appointed to estimate the value of property for the purpose of taxation.

assets—Things of value; all the property of a person, company, or estate that may be used to pay debts.

automation—The automatic control of production processes by electronic apparatus.

B

backup—A spare copy of data or a program.

baker's balance scale—An instrument to weigh ingredients used in baking.

balance—Difference between the debit and credit sides of an account; an amount leftover.

balance sheet—A written statement made to show the true financial condition for a person or business by exhibiting assets, liabilities or debts, profit and loss, and net worth.

bank note—A note issued by a bank that must be paid to the bearer upon demand. Bank notes are used as money.

breading—A process of passing an item through flour, egg wash (egg and milk), and bread crumbs before it is fried.

break-even analysis—A mathematical method used to find the dollar amount needed for a food service operation to break even.

budget—A plan of systematic spending; to plan one's expenditures of money, time, and so forth.

C

calculate—To reach a conclusion or answer by a reasoning process.

calculator—One who computes; a machine that does automatic computations.

calendar year—A period that begins on January 1 and ends on December 31; consisting of 365 days—in a leap year, 366 days.

capacity—Power of holding or grasping; room; volume; power of mind; character; ability to hold cubic content.

capital—Amount of money or property that a person or company uses in carrying on a business.

captain—A service individual in charge of a station or stations.

carryover—Have left over; keep until late.

cashbook—A book containing records of all income and expenses of a business operation.

cashier's daily report—A tool used by management to keep track of cash and charge sales.

Celsius—A term used to measure temperature in the metric system of measuring; graduated or divided into 100 equal parts called degrees; previously called centigrade.

cent—A term used to represent the value of one-hundredth part of a dollar.

centigrade—A term used to measure temperature in the metric system of measuring; graduated or divided into 100 equal parts called degrees. The term now used is Celsius.

centimeter—The one-hundredth part of a meter.

certificate—Issued by a bank to a depositor indicating that a specific amount of money is set aside and not subject to withdrawal except on surrender of the certificate, usually with an interest penalty.

chaud-froid—Jellied white sauce, used for decorating certain foods that are to be displayed.

check—A written order directing a financial institution to make a payment for the depositor.

check register—A form given to the depositor by the financial institution so the depositor can record deposits and checks, knowing the balance of money on hand.

cipher—Zero.

commission—Pay based on the amount of business done.

compensation—Something given in return for a service or a value.

competency—The state of being fit or capable.

complex—Not simple; involved; intricate.

compound interest—Money that is added to the principal (with interest then paid on a new principal).

compressed—Made smaller by applying pressure.

computer—Any of various mechanical, electrical, or electronic devices for computing; specifically one for solving complex, mathematical problems in a very short time.

computerized—To use, perform, operate, etc., by means of a computer or computers.

concept—A mental idea of a class of objects.

configuration—A group or series of machines and programs that make up a complete data processing system.

constant function—A calculator key used to multiply or divide repeatedly by the same number.

convert—Change; to turn the other way around.

corporation—A group of persons who obtain a charter giving them (as a group) certain legal rights and privileges distinct from those of the individual members of the group.

cost of food sold—monetary value of food on hand at beginning of the month, plus the purchases for the month, minus the monetary value of food in the final inventory.

cover charge—An admission fee charged for entertainment.

cubic centimeter—A measure of volume in the metric system with sides 1 centimeter long.

cubic meter—A measure of volume in the metric system with sides 1 meter long.

currency—Money in actual use in a country. In the United States, the term usually applies to paper money, although technically, it is both coins and paper money.

cursor—A short, blinking line that appears underneath the space where the next character is to be typed or deleted. The cursor indicates that the computer is ready for the input of the command.

D

daily food cost report—A tool to show management the exact cost and amount of food used on any given day.

data—A collection of information, facts, statistics, or instructions arranged in definite terms suitable for processing by manual or automatic means.

database management—The sorting and categorizing of information or data.

debit—The entry of an item in a business account showing something owed or due.

decimal—A system of counting by tens and powers of 10. Each digit has a place value 10 times that of the next digit to the right.

decimal fractions—Fractions that are expressed with denominators of 10 or powers of 10.

decimal point—A point (.) used to indicate a decimal fraction.

decimeter—A metric measure of length equal to one-tenth of a meter.

deduction—The process of taking away.

default—Failure to pay when due.

dekameter—A metric measure of length equal to 10 meters.

denominator—The bottom number of a fraction.

deposit—Put in a place for safekeeping. Money put in a bank is a deposit.

deposit slip—A form that provides the depositor and the financial institution with a record of the transaction when money is deposited in the checking account.

depreciation—Lessening or lowering in value.

designate—Point out; indicate definitely.

diameter—The length of a straight line through the center of a circle.

difference—the answer in a subtraction problem.

digit—Any one of the figures 0-1-2-3-4-5-6-7-8-9.

direct purchases—Those foods that are usually purchased each day or every other day.

disc—A flat, circular plate used in computers for the purpose of magnetically recording information on one or both sides.

diskette—A thin, flexible magnetic disk, sometimes called a floppy disk. Information can be recorded onto and played back from a diskette.

dividend—(1) Money to be shared by those to whom it belongs. If a company shows a profit at the end of a certain period, it declares a dividend to the owners of the company. (2) Also the number to be divided by the divisor.

division—Act of giving some to each. Process of dividing one number by another.

divisor—A number by which another (the dividend) is divided.

E

economic—Pertaining to the earning, distributing, and using of wealth and income, public or private.

entree—The main dish of a meal.

E.P. weight—Edible portion weight. The usable portion after processing.

equation—To make equal.

equivalent—Equal in value or power.

estimate—A judgment or opinion in determining the size, value, and so forth, of an item.

evaluate—Find the value or amount of; fix the value.

expenditure—That which is spent.

extension—To stretch out, lengthen, or widen.

F

fabricated—Made up; in food service, standardized portion.

facsimile—To make an exact copy of. A rapid way of communicating, allowing one to send and receive any type of text or graphic information over telephone lines.

factor—One of the two or more quantities, which, when multiplied together, yields a given product. Example: 2 and 4 are factors of 8.

Fahrenheit—A term used to measure temperature in the standard system of measuring; graduated or divided into 212 equal parts called degrees.

file—Put away and kept in any easy-to-find order.

final inventory—The total value of all goods on hand (e.g., in the storeroom). It is the food that has not been sold during the inventory period.

finances—Money; funds; revenues; financial condition.

financial—Having to do with money matters.

financial statements—Instruments used in a business operation to let management know its exact financial position.

fiscal year—The time between one yearly settlement of financial accounts and another. In the United States, a fiscal year usually starts July 1 and ends June 30 of the following calendar year.

fixed assets—Those assets (things of value) that stay firm and do not change.

fixed costs—Those costs (price paid) that stay firm and will not change.

fluctuate—Change continually.

food cost percentage—The cost of food as it relates to the amount of dollars received in sales.

food production report—A form used to find how much product is produced and sold.

forecast—A prophecy or prediction.

format—Size, shape, and general arrangement of a book, magazine, and so forth.

formula—A rule for doing something; a recipe or prescription.

fraction—One or more of the equal parts of a whole; a small part or amount.

function—A quantity, the value of which varies with that of another quantity.

G

garnish—To decorate, such as food.

gelatin—An odorless, tasteless substance obtained by boiling animal tissues. It dissolves easily in hot water and is used in making jellied desserts and salads.

gourmet—A lover of fine foods.

graduated—Arranged in regular steps, stages, or degrees.

gram—Metric system unit of weight (mass). Twenty-eight grams equal one ounce.

gratuity—A present or money given in return for a service; also called a tip.

gross—With nothing removed or taken out. Gross receipts are all the money taken in before costs are deducted.

gross margin—Sales less the cost of food gives the gross margin. It is the margin before other deductions are taken.

gross pay—Money earned before any deductions are removed or subtracted.

gross wages—Money paid to an employee for services before deductions.

guest check—The bill or bill of sale used in a restaurant.

H

hectometer—Measure of length in the metric system equal to 100 meters.

horizontally—Parallel to the horizon; at right angles to a vertical line.

host/hostess—An individual who receives guests at a private or public function.

hypothetical—Something assumed or supposed.

I

improper fraction—A fraction whose numerator is larger than its denominator and whose value is greater than a whole unit.

income—All payments received for services provided.

indicator—One who, or that which, points out.

ingredient—One part of a mixture.

installment—Part of a sum of money or debt to be paid at certain regular times.

interest—Money that is paid for the use of borrowed money.

inventory—A detailed list of items with their estimated values.

invert—To turn upside down.

invoice—A list of goods sent to a purchaser showing prices and amounts.

itemize—To state by items, as to itemize a bill.

K

keyboard—A bank of numeric, alphabetic, or function keys of a typewriter or computer. On the computer, they are used to enter information into the computer terminal.

kilogram—A metric measure of weight equal to 1,000 grams.

kilometer—A measure of length in the metric system equal to 1,000 meters.

L

ladles—Tools used to serve foods or to control portion size.

lease—A written contract whereby one party grants to another party the use of land, buildings, or personal property, for a definite consideration known as rent, for a specified term.

least common denominator—The smallest number that is a multiple of both denominators.

legumes—Vegetables; also refers to dried vegetables such as beans, lentils, and split peas.

liability—A state of being under obligation; responsible for a loss, debt, penalty, or the like.

licenses—A form of taxation that individuals or businesses are required to obtain in order to conduct business.

like fractions—Fractions that have the same denominator.

liter—A measure of volume in the metric system. One liter equals 1.0567 quarts in customary liquid measure, or 0.908 quarts in dry measure.

M

maitre d'—Person in charge of dining room service.

manual—Pertaining to, or done by hand.

margin—The difference between the cost and the selling price of an article.

markup—Marked for sale at a higher price.

Medicare—A federal health insurance program for people 65 or older and certain disabled people.

memory function—A calculator key used to retain figures.

menu—A list of the various dishes served at a meal.

meringue—Egg whites and sugar beaten together to form a white, frothy mass; used to top pies and cakes.

meter—Unit of length in the metric system equal to 39.37 inches.

metric system—The system of measurements based on the meter.

mill—The third place to the right of the decimal when dealing with monetary numbers. It represents the thousandth part of a dollar, or one-tenth of one cent.

milligram—Pertaining to the metric system of measure. It is the thousandth part of a gram.

milliliter—Pertaining to the metric system of measure. It is the thousandth part of a liter.

millimeter—Pertaining to the metric system of measure. It is a lineal measure equal to the thousandth part of a meter.

minimum charge—A fee charged to the guest who is required to spend a certain amount of money even if the total check amounts to less.

minuend—The original number in a subtraction problem.

mixed decimal fraction—A number that is made up of a whole number and a decimal fraction.

mixed number—A whole number mixed with a fractional part.

modem—An electronic device that makes possible the transmission of digitized data from one location to another over telephone lines.

monetary—Pertaining to money or coinage.

monitor—A computer output device. Various information is shown on the monitor.

mortgage—Claim on property given to a person who has lent money in case the money is not repaid when due.

mouse—A computer device that will fit in the palm of your hand. When rolled on a flat surface, it will move the computer cursor. It relays signals that move the cursor on the computer screen.

multiple—A number that contains another number a certain amount of times, without a remainder; example: 16 is a multiple of 4.

multiplicand—In multiplication, the number or quantity to be multiplied by another number called the multiplier.

multiplier—Number by which another number is to be multiplied.

multiplier effect—A method used to obtain a menu price.

N

net—Amount remaining after deducting all necessary expenses.

net pay—Money paid to an employee for services after deductions.

net worth—Excess value of resources over liabilities; also called net assets.

numeral—Symbol for a number.

numerator—The top number of a fraction.

O

occupational tax—A fee that must be paid in order to operate any business within a certain city.

operating system—Directs the flow of information to and from various parts of the computer and is needed by the computer to run programs.

overdrawn—To draw from an account (bank) more than one has a right.

overtime—Time beyond the regular hours.

P

P and L sheet—Another name for a profit and loss statement.

pasta—A dried flour paste product. Example: spaghetti, vermicelli, and lasagna.

payroll—List of persons to be paid and the amounts that each one is to receive. Total amounts to be paid to them.

percent—Rate or proportion of each hundred; part of each hundred.

period—A group of three digits set off by commas in a large number.

periodical—Magazine that is published regularly.

perpetual inventory—A continuous or endless record to show the balance on hand for each storeroom item.

physical inventory—A count taken of all stock on hand.

portion—A part or share.

portion control—A term used to ensure that a specific or designated amount of an item is served to a guest.

portion scale—A tool used for measuring food servings.

portion size—The amount or quantity of prepared food.

prefix—A letter, syllable, or group of syllables placed at the beginning of a word to modify or qualify its meaning; example: deci in front of meter indicates 1/10 of a meter.

primal cut—One of the primary divisions for cutting meat carcasses into smaller cuts.

primary—First in time; first in order; first in importance.

principal—Sum of money on which interest is paid.

printer—An output device for the computer. Prints out required information.

procedure—A way of proceeding; method of doing a task.

product—The result obtained by multiplying two or more numbers together.

production formula—A standardized formula used to prepare foods in quantity.

profile—An outline or contour.

profit—Gain from a business venture. What is left when the cost of goods and carrying on the business is subtracted from the amount of money taken in.

program—Pertaining to the computer, a plan of related instructions or statements that is brought together as a task.

proper fraction—A fraction whose numerator is smaller than its denominator.

property tax—An amount of money collected from individuals or businesses based on the present value of the property.

proportion—Relation in size, number, amount, or degree of one thing compared to another.

proprietorship—Ownership.

purchase order—A written form that indicates to the vendor how many items are to be delivered to an establishment, and lists the prices for each item.

purchase specifications—A detailed description of requirements for items being purchased.

purveyor—One who supplies provisions or food.

Q

quantity—Amount; how much.

quotient—Number obtained by dividing one number by another; the final answer of a division problem.

R

ratio—Relative magnitude. The ratio between two quantities is the number of times one contains the other.

real estate tax—See *property tax*.

receipt—A written statement that money, a package, a letter, and so forth, has been received.

recipe—A set of directions for preparing something to eat.

recipe file number—The number placed on the recipe for easy access when it is filed.

reconstitute—To rebuild the way it was originally, to put back into original form. Example: to reconstitute dried milk, the water is put back.

recourse—Person or thing appealed to or turned to for help or protection.

reduce—To make less in value, quantity, size, or the like.

remainder—The number less than the divisor that remains after the division process is completed.

report—An account officially expressed, generally in writing.

requisition—A demand made, usually in written form, for something that is required.

revenue—Money coming in; income.

rotating menu—Menu that alternates by turn in a series. The series is usually set up on a yearly basis.

roux—A thickening agent consisting of equal parts of flour and shortening.

royalty—Share of the receipts or profits paid to an owner of a patent or copyright; payment for use of any of various rights.

S

salary—A regular, periodical payment for official or professional services rendered.

sales revenue—Money coming in from the sale of certain items.

sales tax—Money collected on purchases of goods from consumers or businesses by governments.

saute—To cook in shallow grease.

scoops or dippers—Tools used to serve foods or to control portion size.

simple interest—Money paid only on the principal.

simplification—A method used to express a fraction in lower terms without changing the value of the fraction.

simplify—To reduce from the complex to the simple; to make plainer to understand.

software—A general term for programs that direct a computer operation. A set of instructions given the computer to perform a given task.

solar—Working by means of the sun's light or heat.

specification—A detailed statement of particulars.

spreadsheet—A printout similar to an accountant's ledger containing rows and columns of important calculations and financial information.

standard recipe—A recipe that will produce the same quality and quantity each and every time.

standardize—To make standard in size, shape, weight, quality, quantity, and so forth.

stations—Serving sections in a restaurant.

status—Condition, state, or position.

stockholder—Owner of stocks or shares in a company.

storeroom requisition—A list of food items issued from the storeroom upon the request of the production crew.

straight line method—The simplest method to use when figuring depreciation on an item, such as a piece of equipment.

subproduct—Sub means under, below, or before. Product is the result of multiplying.

subtraction—An operation that tells the difference between two numbers.

subtrahend—The number removed from the minuend.

sum—Total of two or more numbers or things taken together; the whole amount.

summarize—Express briefly; give only the main points.

symbol—Something that stands for or represents something else.

T

table d'hôte—A meal of several courses at a set price. The dinner menu in most restaurants is served table d'hôte.

taxes—Money collected from individuals or businesses by governments to pay for public services.

technology—The application of science and technical advances in industry, the arts, and so forth.

terminology—The special words or terms used in a science, art, business, and so forth.

trading (borrowing)—To make a group of 10 from one of the next highest place value, or one from 10 of the lowest place value.

triplicate—To make threefold; three identical copies.

U

unit—A standard quantity or amount.

unit cost—The amount that one serving of a particular food costs to prepare.

unlike fractions—Fractions that have different denominators.

utilities—Companies that perform a public service. Railroads, gas and electric, and telephone companies are utilities.

V

variable cost—Costs that are changeable.

variation—The extent to which a thing changes.

vendor—One who sells a product.

verbally—Stated or expressed in words.

versatile—Turning easily from one action, style, or subject, and so forth, to another; able to do many tasks well.

vertical—Straight up and down.

volume—Space occupied.

voucher—A written evidence of payment; receipt.

W

wages—That which is paid or received for services.

whole numbers—Numbers such as 0, 1, 2, and so forth, that are used to represent whole units rather than fractional units.

withholding tax—A deduction from a person's paycheck for the purpose of paying yearly income taxes.

word processing—The system of recording, storing, and retrieving typewritten information.

Y

yield—Amount produced.

Index

A

Accountants, 224
Accounts payable, 299
Accounts receivable, 298
Accuracy, 36–37
Addition, 34–37
  on calculator, 6, 14
  decimal fractions, 65
  fractions, 58–60
  guidelines, 36–37
  by percent, 14
  symbols, 29–30
  terminology, 34
Add—start of shift money
    (bank), 262
Advertising, 294
Allen, Gail, 226
All-inclusive pricing, 268–272
American Culinary Federation
    Chef of the Year
    award, 170
Andrie Rose Inn, Ludlow,
    Vermont, 114
A.P. *See* As purchased weight
    (A.P.)
Arithmetic operations,
    guidelines for, 36–37
Artist Point, Lake Buena Vista,
    Florida, 234
As purchased weight (A.P.)
  costing out recipes using, 165
  definition of, 81
  portion control and, 126–127
  yield determination
    using, 135–136
Assets, 296, 299
Automobile, worth of, 297
Average sales, 182

B

Backing out sales tax and
    gratuity, 269–272
Baker's balance scale, 80,
    87–89, *88, 89*
Baker's percentage, 153–156
Baker's production report, 239,
    240

Balance sheet, 296–299, *298*
Banking, 273–278
  bank statements, 276–278
  checking accounts, 274
  check registers, 275–276
  check writing, 276
  deposits, 273
  deposit slips, 274–275
Bank notes payable, 299
Bank statements, 276–278,
    277
Beau Rivage Resort and
    Casino, Biloxi, Mississippi,
    25
Beef, cuts of, *74,* 74–75
Beginning inventory, 212
Benamati, Greg, 234
Bigley, James, 260
Bookkeepers, 228, 230
Borrowing, 39–40
Break-even analysis, 300–303
Break-even point, 300
Brenenstuhl, Gary, 81
Budgeting, 306–308, *307,* 308
Bush, George H. W., 99
Business forms. *See* Record
    keeping
Buying, portion control and,
    111–112

C

Cake
  division of, 56
  yield determination for,
    146–147
Calculator
  addition, 6, 13
  basic operations, 5–7
  chain calculations, 7–9
  change sign key, 21
  constant function, 9
  division, 7, 13
  hand-held, 3
  keys, *4*
  memory function, 15–20
  multiplication, 6–7, 12–13
  percent, 12–15, 19–20
  plus/minus key, 21

  purchasing decisions, 2–3
  solar-powered, 2–3
  subtraction, 6, 13–14
  using, 3–5
Canada Cutlery, 75
Canceling, in multiplication
    of fractions, 60
Can cutting, 85
Can sizes, 85
Capacity, in metric system,
    102
Capital, 296
Carryovers, 36, 47
Cashiers, 259–268
  daily reports, 259–262, *261*
  returning change, 267–268
Cash paid outs, 262
Celsius, 100, 101, 103–104
Cent, 30
Centimeter, 101
Certified master chefs, 170
Chain calculations, 7–9
Change, giving customers,
    267–268
Change sign key, 21
Checking accounts, 273–274
Checking work
  addition, 36
  division, 52–53
  estimation, 69
  multiplication, 46–47
  subtraction, 40–41
Check registers, *275,* 275–276
Checks
  definition of, 274
  writing, 27, *27–28,* 276, *276*
Chef's Magic Circle, *197,*
    197–198
Ciphers, 66
Commas, in writing numerals,
    26, 100
Commission, 289–290
Community College of
    Southern Nevada, 197
Computers
  food purchasing, 233
  inventory applications,
    217–218, 232–233
  point-of-sale, 232–233, 251,
    253

Constant function, 9–11
Contribution rate, 303–304
Contribution rate percentage, 303–304
Controllers, 289
Conversions
  baker's percentage, 153–156
  Celsius-Fahrenheit, 103
  common sense and, 142
  decimal weights into ounces, 96–97
  metric, *105*, 105–107, *106*
  ratios and proportions, 150–151
  recipe yield, 145–148
  standard recipes, 139–142
Cook's production report, *236*, 236–237
Costed out, 160
Costing
  average sales, 182
  daily reports, 181–182
  food and labor cost percentages, 183–184
  total sales, 182
Cost of ownership, 301
Cost percentages, *180*
  food, 180–181
  labor, 180–181
Costs, 159–175
  food, 159–161, 179
  labor, 159, 171–173, 179
  meat and fish portions, 162–163
  per serving, 117–118
  recipe, 165–168
  unit, 160–161, 165
Counter production report, 245, *245*
Cover charge, 253
"Cracking the nut," 300
Credit card sales, 260
Cubic centimeters, 102
Cubic meters, 101, 102
Cuts of meat, *74*

D

Daily food cost report, 181–182, *182*
Daily labor cost report, 181–182
Daily production reports, 235
Decimal fractions, 64, 73
Decimal point, 64

Decimals, 64–67
  adding and subtracting, 65–66
  converting weights into ounces, 96–97
  dividing, 66–67
  fraction equivalents, 64
  reading, 65
Decimeter, 101
Dekameter, 102
Denominator, 57
Deposit slips, 273–275, *274*
Depreciation, 294–295
Difference, 39
Digits, 25–26
Dippers. *See* Scoops
Direct purchases, 181
Dividend, 49
Division, 49–53
  on calculator, 7, 13
  checking, 52–53
  constant function, 10–11
  decimal fractions, 66–67
  fractions, 61
  by percent, 13
  step-by-step, 51
  symbols, 29–30, 50
  terminology, 49–50
Divisor, 49
Drained weight test, 85

E

Edible portion weight (E.P.)
  costing out recipes using, 165
  definition of, 81
  portion control and, 127–129
  yield determination using, 135–136
Employees
  payment methods for, 171
  taxes on, 282–286
E.P. *See* Edible portion weight (E.P.)
Equivalents, of weights and measures, 81–83, *82*, *83*, *107*
Expenditures, 273, 306
Extension cost, 166

F

Factor, 57
Fahrenheit, 103–104

Faller, Robert S., 292
Federal Highway Administration, 99
Federal Insurance Contributions Act, 283
Federal taxes, 282–284
  employee's withholding tax, 282–283
  FICA tax, 283–284
  income tax, 283
FICA (Social Security) tax, 283–284
Final inventory, 204, 212
Financial statements, 291
Fiscal year, 296
Fish
  costing portions, 162–163
  market form, *134*
  purchasing fresh, 133–134
Fixed cost, 302
Food cost percentage, 180–181, 183–184, 194, 197–198, 204–205, 213
Food costs
  daily report, 181–182
  definition of, 159, 179
  percent, 180–181, 183–184, 194, 197–198, 204–205, 213
  raw, 187
  units cost calculation, 160–161
Food in production, 204
Food preparation
  portion control and, 123–124
  unit cost calculation, 160–161
Food production reports
  baker's report, 239–240
  cook's report, 236–237
  counter report, 245
  daily, 235
  definition of, 233
  salad report, 242–243
Food transfers, 204
Ford, Gerald, 99
Forecasting, 235, 237
Formulas, 321–322
Formula yield, 145
Fractions, 56–61
  adding and subtracting, 58–60
  decimal, 64
  decimal equivalents, *64*
  dividing, 61
  like, 58
  multiplying, 60–61

proper versus improper, 57
simplification, 58
terminology, 57
unlike, 59

G

Gisslen, Wayne, 100
Goldoff, George R., 25
Grams, 100, 101, 103
Gratuity, 256–258,
    269–272, 283
Gross receipts, 262
Gross wages, 171, 172–173,
    286–288
Guest checks, 251–255,
    252, 254
  calculating, 253
  responsibility for, 251–253
  sales tax, 255

H

Halston, Andre, 160
Hectometer, 102
HMB Consultants, 260
Home, worth of, 297
Home furnishings, worth
    of, 297
House accounts, 262
Houseboat, worth of, 297
Huebner, Peter, 75

I

Improper fraction, 57
Income books, 292
Income tax, 283, 285–286
Installment accounts, 299
Interest, on bank deposits,
    273
"In the black," 305
"In the red," 305
Inventory
  beginning, 212
  computer applications,
      217–218, 232–233
  definition of, 201
  final, 204, 212
  perpetual, 201–203
  physical, *203*, 203–204, *205*
Invoice, 181
Invoices, *227*, 227–228

K

Kaperka, Matthew J., 202
Kelvin scale, 103
Kilograms, 101, 103
Kilometer, 102

L

Labor cost percentage,
    180–181, 183
Labor costs
  daily report, 181–182
  definition of, 159, 179
  gross wages calculation,
      172–173
  methods of payment, 171
  payroll, 171–173
  percent, 180–181, 183
Ladles
  measuring with, 87
  portioning with, 120–122
  sizes, *87, 120*
Least common denominator,
    59, 60
Leaver, William, 12
Length, in metric system,
    101–102
Liabilities, 296
Like fractions, 58
Liquid measures, 81
Liquids, weights of, 83
Liters, 100, 101, 102

M

Manager's mathematical
    functions, 268–272
  all-inclusive pricing, 268–269
  backing out sales tax and
      gratuity, 269–272
Markup
  definition of, 193
  using fraction, 193
  using percent, 193–194
Masi, Noble, 91
Mass, in metric system, 102
Maston, Irene, 114
Math skills, necessity of, 79
Meal, portion sizes for, *117*
Measures. *See* Metric system;
    Weights and measures
Meat
  costing portions of, 162–163
  percent of cuts, 74–75

Medicare, 283
Memory function, 15–20
Menu, 186. *See also* Pricing the
    menu
Meters, 100, 101
Metric system, 98–110
  conversions, *105*, 105–107,
      106
  equivalents, 107
  history of, 98–99
  industry use of, 99–100
  lengths, 101–102
  mass or weight, 102
  symbols, 103
  temperature, 103–104
  units of measure, 101,
      103
  volume and capacity, 102
Mill, 30–31
Milliliters, 100
Millimeter, 101
Minimum charge, 253
Minuend, 39
Mixed decimal fraction, 65
Mixed number, 57
Monthly food cost percentage,
    204–205, 213
Multiplicand, 42
Multiplication, 42–47
  on calculator, 6–7, 12–13
  constant function, 9–10
  decimal fractions, 66
  fractions, 60–61
  guidelines, 47
  by percent, 12–13, 19–20
  symbols, 29–30
  table for, *43, 44, 45*, 45
  terminology, 42–43
Multiplier, 42
Multiplier effect, 194–195

N

Neatness, 36, 47
Net pay, 286–288
Net worth, 296
Newell, Bob, 34
New York State Office of
    Nutritional Services for
    correctional facilities, 12
Numbers, 24–29
  digits, 25–26
  large, 28
  numerals, 25
  reading, 28

Numbers *(continued)*
  units, 24–25
  whole, 24
Numerals
  definition of, 25
  writing, 26, 100
Numerator, 57

O

Oahu Country Club,
    Honolulu, Hawaii, 101
Occupational expenses, 301
Ordering food
  portion control and, 131
  yield percentage and, 136
Otesaga Resort Hotel,
    Cooperstown, New
    York, 292
Ounces, converting decimal
    weights into, 96–97
Overdrawn accounts, 274
Overtime, 171, 172–173

P

Payment methods, for
    employees, 171
Payroll, 171–173
Percents, 72–78
  addition by, 14
  on calculator, 12–15, 19–20
  changing to decimal, 9
  decimal fractions and, 73
  definition of, 72
  division by, 13
  of meat cuts, 74–75
  multiplication by, 12–13,
    19–20
  subtraction by, 13–14
Period, 26
Perpetual inventory, 201–203
Physical inventory, *203*,
    203–204, *205*
Pie, division of, 56
Place value, *26*, 28
Plus/minus key, 21
Point-of-sale computers,
    232–233, 251, 253
Portion chart, *115–117*
Portion control, 111–138
  achieving, 111–112

amounts to prepare, 123–124
A.P., 126–127
cost per serving, 117–118
E.P., 127–129
fresh fish purchases, 133–134
importance of, 111
methods, 112–113, 113
number of servings, 125–129
ordering food, 131, 136
policy, 113–117
portion sizes for meal, *117*
presentation and, *126*
scoops/ladles, 119–122
standardized portion chart,
    115–117
Portions, 91
Portion scale, 91–92, *92*
Prefixes, in metric system,
    101–102
Preparation. *See* Food
    preparation
Presentation of food, *126*
Pricing the menu, 187–198
  food cost percent, 194,
    197–198
  formula for, 10, 32
  large versus small operations,
    187
  markup using percent,
    193–194
  multiplier effect, 194–195
Primary expenses, 301
Primary vendors, 230
Problem solving
  proportions used for, 70,
    150–151
  ratios used for, 150–151
Product, 42
Production reports. *See* Food
    production reports
Professional Baking (Gisslen),
    100
Profit and loss (P&L)
    statement, 291–295, *293*
Proper fraction, 57
Proportions, 70, 150–151
Proprietorship, 296
Purchase orders, 229–231,
    230
Purchase specifications, 229
Purchasing, computers used
    for, 233
Purchasing agents, 229–230
Purveyors, 233

Q

Quotient, 49

R

Ratios, 69, 150–151
Raw food cost, 187
Ready-to-cook portions, 112,
    127
Recipes
  approximate yield,
    determining, 145–151
  converting, 139–142
  file numbers for, 236
  See also Standard recipes
Record keeping
  importance of, 224
  invoices, 227–228
  purchase orders, 229–231
  requisitions, 224–225
Remainder, 50, 52
Renshaw, Rodney, 196
Rent, 294
Requisitions, 224–225, *225*
Roll dough, yield
    determination for, 147
Rosenberger, Thomas, 197
Rounding to whole number,
    30–31
Rounding up, 31–32
Routing number, 275

S

Saddle, of lamb carcass, 74
Salad production report,
    242–243, *243*
Salary, 171
Salary plus commission,
    289–290
Sales
  average, 182
  total, 182
Sales revenue, 300
Sales tax, 255, 269–272
Savings accounts, 273
Savoy, Washington, D.C., 196
Scoops
  examples, *120*
  measuring with, 86
  portioning with, 119–122
  sizes, *86, 120*

Self-employed individuals, FICA taxes on, 283, 284
Serving expenses, 301
Shrinkage, 127
Side of meat, *74*, 74
Simplification of fractions, 58
Social Security tax, 283–284
Software, for inventory, 217–218
Solar-powered calculator, 2–3
Soltner, Andre, 144
Sonnenschmidt, Fritz, 170
Speed, 36–37
Standard recipes
  benefits of, 165
  converting, 139–142
  costing out, 165–168
State taxes, 285–286
  employee's withholding tax, 285
  income tax, 285–286
Stewards, 225, 230
Storage areas, 224–225
Storeroom operation, *202*
Storeroom requisition, 181
Straight line method, 295
Subproducts, 43
Subtraction, 38–41
  on calculator, 6, 13–14
  checking, 40–41
  decimal fractions, 66
  fractions, 58–60
  by percent, 13–14
  symbols, 29–30
  terminology, 39
  trading (borrowing), 39–40
Subtrahend, 39
Sum, 34
Supplies, 294
Symbols of operations, *29*, 29–30, 50
SYSCO Foods, 226

T

Taxes
  federal, 282–284
  in food service operations, 281
  state, 285–286
Temperature
  Celsius, 100, 101, 103–104
  common, *104*
  conversions, Celsius-Fahrenheit, 103
  Fahrenheit, 103–104
  Kelvin, 103
Tice, George, 160
Time card, *172*
Time clock, 172
Tips. *See* Gratuity
Total sales, 182
Total variable profit, 302
Trading numbers, 36, 39–40, 47
Transfers, food, 204

U

Uniform size, *167*
Unit cost, 160–161, 165
Units, 24–25
Unlike fractions, 59
Utensils, weighing and measuring, *84*, 86–92, 111

V

Variable cost, 300
Vendors, 230
Volume measures
  liquid versus dry ingredients, 81
  metric system, 102

W

Wages, 171, 284, 286–288
Wagner, Richard, 101
Waitstaff
  gratuity/tip, 256–258
  guest checks, 251–255
  mathematical operations for, 251
Weight, in metric system, 102
Weights and measures, 80–97
  A.P., 81
  common abbreviations, *81*
  common foods, *93–95*
  converting decimal weights into ounces, 96–97
  devices, *84*, 86–92, 111
  E.P., 81
  equivalents, 81–83, *82*, *83*
  importance of, 80
  liquid measures, 81
  metric conversions, *105*, 105–107, *106*
  metric equivalents, *107*
  use of, 80–81
  volume measures, 81
  See also Metric system
Whispering Canyon Café, Lake Buena Vista, Florida, 234
Whole numbers, 24
Withholding tax, employee, 282–283, 285
Wolkoff, Melanie, 160
Working factor, 139–140, 156
W-2 wage and tax statement, *282*, 283

Y

Yield
  formula, 145
  percentage of A.P., 135–136
  recipe, 145–151
  servings from E.P., 127–129